PERSPECTIVES ON WRITING
Series Editor, Susan H. McLeod

PERSPECTIVES ON WRITING
Series Editor, Susan H. McLeod

The Perspectives on Writing series addresses writing studies in a broad sense. Consistent with the wide ranging approaches characteristic of teaching and scholarship in writing across the curriculum, the series presents works that take divergent perspectives on working as a writer, teaching writing, administering writing programs, and studying writing in its various forms.

The WAC Clearinghouse and Parlor Press are collaborating so that these books will be widely available through free digital distribution and low-cost print editions. The publishers and the Series editor are teachers and researchers of writing, committed to the principle that knowledge should freely circulate. We see the opportunities that new technologies have for further democratizing knowledge. And we see that to share the power of writing is to share the means for all to articulate their needs, interest, and learning into the great experiment of literacy.

Recent Books in the Series

Sarah Allen, *Beyond Argument: Essaying as a Practice of (Ex)Change* (2015)

Steven J. Corbett, *Beyond Dichotomy: Synergizing Writing Center and Classroom Pedagogies* (2015)

Christy I. Wenger, *Yoga Minds, Writing Bodies: Contemplative Writing Pedagogy* (2015)

Terry Myers Zawacki and Michelle Cox, *WAC and Second-Language Writers: Research Towards Linguistically and Culturally Inclusive Programs and Practices,* (2014)

Charles Bazerman, *A Rhetoric of Literate Action: Literate Action Volume 1* (2013)

Charles Bazerman, *A Theory of Literate Action: Literate Action Volume 2* (2013)

Katherine V. Wills and Rich Rice (Eds.), *ePortfolio Performance Support Systems: Constructing, Presenting, and Assessing Portfolios* (2013)

Mike Duncan and Star Medzerian Vanguri (Eds.), *The Centrality of Style* (2013)

Chris Thaiss, Gerd Bräuer, Paula Carlino, Lisa Ganobcsik-Williams, and Aparna Sinha (Eds.), *Writing Programs Worldwide: Profiles of Academic Writing in Many Places* (2012)

Andy Kirkpatrick and Zhichang Xu, *Chinese Rhetoric and Writing: An Introduction for Language Teachers* (2012)

Doreen Starke-Meyerring, Anthony Paré, Natasha Artemeva, Miriam Horne, and Larissa Yousoubova (Eds.), *Writing in Knowledge Societies* (2011)

Martine Courant Rife, Shaun Slattery, and Dànielle Nicole DeVoss (Eds.), *Copy(write): Intellectual Property in the Writing Classroom* (2011)

CRITICAL EXPRESSIVISM: THEORY AND PRACTICE IN THE COMPOSITION CLASSROOM

Edited by Tara Roeder and Roseanne Gatto

The WAC Clearinghouse
wac.colostate.edu
Fort Collins, Colorado

Parlor Press
www.parlorpress.com
Anderson, South Carolina

The WAC Clearinghouse, Fort Collins, Colorado 80523-1052
Parlor Press, 3015 Brackenberry Drive, Anderson, South Carolina 29621

© 2015 by Tara Roeder and Roseanne Gatto. This work is licensed under a Creative Commons Attribution-NonCommercial-NoDerivatives 4.0 International.

Printed in the United States of America

Library of Congress Cataloging-in-Publication Data

Critical expressivism : theory and practice in the composition classroom / edited by Tara Roeder and Roseanne Gatto.
     pages cm. -- (Perspectives on writing)
   Includes bibliographical references.
   ISBN 978-1-60235-651-1 (pbk. : acid-free paper) -- ISBN 978-1-60235-652-8 (hardcover : acid-free paper)
   1. English language--Rhetoric--Study and teaching. 2. English language--Composition and exercises--Study and teaching 3. Expressivism (Ethics) 4. Authorship--Study and teaching. I. Roeder, Tara, 1980- editor. II. Gatto, Roseanne, 1975- editor.
 PE1404.C748 2015
 808'.04207--dc23
                              2015006807

Copyeditor: Don Donahue
Designer: Tara Reeser
Series Editor: Susan H. McLeod

This book is printed on acid-free paper.

The WAC Clearinghouse supports teachers of writing across the disciplines. Hosted by Colorado State University, it brings together scholarly journals and book series as well as resources for teachers who use writing in their courses. This book is available in digital format for free download at http://wac.colostate.edu.

Parlor Press, LLC is an independent publisher of scholarly and trade titles in print and multimedia formats. This book is available in paperback, cloth, and Adobe eBook formats from Parlor Press at http://www.parlorpress.com. For submission information or to find out about Parlor Press publications, write to Parlor Press, 3015 Brackenberry Drive, Anderson, South Carolina 29621, or email editor@parlorpress.com.

In memory of Anthony Petruzzi

Acknowledgments

Many thanks to Matthew T. Bird.
We are tremendously grateful for your time, knowledge, and patience.

CONTENTS

Preface: Yes, I Know That Expressivism Is Out of Vogue, But 3
    Lizbeth Bryant

Re-Imagining Expressivism: An Introduction.......................7
    Tara Roeder and Roseanne Gatto

SECTION ONE: CRITICAL SELF-CONSTRUCTION 13

"Personal Writing" and "Expressivism" as Problem Terms............15
    Peter Elbow

Selfhood and the Personal Essay: A Pragmatic Defense 33
    Thomas Newkirk

Critical Memoir and Identity Formation: Being,
Belonging, Becoming...55
    Nancy Mack

Critical Expressivism's Alchemical Challenge 69
    Derek Owens

Past-Writing: Negotiating the Complexity of Experience
and Memory..79
    Jean Bessette

Essai—A Metaphor: Writing to Show Thinking 93
    Lea Povozhaev

SECTION TWO: PERSONAL WRITING AND SOCIAL CHANGE 105

Communication as Social Action: Critical Expressivist
Pedagogies in the Writing Classroom 107
    Patricia Webb Boyd

From the Personal to the Social 123
    Daniel F. Collins

"Is it Possible to Teach Writing So That People Stop Killing
Each Other?" Nonviolence, Composition, and
Critical Expressivism 131
    Scott Wagar

Contents

The (Un)Knowable Self and Others: Critical Empathy
and Expressivism 149
    Eric Leake

SECTION 3: HISTORIES 161

John Watson Is to Introspectionism as James Berlin Is to
Expressivism (And Other Analogies You Won't Find on the SAT) 163
    Maja Wilson

Expressive Pedagogies in the University of Pittsburgh's
Alternative Curriculum Program, 1973-1979 189
    Chris Warnick

Rereading Romanticism, Rereading Expressivism: Revising
"Voice" through Wordsworth's Prefaces 201
    Hannah J. Rule

Emerson's Pragmatic Call for Critical Conscience:
Double Consciousness, Cognition, and Human Nature 219
    Anthony Petruzzi *

SECTION FOUR: PEDAGOGIES 247

Place-Based Genre Writing as Critical Expressivist Practice 249
    David Seitz

Multicultural Critical Pedagogy in the Community-Based
Classroom: A Motivation for Foregrounding the Personal 261
    Kim M. Davis

The Economy of Expressivism and Its Legacy of
Low/No-Stakes Writing 281
    Sheri Rysdam

Revisiting Radical Revision 289
    Jeff Sommers

Contributors 305

CRITICAL EXPRESSIVISM: THEORY AND PRACTICE IN THE COMPOSITION CLASSROOM

PREFACE: YES, I KNOW THAT EXPRESSIVISM IS OUT OF VOGUE, BUT ...

Lizbeth Bryant
Purdue University Calumet

Critical Expressivism: Theory and Practice in the Composition Classroom offers those of us with "Yes-But" syndrome a solution. I was reminded of this syndrome in a webinar in which Richard Johnson-Sheehan claims, "I think Chuck [Paine] and I are still process people despite some of the theoretical arguments for post-process. We still believe we are teaching students a writing process, and in a sense, genres guide us from the beginning of the process to the end." Johnson-Sheehan and Paine explain and justify their decision to teach writing as a process with a "yes-but" approach: Yes, I know that in our growth as a discipline we have moved from a focus on writing as a process to the social and cultural factors that impact language in our electronic worlds, but I still teach writing as a process and assist my students with developing their processes.

Johnson-Sheehan, a scholar in rhetoric and composition, admits in 2012 that he knows this approach to writing has been trashed by scholars who have controlled our meta-narrative, but admits that he sees a need for it. I have faced the same struggle to justify how I teach writing and what I study. Colleagues have asked, "Liz, how can you still focus on teaching expressivism and voice when there are new theories to study?" That's simple—I build new theories and practices into my meta-narrative of Composition Studies. This either/or epistemology doesn't work.

But, composition scholarship leads us to believe that we "are" one or the other. In our scholarship one cannot "be" both/and because the significant scholars in our field have said that a social epistemic view of writing precludes an Expressive and Cognitive view of writing. However, as I work with the myriad of writers in my classes from first-year writing to graduate thesis writing, I experience writers thinking and composing in various paradigms. Havier from East Chicago struggles with translating his mixture of black dialect and Spanglish into Standard American English. When Paul asks me if he should include a piece of research and a quote in his report, I ask him to see his writing situation from the cognitive paradigm: "Does your audience need this information to understand and be convinced of your position?" Charmaine struggles to write the findings from her original research into the final drafts of her thesis. She asks, "Can I really tell philosophy professors how I think they should teach writing?" To assure her that this is what she is supposed to do, I draw on M. M. Bakhtin's idea of writing as a conversation that she can join, and how voice has both expressive as well as social dimensions.

As a teacher and writer, I use various theoretical paradigms to give me different views of the phenomena of writing. Each of these theories is a slice of the writing pie—one aspect of this intricate, analytical, emotional practice we use to bring thought to language. One of these theories does not explain it all, so we keep studying writers and writing, trying to figure it out in its entirety.

Can we create a new metanarrative, one based in building on the theories of others? Certainly. We can view this phenomenon of writing that we teach, study, and practice as composed of the many theories and practices that have been and are being developed in our scholarship. This is the mission of *Critical Expressivism: Theory and Practice in the Composition Classroom*. Its writers and editors are building on Sherrie Gradin's *Romancing Rhetorics: Social Expressivist Perspectives on the Teaching of Writing* from 1995 that theorizes a relationship between expressivism and social-constructivism (xviii). The problem with accomplishing this is that academia has been built on one-upmanship: if my theory is going to be given any credit, I have to trash the ones before me.

For example, James Berlin's words in "Rhetoric and Ideology in the Writing Class" set up his classical "trashing" of expressive rhetoric. In closing his essay Berlin writes, "it should now be apparent that a way of teaching is never innocent. Every pedagogy is imbricated in ideology, is a set of tacit assumptions about what is real, what is good, what is possible, and how power ought to be distributed." He then reiterates the ideology behind cognitive and expressive rhetoric, and ends with his support of social-epistemic rhetoric in which, "social-epistemic rhetoric attempts to place the question of ideology at the center of the teaching of writing. It offers both a detailed analysis of dehumanizing social experience and a self-critical and overtly historicized alternative based on democratic practices in the economic social, and political, and cultural spheres. It is obvious that I find this alternative the most worthy of emulation in the classroom, all the while admitting that it is the least formulaic and the most difficult to carry out" (492). In the last sentence Berlin reminds every writing teacher that "a rhetoric cannot escape the ideological question, and to ignore this is to fail our responsibilities as teachers and as citizens" (493).

Here is the subtle yet evident belief that if teachers choose to employ a cognitive or expressive teaching practice, they have failed. Not wanting to be complete failures, one might employ the "yes-but" strategy: "Yes. I know that Berlin says this strategy is not good, but it certainly works in this class right here, right now."

James J. Sosnoski labels these spaces for trashed theories as theory junkyards. We reach back into our theoretical junkyards to choose a theory and teaching practice that works for us in individual teaching situations, going to the "hard-to-reach basement shelves, boxes in attics, files, that our current word processors barely recognize" (Sosnoski 25). In my attic, I have blue milk crates of articles on student conferencing and archetypal criticism. My husband asks me each year if we can get rid of the crates because he's tired of moving them; my department chair, the narratologist, tells me that no one does that type of criticism anymore: "Liz, come on, do you really believe that archetypes are passed down in our unconsciousness?" And I respond, "You know, I'm not sure about that collective unconscious, but I do know that I can teach *The House on Mango Street* from the perspective of Esparanza's quest myth." Here's another yes-but justification for using tools that have been discounted and trashed.

Literary Criticism is also built on this pattern of trashing the current theory to propose the new. The New Critics burst onto the academic scene in the 1940s with their criticism of the biographical critics. Because the New Critics forbade the study of the author, they trashed the biographical critics. In "The Intentional Fallacy" W. K. Wimsatt and Monroe Beardsley claim that it is a fallacy to determine the meaning of a poem by looking to the intentions of the author. Wimsatt and Beardsley argued that embedded in the poem are meanings that the well-trained critic can interpret. Through the 1940s, 1950s, and 1960s, the New Critics were in vogue until the Marxists, feminists, and new historians came along to tell us what was wrong with the New Critics and why they should be banished to the theory junkyard.

But if we stay with the theory junkyard, we trash many theories that explain how, why, when, and where writing happens. Each of the expressive, cognitive, and social-epistemic rhetorics, as well as Thomas Kent's theory of hermeneutic guessing that moved us into the post-process movement, explains just one aspect of producing texts. The theories build to give us more insight into what humans do as they compose and what teachers do to build writers. Our theories build; they are not trash. And each time a theory is added, our pie gets larger and larger with many more slices for everyone when they need it.

The irony is that in the midst of this supposed trashing there is building. Richard Fulkerson's study of composition at the turn of the twenty-first century reports on "the quiet expansion of Expressive approaches to teaching writing" (654). In 2005 Fulkerson offered his "metatheory" of composition scholarship in which he discerns that Expressivism is alive and well "despite numerous poundings by the cannons of postmodernism and resulting eulogies" (655).

Composition's metanarrative is in need of a revision that integrates all that we have discerned about writing and the teaching of writing: a metavision of our field that encompasses the places we have been and the theories and rhetorics that we have practiced. And this is what the editors and authors of *Critical Expressivism: Theory and Practice in the Composition Classroom* offer us. Their classroom stories build a both/and metanarrative of composition as they theorize how the expressive practices are embedded in the social practices and how the social practices are imbedded in the expressive practices of writing and learning.

REFERENCES

Berlin, J. A. (1988). Rhetoric and ideology in the writing class. *College English, 50*(5), 477-494.

Fulkerson, R. (2005). Composition at the turn of the twenty-first century. *College Composition and Communication, 56*(4), 654-687.

Gradin, S. L. (1995). *Romancing rhetorics: Social expressivist perspectives on the teaching of writing.* Portsmouth, NH: Boynton/Cook.

Johnson-Sheehan, R., & Paine, C. (2010). *Teaching with genre: Cure for the common writing course.* Retrieved from Pearson Online Professional Development Web site: http://www.englishinstructorexchange.com/2012/03/15/teaching-with-genre-cure-for-the-common-writing-course-by-richard-johnson-sheehan-charles-paine-created-october-2010/

Kent, T. (1989). Paralogic hermeneutics and the possibilities of rhetoric. *Rhetoric Review, 8*(1), 24-42.

Sosnoski, J. J. (2002). The theory junkyard. In J. J. Williams (Ed.), *The Institution of Literature* (pp. 25-42). Albany, NY: SUNY Press.

Wimsatt, W. K., Jr., & Beardsley, M. (1946). The intentional fallacy. *Sewanee Review, 54,* 468-488.

RE-IMAGINING EXPRESSIVISM: AN INTRODUCTION

Tara Roeder and Roseanne Gatto
St. John's University

It's no secret that the term "expressivism" has been a divisive one in the field of composition and rhetoric. In order to avoid simply rehashing old debates, we began this project with the rejection of an overly simplified "social epistemic"/"-expressivist" binary. Our goal here is to begin a new conversation, one in which established and emerging scholars united by a belief that the term expressivism continues to have a vitally important function in our field can explore the shape of expressivist theory, research, and pedagogy in the twenty-first century.

While our project undertakes the question of what it might mean to re-appropriate the term expressivism, an equally important one might be: why bother? As Peter Elbow himself writes in his contribution to this volume, "As far as I can tell, the term 'expressivist' was coined and used only by people who wanted a word for people they disapproved of and wanted to discredit." As Sherrie L. Gradin points out in her groundbreaking book *Romancing Rhetorics: Social Expressivist Perspectives on the Teaching of Writing* (a book to which we are greatly indebted, and which in many ways began the conversation we are continuing today), "the expressivist emphasis on imagination, creativity, and process ... has often resulted in a charge of anti-intellectualism" (1995, p. 7).

In an email exchange several of us participated in while working on this project, Peter Elbow raised a concern about the value of the term expressivism itself, along with the intriguing question: "Could it be an instance of disparaged people deciding to use the term of disparagement out of pride?" That certainly resonated with the two of us, who have indeed heard disparaging criticism from colleagues who view expressivism as outmoded, elitist, or uncritical. The term "expressivism" seems quaint, somehow; identifying as "expressivist" naïve. So while it makes sense to challenge the very use of the term, it also began to make sense that reclaiming it (or, claiming it for the first time, since it was, as Elbow reminds us, not "ours" to begin with) might be a gently subversive act. (Or a perversely ironic one?) Or, as Nancy Mack put it, "building on the term by attaching the word 'critical' is a rebellious action—and not just reactionary. How terms accrue meaning is Bakhtinian. We can only hope to appropriate the word momentarily and utter it with our accent."

So it is with our accent that we offer this exploration of not only how the term expressivism came to mean, but also how it might come to mean anew. We believe that the best expressivist practices have always been about complex negotiations between self and other, and the dismantling of the "public"/"private" binary that still seems to too often haunt our conversations about writing and pedagogy. But we also want to push our theory and practice further, conceptualizing the ways in which our expressivist values inform our scholarship and our teaching in an increasingly corporatized educational system.

So what exactly do we value? Our contributors have no one, uniform voice or approach, and we think this is a good thing. We notice that when the two of us talk about teaching and writing, we spend a lot of time questioning handbooks and guides for the "novice" writer, where race and gender and class and sexuality are erased in the name of an increasingly ludicrous concept of "correctness." We know we don't believe in prescriptions or generalities; we believe in a localized, context-specific pedagogy where one size never fits all. And we fiercely value our students and the complex embodied knowledge they bring to our classrooms. We think that when their experiences are at the forefront of our classrooms, exciting thoughts, relevant research, and meaningful connections can take place via a variety of platforms, from handbound books to conversations to YouTube videos.

So what makes this "expressivist"? We are indebted to a tradition in which scholars such as Peter Elbow, Sherrie Gradin, Nancy Mack, Thomas Newkirk, Thomas O'Donnell, Michelle Payne, Lad Tobin, and Robert Yagelski have demonstrated the complex ways in which the "social" and "personal" are not two poles in a binary system. We are also indebted to the feminist maxim, "the personal is political." We hope that this will be the beginning of a new discussion, one in which the complex interactions between self and other are contextualized in a way that values the individual circumstances of our students' lives and the ways in which they make meaning of their experiences and interrogate the culture in which they live.

Our contributors focus on both how to position expressivism theoretically within twenty-first century composition studies, and how specific assignments and pedagogies can facilitate our understanding of what expressivist practices mean to our students and ourselves. While many of the essays share similar themes, and there is some overlap between the sections, we identified four major strands surfacing in our contributors' work.

Section One, entitled "Critical Self-Construction," complicates the notion that "personal" writing and "academic" writing occupy separate categories on some hierarchy of sophistication. It opens with Peter Elbow, who problematizes the very terms "expressivism" and "personal writing" that have so long been connected with his work. He questions what the term "personal" means, pointing out that when we are truly invested in "academic" topics, our own feelings, histories, experiences, and languages will inevitably shape our texts: "I may not be writing here about my sex life or my feelings about a sunset, but it's a personal story nevertheless." This insight sheds a meaningful light on the collective project we are undertaking here, one in which each contributor was compelled to become involved because of her or his own beliefs and experiences as teachers, writers, and thinkers.

Thomas Newkirk analyzes the sources of some teachers' "discomfort" in the face of "personal" writing, exploring the complexity involved in responding to the traumatic and the moralistic in student texts. He also makes a powerful case against dismissing the "personal essay" through the words of his student Brianna, who reminds us that "by turning a blind eye to these types of [personal] essays, we might as well be turning a blind eye to literature itself." Nancy Mack and Derek Owens also challenge the idea that writing about the self is necessarily a solipsistic or uncritical act. Mack looks at the critical function of memoir, a genre that allows writers and readers to question stability and essentialist notions of identity: "a critical memoir approach asks the writer to continually reconsider one's own master narratives," raising questions about how such stories "could be actively re-interpreted and revised to represent a newly constructed, more ethical truth." Such an insight is exciting in the face of the kind of stereotypical "progression" Owens sees as characteristic in many composition courses: "One might picture the progression like some kind of game board—each student entering via their own unique paths and histories, engaging with them along the way, but ultimately everyone coming closer and closer to a common finish line where it's not their 'expressed' personal histories that matter but, say, the way they marshal evidence, cite sources, make inferences, assemble claims. Establish authority." The fact that personally meaningful work is, at its best, also "critical" work is evidenced by Owens' own experience composing his memoir about his mother, a process through which he "became interested in the strangeness of memory and the slipperiness of identity." Jean Bessette also stresses the "dynamic slipperiness of memory" in her contribution to this volume, exploring the ways in which feminist conceptions of memory as "necessarily social and discursive" can contribute to an enriched understanding of the ways in which asking students to write themselves is an inherently critical act, one in which we need to face head on static and limiting notions of what our experiences signify. Lea Povozhaev also tackles the tidy divides between "creative," "personal," and "academic" writing, pointing out that the diverse work of "children creating art, prisoners writing poems, and students writing" evidences the fact that creative acts can be "pleasurable, therapeutic, and educational." The act of eschewing rigid generic distinctions can, our contributors evidence, be both liberatory and pedagogically useful.

Section Two, "Personal Writing and Social Change," explores some of the multiple ways in which expressivist theory and practice are connected to larger political and social goals. For Patricia Webb Boyd, in a period when "many may feel unable to control their own lives, much less effect change in larger society," the question at hand becomes: "How can we imagine creative alternatives where students and teachers can ... see themselves as active participants in public spheres/discourses who can co-create change rather than be passive consumers?" Boyd sees the role of critical expressivism as one that encourages our students to feel connected to their own experiences, and thus to larger goals and communities. Daniel Collins, in his lyric collage, maintains that "expressivist writing theory ... upholds the idea that to write is to discover oneself amidst an array of others." It is through our students' writing about their lived experience that they can forge connections to a larger culture, and begin to enact change. Scott Wagar and Eric Leake both focus on the relationship between expressivist practice and empathy. For Wagar, the goals of non-violence and recognition of interdependence can be facilitated through a pedagogy based on the insights of theorists such as Mary Rose O'Reilly, who asks "Is it possible to teach English so that people stop killing each other?" A fraught question, but one that is essential to the goals of critical expressivist pedagogy—a pedagogy in which we might "consciously re-frame our work in non-violent terms." This is not to suggest that we "critical expressivists" have all the answers: as Eric Leake reminds us in his nuanced examination of the role of empathy in successful expressivist teaching, "a critical empathy continually reminds us that empathy is always at best a careful and purposeful approximation of another's experience." However, by working together with our students, we may find the kind of ground in which our empathy can be at once nourished and examined.

Section Three, "Histories," provides valuable insight into the ways in which expressivist pedagogies and ideas have developed contextually. Maja Wilson instructively teases out the links between Berlin's "battle with the expressivists and Watson's battle with the introspectionists." Her playful and salient piece urges us to locate our theories of composition on solid ethical territory, while providing insightful, contextualized readings of Berlin in light of John Watson's theories of behaviorism. Chris Warnick's essay takes up Karen Surnam Paley's call to "research actual 'expressionist' classroom practice" by delving into materials from The University of Pittsburgh's "Alternative Curriculum" of the 1970s, examining the ways in which the innovative program drew on expressivist philosophies, practices, and assignments. Warnick's essay leaves us with a valuable call to continue the kind of archival research that will better allow us to understand the practical results of expressivist pedagogies. Hannah Rule explores the rich historical relationship between Romanticism and expressivism, arguing that particular "pedagogies and rhetorics are deemed untenable because they are labeled romantic or expressivist, or romantic-expressivist." Rule's essay complicates the neat divides between the various composition "camps" through a careful reading of both the Romantics and the "expressivists." Anthony Petruzzi similarly looks to locate expressivist practice within a history of "critical conscience" as defined by Emerson, offering a nuanced reading of the role of pragmatism in the development of expressivist philosophy.

Our final section, "Pedagogies," explores specific expressivist assignments and classroom practices in hopes of illuminating what exactly some of us do as critical expressivists. David Seitz questions the value of having our students "consume academic texts … and only reproduce their discourse and generic forms." He instead offers assignments "supported by principles of place-based education and theories of genre as textual sites of social action," exploring the ways in which students can use writing as a way to mediate between the expectations of the academy and their own sense of the cultures and communities they occupy. Kim M. Davis urges us to value the "intersection of community-based learning and critical pedagogy." Davis' ethnographic study of her students in Detroit perfectly illustrates the ways in which "personal writing became the vehicle to help bridge the connection between students' lived realities regarding race and place and the critical pedagogy goal of multiculturalism." Sheri Rysdam turns to the expressivist legacy of "low/no stakes writing" as she examines the ways in which low-stakes assignments have a particularly valuable function for emerging student writers. Jeff Sommers re-visits the concept of radical revision in concrete terms, drawing on his own students' positive experiences with acts of meaningfully re-entering their texts and discovering the "rich possibilities open to them through revision."

There's no doubt that we and our students face new challenges as we move through the twenty-first century together. We certainly don't have all the answers to the questions the writers in our courses will grapple with as they continue to make sense of their experiences, their educations, and the culture of violence in which they live. But we do hope that we can offer assignments, approaches, and responses that are worthy of them, and that enable them to make sense of their experiences and the world around them in meaningful, innovative, and self-directed ways.

REFERENCE

Gradin, S. (1995). *Romancing rhetorics: Social expressivist perspectives on the teaching of writing.* Portsmouth, NH: Boynton/Cook.

SECTION ONE:
CRITICAL SELF-CONSTRUCTION

"PERSONAL WRITING" AND "EXPRESSIVISM" AS PROBLEM TERMS

Peter Elbow
University of Massachussetts Amherst

When dispute about something goes round and round without resolution, it's often a sign that the key term has too many unexplored meanings. I aim to show a kind of hidden ambiguity in "Personal Writing" and "Expressivism," and show how this leads to confusion and bad thinking. First, I'll explore the ambiguity in "personal writing." Then I'll explore "expressivism." James Berlin said that personal writing—writing about the self—is the hallmark of expressivism and named me as a prime expressivist. I'll try to explain why I and other so-called "expressivists" made a prominent place for personal writing but didn't consider it better or more important than other kinds of writing.

PART I: DIFFERENT DIMENSIONS OF PERSONAL WRITING

The term personal writing has caused needless argument and confusion because in fact there is no such thing as "personal writing" in itself. There are three different dimensions of the personal and they can be present in various combinations in any piece of writing. The *topic* can be personal or not; the language can be personal or not; and the thinking can be personal or not.

Typical personal topics are the feelings or experiences of the particular writer.

Typical personal language is everyday spoken, colloquial, vernacular, or low-register language and syntax.

Typical personal thinking makes use of metaphors, feelings, associations, hunches, and other such processes that are not systematic or disciplined.[1]

The Topic Can Be Personal—or Not

A personal topic might be "My Experiences with Revising" or "My Experiences in the Peace Corps in Haiti." A striking example is Margaret Bullet-Jonas' *Holy Hunger*, a penetrating account of her struggles with an eating disorder. Personal topics contrast with nonpersonal topics like these: "The Revising Practices of First-Year Students" or "How the Peace Corps Works" or "Conditions in Haiti after the Hurricane" or "Cultural Causes of Eating Disorders." Essays on these nonpersonal topics might never treat the writer or her experience at all.

Obviously there is a continuum or spectrum between completely personal and nonpersonal topics. One example is common in journalism or magazine writing and some books: the writing is based on interviews and it almost floods the reader with the most deeply personal details of someone's life, often using lots of personal language from the interviewee. Yet the writer remains completely hidden and uses no personal language in his or her own voice. Here's another marginal case: a writer takes a seemingly personal topic—say his or her own alcohol use—and make it nonpersonal by taking a wholly detached, medical, or phenomenological approach. (Sometimes this is not so much a way of making the topic impersonal as using highly detached impersonal thinking or language for a personal topic.)

There's a kind of hybrid between personal and nonpersonal that has become a recognizable genre in first-year writing courses: teachers have discovered that students often do a better job with "academic research"—e.g., eating habits or college study habits—if the writer also uses the paper to explore his or her own personal experiences in the area. Of course adults and professionals do the same thing. Jane Hindman, in "Making Writing Matter," writes of the personal topic of her own drinking in an essay that's also about the impersonal topic of human discourse and agency. Nancy Sommers, in "Between the Drafts," writes of the personal topic of her own revising in an essay that's also about revising in general. Keith Gilyard uses alternate chapters to focus on the personal and nonpersonal as a topic in *Voices of the Self.*

Though we thus see marginal or mixed topics, the main point bears repeating: the topic can be personal or not regardless of whether the thinking or language is personal.

THE LANGUAGE CAN BE PERSONAL—OR NOT

What is personal language? We usually call language personal if it uses slang or colloquial forms or an informal register. There's a natural implied metaphor here of physical closeness and presence (a "metaphor we live by"): when someone gets very close it feels personal. What's closest and most personal is a hug or embrace. Distance and absence feel more impersonal or formal. Colloquial language sounds like speech, and speech gives us more sense of the writer's physical presence sitting next to us—more intimate and therefore more personal.

A word like "talky" feels more personal than "colloquial;" "figure out" than "conclude." A certain number of teachers and academic journals ban contractions: contractions give the sound of speech; non-contractions give a sound less heard in speech. The first person "I" calls attention to the presence of the writer and presumably this explains the ritual prohibition against it in many academic situations—especially in science (APA guidelines to the contrary notwithstanding). "We" somewhat dilutes the stain of first person. The second person "you" calls attention to the reader as a person, and even that seems enough to be regarded as too personal for some academic writing. Because most of these features give a greater sense of presence or of contact between writer and reader, Deborah Tannen and other linguists call them "involvement" strategies.

The use of a question can make language more personal by implying conversational contact between writer and reader. Compare these two passages:

> There is only a faint and ambiguous correlation between prostate cancer and a high PSA reading.
>
> But how about PSA tests for prostate cancer? How much can we trust them?

Again it must be remembered that there's no black/white dividing line between personal and nonpersonal language, but rather a continuum.

Personal language can be used for nonpersonal topics. The most obvious site is in much note-taking, freewriting, rough exploratory writing, and informal letter writing when the topic is wholly nonpersonal and perhaps scholarly—for example even some technical scientific topic. Email has increased the amount of personal language and personal thinking used for nonpersonal topics.

But do we find personal language in published writing about nonpersonal topics? If we look back over the last fifty years or so at newspapers, magazines, and nonfiction for a wide audience, we notice a general drift along the continuum towards more informal, personal registers in published writing. Such informality of language was often experienced as a violation of "proper standards for writing." But popular nonfiction has come to use more and more personal registers—even about nonpersonal topics. Literary nonfiction in particular (for example in nature writing) often uses some of the more linguistically personal resources of fiction.

In *The New Yorker*—a magazine that's always been fastidious about language—we find a growing use of informal colloquial language. Look at the first sentence in the second paragraph below:

> There is nothing wrong with cars, TV sets, and running shoes. What's wrong is the waste—chemicals, heavy metals, CO_2—that's produced when we make them, use them, and, eventually, throw them away. Eliminate that waste, and you eliminate the problem.

> Right, and why not cure cancer while you're at it? Last time we checked, waste—landfills, smog, river sludge—was the price we paid for a healthy economy. (Surowiecki, 2002, p. 56)

William Safire often took a conservative line about language in his *New York Times* columns, so it's striking to see how much personal language he used for the nonpersonal topic of correct and incorrect language. His writing was often conversational, casual, first person, sometimes slangy. He celebrated the clash of registers and liked sudden swerves into the personal, especially in asides: "In the age of multiculturalism and interdisciplinarianism (there's a new one), most of the nonscientific uses of the term have been pejorative." In the same column, he started a section with a one-sentence paragraph: "You pay for good linguistic lawyering, you get it." And he ends the section with yet a shorter paragraph: "I spell it tchotchki. Do I need a lawyer?"

Students often use informal language for impersonal topics even if they have been directed to avoid it. But teachers should note how often good writers in the world bring to bear personal language and personal thinking on nonpersonal topics—and that most of our students will do virtually all of their future writing outside the academy. Anne Herrington writes: "Failing to recognize the presence of [linguistic] rendering [of personal experience] in some academic writing—including writing within composition studies—contributes to dismissing its value in undergraduate writing" (2002, p. 233). A number of business genres, however, are notable for strenuously resisting personal language.

In published academic writing we also see a gradual slide toward informal language over the last fifty years. Changes might seem subtle if you are in the middle of them, but I gather that scholarly writing in, say, Spain and Germany retains a formality that has been abandoned here. On the other hand, it's interesting to note nontrivial movement in the other direction toward a formal register in academic writing in our field. Essays from the early days of *College Composition and Communication* tended to use a more personal register than what we've seen since the field has worked harder at professionalism. Think about some of the essays by, say, Edward Corbett and James Corder—esteemed scholars who nevertheless pulled their chair up close to readers and talked fairly personally and directly to them. Also, older scholarship in English studies tended to follow a British tradition of scholarly writing that was slightly talkier than the more formal nonpersonal Germanic tradition in scholarship adopted in the academic world some time in the twentieth century. (Essays for a student audience are more likely to use more personal language, yet oddly enough, it can work the other way too. When Martha Kolln addresses other teachers in the instructor's manual of her *Rhetorical Grammar* (1991, p. 15), she is willing to write more personally than she does to students: she talks personally about an anecdote from her life, but doesn't permit herself this kind of informality in the book intended for students.)

When academics publish a talk or speech, they are likely to use more informal colloquial personal language (though I've often been asked by copy editors to remove such language when I've had a talk accepted for publication).

Nonpersonal language can also be used for personal topics. We often don't notice impersonal language when the topic or content is blatantly self-disclosing. But most people are far more conservative about language than about ideas or content, and the language habits of writers are often especially strong. Training in academic discourse goes deep. Copy editors may weed out locutions in a personal or informal register that remain in the writer's final draft. Consider Jane Hindman's amazingly personal essay that also uses an experimental form: three different type faces for three different voices. It's deeply confessional about personal matters that few are willing to address. Yet not much of the language itself is particularly personal; most of it is either standard edited English or even quite academic. I noticed only three exceptions: three short italicized paragraphs of inner speech dropped in at different points that use distinctly personal writing. For another example, Mary Louise Buley-Meissner speaks of a writer's personal essay where "The word I appears twenty-nine times in thirty-four sentences, yet the self written into her text is voiceless, anonymous" (1990, p. 52).

The most striking example of nonpersonal language used for personal topics is illustrated when professionals like psychiatrists, psychologists, or doctors write professionally about very personal issues like sexuality or divorce—albeit the personal issues of other people. The topic is a very personal story, but the language will usually be in the rubber-gloved, nonpersonal register of their discipline.

THINKING TOO CAN BE PERSONAL—OR NOT

What is personal thinking? The notion might seem counterintuitive and a few people might argue that thinking is only thinking if it follows rules of deductive logic. But the word "thinking" is not normally used so narrowly in English. Common parlance applies the term to a broad range of cognitive processes: metaphorical thinking, trains of feelings, story telling, illustrative examples or anecdotes, inferences based on association rather than strict logic, and perhaps even mere hunches. Andrea Lunsford speaks of how writing can make a space for intuition, emotion, and the body in writing and in the construction of knowledge—what Kenneth Burke calls the paralogical, to go along with the logical that has had a stranglehold on the teaching of writing (1998, p. 24). And feminists have written about how the term "thinking" has been too narrowly defined in ways that represent patriarchy (Falmagne).

A particular kind of personal thinking could be called narrative thinking. Jerome Bruner made his reputation and pretty much defined the field of cognitive psychology by defining thinking or cognition as the abstract process of forming abstract categories. But late in his career he wrote a notable and influential book, *Actual Minds*, arguing that narrative thinking is equally central in human thinking (1986). Anthropologists like Lévi-Strauss showed how myths are examples of vigorous thinking about large nonpersonal issues. Mina Shaughnessy praised Richard Hoggart and James Baldwin for their skill in using autobiography to do intellectual work (Bartholomae, 1980). See also the special issue of *Pre/Text* devoted to personal and expressive writing doing the work of academic discourse (Elbow, 1990).

Again, it's obvious that there is an extended continuum between nonpersonal and personal thinking.

In addition, personal thinking is often applied to nonpersonal topics. Montaigne enacted and celebrated what can only be called personal thinking, even when his topic was nonpersonal (the education of children, for example). Because he actually invented the essay and named it with a word that means "an attempt," many have argued that the essay itself is a genre with an inherent link to informal personal thinking. He associated what is "human" with what is not "ordered" by a strict (French) "method." Naturally, much poetry too applies personal, intuitional, associative thinking to nonpersonal topics (for example, Wallace Stevens' "The Idea of Order at Key West").

Ken Macrorie made an important contribution to our field with his "I Search Essay," showing countless students how to get more invested in serious research by bringing personal intuitive thinking to bear. And there has been an explosion of interest in creative nonfiction, a genre that often applies personal thinking to nonpersonal topics. William Safire liked to do policy analysis by pretending to get inside the feelings of public figures:

> I am John Kerry, falling farther behind in the polls with only six weeks to go.
>
> I've already shaken up my staff again …
>
> The "fortunate son" business hasn't hurt Bush—and I wasn't exactly born in a log cabin. (2004)

When Nicholas Baker writes about the impersonal topic of punctuation he conveys lots of history and technical information, but his actual mode of thinking about it is often strikingly personal. And his language slides toward the colloquial and personal. Peter Medawar, Nobel prize winner in biology, writes eloquently about the difference between the associational and intuitive thinking that scientists use to figure out their hypotheses, and the nonpersonal disciplined form in which they typically present their findings. Nancy Sommers uses her feelings to help her think about the nonpersonal topic of revising. Jane Hindman thinks with her experience—noticing one feeling and then probing and waiting to find another feeling underneath it—in order to wrestle with the abstract nonpersonal issue of the degree to which the self is constructed by discourse. Fontaine and Hunter's *Writing Ourselves into the Story* is one of various collections of essays that use personal experience for thinking about academic topics in composition.

Is this Differential Analysis Necessary?

This is not just an exercise in casuistic categorizing for its own sake (which might occasionally have been a temptation for Aristotle). I see the same practical consequences for this analysis as I argued in my discussion of five species of voice (1994b) and multiple species of academic discourse (1991). When people fail to notice that a single term is hiding multiple meanings, they often think carelessly and argue fruitlessly past each other: they are unconsciously assuming different definitions of personal writing, voice, or academic discourse.

For example, readers often assume that a text is personal because it is more or less dominated by, say, strongly personal language (what a reader might call "flagrantly personal"). They fail to consider the nonpersonal nature of the topic and even the thinking. This kind of misjudgment is particularly harmful when a teacher tells the student, "this is too personal." The student is liable to try to push the thinking and the focus of the topic even further towards the impersonal—often making the essay ineffectively general and abstract. How much better if the teacher could have said, "It's only your language that is too personal for this context." It might even be that the essay would have been better if the student nudged the thinking and topic focus a bit more in the personal direction. By the same token, an essay might be almost embarrassingly self-disclosing in topic—but not in language or thinking. (I'd say that Jane Tompkins sometimes wanders in this direction.)

When teachers or other readers take enough care to notice, for example, the differences between personal elements among the three dimensions of writing, they also have a better chance of attending to their own personal reactions and engaging in careful thinking: "This paper really irritates me. I wonder why. Has it touched on a sore spot for me, or is there in fact a feature in the text that asks readers to experience something challenging or 'in your face'?"

The kind of differential analysis I've been using here has led me to argue more generally for rubrics in teacher response and assessment (and sometimes even peer response). Readers who fail to distinguish among the dimensions of a text (e.g., thinking, organization, clarity of sentences, mechanics) often fall into snap holistic judgments. This kind of unthinking interpretation is particularly harmful when a paper is full of errors in grammar and spelling—especially grammar that a teacher unconsciously associates with "stupid." Such a teacher fails to see many genuine strengths in the paper and therefore gives misleading and actually damaging feedback—or an invalid grade. Here's a sad comment by an experienced teacher about a piece of writing by speaker of African-American English: "Only now can I really address the underlying thinking and understanding problems—because previously the writing was so atrocious that I couldn't see them." (I took this from a composition listserv.) In a comparable way, an entire essay can seem to be tainted for some readers because it embodies political or religious or cultural views that the teacher experiences as toxic.

PART II: MY RELATIONSHIP WITH PERSONAL WRITING AND EXPRESSIVISM

I wonder whether you noticed that my own writing throughout Part One is almost entirely nonpersonal—in topic, thinking, and language. Perhaps the language might be experienced by some readers as slightly personal because I avoided a "formal" or "high" register—and occasionally used "I." But does that make it "personal"? I'd say no. Still, in the next section I want to let my writing be personal on all three dimensions: personal topic, personal thinking, and (fairly) personal language.

I'm not using Part Two merely as an illustration of the analysis in Part One. No; I've written this stylistically schizophrenic essay in order to enact my divided loyalties to personal writing. For I keep bouncing back and forth in my feelings about personal writing:

First bounce. I tried to keep anything personal out of Part One because I want you to assess it entirely in terms of the logic of its analysis. For example, when I pointed out how many writers mix the personal and nonpersonal in the same essay, I hope it was clear that I wasn't expressing approval—just making an empirical claim in order to bolster my main analytic argument about how the different dimensions of the personal are separate and can be mixed.

Second bounce. But I know it's impossible to make a purely rational disinterested argument that works entirely on its own logic. You could even say that it's intellectually dishonest to pretend to do so. Any attempt to argue in this way will always be surreptitiously slanted by the writer's position. This principle implies that we have a duty, as writers, to reveal our personal stake; to acknowledge that readers can't assess our argument unless they know something about the position we write from.

I agree with this view in many situations. I get irritated with argumentative writing (especially by academics) where the writer pretends to be making a disinterested or objective case, yet that case is permeated by surreptitious personal feelings: the writer is secretly trying to settle a score with a critic, or trying to defend a pet theory that he himself has a big stake in, or trying preen his or her erudition, or salve a wounded ego. When an academic is good at this game, only readers "in the know" will see these backstage hidden agendas. Why do the conventions of academic discourse still reflect a pretense of objectivity, when academics themselves are so busy saying that objectivity is impossible?

Third bounce. Still, I want to push back against my argument in the second bounce. I'm deeply committed to the idea no one has an obligation to reveal themselves more than they want. One of the great glories of writing is that it permits us to disguise our voices or hide our feelings. An argument can be good or bad apart from who makes it or what the personal motivation might be. The anonymity that is possible through the technology of writing has made it possible for countless people, especially in stigmatized groups, to persuade readers who would not otherwise have listened to them. Just because perfect objectivity is not possible, that doesn't mean that we can't strive toward it and make good headway.

Fourth bounce. Still, any attempt I might make to hide behind impersonal writing was probably wasted on many readers, since I have come to be so widely identified with personal writing. In the early 1980s, Berlin defined me as a prime expressivist, and this characterization was widely accepted. So it's not really possible for me to pretend to be disinterested.

So now I want to tell the story of my relationship to expressivism and personal writing. I will invite all three personal dimensions into my text. I may not be writing here about my sex life or my feelings about a sunset, but it's a personal story nevertheless. The topic is personal: like most of us, I have personal feelings about certain "academic" topics. The thinking is personal too: it reflects not just my thinking but my feelings and intuitions and how my personal position influences my take on personal writing and expressivism. And so too, the language is fairly personal: it may not be slangy or "colloquial," but it's not far from my "vernacular"—the language that comes most naturally to my white middle class academic mouth. (Perhaps the language in Parts One and Two is pretty much the same: kind of halfway between personal and impersonal.)

*

When Berlin called me a poster boy for expressivism in the 1980s, he must have been thinking mostly about my *Writing Without Teachers*, published in 1973. For his later article in 1988, he also looked at *Writing With Power* (1985), but that book is remarkably impersonal compared to the 1973 book. So I will be referring here mostly to *Writing Without Teachers* in trying to figure out why

23

I was so identified with personal writing.

Actually, there are two questions that need exploring: Why did Berlin and so many readers think that *Writing Without Teachers* itself was personal? And why did Berlin and so many readers think my goal in the book was to advocate or preach personal writing?

1. I don't think the book was very personal, but I understand now why it was so often felt that way. Let's look at the three dimensions:

Language. Not very personal, I'd say. Here's a typical example. You'll see "I" a number of times, but the word is not really very personal; it's functioning as a generalized claim about people in general.

> We all tend to believe in word-magic: if I think words, my mind will be tricked into believing them; if I speak those words, I'll believe them more strongly; and if I actually write them down, I am somehow secretly committed to them and my behavior is determined by them. It is crucial to learn to write words and not believe them or feel hypnotized at all. It can even be good practice to write as badly or as foolishly as you can. If you can't write anything at all, it is probably because you are too squeamish to let yourself write badly. (1973/1998, p. 70)

"I" is a called a "personal" pronoun, but it's pretty clear in this passage that it refers not to me but to other people who have feelings different from mine. (I fear I've always had a weakness for overusing "I" and "we" in ways that are theoretically suspect—betraying a tendency to assume "we're all alike.") But despite all the "I"s in that passage, I'm struck with how seldom I used the word throughout the book.

Perhaps in 1973, my language might have struck academic readers as personal or speech-like, but I was trying to talk to a popular audience. When I wrote the book, I didn't foresee that so many academics would read it. I had taught for almost twenty years, but had never been in an English department nor identified with the field of composition. It's ironic that this least academic of all my books would be read more often than any of the others in graduate seminars.

Thinking. The thinking in *Writing Without Teachers* was indeed very personal, and I think that's the biggest reason why so many readers experienced the book as personal. What interested me most, and still does, is thinking. (I'm hoping that my tombstone will read, "He loved thinking.") I wanted to show that our thinking doesn't have to be formal and impersonal or strictly logical when we work on nonpersonal or academic topics.

I was trying to describe the writing process as a personal process—and make my description informal too. I used lots of homely details from everyday life. At the conceptual center of the book were two homely metaphors: "cooking" and "growing"—idiosyncratic and personal. (My Oxford editor advised me to drop those metaphors.) At one point I used a kooky childish analogy for the mystery of the writing process: I asked readers to imagine a land where people couldn't understand how to touch the floor with their fingers because the traditional belief was that one did it by reaching upwards. Thus their traditional process for floor-touching never worked. Yet there were a few people who had actually learned to touch the floor—by instinct or trial and error—but they couldn't explain how they did it because their whole conceptual system was confused about up and down (1973/1998, p. 13).

After this book came out in 1973 I began to get a trickle of letters from strangers addressing me quite personally, as though they felt they knew me. I didn't mind; indeed I felt kind of touched, but it's always seemed a little curious. For I hadn't revealed much about me in *Writing Without Teachers*. Yes, I acknowledged—quite briefly—that my interest and relationship to writing grew out of my own difficulties and struggle and even failure. But I told almost nothing of what actually happened—which was in fact a very personal story. Nor did I tell virtually anything about my life.

But though I didn't let my life or my "self" show, I let my mind show. It was because my thinking was so personal that some readers felt they knew me. And why not? It turns out that when someone gives an accurate picture of their thinking processes—with all its idiosyncratic twists and turns rather than the neatened picture of thinking that writers often publish, especially academic writers—readers often feel they know the writer. (My wife once quipped that the book invited the reader into bed with me. But this had to be based only on my thinking. A fun idea: thinking as sex appeal?)

Topic. In *Writing Without Teachers*, I let my mind show, but my mind was not at all the topic of the book—nor my self nor my feelings. The topic of *Writing Without Teachers* was squarely nonpersonal: the process of writing. I used the book to tell people—obsessively—what they should do to make their writing go better. I may have started by acknowledging that I was making generalizations based on a sample of one, but even to the small degree that my experience shows, it was always a means to a nonpersonal end—generalizations of wider import. It wasn't till 1998, when I wrote "Illiteracy at Oxford and Harvard" and also the Preface to 2nd edition of *Writing Without Teachers*, that I told my personal story of failing and then gradually figuring out a way of writing. Of course it was easier in 1973 to qualify as a flaming show off than it is now—especially in the light of the all the recent self-disclosure by academics.

In short it was not at all a "me me me book." (Berlin wrote in 1982 that "expressionistic rhetoric" involves the "placement of the self at the center of communication" [p. 772.]) It was, however, a kind of "you you you" book. I couldn't stop talking about what "you" should learn to do to make the writing process more successful and satisfying. Maybe this gave a kind of personal feeling to the topic. Of course I didn't know anything at all about my readers, but maybe my strategy led them to think a lot about themselves. I guess by saying "you you you," I was using an "involvement strategy."

So was *Writing Without Teachers* a piece of personal writing? The question has no answer. It illustrates why we need the analysis I gave in Part One. The book was notably personal in thinking, but not personal in language, and mostly not in topic. The reception of the book as personal by so many readers confirms my hypothesis at the end of Part One: readers are sometimes tempted to ignore nonpersonal dimensions when one dimension seems strikingly personal.

2. Why did so many readers think my goal in the book was to advocate or preach personal writing? Why did Berlin consider me an archetypal expressivist—someone committed to writing about me, me, self, self, feelings, feelings—only what is internal? And why does he name me as the central figure of expressivism (1988)—a school he said is based on this premise: "Truth is conceived as the result of a private vision" (1982)?

In his later essay ("Rhetoric and Ideology") he quotes my 1985 *Writing With Power* to argue that I "consistently" preach personal writing. But to make his case, he purposely misquotes me to pretend that my words champion personal, expressive, self-oriented writing when they are actually saying the opposite. Berlin writes:

> This power [that Elbow advocates] is consistently defined in personal terms: "power comes from the words somehow fitting the writer (not necessarily the reader) ... power comes from the words somehow fitting what they are about. [Berlin's ellipses] (1988, p. 485)

Look at the words I actually wrote—by way of introducing two chapters about power coming from nonself:

> ... I think true power in words is a mystery.... In [the previous] Chapters 25 and 26 about voice, I suggest that power comes from the words somoew fitting the writer (not necessarily the reader).... In [the following] Chapters 27 and 28 about breathing experience into writing, I suggest that power comes from the words somehow fitting what they are about. The words so well embody what they express that when readers encounter the words they feel they are encountering the

objects or ideas themselves.... (280)

And if he had read the chapters these words were introducing, he would have found passages like these. First the epigraph by Basho:

> Go to the pine if you want to learn about the pine, or to the bamboo if you want to learn about the bamboo. And in doing so, you must leave your subjective preoccupation with yourself. Otherwise you impose yourself on the object and do not learn. Your poetry issues of its own accord when you and the object have become one.

And then this passage in a subsection titled "A Warning about Feelings:"

> But strong feelings in themselves, don't help you breathe experience into words. In fact some of the worst writing fails precisely because it comes too much out of feelings rather than out of the event or scene itself—out of the bamboo. (1988, p. 334)

How can someone pretend to be a scholar and use manipulative ellipses to pretend that a passage fits his ideological thesis when it actually contradicts it?

I was angry and even hurt to see such an unscholarly distortion of my work. I've never recognized myself in his picture—nor the stereotypical pictures of the other main expressivists like Macrorie, Britton, and Murray. Indeed, I'd say that Berlin's characterization of expressionism was harmful for the field. I considered trying to write back and argue against his reading, but whenever I've seen people do that, they always sound like wounded ineffectual whiners. One friend told me that I looked arrogant not to argue against Berlin in print—as though I didn't design to enter the fray—but I ended up feeling that it would have been futile; that the only constructive thing I could do was to carry on with my own work and not be deflected or thrown off course.

It's intriguing that his picture of me and the field persuaded so many people in composition studies. His division of the field into one right school and three wrong ones somehow took deep root and finally became an almost universally unexamined assumption. (See, for example, Victor Villanueva's "The Personal," (2001, p. 52), and Greg Myers (1986, p. 64).)

But as I put away my anger at his wrong-headed picture of my work—and his rhetorical brilliance in making everyone accept his picture of the field—perhaps I can see how it happened.

In truth I was preaching personal writing—in a sense. That is, I was preaching freewriting (among other things), and that seems like mostly personal writing. Freewriting gives you no time to plan, and in its default exercise form there is no specified topic. In those conditions, people tend to freewrite personally. I guess he was hypnotized by what seems like the inherently personal nature of freewriting (it seemed much more controversial and dangerous than it does now).

But in preaching freewriting, I was preaching a process—a process designed to lead to any kind of product, not personal writing. Freewriting is a means to an end—to help you learn to write more fluently and easily and to find more words and thoughts. The process has no bias at all toward personal writing. In fact, freewriting as a process is not inherently personal. Many people use freewriting to explore completely nonpersonal topics. I'd guess that most of the freewriting I've done in my life (excluding journal writing) is nonpersonal in content (though using personal language).

Berlin quotes words from the opening of *Writing Without Teachers* about my goal in the book: "to help students become 'less helpless both personally and politically' by enabling them to get 'control over words'"(1973/1998, p. 485). He pretends this means that the goal is personal writing and can't see how that goal (as with freewriting) pertains to all kinds of writing, not just personal writing.

In fact, as I look back at *Writing Without Teachers*, I'm amused to notice how narrow and bookish were the examples of writing tasks that I tended to use. I think I spoke about an essay on the causes of the French Revolution. My editor at the time joked that even though the book pretended to be about writing without teachers, really I hadn't yet learned to escape the classroom. I remember inserting, late, some examples of fiction, poetry, and memoir, but they were token examples. I knew nothing about that kind of writing; school writing was all I knew.

Of course freewriting often does lead to personal writing. But I'd say that my main goal in making lots of space for personal writing was to help inexperienced or timid writers take more authority over their writing: not to feel so intimidated by it and not to write so much tangled or uninvested prose or mechanical or empty thinking. The various dimensions of personal writing seemed to me then, and still seem, the most powerful tools for getting authority over writing and thinking in general. When we invite personal topics, we invite people to write about events or experiences that they know better than any reader—even the teacher reader. Thus they have more authority about the topic.[2] And when we invite personal thinking, we invite people to develop ideas by following their own personal and idiosyncratic thought processes—using hunches, metaphors, associations, and emotional thinking. Most people can produce richer and more interesting ideas this way than by trying to conform to disciplined thinking untainted by personal biases and emotions. Of course disciplined thinking is also necessary, but as I argued, it needs to come afterwards in a writing process that consciously separates noncritical generating from detached critical judging.

*

When we invite personal language, we invite people to write by using whatever words come most comfortably to tongue—instead of always pausing, erasing, changing and worrying that they've probably used the wrong word. Of course I made it clear that one eventually had to turn around and criticize and edit many of one's freely written words ("taking a razor to one's own flesh" was one way I put it in another metaphor of personal thinking), but that critical process didn't need to interfere with a happy and self-confident process of generating words and ideas.

I was also preaching the teacherless writing class. Like freewriting, it was designed to help people do all kinds of writing and it carried no bias toward personal writing. But like freewriting, the process itself must have seemed flagrantly personal: no teacher; no one with sanctioned expertise; people (often personal friends) sit around talking about the feelings and thoughts that come into their minds as they hear or read each others' texts. Joe Harris complained that "the students in [a teacherless class] … do not seem to be held answerable to each other as intellectuals" (1997, p. 31). In this age of the internet and Wikipedia we can forget how unusual it was to propose a teacherless writing class in 1973. Perhaps it was asking too much of Berlin even in the 1980s to read carefully enough to see the that the teacherless peer process I laid out was quite disciplined and methodical—and not especially personal. For example, if a responder in a teacherless class talks about her feelings that occur as she reads a writer's text, her topic is not her feelings; her topic is the writer's text and what those feelings reveal about it.

*

In this second half of the essay, then, my point is that "expressivism" is a seriously misleading word. It has led countless people to skewed and oversimplified assumptions about a period and a group of people—for I think that what I'm saying here goes for Macrorie, Britton, and Murray too. I'd say that all of us defended and even celebrated personal writing in a school context where it had been neglected or even banned. But we didn't call personal writing any better than nonpersonal writing. Unfortunately, the term expressivism has been sold and widely bought as a label for the essence of my work—and that of a whole school of others—allegedly preaching that students should always use personal language and thinking and take the self as the topic of their writing—and not consult any standard of truth but what they find inside.

I can't remember that I (or Macrorie, Britton, or Murray) ever used the word "expressive" for our goal or approach in teaching writing. Of course Britton pointed out that "expressive language" shouldn't be neglected in school over "transactional" and "poetic" language; Kinneavey spoke of "expressive discourse" as one of four kinds. But neither of them or any of the others, as far as I know, ever used the term as a label for people. They wouldn't have spoken of a teacher or method as "expressive" or "expressivist." As far as I can tell, the term "expressivist" was coined and used only by people who wanted a word for people they disapproved of and wanted to discredit.

Summing up the two parts of this essay, I see the two terms, "personal writing" and "expressivism," suffering from different problems. "Personal writing," as a single term, tempts one to assume that there's a single kind of writing that can be so described—instead of recognizing how the personal and the nonpersonal are often mixed across three dimensions.

I'm afraid that "expressivism" is hopelessly infected by narrow and usually pejorative connotations. I don't see any way to use the term validly. Historians of composition need to find more accurate ways of describing the views of the people it was pinned on. I'm not a historian, but I don't see what's wrong with the term "process." We were all newly preoccupied with exploring the complex things that go on when people write and eager to help people become more consciously strategic in managing their writing process. I think we all had a new and heightened interest in invention, particularly in helping people take more authority over themselves as writers by writing more from the self—but not necessarily about the self.[3]

NOTES

1. My analysis could be called Aristotelian. Aristotle loved to increase clarity and precision by dividing entities into sorts or parts or species. In past essays, I've found this strategy helpful for clarifying controversies about voice and academic discourse. I tried to reduce confusion and dispute about the concept of voice in writing by showing that there are actually five kinds of voice that can exist in a text: audible voice or intonation—the sounds in a text; dramatic voice or the sense of a person or character or implied author; recognizable or distinctive voice—a voice characteristic of a particular writer; voice with authority—"having a voice"; and resonant voice or presence. I applied the same strategy to academic discourse, arguing that we can reduce confusion and needless dispute if we notice differences between different species of academic discourse and always specify which kind we are talking about. For example, different disciplines use significantly different conventions and kinds of language (i.e., kinds of organization, reasoning, and what counts as evidence). Look even at the single discipline of English where there are significant differences among the conventions used in textual criticism, biographical criticism, psycho-

analytic criticism, reader response criticism, phenomenological, and postmodern criticism. (Here's an amusing but nontrivial difference: most literature teachers will consider a student hopelessly naive about academic discourse if he or she refers to Hemingway as "Ernest." Yet if it's a paper in biographical criticism, the usage can be perfectly appropriate.)

2. Bartholomae is interested in the dilemma of student authority over writing: the "central problem of academic writing, where students must assume the right of speaking to someone who knows more about baseball or 'To His Coy Mistress' than the student does" (1985, p. 140). He can't seem to imagine that a student could know more about baseball than he—or if not baseball, then perhaps her father's experience in Vietnam or her brother's way of negotiating Asperger's. He can't seem to accept the possibility of inviting students to enter a rhetorical space where they have more authority than he.

3. But Tom Newkirk has hope for the word: "The term 'expressionist' may eventually serve us well. Maybe it has the same fate as "impressionism"—which was coined as a satiric term by the journalist Louis Leroy in reference to a painting by Monet" (personal communication, 2012).

REFERENCES

Bartholomae, D. (1985). Inventing the university. In M. Rose (Ed.). *When a writer can't write* (pp. 134-165). New York: Guilford Press.

Bartholomae, D. (1980). The study of error. *College Composition and Communication, 31,* 253-269.

Berlin, J. (1982). Contemporary composition: The major pedagogical theories. *College English, 44,* 765-777.

Berlin, J. (1988). Rhetoric and ideology in the writing class. *College English, 50*(5), 477-494.

Booth, W. (1974). *Modern dogma and the rhetoric of assent.* Chicago: University of Chicago Press.

Bruner, J. S. (1986). *Actual minds, possible worlds.* Cambridge, MA: Harvard University Press.

Buley-Meissner, M. L. (1990). Rhetorics of the self. *Journal of Education, 172,* 47-64.

Elbow, P. (1994a). Introduction. In *Landmark essays on voice and writing* (pp. xi-xlvii). Mahwah, NJ: Hermagoras Press/Erlbaum.

Elbow, P. (1994b). Introduction: Voice and writing. *Voice and writing* (pp. xi-xlvii). Mahway, NJ: Hermagoras Press.

Elbow, P. (1990). Foreword: About personal expressive academic writing. *Pre/Text: An Interdisciplinary Journal of Rhetoric, 11*(1-2, 7-20).

Elbow, P. (Ed.). (1990). *Pre/Text: An Interdisciplinary Journal of Rhetoric, 11*(1-2).

Elbow, P. (1991). Reflections on academic discourse: How it relates to freshmen and colleagues. *College English, 53*(2), 135-55.

Falmagne, R. J., Iselin, M-G., Todorova, I. G., & Jen Arner, J. *Reasoning and personal epistemology: A critical reconstruction.* Unpublished manuscript.

Harris, J. (1997). *A teaching subject: Composition since 1966.* Upper Saddle River, NJ: Prentice-Hall.

Herrington, A. (2002). Gone fishin': Rendering and the uses of personal experience in writing. In P. Belanoff, M. Dickson, S. I. Fontaine, & C. Moran (Eds.), *Writing with Elbow* (pp. 223-238). Utah State University Press.

Hindman, J. (2001). Making writing matter: Using "the personal" to recover[y] an essential[ist] tension in academic discourse. *College English, 64*(1), 88-108.

Kinneavey, J. L. (1971). *A theory of discourse.* Englewood Cliffs, NJ: Prentice-Hall.

Kolln, M. (1991). *Rhetorical grammar: Grammatical choices, rhetorical effects. Instructor's manual.* New York: Macmillan.

Lunsford, A. A. (1998). Toward a mestiza rhetoric: Gloria Anzaldua on composition and postcoloniality. *Journal of Advanced Composition, 18*(1), 1-27.

Medawar, P. (1982). *Pluto's republic.* New York: Oxford University Press.

Myers, G. (1986). Reality, consensus, and reform in the rhetoric of composition teaching. *College English, 48*(2), 154-171.

Safire, W. (1999, February 21). On language: Need not to know. *New York Times Magazine,* pp. 18-19.

Safire, W. (2004, September 21). Inside Kerry's battle plans. *Fairbanks Daily News-Miner,* 7.

Said, E. W. (1999). *Out of lace: A Memoir.* New York: Knopf: Distributed by Random House.

Sommers, N. (1992). Between the drafts. *College Composition and Communication, 43,* 23-31.

Surowiecki, J. (2002, May 6). Waste away. *The New Yorker,* p. 56.

Tannen, D. (1982). Oral and literate strategies in spoken and written narratives. *Language, 58,* 1-21.

Tobin, L. (1993). *Writing relationships: What really happens in the composition class.* Portsmouth NH, Boynton/Cook Heinemann.

Villanueva, V. (1993). *Bootstraps: From an American academic of color.* Urbana, IL: NCTE.

Villanueva, V. (2001). The personal. *College English, 64*(1), 41-62.

SELFHOOD AND THE PERSONAL ESSAY: A PRAGMATIC DEFENSE

Thomas Newkirk
University of New Hampshire

There are many plausible reasons to dislike the personal autobiographical essay—and to refuse to teach it in a writing course. There is the sameness of the topics: eating disorders, deaths and traumas, challenges and successes. There is the predictable moralizing, what David Bartholomae has termed "sentimental realism," with culturally accepted commonplaces employed as learning lessons. There is the mismatch between the personal essay and the kinds of writing expected in the university, where there is a limited tolerance for autobiographical narratives. Any program that stresses this genre risks the disdain of colleagues in more established disciplines. With composition already perceived as a feminized "soft" discipline, it can become doubly feminized (and intellectually vulnerable) by any taint of sentimentality, a term with a long historical association with women's writing and reading. There is the understandable reluctance of teachers to take on any role that resembles psychotherapy and draws them into relationships that they feel unqualified to sustain. As Richard Miller has argued, there is a physiological unease involved in responding to writing (or speaking) that deals with trauma:

> The bodily discomfort arises, I believe, because it is unclear,
> exactly what is being asked of those who are within reach of
> the speaker's words: beyond saying, "I can hear you. I can see
> you," beyond authorizing the speaker's version of events, what
> can listeners do? What role can they play? (1996, p. 277)

And even Montaigne himself had doubts about the value of his essays for readers—what, after all, did the reflections of an unknown, retired lawyer matter? These reservations are shared by a wide swath of composition teachers, and I respect these concerns and would never endorse a program that imposed this genre upon them.

My focus in this essay is on a more profound philosophical challenge to the personal essay that was part of the "social turn" in composition studies in the 1990s, particularly the critiques of Lester Faigley, James Berlin, and David Bartholomae. I will focus on the detailed attention that Faigley gives to the personal essay in his book, *Fragments of Rationality: Postmodernity and the Subject of Composition*. Faigley examines a set of exemplary student essays (with teacher commentary) published in William Coles and James Vopat's *What Makes Writing Good*. A majority of these essays seemed to embody values of an ideology that Berlin would call expressionism (often later altered to expressivism). The writers of these personal essays seem to be free agents, operating outside of culture, or systems of power, or genres; writing originates from a "self," a uniform consciousness. The measure of "authenticity" was how honestly the writing represented or portrayed that self. And as Emerson claimed, the more truthful the writer is in representing this inner thought and experience, the more the expression speaks for others, the more universal it is.

The term "authentic," according to Faigley, is fraught with problems. How, after all does a teacher determine if a piece of writing is "authentic;" how does the process of authentication work—are we speaking of accuracy of memory (which, as psychologists have shown, is altered with retellings)? Is it the expression of emotion? Is it a personal voice? Is it a stylistic preference of teachers? What is the touchstone, the stable pre-discursive self, that is the measure of authenticity? The term itself (like the term "natural") disguises its own ideological and historical roots, the "unstated assumptions about subjectivity," which Faigley tried to make explicit:

> Modern American notions of the individual self derive in part from nineteenth-century liberalism and utilitarianism, which in turn drew on Thomas Hobbes' theory of the atomic, self-interested self. The blend of economics and psychology in these notions of self remains evident in writing pedagogy …. two notions of the individual are often conflated—the self-aware Cartesian subject possessing a unified consciousness and the "freely" choosing competitive individual of capitalism. (1992, p. 128)

Faigley suggests a criticism that James Berlin makes far more bluntly: that the expressivist pedagogies which promote the "free choices" involved in personal essay are complicit with capitalism which also promotes the free choices of the consumer.

From a practical standpoint, the personal essay presents students with a complex task—to speak about their experiences without the critical tools that would help them examine the discourse they are using. Consequently Faigley and Bartholomae claim that they ventriloquise, and echo the moral language of parents and coaches:

> To ask students to write authentically about the self assumes that a unified consciousness can be laid out on the page. That

the self is constructed in socially and historically specific discursive practices is denied. It is no wonder, then, that the selves many students try to appropriate in their writing are voices of moral authority, and when they exhaust their resources of analysis, they revert to moral lesson-adopting, as Bartholomae has noted, a parental voice making clichéd pronouncements where we expect ideas to be extended. (1992, pp. 127-128)

To critics like Faigley and Bartholomae, nothing could be more inauthentic (and one senses, irritating) than the moralisms that close down thinking and end many personal essays.

Finally, drawing on the work of Foucault, there is the question of intrusive institutional power—the ways in which practitioners of the personal essay, while claiming to grant freedom to the writer, are imposing a set of values and expecting students to reveal insecurities, traumas, family difficulties, health issues, and personal details of their lives. No trauma, no good grade. The personal essay becomes a form of confession, with the archetypal confession being the omnipresent "Shooting an Elephant." In effect, Faigley wants to call the bluff of expressivist teachers: they claim to give "ownership" to the student, to give up authority to the student, yet by passing judgment on the authenticity of these personal accounts, they assume a power of surveillance that can be more invasive than the traditional pedagogies they originally opposed.

Faigley's challenge, then, is a profound one. Proponents of the personal essay are revealed as naïve, as blind to the situated, social, ideological nature of language use. There is the troubled quest for an essential, pre-social "self," for a language that is "free," for a "voice" that is unique—even for writing in the absence of any sense of audience. This free space just doesn't exist. Faigley and others argue that the "self" of expressivist pedagogy is a social construction, constituted by language and culture, located in history—and as Anis Bawarshi has argued in his brilliant book, *Genre and the Invention of the Writer*, even our desires are shaped by social genres (which also fulfill those desires).

The persistence of expressivist key terms like "voice" and "authenticity" represent, in Faigley's views, a disciplinary problem in the field of composition studies—the failure to engage with the more satisfactory, generative, and defensible descriptions of writing as informed by postmodern theory. Hence the tendency to write the narrative of composition studies as a progress narrative, and to treat the "social turn" as a paradigm shift, a rejection of deeply flawed views of composing that could now be treated as a kind of historical artifact. The term "post-process" is emblematic of this view—a rhetorical move that casts expressivism as a discredited tradition, that must give way to a fuller, richer, more defensible view of writing instruction. In fact, the critique is profoundly ethical: the charge is that those who teach the personal essay engage in inappropriate and intrusive relationships with their students—and they promote an individualistic view of authorship that is naïve and ultimately disempowering.

In this essay I will attempt a defense of the personal autobiographical essay, drawing on a powerful line of psychological research, led by Martin Seligman and Stephen Maier, and more recently extended by Carol Dweck. This body of work examines the explanatory styles and attitudes of resilient, "healthy" individuals—and, I will argue, helps explain the enduring appeal (and psychological utility) of the type of essay writing that Faigley and others criticize—that which stresses individual agency.

We can begin with what I consider one of the weaker parts of this challenge to expressivism and the personal essay: the charge that it is easily appropriated by the powers of consumerism, since both associate identity with personal choice. This is, in the end, an argument from similarity, since it would be difficult to establish any solid cause-effect relationship. One might just as easily argue that the sophisticated awareness of the social construction of needs could also be co-opted by advertisers and marketers (the similarity is there too). In fact, it is very hard to predict how ideas will be taken up and used in other situations. To my knowledge there is no empirical evidence of a connection between expressivism and capitalism—it is sheer speculation. The only major study I know of that even attempts to trace the ways in which literacy practices contributes to career development is Jonathan Rose's *The Intellectual Life of the British Working Class*, which among other things traces the reading histories of many militant leaders of the labor movement. These leaders were radicalized not by the indoctrination of Marxists (whom many found rigid and uninteresting) but from reading classic authors, particularly Charles Dickens, whose belief in personal altruism would seem at odds with the collective movement they would help build. George Orwell, in his magnificent essay on Dickens, describes a similarly complex act of appropriation and influence. There is no neat, clean, determinist, ideological line that can be drawn.

The claim of "surveillance" is similarly weak, and rests primarily on the rhetorical power of the term itself, evoking Foucault and Bentham's panopticon. The problem has to do with the virtually unbounded way in which the term can—and has been—used. Is there any act of teaching or assessment that is not, in some form, an act of surveillance? Were my conferences with my children's teachers not an act of surveillance? Monitoring is occurring no matter the genre of writing we assign: as teachers we ask for accounts of the writing process, we read drafts, we monitor the thought processes of our students. It is impossible to imagine the work of education (or participation in any social unit) without these forms of attention and assessment. So the fact of surveillance is a given (which I think is Foucault's point). It is inescapable. The ethical question is the manner and purpose of the surveillance, and here the case needs to be made that a student writing about significant events in an essay, read and evaluated by the teacher, is likely to be personally harmful. I won't deny that this is a possibility, though I would add that teachers can be insensitive working in any genre. Obviously, any teacher who feels uncomfortable responding to papers like the ones in the Vopat and Coles collection should not be assigning that kind of writing. I am not at all arguing that it should be a universal requirement. But on the other hand I have seen generations of teachers at my own university handle such writing with tact and sensitivity. I have read thousands of evaluations and the issue of surveillance is virtually non-existent in student accounts. It is raised almost exclusively by academicians criticizing the genre.

It is also tempting to respond to Faigley by challenging his linking of the personal essay and the "unified consciousness." One could easily argue the reverse: associate the essay instead with the "fragmentation," the deconstructive impulse of postmodernism. The essay is a perfectly fine vehicle for exploring the multiplicity, fragmentation, and constructedness of the "self." The essay, as Montaigne deployed it, celebrated the instability and inherent irrationality of the self; human claims to be rational, were, in his view, a form of presumption and vanity. Human beings are too temperamentally volatile and self-interested, and language too imprecise, to claim steady rationality. In his long essay "An Apology for Raymond Seybond," he has long satiric passages where he rebuts claims about human reason by citing evidence (much of it fabricated by Plutarch) about identical abilities in animals. Men praise their analytic ability to distinguish plant types; well, goats can do that too. And despite his claim in the famous address to his readers, that he would prefer to portray himself naked—as if self-presentation was a matter of disrobing—his project was clearly a complex act of discursive construction, one that he commented on frequently in his many additions to the original essays. In one addition he commented on his tendency to make additions:

> My first edition dates from fifteen hundred and eighty: I have long since grown old but not one inch wiser. "I" now and "I" then are certainly twain, but which I was better? I know nothing about that. If we were always progressing toward improvement, to be old would be a beautiful thing. But it is a drunkard's progress, formless, staggering, like reeds which the wind shakes as it fancies, haphazardly. (Montaigne, 1595/1987, p. 1091)

Montaigne resembles Laurence Stern in that he seems to push to the limits, even undermine the genre he is in the process of creating. There has been no more strenuous critic of "unified consciousness" than Montaigne, and the personal essay, with its openings for amendments and cycling back, became the vehicle for making this challenge.

Such a defense, though, would sidestep the objection many compositionists have concerning the personal essay. Simply put, the deep, and often amusing, skepticism of Montaigne's essays bears little resemblance to the efforts of students. In the introduction to his collection, *The Art of the Personal Essay*, Phillip Lopate argues that the most successful essayists are either older, or like Joan Didion and James Baldwin, they assume, early on, an older persona—they have outgrown or abandoned beliefs in human perfectibility and distanced themselves from the assurances of true believers, heroes, and reformers. Yet in student essays it is precisely this belief in perfectibility, personal agency—this optimism—that regularly animates their essays (and often embarrasses their teachers). Every difficulty is a learning experience; every death a reminder of the preciousness of life. The "self" that is portrayed is not exactly a "unified self" but a progressive one, part of a constructed coherent narrative of self-development (the very kind of narrative Montaigne refused to write). Any defense of the personal essay needs to address this sensibility, this propensity for belief and affirmation that animates their writing. To defend the personal essay—as young students write them—entails defending this bias toward affirmation.

FAITH, OPTIMISM, AND "SENTIMENTAL REALISM"

> Normal human thought is distinguished by a robust positive bias.
> —Shelley Taylor

In 1896 William James published his great essay, "The Will to Believe" (which he later regretted titling, preferring "The Right to Believe.") In it he debunks a view prevalent in his time: that beliefs should be the product of an objective and dispassionate review of the facts. To accept unsupported opinion is to be duped and we are to "guard ourselves from such beliefs as from a pestilence which may shortly master our body then spread to the rest of the town" (James, 1997, p. 74). Intelligence, according to this viewpoint, was strongly associated with skepticism, doubt, coolness, withholding affiliation. James turns the argument on its head claiming that even this position represented a form of belief—and that passion, commitment, and belief are essential in making the pragmatic tests of truth. The scientist's passionate belief in an ordered, explainable universe is a crucial tool in helping him or her to extend that explanation. And if beliefs lead to mistakes, then "our errors are surely not such awfully solemn things"(1997, p. 19).

One of the glories of James' career was his openness to the psychological utility of a vast range of religious beliefs, from mesmerism to Buddhism to evangelism—all of which he treated with elaborate respect. In the early 1970s, Peter Elbow reactivated this argument in his essay on the believing game, arguing that the academic culture held a bias against the functionality of belief, and a bias in favor of skepticism and critique which are often seen as the mark of perceptive thought and real academic work. By contrast, assertions of belief, whether based on a religious faith or a personal code, are often viewed within the academic culture as dogmatic, unsophisticated, simplistic; they are evidence that the student is "written" by his or her culture and helpless to push back against it. Students are victims of what James would call "dupery." David Bartholomae, in particular, would claim that these assertions are usually nothing more than moral commonplaces that are passively absorbed by students, and handy for "wrapping up" their personal essays.

The capacity to self-monitor in matters of taste—to identify and resist the appeals of sentimentality—is part of the identity equipment of academics, particularly in the humanities (Newkirk, 2002). It is a form of cultural capital, an ingrained preference for the ironic, distanced, critical, and complex that, as Bourdieu demonstrated, serves to establish class distinctions. Even the poorly paid adjunct, teaching a literature survey, has the satisfaction that she can avoid dupery, that she is alert to the intellectual softness of sentimental appeals with the attendant clichés and commonplaces. As Suzanne Clark writes, few criticisms are as damaging as the use of the epithet "sentimental":

> The author's rationality is in question, and so is the credibility of the argument. If you are the victim of a "sentimental" epithet, you have been excluded from the magic circle. It is as if your readers are too tough for you, and you are too much of a sissy for them .... (1994, p. 101)

Richard Miller has argued that these judgments and preferences are not purely intellectual; they are experienced bodily as forms of discomfort, even revulsion. There are a range of terms (including "taste" itself) which register this physical reaction, many dealing with oversweetness ("syrupy," "sappy," "saccharine"). A more dated term, "schmaltzy," has the root meaning of rendered chicken fat, what one might imagine at the base of the stomach. Miller's point is that our reactions to emotional autobiographical writing is often instant and visceral, experienced in the gut; our sense of taste is embodied, instinctive, and employed without disengaging from our own perspective (as our own theories of social construction would require us of).

The issue may not be whether a writer uses commonplaces, for all discourse communities rely on claims and commonly agreed upon warrants; this essay is littered with them. The issue is that personal essays of young students often employ a type of commonplace that jars or irritates (or nauseates) a type of reader. They run against an aesthetic; in their wholehearted affirmation, they position the writer in (and ask the reader to endorse) a discourse community of motivation and self-help, a place of coaches and graduation speeches that represents everything the academic reader habitually defines himself or herself against. It is not genuine thought but ventriloquism—the student being written by culture. This discourse of self-efficacy and optimism simply has no cultural capital for these readers.

Yet paradoxically, there is now abundant evidence of the psychological utility, even necessity, of the very narrative patterns—of uplift, and overcoming obstacles—that many writing teachers find so annoying and unthinking. In her book *Positive Illusions: Creative Self-Deception and the Healthy Mind*, psychologist Shelley Taylor summarizes a range of studies to argue that an "unrealistic," even "self-aggrandizing" view of the self has major positive benefits for personal happiness. This exaggerated sense of personal agency emerges so powerfully and quickly in early childhood that it is very likely "natural [and] intrinsic to the cognitive system" (Taylor, 1989, p. 44). Like the evolution of organs or immune systems, it may be hardwired to support the perpetuation of the species—as anthropologist Lionel Tiger has argued, "optimism is a biological phenomenon" (Taylor, 1989, p. 40). The key beneficial illusion is a heightened sense of being able to master one's environment:

> The illusion of control, a vital part of people's beliefs about their attributes, is a personal statement about how positive outcomes will be achieved, not merely by wishing and hoping that they will happen, but by making them happen through one's own capabilities. (Taylor, 1989, p. 41)

Of course, events are not in our control, and humans face trauma and tragedy. But even victims of terrible illness and loss are often able to derive meaning and benefit from their situation, perhaps working to inform or help others in their same situation. Or to find that their tragedy brings an existential clarity to their lives. Taylor quotes a 61-year-old cancer patient:

> You can take a picture of what someone has done, but when you frame it, it becomes significant. I feel as if I were, for the first time, really conscious. My life is framed in a certain amount of time. I always knew it, but I can see it, and it's made better by the knowledge. (1989, p. 195)

A commonplace, perhaps, but a profoundly functional one.

Taylor's argument is supported by a line of research on "explanatory style" conducted by Martin Seligman and his colleagues. Explanatory style refers to the ways in which individuals account for the difficulties they face; for example whether they see themselves as victims or agents, whether they posit the cause as a pervasive personality flaw, and what kind of flaw. In effect, Seligman is looking at narrative patterns which have relevance for the ways students write about trauma and difficulty. He identifies three crucial dimensions of explanatory style:

> Stability. Causes can be accounted for as stable in time (and thus likely to reoccur indefinitely) or they may be temporary and remediable.
>
> Range. Causes may be perceived as a global trait of the individual ("I'm stupid," "I'm not a people person."). Or they may relate to a specific, local, and limited kind of problem or situation.
>
> Locus. Causes can be seen as internal or external—as arising from purely individual failures or flaws in judgment or personal weakness, or as arising, at least partially, from outside circumstances.

According to Seligman a great deal rides on the kind of explanatory style an individual comes to adopt. The condition he has called "learned helplessness" is characterized by a particular pattern where people "explain bad events by internal, stable, and global causes and explain good events as external, instable, and local" (Seligman, 1988, p. 92). Success is the unstable result of luck; failure is the product of character. Marvin Minsky captured the spirit of this argument as follows:

> Thinking is a process, and if your thinking does something you don't want it to you should be able to say something microscopic and analytic about it, and not something enveloping and evaluating about yourself as a learner. The important thing in refining your thought is to try to depersonalize your interior; it may be all right to deal with other people in a vague global way, but it is devastating if this is the way you deal with yourself. (as quoted in Bernstein, 1981, p. 122)

Seligman's research identifies the devastation Minsky refers to, the profound consequences—for physical and mental health—of the explanatory style associated with learned helplessness. In addition to a longstanding association with depression, researchers now believe that this explanatory style is an ineffective way of dealing with stress that compromises the immune system, leaving the individual susceptible to a range of infectious diseases. Not surprisingly, a "healthy" explanatory style is associated with increased motivation, persistence, and educational achievement.

All of which suggests a fundamental dilemma for academic readers. It is hardly surprising that young writers employ commonplaces of effort, overcoming obstacles, learning from difficulties, naming heroes and saints in their lives—that they construct their narratives as a form of heroic progression. There is now a huge body of research to document the benefits—even the evolutionary necessity—of such formulations. And as William James and Peter Elbow argue, this positive bias can be self-verifying. If a student believes that an obstacle like a failing a test is a learning opportunity (clichéd as that view is), she is likely to be more successful in gaining a benefit from it than someone who treats that failure as one more sign she is not good at the subject (a global reaction). Yet aesthetically these formulations in personal essays, as I have noted, frequently fail to satisfy, and even repulse, the academic reader who is gratified by an entirely different, more nuanced, ambivalent, ironic sensibility.

STUDENT AS CO-THEORIST

To illustrate this dilemma I will quote extensively from a paper of one of my own students written early in a first-year course. The assignment which I call the "Right to Speak" paper requires them to pick a public issue on which they have personal experience that has caused them to have some viewpoint; the goal of the paper is to show how this viewpoint arises out of the experience. In preparation we read Sallie Tisdale's "A Weight Women Carry" and "Grade A: The Market for a Yale Woman's Eggs," an award-winning essay by Jessica Cohen. I also read aloud an essay on euthanasia in which I recount the last days of my mother's life when she refused food and water for twelve days. I suggested additional topics, reminding them that they are all experts on their own education, and have a right to comment on it. One student, Brianna, chose to write about the cruelty and shunning she endured in middle school. The paper begins with a description of the bodily experience of depression she felt each day as she got ready for school:

> The pain I went through those four years is nearly indescribable. Every morning I would wake up with a heavy chest. It literally weighed me down. My heart in particular would feel heavy and burdened. I could feel it struggle with every pulse.

It was like my heart was forced to beat against its will. I could feel the disdain in its pounding, its unwillingness to keep going. In response to this weight my shoulders would slump forward, pulling the rest of my upper body down with it. My head hung low. My eyes drooped. It never ceased to astonish me how my emotional pain managed to manifest itself into physical mannerisms.

The main body of the paper is a description of a set of humiliating encounters in school.

> I seemed to be the bearer of silence. I would go over to a group of kids who were laughing and giggling in order to play with them, and the giggling would immediately stop. I would ask some people to play something with me, and they would always have something to do. Recess time was the worst. I always seemed to try to join a game of four-square just a little too late, as there was never any room for another person …. And I especially was never able to penetrate the wall of backs and shoulders of the kids standing around in a circle talking to one another. This left me standing alone against the school's wall observing all the other kids at play, desperately wishing I could be them.

One particularly painful scene, so vivid in her mind that she had to interrupt her writing and cry when she was composing it, involved her not being chosen to help in a cooking project:

> I remember one day during home base, a time during the day where each specific section gets together to talk about random nonsense, a girl named Susanna from another home base came in to announce she was baking cookies. Her home base teacher had told her that she could pick one friend to bake cookies with her. She asked all of us who wanted to be that lucky person. Of course, everyone raised their hands and eagerly began pleading to pick them. She ended up picking a girl named Megan, who immediately hopped out of her seat and ran to Susanna's side. I sadly lowered my hand and gave Susanna a look of grief. She smiled at me and said "Hmmm, well maybe you can bake with me too, Brianna". Before I could allow any sort of happiness ease my hurt body, Megan immediately straightened up, flung her eyes open,

and involuntarily hushed "No! No!" in Susanna's ear. She caught herself and slowly turned to look at me and gave me a nervous giggle.

My stomach sank so low it might as well have fallen to my feet. I had to try so hard to not cry in that moment. An intense, sharp pain stabbed into my heart and stomach. It hurt so much that I felt like puking for a split second. That was the first moment I realized how alone and unwanted I truly was. It had manifested before my eyes. I had never actually seen or heard anyone display their disapproval of me before. To this day, I still cannot look Megan in the eyes without thinking about the cookie incident. To this day, I feel the same stab in my heart and stomach when I think about it.

The rest of sixth grade and seventh grade continued on very much the same way. There were endless displays of "No! No!" detonating in my face every day. Whether it was a hushed giggle accompanied by a finger pointing in my direction amongst a couple of girls, the rumors about how I was a compulsive liar and ate lard for breakfast, or even the obese, ugly cartoon drawings of me that were left in my locker, it was made clear to me that my loneliness and pain would last for a long time.

She completely closed herself off from the rest of the world. "I was a bottle of thoroughly shaken soda pop just waiting to explode." And in fact, near the end of the paper she describes cutting herself:

I took my razor from the shower and slashed my wrist with it three times. It felt good. The release of pain was extraordinary. I wanted to cut more. I wanted to go all up and down my arm, but I knew I would get caught cutting myself if I did that, so I stopped after three cuts. I carefully put my razor back in the shower, turned the water on, and washed away all the blood, snot, and tears, cleansing myself once more.

At this point her paper shifts abruptly to the insight or understanding she wants the narrative to convey:

While I never acquired scars from my razor-incident, I've never fully recovered from those four years. My body is still an open wound that I don't think will ever be healed. And as much as I wish I had a happy and normal adolescence, I wouldn't change the past even if I had the power to. While I will never fully recover from my trauma, I have taken away something so positive that it far outweighs all the negatives of my middle school experience: kindness and compassion. My agony has molded me into a far better person than I could have ever been had I not been so scorned and neglected.

During my four years of misery, I would think to myself if only they knew. If only they knew how I feel right now. If only they knew what happened behind closed doors, maybe they wouldn't be so mean and cruel. I think about this every time I interact with a person. I don't know their back-story. I don't know the emotional baggage they carry around with them. All I know is that I need to be sensitive towards their feelings.

I think about the how complicated and intense my pain and emotional grief was, and all because people weren't nice to me. It's such a simple thing, really. Just be a good, kind person. Something as simple as a smile or a "hello" can brighten up someone's day. And who knows, maybe that person really needs it. Because of my past, I am now able to possibly better someone's future—a fair trade-off for my pain, I think.

In this final section we can see Brianna's attempt to take agency and assert that she has made constructive use of this experience, while acknowledging that she still lives with the trauma of those years. One of her fears in writing the paper was that it would elicit "pity," that it would receive an undeserved high grade "out of pity or awkwardness." By claiming a positive outcome she finally becomes an agent in her own story; it is the pattern of explanation that Seligman and Taylor associate with a healthy resilient reaction to difficulty.

When, with her permission, I shared the paper with a group of teachers, one reaction was doubt about her claim that she wouldn't "change the past" if she could because of what she had gained. I had kept touch with Brianna in the year since she was in my class, and knowing her interest in introspection and psychology, I invited her to respond to this concern about her paper. She wrote:

> I suppose I would have preferred to avoid all that pain. Who wouldn't? But I truly believe I would not be the person I am today had I not endured what I did. I firmly believe that every evil is accompanied with a good, and vice-versa. With all that pain came an incredible sense of sympathy and caring towards

> others. Yes, I am still hurting and not fully recovered (and may never be) be from my experience. I have been greatly impacted psychologically and it's going to take a lot of hard work to be able to function as I would like to be able to. But this is balanced with a gift of compassion that I think more people in this world need. If that pain was what I needed to go through in order to attain this gift, then so be it, because that makes me one more person who will treat others the way they deserve to be treated and hopefully I can spare them some of the pain I endured.

In her commentary on this paper, she said that the process of writing was an "emotional rollercoaster," and not one that brought her the sense of catharsis that she had hoped for. So I wanted to get her reaction to the question of whether this kind of writing should have a place in a writing course:

> I completely understand where these concerns come from, and I can certainly appreciate them. But I think the purpose of (good) literature is to bring up these sorts of issues and topics; topics which are uncomfortable, topics that are important and relevant to many people, and topics which evoke strong emotions so that we may recognize and discuss them. The great thing about personal essays is that if some topic is true for one person, there is more than likely at least one other person out there who can relate and identify with that person, and therefore the topic is worth sharing and discussing. By turning a blind eye to these types of essays, we might as well be turning a blind eye to literature itself. Now obviously if a student or teacher is truly uncomfortable with this sort of thing, then guidelines or alternate assignments can be made. But I don't think the personal essay should be dismissed from classrooms.

As a final question, I asked her if she saw any relationship between personal essay writing and the other writing that she had done in academic courses.

> I absolutely believe there is a connection between this type of writing and the writings in other courses. This kind of writing is very personal and therefore may evoke strong feelings and emotions. One of the hardest things to do in writing, which is one of the challenges a personal essay presents, is write a well-written paper about a topic you are passionate about. In most cases when someone is passionate about a certain

subject, they have so much to say that it's difficult to discipline themselves into writing a paper that is coherent. This is a very critical skill to be able to achieve: to be able to release your emotions and take a step back to look at a subject from a disciplined and impartial point of view. This is a skill that is required in many, if not most, types of writing, such as persuasive essays or debates, or even analytical and critical papers. I would argue that this skill is one of the most basic and important skills to have in writing. The personal essay without a doubt exercises this skill, and therefore is very relevant to other types of writing.

This response situates Brianna in the complex debate concerning "transfer" from a first-year writing course. Her position seems to align with those who argue for the possibility of "far transfer" (Wardle, 2007): the capacity of learners to develop a meta-awareness of writing processes—in this case her sense of managing complex emotional material—that can be of use in writing assignments which do not closely resemble the personal essay.

TOWARD A HERMENEUTICS OF RESPECT

But to return to "the nervous system." This student paper can create a discomfort for writing teachers, and it is important to speculate about the source of that discomfort. I would argue that it does not arise from the personal material—which for the most part is handled with narrative skill, particularly as she describes the bodily sensation of her depression and exclusion. Her occasional use of metaphor is also compelling ("I seemed to be the bearer of silence;" "I was a bottle of thoroughly shaken soda pop just waiting to explode"). The reader's discomfort does not arise from a concern about acting the therapist—the paper is clearly not asking for this. No, the discomfort most likely comes from statements like this:

> If there's one positive thing I took from middle school, it's that you should be a kind person.

Or this:

> While I will never fully recover from my trauma, I have taken away something so positive that it far outweighs all the negatives of my middle school experience: kindness and compassion. My agony has molded me into a far better person than I could have ever been had not been so scorned and neglected.

At moments like these, the writer locates the paper within a form of moral, even moralizing discourse that academic readers are often deeply suspicious of—and embarrassed by ("what would the comp director think of this?") This is the language of self-help, or therapy, or guidance counselors, or graduation speeches. Brianna clearly locates herself in this discourse at the end of the paper, where she quotes what she wrote in her senior yearbook four years after these events took place:

> My life's philosophy is a simple one, but extremely important. In my high school senior yearbook I leave with one very important message to all. I like to think of it as a summary of my entire grade school experience. Under my picture you will see the quote "Be nice to people—they outnumber you 6.6 billion to one." True, no?

The academic reader is deflated by words like "simple," "nice," and "very important message." Our mission, after all, is to disrupt the view that any life philosophy can be simple, or that morality can be reduced to such truisms. One reader of Brianna's paper suggested that with more time and reading in a writing course, she would develop more "distance" on the topic. Yet she is writing from the perspective of five years, and in her comments a year after the paper was written, the moral core of her essay is consistent. It may be that it is the readers of this essay that want "distance"—because the essay puts them in too close proximity to a form of moral assertion that makes them uncomfortable, as if they have wandered into a meeting where they had hoped to listen to Joan Didion and they get Dr. Phil.

One way to respond to an essay like this one is to employ a hermeneutics of distrust, to treat the moral assertions of the paper as mere clichés and copouts; this is what David Bartholomae seems to do when he calls them "commonplaces." In some of the earlier versions of a critical studies approach, as these commonplaces were viewed a form of "false consciousness," a passive acceptance of cultural truisms that served dominant interests—a manifestation of James' "dupery." The task of instruction was to help students play the "doubting game"—to deconstruct or problematize these beliefs, to show their arbitrary constructed nature, and expose the political interests they serve. As should be clear by now, I am arguing that this approach would be counterproductive in the case of this essay; it would be to challenge its core, its very reason for being—and to dismiss the profound functionality of this "simple" belief system for the writer. It would be a form of violence and disrespect, a failure of imagination and empathy, an ethnographic tin ear. It would also be a failure to use the self-critical tools of cultural criticism that would ask readers to interrogate their own discomfort.

But this greater openness to these moral commonplaces does not mean that all the reader can do is say, "I can see you, I can hear you." Like any discourse, "sentimental realism" can be performed well, and it can be performed poorly. Not all writers can write "in your face" scenes as Brianna has, or be as attuned to bodily response. The effect of her paper rests on this ability, as she says near the end, to reveal to readers the depth of distress that these too-typical middle school behaviors can create. At the same time there are perspectives missing in the paper: one teacher who read the paper asked why parents and teachers didn't intervene (think of the clumsy move of Susannah publicly choosing a peer to do the cooking). Surely they bear some responsibility. I wished I had posed this question to her during our conference on the paper, so I asked her this question a year later in our email exchange. She acknowledged that her parents could have stepped in earlier, but she understood why her teachers didn't:

> I put on a really terrific front at school ... they were SHOCKED when my mom told them that I was miserable in middle school. Even to this day, when I talk to them about it they are completely dumb-founded. They say things like "You were always so happy and bubbly all the time. I just can't believe that you hated middle school so much." So to be fair, my teachers didn't have anything to pick up on and intervene in. But the bottom line is that people are responsible for their own actions. Besides, anyone who has experienced the public school system understands that it's almost like its own separate society. You're expected to deal with things on your own. Allowing for an adult to step in is like cheating or breaking the rules, and you are immediately coined as a target for bullying. While I would agree that adults should have stepped up, I would also argue that there shouldn't have been the need to do so.

I regret that we didn't explore this "front" in our conference because her descriptions of it might have heightened the pathos of her situation. In addition to enduring the shunning, she had to maintain a front that would keep the adults around her from guessing her distress. But she rejects as a digression the suggestion that she explore the responsibility of adults in this situation because it was the behavior of the girls, her peers, that is criticized. There should have been no need for adults to intervene. The more "mature" or sociological move to view the situation in a systematic way, spreading the blame to adults, would blunt her moral criticism.

I realize that papers of this kind raise anxieties among teachers, particularly those new to the profession, about crossing the line into being a therapist (although as Lad Tobin has written, we fool ourselves if we think this is a clear line). I don't want to minimize this concern, but in my experience it need not be an obstacle. To begin with, students who choose write about traumatic issues are, almost without exception, not asking us to be therapists. They want us to be sensitive and curious readers who help them elaborate and explore topics they have chosen to write about. I will often begin my questions about their papers by saying that I respect them for taking on a difficult and emotional topic and that if any of my questions make them uncomfortable not to answer them—but almost invariably students welcome the questions. Michelle Payne comments in her study, *Bodily Discourses*, that allowing this kind of writing to be done in a course has the effect of normalizing the subject matter—it is not shameful, unspeakable. It can be the subject of a paper; writing is therapeutic by not being therapy, but normal school work. She writes: "It is especially important, I think, for women who have suffered bodily violence to believe a 'unified, normal' self is possible through writing in an academic context" (Payne, 1997, p. 206).

It is also important to remember that this essay is part of a sequence that led, as it does in many first year classes, to assignments that dealt with responding to reading and to research. An essay like this one can help a teacher in directing students to topics that can combine the personal and academic, building on what Michael Smith and Jeffrey Wilhelm call "identity markers." In Brianna's case, this paper clued me in to her interest in the psychology of distress, her fascination with the ways in which social stress is experienced bodily. In another paper she describes playing the role of Nurse Ratched in *One Flew Over the Cuckoo's Nest* and finding the way of walking to convey her emotional stiffness. When she chose later in the semester to research panic attacks, which she also has experienced, I knew from her previous writing that this was a good topic for her (and it was a very successful paper). As Marcia Curtis and Anne Herrington argue in *Persons in Process*, the most engaged and committed undergraduate writers are those who have a personal stake in their academic subject; they are the ones who dismantle the personal/academic binary. And for me this essay was a key to helping Brianna do that.

*

Finally to the issue of power. One charge against the personal essay is that it can become solipsistic, so self-preoccupied and individualistic that the writer is powerless to appreciate or challenge systematic social evils. One thing academic language provides is a more powerful capacity to critique and challenge injustice. I would not deny this is sometimes the case (virtually every "travel" paper I have received fails in this way). But this argument can be turned on its head—that much of the writing in the "academy" insulates practitioners from the way rhetorical power actually operates in the wider culture. There would not be a need to argue for "public intellectuals" if most of us were good at public discourse. A dismissal of "sentimental realism" can alienate academics from the way writing (and narrative) functions in the wider culture—to commemorate, provide solace, entertain, persuade, inform. One can easily imagine a public function for Brianna's essay—to help teachers be alert to the excluded child, or to make middle school girls aware of the pain that the ostracized girl can feel. While essays like Brianna's may be therapeutic, they are also forms of public moral writing, as witnessed by the considerable popularity of "This I Believe" series on National Public Radio. To the extent that composition studies has embraced the public, non-academic uses of language, it should pay serious attention to the power of moral discourse like hers.

I personally experienced this removal from public discourse several years ago at an annual NCTE conference. Somehow I was on the "research strand," which as anyone familiar with the conference knows is the kiss of death, a kind of consumer warning. A group of us were scheduled to present in a huge ballroom, and as the scheduled time approached it became clear that the panel outnumbered the audience—so we pulled together a few chairs in a pathetic huddle to make the session feel more intimate. In the session I was criticized by a prominent researcher for promoting narrative and descriptive writing, and not the more powerful "language of the academy." I was, in effect, disempowering my students.

I remember thinking at the time, "If we and our language is so powerful, why isn't anyone here?" For I knew in some other ballroom, my colleague Donald Graves would be speaking to an audience of over a thousand, which would respond enthusiastically to his humor, his stories of children in his study, his descriptions of their writing, and his ability to mimic conversations with these children. At times these stories had the weight of parables, exemplary stories. He would alternate from humor to pathos to indignation without any notes, and never losing his audience. And he changed the face of elementary education.

Who, I was thinking, really has a handle on the "language of power"?

REFERENCES

Bartholomae, D. (1985). Inventing the university. In M. Rose (Ed.), *When a writer can't write* (pp. 134-165). New York: Guilford.

Bawarshi, A. (2003). *Genre and the invention of the writer*. Logan, UT: Utah State Press.

Berlin, J. (1988). Rhetoric and ideology in the writing class. *College English, 15*(5), 477-494.

Bernstein, J. (1981, December 14). Profiles: Marvin Minsky. *The New Yorker*, pp. 50-128.

Bourdieu, P. (1987). *Distinction: A social critique of the judgement of taste*. Cambridge: Harvard University Press.

Britton, J. (1982). Shaping at the point of utterance. In G. M. Pradl (Ed.), *Prospect and retrospect: Selected essays of James Britton* (pp. 139-145). Montclair, NJ: Boynton/Co. (Reprinted from A Freedman and I. Pringle (Eds.), *Reinventing the rhetorical tradition*, 1980, Conway, AR., L & S Books., for the Canadian Council of Teachers of English).

Burke, K. (1969). *A grammar of motives*. Berkeley, CA: University of California Press.

Burke, K. (1968). *Language as symbolic action: Essays on life, literature, and method*. Berkeley, CA: University of California Press.

Clark, S. (1994). Rhetoric, social construction, and gender: Is it bad to be sentimental. In J. Clifford & J.Schlib (Eds.), *Writing Theory and Critical Theory* (pp. 96-108). New York: Modern Language Association.

Cohen, J. (2002, December). Grade a: The market for a woman's eggs. *Atlantic Monthly*, pp. 76-78.

Coles, W. E. & Vopat, J. (1985). *What makes writing good: A multiperspective*. New York: D. C. Heath.

Dweck, C. (2000). *Self-theories: Their role in motivation, personality, and development*. London: Psychology Press.

Elbow, P. (1973/1998). *Writing without teachers*. New York: Oxford University Press.

Emerson, R. W. (1982). *Nature and selected Essays*. New York: Penguin Books.

Faigley, L. (1992). *Fragments of rationality: Postmodernity and the subject of composition*. Pittsburgh: University of Pittsburgh Press.

Foucault, M. (1995). *Discipline and punish: The birth of the prison*. New York: Vintage.

Herrington, A., & Curtis, M. (2000). *Persons in process: Four stories of writing and personal development*. Urbana, Illinois: NCTE.

James, W. (1892/1985). *Psychology: The briefer course*. Notre Dame, Indiana: Notre Dame University Press.

James, W. (1997). The will to believe. In L. Menand (Ed.), *Pragmatism: A reader* (pp. 69-92). New York: Vintage.

Lopate, P. (1994). *The art of the personal essay*. New York: Doubleday.

Miller, R. (1996). The nervous system. *College English, 58*(3), 265-286.

Montaigne, M. de. (1595/1987). *The complete essays*. (M. A. Screech, Trans.). New York: Penguin.

Newkirk, T. (2002). Sentimental journeys: Anti-romanticism and academic identity. In P. Belanoff (Ed.), *Writing with Elbow* (pp. 21-33). Logan, Utah: Utah State University Press.

Orwell, G. (1940/2002). Charles Dickens. In J. Carey (Ed.), *Essays* (pp. 135-184). New York: Knopf (Everyman's Library).

Payne, M. (1997). *Bodily discourses: When students write about sexual abuse, physical abuse, and eating disorders in the composition classroom.* (Doctoral dissertation, University of New Hampshire).

Rose, J. (2002). *The intellectual life of the British working class.* New Haven: Yale University Press.

Seligman, M. E. P., Kamen, L. P., & Nolen-Hoeksema, S. (1988). Explanatory style across the lifespan: Achievement and health. In E. M. Heatherington, R. M. Lerner, & M. Perlmutter (Eds.), *Child development in lifespan perspective* (pp. 91-114). Hillsdale, NJ: Lawrence Erlbaum.

Smith, M. & Wilhelm, J. (2002). *Reading don't fix no Chevys: Literacy in the lives of young men.* Portsmouth, NH: Heinemann.

Taylor, S. (1989). *Positive illusions: Creative self-deception and the healthy mind.* New York: Basic Books.

Tiger, L. (1979). *Optimism: The biology of hope.* New York: Kodansha.

Tisdale, S. (1998). We do abortions here. In D. Cavitch (Ed.), *Life Studies: An Analytic Reader* (pp. 471-478). Boston: Bedford.

Tobin, L. (1993). *Writing relationships: What really happens in a composition class.* Portsmouth, NH: Boynton Cook/Heinemann.

Wardle, E. (2007). Understanding "transfer" from FYW: Preliminary results of a longitudinal study. *Writing Program Administration, 31,* 65-85.

CRITICAL MEMOIR AND IDENTITY FORMATION: BEING, BELONGING, BECOMING

Nancy Mack
Wright State University

Critique can function as more than a scholarly pursuit; it can become a valued skill for surviving as an outsider within an academic context. Because universities are complex, largely reproductive systems, being a hard worker and following the rules does not necessarily lead to reward or even much notice. Increasing demands and multiple layers of political machinations foster disillusionment and alienation. Participating in programs, grants, and other initiatives only increases the perils, not to mention running the gauntlet of publishing and tenure. As egotistical as I may be, it is best to remember that the academic universe is not the only place fraught with crushing hegemonic pressures. Being a parent, teenager, or restaurant server all necessitate the ability to analyze the forces that impose limitations and subvert one's agency to author ethical, answerable acts. Fortunately, critique has long been expressed through many productive means such as music, cartoons, jokes, parodies, postings on social media, clothes, hair styles, body art, gestures, and of course, various types of composing and writing.

This chapter forwards memoir as a writing assignment that can be informed by a critical notion of subject formation. The heuristic activities that I describe were developed for courses on different levels: first year composition, English education writing pedagogy, and several graduate seminars. Recently, I incorporated a few of these generative strategies into an online graduate course about critical memoir. After commenting on the constraints of theoretical taxonomies, a series of heuristic strategies are outlined to increase awareness of identity as a conflicted representation that is always open to revision through writing.

TROUBLING TAXONOMIES

Regretfully, labels reinforce power relations behind reified categories. Nevertheless, taxonomies may come in handy when trying to wrap one's head around a huge amount of information during an introductory course about composition theory (Mack, 2009). A disclaimer always needs to be fronted when using such devices that taxonomies are cultural generalizations that in most cases rewrite history to benefit the reigning group. Fulkerson's (1979, 1990, 2005) serial glosses relate an overly dramatic, progress-narrative of the field. A people's oral history always varies from the official, printed versions, with some of the old timers choosing silence rather than the futility of constructing an alternative narrative. I merely wish to trouble the master narrative for the field by pointing out that the names commonly representing the theory camps in what is called Rhetoric and Composition should be contested. Bruce Horner and Min-Zhan Lu (2010) astutely argue that these two words that represent the field itself deserve critique. We might question which term should come first and whether the "and" implies equality or mere addition. The names for individual theory groups did not precede the development of a particular perspective, nor did these labels emerge from individual scholars meeting as a group, voting on an identifier, and donning T-shirts with slogans to represent their mutual ideology. At the time that some of these camps supposedly came into being, I would have bet on totally different names as gaining popularity. For example, I would have suggested "transformative pedagogies" rather than the cumbersome "social epistemic rhetoric," but James Berlin never requested my advice.

History is far more complex than any taxonomy can represent. Most scholars have careers that span decades with their positions developing if not taking twists and turns related to forces that may not be fully revealed. Proffering a new position will always come with great political risk and may indeed necessitate the Foucauldian moment of labeling others to create a somewhat undeserved distinction. Maybe the academic desire to coin a new concept leads to the emphasis on difference so we can offer a new and improved concept. Yet such stress on difference also may lead to categories that imply binaries and warring factions, even when they may not exist. Raul Sanchez comments on the need for a progressive cause and effect claim when forwarding a new theory:

> We might even say that process theory was invented by postprocess theory in the same way that, according to Susan Miller, current-traditional theory was invented by process theory …. In a sense then, to participate in a discussion about the relative merits of process and postprocess theories is to use the apparatus, to perform the same act of piety. More importantly, it is also to forego the opportunity to redefine the historical and theoretical terms by which writing will be studied. (2011, p. 187)

Even claims of members' alienation or affiliation may be political projections. These fossilized monikers are hardly accepted team names that rally scholars under their banners to battle the opposition in disciplinary skirmishes. Taxonomies of theory groups are misrepresentations at best and divisive propaganda at worst. Our critiques should historicize such labels to make these groups more dynamic and even revisable.

Richard Weaver (1953) warns against an over-emphasis on theory godterms. These potent terms are vague and therefore discount the complexities of the daily classroom experience. Patricia Harkin (1991) has forwarded a more grounded notion of teacher lore as employing multiple theoretical approaches in service of the teacher's many responsibilities. Thus, a theoretically informed teacher might devise a writing course that draws from multiple approaches: traditional skills, process procedures, expressive needs, cognitive development, academic initiation, critical concerns, rhetorical demands, logical argumentation, genre practices, civic responsibilities, disciplinary knowledge, local imperatives, postmodern alienation, and real-world communicative activities. To make such determinations in curriculum design is not eclectic but rather dynamic in which multiple theories must interplay in a changing, local context. As someone who might be labeled as a practitioner, I am advocating for more theory to complicate our practices, rather than pitting one mythologized theory group against the other.

CRITICAL MEMOIR AND IDENTITY FORMATION

I am somewhat surprised that the personal narrative survives as a writing assignment. Although students favor it, the personal narrative has been critiqued for promoting a naive notion of a singular, static, authentic self. Abandoning the personal narrative in favor of the combative, polarizing argument assignment seems to be in fashion in first-year college writing courses and has trickled down into high school assignment initiatives and the Common Core standards. Some teachers will even say that the personal narrative is too easy for students to write because it is organized chronologically while others would counter that using a familiar structure makes it possible to focus on other more important skills. The personal narrative has been condemned as everything from too emotive to too culturally scripted. While examining her teaching in a personal essay course, Amy Robillard reveals her disciplinary guilt:

> Personal essay assignments become subject to the same by now well-honed critiques of personal narrative assignments. The personal narrative is too easy, uncritical. We shouldn't assign personal narratives because we're only inviting students to confess their most embarrassing experiences to us. We're

not therapists, after all. (Sharp-Hoskins & Robillard, 2012, p. 324)

I respect Robillard's distinction between the personal narrative and the personal essay as a revision that comes from a more critical understanding of subject formation, including her own narrative of herself as the "good" teacher. From this article, both Sharp-Hoskins and Robillard model their critical reflection process: "We argue, then, that it is only by recognizing our own implication, our own attachments, in the economies of emotion that circumscribe us that we can begin to challenge the master narratives of the 'good teacher'" (2012, p. 333). Disciplinary critiques should motivate teacher scholars to interrogate and revise their assignments in an ongoing dialectic between theory and practice.

My revision of the personal narrative assignment derives from an eclectic mix of Russian cognitive psychology and critical theory. As a first generation college student, I cannot avoid thinking about students' motives for enrolling in college courses. Most enroll in degree programs to make a change in identity, be it from local high school student to a more cosmopolitan college student, from one career to another, or more hopefully from one economic stratum to another. In his textbook about educational psychology for teachers, Vygotsky's last subheading in the last chapter is entitled "Life as Creation"(1997). Vygotsky argues for a type of subject formation that is a social process throughout one's lifetime that requires active participation it its creation. Thus, it is no surprise that for Vygotsky, self-regulation is about the development of metacognitive thinking versus controlling discrete behaviors. Self-regulation is about self-formation and becoming the person one wants to be within a given social milieu. Certainly, enrolling in college can be an act of agency to change one's circumstances that implicates identity formation as a context for inquiry, reflection, and revision through writing.

To create what might be an artificial difference from the personal narrative, I have chosen to label this type of writing assignment a critical memoir. I started with Lucy Calkins' (1986) delineation of narrative as what happened, autobiography as when it happened, and memoir as who it happened to and how that experience represents an important theme in that person's life. As I became more versed in postmodern subjectivity, I started to think of memoir as constructed from multiple subject positions:

- The naive self who was present at the time of the experience.
- The subjective self who interprets the experience as the culture would suggest.
- The future self who imagines the person that the author wishes to become.

- The author self who negotiates among the other selves and constructs meaning (Mack, 2007).

Memoir encourages selectivity of experience, multiple interpretations, future orientation, and agency in representation. To push the memoir genre to become more critical, identity formation should be complicated further. Thus, writing activities should promote reflection about identity as being (Mack 2006)
- multiple in various cultural roles,
- conflicted by acts of accommodation, resistance, and opposition,
- temporal within larger historical and economic forces,
- materially situated in a local, dynamic space,
- embodied in emotionally-laden, lived experience,
- interpreted and co-created by society,
- mediated through language that is culturally ideological,
- developmental through continual maturation and education,
- revised by intentional and willful agency, and
- connected to literacies that are larger than the classroom.

This is indeed a tall order. In some regards a critical memoir approach asks the writer to continually reconsider one's own master narratives, questioning the who, what, when, where, and why of the potential ways that the stories could be told. More than questioning whether the story is true are the questions about how the story functions and how it could be actively re-interpreted and revised to represent a newly constructed, more ethical truth. The emphasis on reflection in composition studies informs my desire to include critical interpretation in all aspects of memoir writing. Kathleen Yancey (1998) and Donna Qualley (1997) are both scholars who have emphasized reflection as primary to the composing process.

CRITICAL HEURISTICS IN PRACTICE

The ten-week graduate course in critical memoir was structured around reading, writing, and reflection in three units: being, belonging, and becoming. The name for the being section of the course was influenced by Mikhail Bakhtin's concept of "being-as-event" that describes the individual's existence as an activity. In one of my favorite quotes about subjectivity Bakhtin makes the analogy to a rough draft in need of an ethically answerable deed to escape endless drafts in order to "rewrite one's life once and for all in the form of a fair copy" (Bakhtin, 1993, p. 44). Writing critical memoir has the potential to be part of a Bakhtinian answerable deed as the writer decides what the memory means by selecting, examining, reflecting, and finally assigning meaning to it.

To return to Vygotsky's notion of ontological development of life as a creation, adults often have moments when they dredge up the past in order to make sense of it. Perhaps the very moments when we do this are moments of identity crisis when we feel the need to revise our selves. Some may do this with a therapist who generally provides the interpretation while others will merely have an uncritical moment of nostalgia. For a memoir writing course, assigning meaning to memory can engage students in critical reflection. Although the teacher plays a powerful role in this reflection, we should not assume the therapist's role of primary interpreter. Consequently, I did not micromanage students' insights by commenting extensively on drafts or in lengthy individual conferences or emails. These strategies, although potentially effective, were not realistic for my intent or workload. My influence was primarily through the selection of the readings and the creation of a series of heuristics. These careful curricular decisions were my means for fostering the students' reflections. My role as a reader was more one of praising their insights rather than forwarding my reflections on their experiences.

The critical reflection required for a re-interpretation of experience benefits from a stance of inquiry similar to ethnographic research in which patterns emerge from a process that is rich in phenomenological details and data. This ongoing hermeneutic inquiry should ideally happen before, during, and after each memoir writing experience. One student explained the inquiry into memoir this way:

> As a writer, memoirs feel deeply personal, almost as if something that could exist without a reader. My understanding of the memoir has been challenged and expanded. Not only do I further appreciate the genre, but the process that must occur in the writing process. Unlike the academic writing process, the memoir writing process is much more an inner experience, requiring the writer to travel through remembrances, trying to find that which real memory is. Victor Villanueva first made me aware of the distinction between memory and remembrances. Memory requires more of a person, and is a process driven activity. It is not until more details and dialogue have surfaced from musing on a remembrance that a memory really begins to shape. Memories are the remembrances that we actually relive, nearly re-creating the experience. True memoir writing comes when that memory is recreated for the reader. I am still working to develop my memoir writing into reader-based prose. It can be emotionally

exhausting to relive remembrances enough to actually meet real memory.

Activities not included here also focused on writing crafts such as details, characters, dialogue, and inner thoughts.

The "being" unit encompassed a wider notion of literacy. Students initially journaled in response to literacy memoirs with a working class focus by Laurel Johnson Black (1995) and Linda Brodkey (1994). Any selection of readings comes with a political agenda. I chose several readings that had a social class theme because class is a major issue for my students; however, I made it clear that students were not required to write about class issues. Also, I wanted readings that did not present tidy, simplistic literacy narratives like those that Jane Greer refers to as "conversion narratives" (2012) or Ishmael Reed critiques as "redemption" narratives (2012). In particular, Black presents a complex understanding of literacy through her value of working class language and the disconnect that her education has caused with her sister. As Patrick Berry proposes, the use of literacy narratives should "move beyond a singular focus on either hope or critique in order to identify the transformative potential of literacy in particular circumstances" (2012, iii). So, the question for the writer becomes how should the literacy narrative function within the individual's unique identity formation.

I assigned a series of brainstorming prompts that first required students to itemize a wide range of literacy experiences throughout their lives both inside and outside of school. The prompts continued with questions about more complex functions of literacy for purposes of escape, friendship, entertainment, peace-making, status, curiosity, and rebellion against authority. Students were to note themes in their development as well as how literacy functioned for their families, friends, and multiple identity groups. Finally, students considered conflicts related to their literacy, including occasions when they were intentionally silent, refused to communicate, or chose not to become literate about something for a strong reason. Students also responded to other working-class academic memoirs from Dews and Law's *This Fine Place So Far From Home* (1995). From the prompts and journaling students developed two ideas, drafted, and revised a literacy memoir about experiences that varied from childhood through adulthood. One student's powerful memoir related the experience of being betrayed by a hate-filled, adolescent diary entry when it was discovered by an abusive stepfather.

The "belonging" unit was named from an article by psychologist Barbara Jensen (2012) in which she characterizes the difference between working and middle classes as "belonging" versus "becoming." Jensen characterizes the working class sense of self as developing from childhood in close relation to others, as including or affiliating others whereas the middle class self emerges as separation from others, as negotiating or competing with others. Although I wanted students to consider class conflicts, I opened the heuristics to other types of identity groups.

This unit took longer to implement and involved many more heuristics than the previous unit. Multiple definitions of memoir, culled from several scholars, were presented. In addition to more readings from *This Fine Place So Far From Home* (Dews & Law, 1995), students read selections from Zandy's *Liberating Memory* (1995) and from Rick Bragg (1997) and Paule Marshall (1983). After modeling my own overlapping identity circles related to gender, class, family, relationships, education, location, generation, health, interests, responsibilities, and career, students made their own webs. Another series of prompts invited students to record experiences with language and identity, such as feeling like an insider or outsider, taking a stand or making peace, being offended or offensive, and defending or inspiring others. Students answered a lengthy questionnaire that identified working class markers related to food, clothing, purchases, childhood, home, work, and school; and viewed a hidden class rules chart (Payne, 1996). Students placed life experiences on a graphic organizer, ranking them as accommodating, resisting, or opposing cultural norms. During revision students also read bell hooks (2012), Frank Dobson (2002), and Victor Villanueva (2004). Students had no problems with selecting topics from diverse identity groups and consequently wrote memoirs about race, music, alcoholism, religion, gender, and disability with only one student selecting social class. These memoirs were more complex than earlier ones. Accordingly, the previously mentioned student observed that social class is "a complex system with many layers and much ambiguity."

The third unit about "becoming" springs from Freire's use of "becoming" as a trope in *Pedagogy of the Oppressed* (1973) for creating a critically conscious, future-oriented, literate identity. In a previous critical pedagogy seminar, I created an activity based on Friere's concept of limit situation that guided students to trace moments of frustration to the larger social forces of oppression. Students frequently connected their procrastination in completing assignments with forces inherent to graduate education.

A positive and negative graph activity (Rief, 1992) assigned students to draw and annotate a time line of experiences in order to analyze critical patterns in their lives. Readings included Jacqueline Jones Royster (1996), Janet Bean (2003), and one of my articles (2007). An expanded limit situation heuristic engaged students in listing personal, professional, and writing goals. Students then selected one goal from each category and critically analyzed the forces that thwarted their progress. Limit situations were described as "physical needs, time constraints, financial problems, power obstacles (permission), social pressures (other people), institutional constraints (rules), historical patterns, and cultural biases." Next, students imagined impractical and practical solutions for each goal and one small, immediate step that could be taken. The next activity, "Emotional Indicators of Stress," requested that students think about social systems in which they had been unrewarded, ignored, given extra duties, trivialized, uninformed, left behind, rated poorly, given misleading information, or told lies. After some explanation of who benefits from this type of cultural hegemony, students tracked their recent negative emotions (rage, anger, passive-aggressive desires, frustration, silence, procrastination, fear, guilt, self-loathing, or despair) as a barometer for subtle forms of oppression. Next, a comparison was made to circumstances that elicit the opposite emotions. Finally, students proposed things that could be changed or that they did have power or control over such as their own reactions. This activity was influenced by my interest in economies of emotion, particularly the scholarship of Lynn Worsham (1998), Julie Lindquist (2004), Donna LeCourt (2004), Laura Micciche (2007), and Michalinos Zembylas (2005). Reading explications of emotional labor has helped me to acknowledge that feelings can be connected to agency in subject formation and pedagogy. In other words, critical analysis of emotion brings the potential "to think, feel, and act differently" (Mack, 2007, p. 22). The critical analysis process can begin with an awareness of a bothersome or intense emotion. Feminist scholar Alison Jaggar defines troubling emotions as "outlaw emotions."

As well as motivating critical research, outlaw emotions may also enable us to perceive the world differently from its portrayal in conventional descriptions. They may provide the first indications that something is wrong with how things are. Conventionally unexpected or inappropriate emotions may precede our conscious recognition that accepted descriptions and justifications often conceal as much as reveal the prevailing site of affairs. Only when we reflect on our initially puzzling irritability, revulsion, anger, or fear may we bring to consciousness our "gut-level" awareness that we are in a situation of coercion, cruelty, injustice, or danger (Mack, 2007, p. 161).

To some extent I wanted students to view their outlaw emotions as an early warning system that alerts them to examine the oppressive forces that may be connected to these emotions.

After drafting a limit situation memoir, students completed a pronoun revision activity based on a presentation by Karen Hollis in which a paragraph is selected that contains the singular pronouns of I, me, or my that are revised to plural pronouns of we, us, and our. Students then pondered how their individual limit situation might be connected to the experiences of a larger group of people. The diversity of memoir topics seemed to widen as the term progressed.

For the limit situation memoir, topics addressed family member's rejection of educated vocabulary, deciding to leaving seminary, dealing with negative comments from a professor, accepting polygamy, financial problems with meeting social obligations, and negative comments about weight.

As part of the final portfolio reflection process, I shared my writing manifesto list and asked students to create one of their own, an activity I hoped would help students reflect on what they wanted their writing to be in the future.

When the only writing you do is school writing, the teacher controls all the assignments, topics, and deadlines. Finding the time, motivation, and support necessary to keep writing outside of school is incredibly difficult. It is as if every other part of our lives conspires to prevent writing. Many other parts of our lives cannot be delayed to give us time to write. What we can control is our attitude. A negative attitude can block all possibilities to write. If the writer cannot believe in the importance of his or her own writing, then nothing will get done. It is time to claim your writing for yourself, for your own projects, for your own purposes, desires and dreams.

In addition to reflective journal entries after each of the three essays, the portfolio cover essay assignment requested that students contemplate insights gained from writing their memoirs as well as themes that connected the individual pieces and their readings. Here are two excerpts from different students:

> Both memoirs make a strong case for the claim that we must constantly reinvent ourselves while fighting against the societal forces that want us to adhere to dominant rules that may not benefit us.

> Bell wrote about the price of an education. She argued that those who are less fortunate will be challenged with having to forget where they came from, wipe their memories clean of anything that is not fit for the educated elite. Unconsciously, I had already done this. If I was going to be successful in the world of academia, I had to learn to cover up my roots with the soil of the high-class. I had to forget that I came from a less than worthy background. I had to accept that education wasn't a right for me, but a privilege. I had to come to terms with being neither black nor white, but instead the grey area that goes mostly neglected; the grey area that the minds of logic detest because it challenges their neatly organized world. I had to forget everything that brought me to where I was if I was going to continue to persevere myself and make my mark in the world.

AGENCY AND THE CRITICAL MEMOIR

Regardless of the mode or genre, the teacher must create writing assignments that critically connect literacy to the student's agency in identity formation. The traits that differentiate critical memoir from the personal narrative are primarily that the writing is more subtly nuanced and critically complex. The writing should open the author to the possibility of agency through the interpretation and representation of memory. The meaning of the memoir is revised from the student's current vantage point of an increased critical awareness and projected towards a hopeful future, thus giving the author some degree of agency in shaping identity.

Discounting that the student has any agency in subject formation relegates literacy to functioning only in a most dismal manner. Vygotskian scholars Dorothy Holland and William Lachicotte make room for agency in identity formation that might open up discursive spaces to new variants:

> People have to create selves that (in the metaphor of residence) inhabit the (social) structures and spaces (cultural imaginaries) that collectivities create, but they produce selves that inhabit these structures and imaginaries in creative, variant, and often oppositional, ways .... And, in the circuits of emerging communities of practice, innovation may play out and regularize the semiotic means for new identities and activities that lie beyond existing structures of power. (2007, p. 135)

This notion of creative variants is similar to Victor Turner's discussion of liminal or in-between spaces in social structures that permit resistance and revision (1977). However, unlike essays, identities take a great deal of time and emotional energy to be revised.

Hope is important, but agency should not be located only within the writing itself. To make the larger connection between writing critical memoir and civic literacy might be too grand a claim. I do important work in the writing classroom, but my goal is more that of increasing critical thought rather than liberating anyone's identity. I agree with Rochelle Harris' insistence that emergent moments of critical thought can happen in students' personal essays, autobiographies, and memoirs:

> Before institutional, community, national, and/or global transformation come the personal commitments and experiences that motivate one to claim the agency necessary to begin social critique. The most important critical work emerges

as students write about the places they have been, the experiences they have had, the books they have read, and the ideas they have pondered. This is one of the most revolutionary of critical acts—to transform and empower one's own words as they are embedded in that most difficult of intertextual histories to negotiate, the history of one's own life. (2004, p. 417)

I must remember that Freire cautioned that the classroom is dominated by the hegemony of the larger society and not really the "lever of revolutionary transformation" (Shor & Freire, 1987, p. 33). Education may not be the great equalizer for my students (or for me, for that matter), but it can help us to compose a more thoughtful draft in the endless revisions of ourselves and our lives.

REFERENCES

Bakhtin, M. M. (1993). *Toward a philosophy of the act*. (V. Liapunov, Trans.). Austin: University of Texas Press.

Bean, J. (2003). Manufacturing emotions: Tactical resistance in the narratives of working class students. In D. Jacobs & L. R. Micciche (Eds.), *A way to move: Rhetorics of emotion & composition studies* (pp. 101-112). Portsmouth, NH: Boynton/Cook.

Berry, P. W. (2011). *Beyond hope: Rhetorics of mobility, possibility, and literacy*. (Doctoral dissertation).

Black, L. J. (1995). Stupid rich bastards. In C. L. B. Dews & C. L. Law (Eds.), *This fine place so far from home: Voices of academics from the working class* (pp. 13-25). Philadelphia: Temple University Press.

Bragg, R. (1997). Prologue. In *All over but the shoutin'* (pp. xi-xxii). New York: Pantheon Books.

Brodkey, L. (1994). Writing on the bias. *College English, 56*(5), 527-547.

Calkins, L. (1986). *The art of teaching writing*. Portsmouth, NH: Heinemann.

Dews, C L. B, & Law, C. L. (Eds.). (1995). *This fine place so far from home: Voices of academics from the working class*. Philadelphia: Temple University Press.

Dobson, F. E., Jr. (2002). Beyond the limits: Reflections of a Black working class academic. *Public Voices, 5*(3), 85-91.

Fulkerson, R. (1990). Composition theory in the eighties: Axiological consensus and paradigmatic diversity. *College Composition and Communication, 41*(4), 409-429.

Fulkerson, R. (2005). Composition at the turn of the twenty-first century. *College Composition and Communication, 56*(4), 654-687.

Fulkerson, R. (1979). Four philosophies of composition. *College Composition and Communication, 30*(4), 343-348.

Freire, P. (1973). *Pedagogy of the oppressed.* Harmondsworth, UK: Penguin Education.

Greer, J. (1995, March). "And now I can see:" The function of conversion arratives in the discourse of cultural studies. Paper presented at the Annual Meeting of the Conference on College Composition and Communication, Washington, DC. Abstract retrieved from http://files.eric.ed.gov/fulltext/ED385838.pdf

Harkin, P. (1991). The postdisciplinary politics of lore. In P. Harkin & J. Schlib (Eds.), *Contending with words: Composition and rhetoric in a postmodern age* (pp. 124-138). New York: Modern Language Association of America.

Harris, R. (2004). Encouraging emergent moments: The personal, critical, and rhetorical in the writing classroom. *Pedagogy: Critical Approaches to Teaching Literature, Language, Composition, and Culture, 4*(3), 401-418.

Holland, D., & Lachicotte, W. (2007). Vygotsky, Mead and the new sociocultural studies of identity. In H. Daniels, M. Cole & J. V. Wertsch (Eds.), *The Cambridge companion to Vygotsky* (pp. 101-135). New York: Cambridge University Press.

hooks, b. (2000). Learning in the shadow of race and class. *The Chronicle of Higher Education*, 14-16.

Horner, B., & Lu, M-Z. (2010). Working rhetoric and composition. *College English, 72*(5), 470-494.

Jagger, A. M. (1989). Love and knowledge: Emotion in feminist epistemology. In E. M. Jagger & S. R. Bordo (Eds.), *Gender, body/knowledge: Feminist reconstructions of being and knowing* (145-171). Rutgers University Press.

Jensen, B. (1997, June). *Becoming versus belonging: Psychology, speech, and social class.* Paper presented at the Youngstown Working Class Studies Conference, Youngstown, OH. Retrieved from http://www.classmatters.org/2004_04/becoming_vs_belonging.php

LeCourt, D. (2004). Identity matters: Schooling the student body in academic discourse. Albany: SUNY Press.

Lindquist, J. (2004). Class affects, classroom affectations: Working through the paradoxes of strategic empathy. *College English, 67*, 187-209.

Mack, N. (2006). Ethical representation of working class lives: Multiple genres, voices, and identities." *Pedagogy, 6*(1), 53-78.

Mack, N. (2007). Being the namer or the named: Working-class discourse conflicts. *JAC: a Journal of Composition Theory, 27*(1-2), 329-350.

Mack, N. (2009). Representations of the field in graduate courses: Using parody to question all positions. *College English, 71*(5), 435-459.

Marshall, P. (1983). The making of a writer: From the poets in the kitchen. In *Reena and other stories* (pp. 1-12). Old Westbury, NY: Feminist Press.

Micciche, L. R. (2007). *Doing emotion: Rhetoric, writing, teaching.* Portsmouth, NH: Boynton/Cook Publishers.

Payne, R. (1996). *A framework for understanding poverty.* Highlands, TX: aha! Process.

Qualley, D. J. (1997). *Turns of thought: Teaching composition as reflexive inquiry.* Portsmouth, NH: Boynton/Cook.

Reed, I. (2010, February 4). Fade to white. *The New York Times.* Retrieved from http://www.nytimes.com/2010/02/05/opinion/05reed.html?_r=0

Rief, L. (1992). *Seeking diversity: Language arts with adolescents.* Portsmouth, NH: Heinemann Educational Books.

Royster, J. J. (1996). When the First Voice You Hear Is Not Your Own. *College Composition and Communication, 47,* 29-40.

Sanchez, R. (2011). First, A Word. In S. I. Dobrin, J. A. Rice, & M. Vastola (Eds.), *Beyond Post Process* (pp. 183-194). Logan: Utah State University Press.

Sharp-Hoskins, K., & E. Robillard, A. E. (2012). Narrating the "good teacher" in rhetoric and composition: Ideology, affect, complicity. *JAC: A Journal of Composition Theory, 32,* 305-336.

Shor, I., & Freire, P. (1987). (1987). *A pedagogy for liberation: Dialogues on transforming education.* South Hadley, MA: Bergin & Garvey.

Turner, V. W. (1977). *The ritual process: Structure and anti-structure.* Ithaca, NY: Cornell University Press.

Villanueva, V. (2004). "Memoria" is a friend of ours: on the discourse of color. *College English, 67*(1), 9-19.

Vygotsky, L. (1997). *Educational psychology.* Boca Raton, FL: St. Lucie Press.

Weaver, R. M. (1953). *The ethics of rhetoric.* Chicago: H. Regnery.

Worsham, L. (1998). Going postal: Pedagogic violence and the schooling of emotion. *JAC, 18*(2), 213-245.

Yancey, K. B. (1998). *Reflection in the writing classroom.* Logan, UT: Utah State University Press.

Zandy, J. (1995). *Liberating memory: Our work and our working-class consciousness.* New Brunswick, NJ: Rutgers University Press.

Zembylas, M. (2005). *Teaching with emotion: A postmodern enactment.* Greenwich, CT: Information Age.

CRITICAL EXPRESSIVISM'S ALCHEMICAL CHALLENGE

Derek Owens
St. John's University

THE PERSONAL-TO-PROFESSIONAL LADDER

From the beginning one of the messages I got (as far as teaching first-year writing was concerned) was that pretty much one begins by "teaching the personal," moves as soon as possible to the "analytical," then closes with the "argumentative." There might be other stops en route—"expository" and "persuasive" and the like could all get slipped in between the bookends. But the trajectory was clear: initially "allow" students to dip into their lives and experiences, with the goal of eventually moving away from all that "personal stuff" into realms more explicitly "academic," "rigorous," "scholarly." Hook the initiates, in other words, by first "letting them" write about their lives and interests, the stuff that floats their boats. Once we've whetted their appetite though, shift gears. "Personal expression" gets left behind as analysis of other people's texts takes center stage. "Dissection" and "critique" and "debate" move in where the personal has been evicted, or at least rendered secondary or subservient to the examination of artifacts, the elucidation of ideas located beyond the writer's local experience. One might picture the progression like some kind of game board—each student entering via their own unique paths and histories, engaging with them along the way, but ultimately everyone coming closer and closer to a common finish line where it's not their "expressed" personal histories that matter but, say, the way they marshal evidence, cite sources, make inferences, assemble claims. Establish authority. Enter into other people's conversations.

Occasionally this "personal-to-professional" path was made quite explicit. In one place where I used to teach, a senior colleague and supervisor laughed disparagingly of how our freshmen were "so in love with their little stories" and needed to be "broken" of such self-indulgences. This was in marked contrast to the fairly progressive graduate program I was in during the late 1980s where considerable attention was placed on designing learning environments where students had the freedom to explore writing on their own terms. And yet even there, once we grad students got to our comps and the dissertation, the notion of incorporating or validating the "personal"—however much that concept had been valued in our conversations about students' rights to their own languages—was regarded as risky and problematic. We were after all training ourselves to enter the profession; to not take seriously the genre conventions of the cover letter, dissertation prospectus, the manuscript, the job interview, would have been self-defeating.

I suppose what bothers me most of all is how seductive this one-directional ladder is. I know because I'm no stranger to it. I have in fact embraced it in the past and at times uncritically enforced it. I used to recommend it to faculty looking for suggestions on how to introduce writing at different stages of the semester. And this supposed progression—it really can be such a seductive little formula, no? I mean, there is a comfortable logic to it. Those early-in-the-semester "personal essays" can be such excellent icebreakers. Everyone gets to find out a tiny bit about each other, tell some "personal" stories. Students find it little easier to open up in their small group discussions, maybe even locate common ground. Then about a quarter into the semester the focus can turn to texts written by real, published writers, the classroom vocabulary turning to matters of "close reading" and "textual analysis" and "unpacking the text." Then, after they graduate from this phase, students are channeled into the even loftier realms of argumentation, and new vocabularies are adopted about "claims," "defining terms," "evidence," "anticipating counter-arguments."

It's not that any of the attendant topics or conversations that take place in this linear continuum is inherently problematic. What's bothersome is the underlying assumption that one inevitably goes in through the Expression door, exits out the Critical door, and that these realms have to occupy rigid, separate geographies.

Of course what I've articulated here is a crude cartoon. I don't personally know anyone who teaches a writing course exactly this way, slavishly marching through these realms in such predictable, lockstep manner. But I feel confident that this trajectory remains alive and well and largely implicit in varying degrees throughout writing curricula and textbooks. (If I'm wrong, we would probably see just as many courses demonstrating the inverse: students beginning with research papers, constructing arguments, analyzing texts, then wrapping up with "personal narratives.")

I also realize that the terms and binaries I'm invoking here—personal/expressive vs. academic/critical—aren't givens. Some in this volume, like Peter Elbow in his opening chapter, challenge the terminology altogether. Still, for me, these terms retain some cash value. Ultimately I don't find either word meaningless or inherently pejorative; instead I want to bear in mind these are working fictions that point to distinct histories and perceptions, not intractable discourse conventions, and that it's in their juxtaposition, their melding, where we find exciting opportunities for imagining writing.

I'm interested in how either end of the spectrum puts pressure on its alleged antithesis, pushing and pulling us to a more hybrid middle arena where "critical" embodies the "personal," and "expressive" eats the "academic"—to a point where the paired construction no longer reinforces either endpoint but actually calls them into question. A binary issuing a challenge for us to recognize the limitation of the very presupposed obligatory continuum. Ultimately this both/and construction—or more accurately, reflective process—calls to mind (for me anyway) the alchemical pairing of opposites referred to as the *coniunctio*, a reasonable metaphor, perhaps, to bear in mind as we explore the possible benefits of conjoining these two modes of inquiry.

FROM MOTHER'S MILK TO SPEED

Before unraveling that further let me take a detour into etymological terrain. There's a richness of meaning in the root "express" that is absent in the manner in which the word is commonly invoked in our field. For while "expressive" in our compositional history has often been linked with, say, "personal," "emotional," and "uncritical," a quick tour through the word's history points to some interesting variations. An incomplete list, courtesy of the OED:

> One of the earliest meanings of "express" is "to press out," specifically to press or squeeze out milk from the breast. An organic, feminine connotation—although express here also means being forced out by mechanical means.

> "Express" also means "to portray, represent," linking it with rendering—and so in this way "expressive discourse" could, one might think, have something in common with the detailed description associated with, say, more clinical, scientific observations.

> The term "beyond expression" is intriguing for it implies that "expression" is the endpoint, a culmination—as there can be no expression beyond expression. Expression thus as the final realm, a pinnacle of—well, expression.

> "Expressionless" of course means "destitute of expression; giving no indication of character, feeling, etc.; inexpressive." It means "expressing nothing, conveying no meaning." Here expression is thus saturated with meaning, the source and conveyor of meaning—whereas expressionless equals absence. No meaning, in other words, without expression.

> Expression is elsewhere defined as "to represent in language; to put into words, set forth (a meaning, thought, state of

things); to give utterance to (an intention, a feeling)." Not only is expression thus meaning saturated, but is here the very creation of meaning—meaning conjured within language. And when it's summarized as "To put one's thoughts into words; to utter what one thinks; to state one's opinion," it comes very close to argumentation, the articulation of a position.

If the earliest roots of "express" carry vestiges of the feminine and maternal, embedded within the term are conventionally masculine connotations as well. For express also means speed, no dillydallying, no time to stop unnecessarily along the way. No pausing for reflection. Hence we have the express train, express delivery, express highway, express messenger, and even the express rifle.

It seems some in our field have chosen to define "expression" and "expressivist" and "expressionist" pretty narrowly. In composition such words have too often been indicators of naive exuberance, narcissism, lack of self-reflection.[1] Interestingly, we have been much savvier about the term "critical." While the OED tells us that "criticism" certainly means "the action of criticizing, or passing judgment upon the qualities or merits of anything; esp. the passing of unfavourable judgment; fault-finding, censure," we're quick to make clear to our students that it is not that kind of criticism we're all about in the academy but rather critique as measured, thoughtful, transparent, honest introspection in the search for truth. Or something like that.

Why has our field been more willing to acknowledge the multiple meanings in the definitional aura surrounding "critical," and not so much "expressive"? What is it about the "personal" that makes the academic so nervous?

OUR (NOT SO CRITICALLY) EXPRESSIVE ACADEMIC DISCOURSE

Which brings me to my second short detour in which I feel compelled to highlight a contradiction we all know but which I don't think gets acknowledged nearly enough: that, despite our professional tendency to reject the "personal" in favor of "objectivity," academia, as a culture and a workplace, is as fraught with as much raw, personal, messy personal emotion as any professional community you can probably think of.

As academics we do an incredible job at portraying ourselves as dispassionate scholars privileging neutral objectivity and reasoned discourse and impartial rigor. More often than not we value the quantitative over the qualitative, "empirical data" over storytelling, measured debate over in-your-face finger pointing. But let's be honest: we are no strangers to the most personal of the personal—as any Human Resources office, dean, general counsel, chair, and most faculty, adjuncts, and grad assistants can tell you. For while in our peer-reviewed journals we might (might) bend over backwards to effect a posture of measured balance—infusing our prose with obligatory phrases like "I would like to suggest" and "an alternative reading might" and "perhaps we ought to consider," we are also people who are no slouches at throwing tantrums in department meetings, dissing colleagues, distributing ad hominem attacks in mailboxes, making students cry in the classroom, making our colleagues cry, crying ourselves in our offices, writing snotty emails, and sparring with colleagues in all manner of venues. Nor are we strangers to favoritism, paranoia masked as overconfidence, jealous petty exchanges, insults, one-upmanship, and character assassination. (It's why, when academics read a novel like Richard Russo's *Straight Man*, they know immediately a text like that has to be grounded in reality.)

I'm not saying the "personal" or "expressive" are synonymous only with these touchier emotions. Obviously much of our "expressive" discourse is also what we would consider laudatory, necessary, and worth celebrating—we are after all a breed of professionals who value academic freedom, speaking truth to power, and pursuing things like "truth" even when it disrupts various status quos. My point is that such more emotionally problematic "expressive," "personal" iterations are alive and well in our academy, always have been, and that a more accurate and comprehensive assessment of "academic discourse" would have to include this richer, messier pool of discourse. To pretend that the discourses of academic culture aren't in a great many ways inherently "expressive" just isn't true.

AN ALCHEMICAL INVITATION

For me the challenge and appeal of "critical expressivism" is in its both/and implications. Alchemically, the *coniunctio* refers to the wedding of opposites, the bringing together of unlike materials or states of being in order to construct some alternate hybrid form or perception that, synergistically, depends upon yet is distinct from its components. For me the bridging of the "critical" and "expressive" domains ultimately leads us to a reflective process where, Uroboros-like, we continually cycle through both opposites to a point where the binary might be left behind and some other, more interesting, complex, queered understanding of introspection, and how it might be imaginatively conveyed, begins to surface. These conjoined twins push us to continually problematize and question our own positionality as we write—moving us to ask such questions as:

What's my own personal, private investment in this? (and if there isn't one, then, why exactly am I engaged in this writing act?) What does this writing task hold for me, personally, and how and why might I acknowledge (or conceal) the degree of that personal investment? Am I sufficiently subjecting my predilections to healthy skepticism, processing them through a critical filter, unwilling to leave anything to assumption? How far am I willing to critique my own ideas, and in the process regard my lived histories that have made them part of who I am? If the discursive arenas I seek to enter and participate within frown upon rhetorical markers others might characterize as too "personal," or likewise too "academic," how far am I willing to go to challenge the expectations of those audiences? When do I acquiesce? How might my concept of "the personal" evolve into something that resembles nothing like all the forms and genres typically, maybe pejoratively associated with that word? And same for "critical," the "academic?" Most of all, how to write, and think through writing in ways that move outside both ends of this spectrum, that don't reject either the "expressive" or the "critical," but engage in a means of trying to make writing within (or outside—?) an arena where personal/academic, critical/expressive begin to drop their meanings, and no longer make all that much sense anyway?

What I like about the concept of the "critically expressive" is how it queers the binary, challenging each half by forcing them into the other's arms. Comparable pairings (although, here, flipped) might be "personally academic," "locally global," "emotionally objective." It's interesting too that in such pairings one of these inverted twins is always the suspect term demanding validation, whereas its partner is typically assumed to be more appropriate. "Expressive," "personal," "local," "emotional"—traditionally, in academic contexts anyway, such gestures have to be justified, excused, permitted. Allowances made. We feel we have to make good arguments for letting them through the door. On the other hand "critical," "academic," "global," "objective"—these are assumed to be self-evident. Ultimately though it's not condemning one side over the other, or even reversing this imbalance, but the invitation to create some wholly distinct third space through writing that I find appealing. An invitation leading, perhaps, to an understanding of writing as, say, art.

So how might this manifest in the classroom? When we find ourselves composing, verbally or in writing, "in the personal"—that is, self-consciously invoking the autobiographical or the local or the personal or even the "emotional"—we might push ourselves and our students to consider never settling for "just" telling the story, venting, confessing, sharing. Not that there's anything wrong with "just" doing any of that. But if the critically expressive is one of our interests, we've an opportunity before us to question the stories we would otherwise "just" tell (the classroom as a conversational, compositional realm distinct from, say, the dinner table or bar). It's a space where we can expect ourselves to keep asking: so why that story? Why convey this personal account? What's the motive behind this desire to share these emotions? What might be some of the as of yet unrealized stories percolating beneath this autobiographical rendering? In other words, not to simply be satisfied with the presentation of story for story's sake, but provoked to keep cracking story open, unraveling and unpacking it.

On the flip side, when we find ourselves operating "in the academic"—that is, attentive to all that critical stuff like evidence, analysis, arguments, and the rest of it—we might seek to be more unabashedly up front about the personal, and maybe even private, motivations and concerns behind the ideas and decisions that grow out of this work. Here, the focus could also be on storytelling, but the stories behind our professional and research needs.

Many of us in composition studies do something like this already. Most of our journals are filled with articles where authors make no apologies for introducing their own autobiographical, "personal" accounts and motives. Still, I'm interested in what happens when we push ourselves further to the point where considering the personal as critical, and the critical as personal, becomes risky, startling, and maybe uncomfortable.

I did this recently in a book I wrote where I struggled to tell a variety of stories and pull together a bunch of research. The process was for me more painful, awkward, invigorating, and ultimately revealing than any other writing project I've undertaken. The book had its genesis in these so-called "recovered memories" my mother started to have in her early fifties—accounts of rather sensational abuse at the hands of grandmother. I wanted to tell these stories, which my mother passed along to me, but needed to present that telling within the context of something larger than "just" her childhood story. And so I found myself researching the history of the region in which she grew up—a weird section of central New York State. This historical mining unexpectedly led me back to the "personal" as I turned up accounts of long lost relatives on my mother's side (including, I discovered, the leader of a religious cult back in the late 18th century).

After a while I realized, somewhat reluctantly, that I would also have to introduce some of my own childhood memories and photos in this narrative as a means of contrasting the horrorshow my mom experienced with the more idyllic childhood my mother, and father too, constructed for me and my sister. This was exceptionally hard for me. To shine a light on myself that way and be so revealing to an outside audience made me incredibly nervous. I was much more comfortable letting the focus be on my mother, dead relatives, and regional histories. As a result I learned that, while the "personal" and "expressive" are often assumed to be problematic in that they invite undisciplined, narcissistic navel-gazing, in truth a rendering of the intimate, the guarded, the innermost, can require no small degree of difficult reflection and self-critique in figuring out how to communicate all that to an invisible, imagined public audience. Being "expressive," in this sense, for me, turned out to be way harder and weirder than any of the academic writing I ever did. Developing that kind of confidence in one's work, one's audience—it's just scary.

As I worked through this business of bridging other people's stories with my own, the focus of this book took on new significance. I became interested in the strangeness of memory and the slipperiness of identity. In doing research into accounts of child abuse as well as controversies surrounding concepts like recovered memory, I found myself realizing I had to rethink concepts like "childhood" and "trauma" from scratch. On top of all this I wanted to introduce as much photographic and visual "narrative" as possible—old photos and postcards—while messing around with the visual arrangement of text on the page in ways that might (if only to me) indiscreetly reflect some of the ideas housed within.

In the end it turned out to be the most difficult thing I've written and will likely ever publish. More than anything else I've tackled in writing, this manuscript represented more fully a sustained engagement with the merging of these two endpoints—the critical, and the expressive. Working within this hybrid, liminal realm now seems to me more challenging than self-consciously choosing to reside within either side. A both/and embrace that seems fraught with difficulties, but also unexpected surprises.

I make mention of my manuscript not because it's how I'm pushing others to write. I mention it because it's an example of what this whole critical/expressive *coniunctio* (or whatever metaphor you prefer) might point to. Ultimately I'm interested in classroom environments, and master's theses, and dissertations, and published articles, where authors (and the faculty, directors, supervisors, editors, and readers who say yea or nay to the worthiness of such work, validating them or not) grant themselves permission to dive into and beyond notions of both "expressive" and "critical," "personal" and "academic," to a point where the writing manifests messily, curiously. "Of its own accord." I've come to realize that I privilege discovery, even when it surfaces in odd and uncomfortable ways. Experimentation borne out of need and desire, not necessarily fashion or convention or tradition. Right now "critical expressivism" seems to me about as exciting a new concept as any surfacing within our field, opening up strange and startling new landscapes for composing.

NOTES

1. And when I say "we" I include myself. Because—and here is my essay's little mea culpa moment—I was often one of those who was too quick to assign pejorative connotations to "expressive" discourse. For the longest time I associated the word with sloppy exuberance, or loud relatives, or the constant barrage of egos run amuck on television and radio. Of course, my resistance to the "expressive" had more to do with my own discomfort with conveying the autobiographical—something touched on in this essay. So I failed to draw a distinction between the kind of obligatory, scripted expressionism one finds in, say, reality television and bad memoir writing and extroverted uncles, with the legitimately self-preoccupied explorations of first-year writers who have every reason to be fascinated with their lives, histories, minds, and emotions. Thanks, by the way, to the editors of this collection for providing me with an opportunity to figure this out.

PAST-WRITING: NEGOTIATING THE COMPLEXITY OF EXPERIENCE AND MEMORY

Jean Bessette
University of Vermont

Early advocates of personal writing sought to use first-year composition to restore authenticity to students who must suffer a "plastic, mass-produced world" outside the classroom (Adler-Kassner, 1998, p. 218). In line with this objective, the rhetoric of early personal writing pedagogy is constituted by tropes of ownership, expression, self-understanding, and "authentic voice," as the title of Donald C. Stewart's 1972 expressivist textbook illustrates. Linda Adler-Kassner contends that, as a result of this goal of authenticity and ownership, expressivism "started with and centered around experience—defined as personal, private, individually felt understanding of the writer" (1998, p. 219).[1] "Experience" however, was almost always framed in terms of the past. Expressivist Gordon Rohmann argued, for example, that it is in the nature of human beings to make analogies between "this experience and others" gone by; we "know anything in our present simply because we have known similar things in our past to which we compare the present" (1965, p. 111). For Rohmann and other expressivists, writing past experience—that is, composing with memory—was a means by which students could achieve the self-understanding expressivists sought.

More contemporary textbooks with calls for personal writing echo these early understandings of "individually felt," authentic access to past experience, making it clear that the reliance of personal writing on the authority of memory persists. Robert Yagelski's 2010 *Reading our World: Conversations in Context*,[2] for example, asks students to write essays "based on memories of [their] childhood" or essays in which they "describe an important memory [they] have of [their] family" (pp. 80; 85). Assignments such as these often link memory writing with present identity, asking students to focus on a "particular aspect of [their] upbringing and how the place where [they] were raised might have influenced [their] sense of identity" (Yagelski, 2010, p. 85). When Yagelski asks students to write the past experience that has constituted them as individuals today, he treats experience as foundational in some way, as a stable referent students can access and articulate in order to better understand their present selves. These assignments invite the writing of narrative, chronological and linear in structure, because the memories often end up in the form of a story, bolstered by the authority of the writer's experience.

This chapter takes a closer look at the "pastness" of the experience students of personal writing are asked to compose. When we refigure "experience" as "memory," we emphasize the slipperiness of our perceptions of the past: the ways in which changing present circumstances reconfigure our sense of what happened. Lynn Z. Bloom explains that writing the past cannot be understood in terms of truth, except in Joan Didion's sense of a subjective truth: the "truth of how it felt to me" (as quoted in Bloom, 2003, p. 278). But even Didion's sense of a truth of feeling is undermined when, as Bloom puts it, "the writer's vision varies over time and intervening circumstances" and when, "as we experience more of life and learn more ourselves and as the world itself changes, we come to understand events and people differently" (Bloom 2003, p. 286). Memory is dynamic and unstable, at odds with our attempts to grab hold of it in writing and make it permanent as a foundation for understanding our present selves. Such understandings of memory upset calls to represent experience as individual, authentic, chronological, and linear.

What becomes of expressivist writing when the pastness of experience complicates its foundational stability for present self-understanding? Rather than view the complexity of writing with memory as support for discontinuing the teaching of personal writing, I consider here how we might approach personal writing in a way that takes into account the dynamic slipperiness of memory. Writing memory with attention to its complexities is important work for students not only because they are already writing with memory in many composition classrooms but also because, as I will show, memory writing offers a unique opportunity for critical analysis of students' social and political locations. As a feminist scholar, I offer in this paper a feminist pedagogical approach emphasizing strategies of alternative discourse as one way to address the complexity of writing with memory.[3] Ultimately, by drawing theories of collective memory into conversation with feminist composition pedagogy, I hope to illustrate how this kind of memory writing might be taught and learned.

Before I describe a sequence of assignments and a course in which I attempted to put into practice my understanding of how writing with memory might best be approached in first-year composition, I will briefly articulate the theoretical perspective that informed the course. Historian and memory studies scholar David Lowenthal argues that we

> select, distill, distort, and transform the past, accommodating things remembered to the needs of the present ... Memories are not ready-made reflections of the past, but eclectic selective

reconstructions based on subsequent actions and perceptions and on ever-changing codes by which we delineate, symbolize and classify the world around us. (1985, p. 210)

Lowenthal's emphasis on the "subsequent actions[,] ... perceptions," and "ever-changing codes" that organize our memories underscores the elusiveness of our grasp on a pure reconstruction of our experience. But it also suggests a second, simultaneous focus for writers of experience to consider: not only the experience "itself" they wish to recall and reproduce in writing but the dynamic "codes" through which the experience becomes legible in the writer's present structure of understanding. Historian Joan Wallach Scott's understanding of experience resonates with Lowenthal's. She objects to uncritical uses of experience because such uses preclude our critical examination of the ideological system in which the experiencer both enacts the experience and later recalls the experience. Instead of analyzing the workings of the system, the authority of experience reproduces the terms of the system, "locating resistance outside its discursive construction" (Scott, 1991, p. 777).

Lowenthal and Scott's theorizations of memory articulate the mediation of our memories, the ways in which the experience itself and our subsequent memory of it are constructed by the "system" or "codes" through which we view the world. When we bring Lowenthal and Scott into conversation with composition scholars of expressivism, the difference becomes apparent between viewing memory as culturally situated and constituted and viewing experience as "personal, private, [and] individually felt," as Adler-Kassner (1998, p.218) characterizes expressivism. Instead, Lowenthall and Scott's theorization of memory shows it to be necessarily social and discursive. As Scott suggests, subjects are constructed discursively through the act and memory of experience, which in turn produces (not merely records) a particular perspective on the experience. This view can be seen as a critique of the individualism implicit in expressivism because it situates the self inextricably in the social and discursive world.

Memory can be described as "collective" because, as Maurice Halbwachs argued in *The Social Frameworks of Memory*, "the mind reconstructs its memories under the pressure of society" (1992, p. 51). Memories hang together in the mind of an individual because they are "part of a totality of thoughts common to a group" (Halbwachs, 1992, p. 52). According to Halbwachs then, individual memories are not necessarily individual; they are produced in the social milieu of the group the individual identifies with. This social memory can "characterize groups" by revealing a "debt to the past" and expressing "moral continuity" (Klein, 2002, p. 130). Taken together, the implications of Lowenthal, Scott, and Halbwachs are that, when we set out to recount past experience, we must attend to the ways in which memories are formed with others in the present as a means of connection, group coherence, and a sense of shared past and future. I see their theorizations as a call to view experience not as such but rather for the social and discursive frames through which we understand the experience and the social (which is to say, identificatory) uses to which we put the experience—the ways we shape memories to fit those we believe we share with others, as a way of cohering more securely as a group.

If students of personal writing are asked to attend to the social, discursive forces and the present identificatory uses that might shape their memories, their approach to expressivism becomes "critical." This attention to how "personal" memories are socially or discursively shaped in service of present identifications begs questions of power and agency. In what narrative forms do the experiences we remember take shape? How are certain experiences remembered and others forgotten? The ability to use a memory and to define for others its use is fundamentally related to historical distributions of power (Connorton, 1989, LeGoff & Nora, 1977). This tension between memory and forgetting reveals the past to be a dynamic, perpetually contested site, constantly open to varying degrees of fluctuation depending on the contingent power of the group in question. Memory is a dynamic, "processional action by which people constantly transform the recollections they produce" (Zelizer, 1995, p. 218). In sum, when we reconfigure experience as memory, the task of expressivism becomes decidedly social and decidedly critical.

Though "personal" memory cannot be extricated from present social forces, composing critically with memory is not without opportunities for agency. As Nancy Mack explains in her contribution to this collection, writing what she calls "critical memoir"

> should open the author to the possibility of agency through the interpretation and representation of memory. The meaning of the memoir is revised from the student's current vantage point of an increased critical awareness and projected towards a hopeful future, thus giving the author some degree of agency in shaping identity.

When we think of memory as dynamic, processual, presentist, and very much situated in the social and discursive world, agency is made possible when such complexity is both represented and interrogated in language. While conventional personal narratives are structured chronologically with a beginning, middle, and end and often conform to familiar plots, a presentist, processual, social, and discursive understanding of memory calls for a disruption of conventional structures. Because such structures can be understood as a present "system" or "code" that produces, rather than records, the experience, adherence to these conventions of narrative inhibit the simultaneous interrogation of memory's social and discursive construction that makes identificatory agency possible.

Thus, writing with memory compels alternative rhetorical strategies to conventional personal narratives. My considerations of alternative discourse are inspired by Kate Ronald and Joy Ritchie's critical reading of Dorothy Allison's creative nonfiction piece, *Two or Three Things I Know For Sure*. Ronald and Ritchie see in Allison's memoir a "model for how to use language to survive and change one's reality" (2006, p. 7). Allison's work takes an unconventional form for writers to imitate, a "method of unfolding and holding on to the paradoxical relationships between fiction and fact, silence and speaking, certainty and doubt, cultural norms and taboos" (2006, p. 7). That is, for Ronald and Ritchie, the rhetorical strategies Allison employs allow her to accomplish seemingly improbable contradictions in the same text, which I reread here in the language of memory: to show through memory writing what is remembered and forgotten, what "was" and what present circumstances reconfigure, and to situate these potential contradictions in the context of "cultural norms and taboos" (that is, how they align with cultural expectations and where they transgress). The use of alternative discourse in writing memory may accomplish what Lisa Ede and Andrea Lunsford call "crimes of reading and writing," the upsetting of normative conventions with the goal of facilitating "transformative agency" (2006, p. 17).

Taking my cues from these feminist pedagogues, I set out to design a pedagogical approach through which students might be taught to read for the rhetorical strategies used by writers of memory who employ alternative discourse, in order to then selectively imitate the strategies in their own personal writing. How do memory writers like Allison, or Susan Griffin, or Gloria Anzaldua, for example, grapple and rhetorically represent their past experience in the context of larger social and historical discourses? What do their particular choices in language allow them to think through that more conventional personal narratives do not? What alternative sentence structures do they employ? How do they position themselves vis-à-vis others, vis-à-vis "history," vis-à-vis their memories, in language?

To examine how this work played out in my own classroom, I will describe how this project was undertaken with Susan Griffin's creative nonfiction/memoir chapter, "Our Secret," published in her collection *Chorus of Stones* (1993). "Our Secret" is a complex, fragmented essay, amalgamating and juxtaposing interpretations of Griffin's memories of her family life with her interpretations of Heinrich Himmler's family life. Himmler was the chief of the SS under Hitler during the Second World War—clearly an unlikely candidate and cultural context for a contemporary American writer to situate her own memories among.

But Griffin does so in order to ask larger questions about where rage comes from, how it emerges and manifests culturally, and how acts of rage disseminate and influence others across time and place. Her inquiry into her own past unearths and analyzes the source of her acts of childish rage against her grandmother and leads her to compare own family's strict childrearing practices to Himmler's context of rigid, almost torturous German childrearing. She asks questions akin to more traditional expressivist writing: she wants to learn "how it is" that people—herself, Himmler, others—"become [them]selves." But she does so in a complex mélange of personal and historical pasts, using her own memories to better understand larger historical happenings and vice versa.

In the classroom, I sought to help students see Griffin's strategies for engaging with and problematizing the past. I designed discussion questions and writing assignments that asked students to attend to her particular rhetorical strategies for identifying and disidentifying with a larger cultural past. We read Griffin's essay for the textual cues of her unique rhetoric of memory—her radical disruption of chronology, use of uncertain speculative language, and strategic shifts in perspective that emphasize the intersections of personal and cultural pasts. As a class, we looked for what "pieces" constituted Griffin's fragmented essay and found it to be an interweaving of interviews; readings of diaries, photographs, and art; scientific facts; and her own familial memories into a tapestry of emotion, tragedy, and perhaps hope.

Looking more closely at particular paragraphs and sentences, we looked for textual cues that indicated how she represented the relationship between individual and collective memory. Students saw fragility and incertitude in her readings of others and her own pasts, revealed in particular choices of language that disrupted any sense of historical accuracy. For example, we focused on a passage in which Griffin describes an interview with a woman who witnessed the aftermath of a German concentration camp as a young child. In her description of the woman's memory, Griffin's language is initially assured, employing jarring imagery of concrete things: she saw "shoes in great piles. Bones. Women's hair" (1993, p. 114). But immediately the woman's memories are called into question: "She had no words for what she saw. Her father admonished her to be still. Only years later, and in a classroom, did she find out the name of this place and what happened here" (Griffin, 1993, p. 114). Students saw the certainty of the woman's experience, represented by lists of objects, threatened by her inability to capture it in language; they saw, through careful close reading for rhetorical strategies in representing memory, that it was only through the later safety of sterilized classroom history that the woman could "understand" what happened.

In close-reading passages like these, students saw a kind of dual representation and interrogation.[4] The woman's memory is of a time when she had no words to understand her experience. The experience, as she can access it, is not foundational because it is only later in school when she realizes what happened—a delayed realization that becomes the foundation for her response to Griffin's interview, and which may be understood as a "system" or "code," in Scott and Lowenthal's terms, through which the experience is constructed legibly. My students began to see the slipperiness of experience because Griffin sprinkles her tapestry with reminders that, though she speaks of and through various historical figures (from Himmler to her grandmother), it is always mediated through her own memory. The aforementioned interview, a form of evidence collection often validated by its claim to direct experience, is called into question when Griffin writes, "I give [the interviewee] the name Laura here," (1993, p.114) suggesting that it is Griffin who controls the representation of "Laura's" memory and that ultimately, it is Griffin's memory to share. In-class close reading practice helps students see how individual memories are constructed retrospectively in different social environments, and that it matters how we represent memory in language, because to do so critically is to interrogate how memories get made and what present needs they serve.

In order to get students close-reading these kinds of rhetorical moves so they could later put them into practice in "personal" writing, I asked them to write an analytical essay first, in which they examined and evaluated the rhetorical strategies Griffin used to "write the past." One student[5] wrote that

> Griffin keeps herself in the story as an 'imaginer' that tries to see how an event transpired. Perhaps this gives her an opportunity to include her own stories of childhood in comparison with Himmler's. For instance, she details Dr. Schreber's [German, WWII-era] advice on childhood parenting: "Crush the will, they write. Establish dominance. Permit no disobedience. Suppress everything in the child." She then compares the childrearing acts with what she had gone through with her grandmother. She too was suppressed: "When at the age of six I went to live with her, my grandmother worked to reshape me ... not by casual example but through anxious memorization and drill."

This student is noticing how Griffin is able to incorporate her personal memories into a larger collective past: by remaining in the story always as an "imaginer" who looks through the same lens of inquiry at historical pasts as she does her own memories.

Another student wrote of rhetorical moves that allow Griffin to evade talking about the past "as though it had actually occurred" and instead allow her to "state them in a way that they were possibilities, using qualifying cues such as 'did…?,' 'must have,' and maybe,' etc." Between seemingly straightforward, traditionally historical statements garnered from interviews, photographs, art, and science, this student noticed that Griffin interjects with her own memory's "I." After definite claims like, "it is 1910. The twenty-second of July," he noticed that Griffin extended into the imaginary, speculating that "his father must have loomed large to him. Did Gebhard lay his hand on Heinrich's shoulder?" (Griffin, 1993, p. 118). "I can see him," Griffin writes of the long deceased Himmler, but it is always, ultimately, herself she sees: through Laura, through her grandmother, through the mélange of fact and fiction that constitute her exploration and generation of the past. The student thought that "the fact that she has produced her own stories" formed a "biased view of Himmler and his childhood" but one that "generates a different perspective on the war and her relationship to it." The student, in other words, was noticing how Griffin's rhetorical strategies for writing the past produced something that other, more traditional strategies could not, despite the accompanying loss of "objectivity." Griffin writes her memories but employs stylistic strategies to perpetually question the certainty of the claims to memory she makes. She situates herself in different perspectives and historical moments, destabilizing herself as a unified, prediscursive self with unmediated access to experience even as she interrogates the larger sociocultural structures that would make the events she remembers (the Holocaust, childhood abuse) possible.

After my students wrote essays analyzing the rhetorical strategies with which Griffin writes her personal past and situates it in a larger cultural/historical context, they were tasked with a project like hers: to write an experimental essay in which they situate and interrogate their own memories in relation to other historical figures and histories. I see this assignment as enacting what Toni Morrison calls the "willed creation" of memory writing (1984). Morrison's use of the term "willed" juxtaposed with "creation" emphasizes how rhetorical choices in representing the past are inventive and painstakingly strategic, rather than a mere record of the past as it was. As Morrison suggests, "there may be play and arbitrariness in the way a memory surfaces but none in the way the composition is organized, especially when I hope to recreate the play and arbitrariness in the way narrative events unfold" (1984, p. 216). The writing of the analytical essay prior to the composition of the more "personal"/experimental essay helps students see that the rhetorical choices we make in writing the past facilitate or inhibit the critical expressivist work we can do.

I will close by describing one student's response to this assignment, for which she was tasked to read her own memories through the art and life of a historical figure, as Griffin did with Himmler and other figures. My student, Dylan Gallagher, was to use the past of a historical figure to raise questions in inquiry into her own past, and to represent this inquiry experimentally: to use unorthodox form and "crimes of writing" to subvert conventional modes of historiography (Ede &Lunsford, 2006). She was to take seriously our discussions of Griffin's stylistic subversions of form and the ways in which Griffin's textual cues undermined historical (and memorial) accuracy in favor of a different project: a complex merging of history and personal writing, a powerful connection between the personal and the political, and a simultaneous interrogation of personal memory and cultural history.

Dylan chose her own unorthodox writer to read her memories against and through: e. e. cummings. Inspired by the visual of Griffin's fragmented, italicized layout, Dylan incorporated images and fragments with her own inventive and imitative twist. She emulated a childhood letter from cummings to his mother that was handwritten with columns, horizontal and vertical writing, and hand-drawn pictures. Dylan replicated cummings' visual layout, typing in columns and interweaving excerpts from his poetry and biography with analysis of her own memories. The strategies of speculation and sentence fragments she learned from Griffin stand out to me: buried in an opening paragraph of seemingly straightforward biography of cummings' early life, she writes "I can picture his mother, Rebecca, looking at one of his letters and laughing at the lopsided drawings of elephants and dinosaurs and planets. At his scattered writing."

But later strategies are of her own invention, inspired by cummings. Using the close reading strategies she learned in her analysis of Griffin, Dylan reads cummings, interweaving interpretations of his poetry with her memories. I quote her at length:

> He did not shy away from writing about death or sex. Death has always been an uncomfortable subject for Many People. Many People refuse to acknowledge death and worms and ceasing to exist. But ee does not. He asks and answers the hard questions through a simple arrangement of words ...
>
> i like my body when it is with your
>
> body. It is so quite new a thing.
>
> muscles better and nerves more.
>
> i like your body. I like what it does,
>
> i like its hows ...
>
> and possibly I like the thrill of
>
> under me you so quite new (cummings 218)

> The first time I had sex I was terrified and uncertain. I was full of questions, about how sex works, how it alters the relationship between two people and also about who I was. But more than that, I was excited. It was thrilling, losing my virginity. Independence is an odd thing to gain from sex. Often, I hear people feel an inappropriately strong attachment to the person with whom they lose their virginity. I experienced no such attachment. As ee describes. An initial attraction to a body, loving perfections and flaws, loving bones and skin, wanting to touch feel, know their body. The physical act of sex. The thrill. And afterwards,
>
> nothing.

From Griffin, she learns to play with visual form (unorthodox layout and fragments), and she learns to amalgamate diverse materials to get at her own memory (she looks to letters, poetry, and biography).

But more importantly, she learns to read cummings' history and work through her own memories, which has an apparent transformative effect. From Dylan's own experience with cummings, a poet who is himself a part of the memories of her upbringing, she learns to play with the combinations of words, capital letters, and punctuation because something about the way he puts words together speaks "her"—but not a unified or static sense of self. The excerpt above implies that at first she was terrified, and then through the experience of reading cummings, she articulates a new memory, one that replaces vulnerable emotion with a detached tactile physicality she finds empowering. Afterwards, when the man's body has left her side, she feels nothing and she fears nothing of the nothingness, unlike "Many People." The past she arrives at is arguably subversive: using cummings' life and work, she arrives at a memory that defies larger sociocultural expectations for what she, as a young woman, should feel. She rejects expectations for sentimentality and attachment through a "crime of reading and writing," subverting conventional sentence structure and spatial layout. I read this as a kind of identity work with a feminist edge. She is putting pressure on the expectations of "Many People" and revising her memory from her initial recollection of "terror," which Many People would expect, to a sense of detachment that might protect her from retrospective and future feelings of fear and dependence.

While Dylan's and my other students' writing was not "perfect" and while there were certainly some students who could or would not break out of conventional modes of personal writing, Dylan's and other students' essays revealed the ways in which writing memory with complexity is something that has the potential to be taught. Students can learn to write with memory to reveal a discursive self in motion, an understanding of a self as always shifting and multiple depending on the memory texts the writer comes into contact with and the present circumstances in which she finds herself. For Griffin, it was through representations of "Laura" and Himmler and so many others; for Dylan, it was through representations of cummings and his work. In the process of examining and imitating cummings' life and work in unorthodox ways, she articulated a transitioned understanding of her own past—against dominant narratives of what a young woman should feel during and after physical intimacy. I want to suggest that Dylan's work be read as a feminist memory, written through feminist means, in a way that does some justice to the complexity of writing with memory.[6] Dylan uses cummings to write herself to an empowering memory of physical intimacy, simultaneously showing us her transformation such that we know this memory is not stable and foundational. It is something to be generated and used for strength in this moment, perhaps to be revised again and again as she continues to find herself in new present circumstances.

When we bring collective memory studies into conversation with feminist composition pedagogy,[7] it becomes clear that memories sit in the intersection between the personal and the social, a location that is always political with real implications for individuals' sense of their relationship to the world. This chapter has contended that memories' location in the intersection between the personal and social is something that can be rhetorically represented and simultaneously interrogated, in such a way that students are called to attention to the role of pasts in their present lives and cultural locations. Unorthodox "crimes of writing" have the potential to help students represent the self that emerges from memory work as one that is as processual and collective as memories themselves and one with the critical potential to challenge the social and discursive frameworks that might be constraining their present senses of self. This chapter is a call to complicate experience, to disrupt traditional, narrative approaches to personal writing, and to help students learn to read and write for a more critically expressivist understanding of the intersections between personal and collective memory and identity.

NOTES

1. Like Adler-Kassner, Wendy Hesford finds in expressivism a point of view that reads "autobiography ... as a doorway to the apprehension of an original experience or an unchanging essence" (1999, p. 65). Instead, she advocates autobiographical acts that attend to the "social signifying practices shaped and enacted within ... ideologically encoded" social and historical forces" (p. 64).

2. Yagelski's is representative of textbooks that do not forefront personal writing as their central pedagogy but nonetheless incorporate assignments that ask students to write with memory, indicating expressivism's subtle but enduring legacy.

3. I want to underscore that feminist pedagogy is only one way to approach the complexity of writing with memory, stemming from my own investments in feminist studies, which have, as the chapter will show, led me to experimental and alternative discourse. Feminist pedagogy and experimental writing may not be, I believe, the only way to address the problem of memory's over-simplification, but they are the methods that inspired the assignment sequence I describe later in this chapter.

4. Students' simultaneous attention to representation and interrogation resonates with Min-Zhan Lu's problematization of experience. Lu argues that uncritical uses of experience, even in the pursuit of feminist goals, can work to subsume differences and essentialize gender as distinct from other cultural- or identity-based vectors of difference. Instead, she advocates a use of personal experience that works on both experiential and analytical levels to disrupt a "false notion of 'oneness' with all women purely on the grounds of gender" (1998, p. 242).

5. I cite three students in this essay. All three were from a recent first-year composition course at the University of Pittsburgh; the first two have allowed me to reference their work but preferred to remain anonymous, while the last, Dylan Gallagher, permitted me to use her full name.

6. Ronald and Ritchie write that a feminist pedagogy "locates theory and practice in the immediate contexts of women's lives," helping students move toward a "resistant, critical stance toward monolithic descriptions of discourse and gender" (1998, p. 219). Writing, through a feminist pedagogy, becomes an act of constant awareness of one's particular location, working "among and between" analytical, experiential, objective, subjective, authoritative and local strategies. I'm contending that Dylan's transformed memory does indeed take a "resistant, critical stance" toward expectations for her age and gender in its very movement "among and between" analytic and experiential, subjective and authoritative strategies: she is analytic and authoritative in her use and reading of cummings and subjective and experiential in her representation of a transitioned memory.

7. Marianne Hirsch and Valerie Smith attest to feminism and memory studies' shared concern with the reception of a version of the past in the context of larger society forces. As Hirsch and Smith put it, "feminist studies and memory studies both presuppose that the present is defined by a past that is constructed and contested. Both fields assume that we do not study the past for its own sake; rather, we do so to meet the ends of the present" (2002, p. 12).

REFERENCES

Adler-Kassner, L. (1998). Ownership revisited: An exploration in progressive era and expressivist composition scholarship. *College Composition and Communication, 49*(2), 208-233.

Allison, D. (1996). *Two or three things I know for sure.* New York: Plume Books.

Bloom, L. Z. (2003). Living to tell the tale: The complicated ethics of creative nonfiction. *College English, 65*(3), 276-289.

Connerton, P. (1989). *How societies remember.* New York: Cambridge University Press.

Ede, L., & Lunsford, A. (2006). Crimes of reading and writing. In K. Ronald, & J. Ritchie (Eds.), *Teaching rhetorica: Theory, pedagogy, practice* (pp. 13-31). Portsmouth, NH: Heinemann/Boynton.

Griffin, S. (1993). *Chorus of stones: The private life of war.* New York: Anchor Books.

Halbwachs, M. (1992). *On collective memory.* Chicago: University of Chicago Press.

Hesford, W. S. (1999). *Framing identities: Autobiography and the politics of pedagogy.* Minneapolis: University of Minnesota Press.

Hirsch, M., & Smith, V. (2002). Feminism and cultural memory: An introduction. *Signs, 28*(1), 1-19.

Klein, K. L. (2000). On the emergence of memory in historical discourse. *Representations, 69,* 127-150.

LeGoff, J., & Nora, P. (Eds.). (1977). *Constructing the past: Essays on historical methodology.* Cambridge, UK: Cambridge University Press.

Lowenthal, D. (1985). *The past is a foreign country.* Cambridge, UK: Cambridge University Press.

Lu, M. (1998). Reading and writing differences: The problematic of experience. In S.C. Jarratt, & L. Worsham (Eds.), *Feminism and composition studies: In other words* (pp. 239-251). New York: Modern Language Association.

Morrison, T. (1984). Memory, creation, and writing. *Thought, 59,* 381-390.

Rohmann, G. D. (1965). Pre-writing: The stage of discovery in the writing process. *College Composition and Communication, 46,* 111.

Ronald, K., & Ritchie, J. (1998). Riding long coattails, subverting tradition: The tricky business of feminists teaching rhetoric(s). In S. Jarratt, & L. Worsham (Eds.), *Feminism and composition studies: In other words* (pp. 217-238). New York: Modern Language Association.

Ronald, K., & Ritchie, J. (2006). *Teaching rhetorica: Theory, pedagogy, practice.* Portsmouth, NH: Boynton/Cook Heinemann.

Scott, J. W. (1991). The evidence of experience. *Critical Inquiry, 17*(4), 773-797.

Yagelski, R. (2010). *Reading our world: Conversations in context.* Independence, KY: Wadsworth Cengage Learning.

Zelizer, B. (1995). Reading the past against the grain: The shape of memory studies. *Critical Studies in Mass Communication, 12,* 214-39.

ESSAI—A METAPHOR: WRITING TO SHOW THINKING

Lea Povozhaev
Kent State University

An "essai" writer responds to the world with a sense of dynamic responsibility. Her task has roots in the European enlightenment and can be understood as a means to critical, personal, and socially relevant writing. My notion of essai (the word means "an attempt" in French) comes from the sixteenth century French essayist Michel De Montaigne who wrote essays to better understand who he was. He wrote in response to ancient philosophers, and he, like them, reflected upon the meaning of one's own life, found in a felt-sense of personal experiences within socially situated realities. His thinking was critical and deep, and it went so far as to inform him on how to live and die. Montaigne valued honest inquiry above word play and verbosity and considered himself a gentleman more than a scholar. For Montaigne, writing was for self-knowledge and understanding of human nature. Consequently, his writing was to actualize improvement in himself and society. In an "essai," one demonstrates self-awareness in the context of socio-cultural situations within which one lives. For example, this article arises naturally from my work as a writer and teacher with the ever-present inquiry: Why write and why teach students to write? From my experiences writing and teaching writing, I find composition is a tool towards understanding social issues in personal ways. I argue that students of composition should be invited to write essais in which they compose first-person life narratives of embodied experiences in the world.

To illustrate my point, allow this small essaistic indulgence. I write true stories of my experiences in a multicultural family, raising three children, and exploring issues of faith. I teach composition at a large state university where I am completing studies for a doctorate in English. As I study writing philosophies and practice pedagogy, the question of why I write merges with questions on the importance of writing for students of various backgrounds studying a range of subjects with different jobs in mind. I consider students' real lives, busy with work and families, as I also teach writing at a community college. Some of my students are adults who have returned to earn their long-awaited college degrees. Particularly adult students alert me to the need (and their ability) to see meaning-making as central to composition. Purpose tends to motivate students to carve out the time and exact the necessary patience from their busy lives and engage in the task of essai writing. I relate with students at this community college ten minutes from my husband's host-family, with whom we have been living since last Christmas. I understand the push-pull of returning to school and fighting to earn a degree with academic objectives and balance family life. I am motivated to write and enter a public conversation when the subject matters in particular ways to my life. For example, researching vaccinations and writing essays on alternative medicine in the face of rising health costs and threats of increasing bodily toxicity. Answers seem further away the deeper one probes and attempts to understand; however, the care deepens and, ultimately, one asserts a stance as knowledge is gathered (both life experiences and facts).

Writing has been a way to locate myself in time and to contextualize others' lives around me by the concrete act of words on a page. Time seems fluid as I live in an old castle on a hill with extended family. My children swim in a pool where once I first met their father. I have composed essays to understand where I am, and why I'm here. By essai writing, my personal life intersects with my academic life and there is liberty to become self-aware, to construct meanings, and to articulate the purposes emerging in a present vision of life. In addition to temporality, writing can be a resource for increasing wellness by lessening isolation and seeking understanding as one's personal realities are made public. Furthermore, individuals writing essais learn to evaluate socially situated meanings, which they may wish to challenge against their own embodied realities. In the process of realizing one's own positions on issues, an essai writer pays critical attention to details of others' arguments. By so doing, an essai writer becomes more conscious of herself as well as others.

For me, an essai writer analyzes aspects of life and constructs meanings for the benefit of self and others. An essai writer engages others with the passion she encounters in writing to understand relationships among aspects of life that might otherwise have seemed unrelated. Accordingly, an essai moves from close-up-and-personal, divulging details of one's own life, to academic and scholarly, whereby one relates to others' ideas and extends them. In addition, one develops notions and continuously connects the personal and the social to render a cohesive and coherent essai. A composer of the essai aims to push past the obvious and delve into the deeply meaningful, and one is ultimately surprised by understandings gained through writing that relates personal experiences to social issues researched.

Essai writing can be pragmatic, particularly for students of composition, because it is a non-foundational approach to writing that enables a critical, searching spirit and invites students to construct personally relevant meanings within the social contexts of their everyday lives. Composing essais can be in line with

Deweyan philosophy as an experimental, hybridizing act that extends students' thoughts and experiences with others. Furthermore, when students develop greater understanding of their own lives, and learn to compose essais that relate this knowledge, their critical thinking and writing skills develop alongside their sense of confidence as intellectuals.

My approach to writing the essai comes from a pedagogical philosophy in line with critical social expressivism. In order to further discuss the benefits in teaching composition with the inclusion of essai writing, I turn now to an account of scholars whose basic pedagogical principles are expressivistic and whose notions lead us to critical social expressivism.

A HISTORY OF RE-FIGURING EXPRESSIVISM

Harkening back to ancient Rome, composition was the capstone of a classical education, "helping students make a smooth transition of the 'play' of the classroom and to the 'business' of real-world civic action" (Fleming, 2003, p. 109). Language informed students' identities and was a source of power. Ancient rhetors argued for social action in civic arguments at court or in the arena where they aimed to persuade the masses. An argument was structured by one's personal style, including word choice, arrangement, and narrative accounts. There was then, as there is now, a dialectic of form and expressiveness. Today, with my proposal for writing essai, one communicates his or her perception of self and relationship of self with the world. An essai is not only a genre but a way of thinking, and a way of demonstrating thoughtfulness by writing.

John Dewey understood that academic work required a balance of one's attention on what was near and what was more distant. His work has been used by figures such as Janet Emig, Stephen Fishman and Lucille McCarthy, Thomas Newkirk, Lad Tobin, and Donald Jones to refigure the social climate of composition studies. Like Dewey, they understood that "to be playful and serious at the same time is possible, and it defines the ideal mental condition. Absence of dogmatism and prejudice, presence of intellectual curiosity and flexibility, are manifest in the free play of mind upon a topic" (Dewey, 1916, p. 224). Dewey explained at the turn of the century how the self and the world were not separate but necessary for one another. He shook loose the rigid boundaries set around personal versus social concerns and suggested pragmatism serve as the loop hole, the means to a negotiated end. According to Deweyan philosophy, what worked in practice took precedence over, even validated, theory. Therefore, Dewey and his followers perceived the social and the personal as cooperative, and "experience, knowledge, and habits of good living" (Dewey, 1916, p. 224) governed educational practices. In this way, nested dualisms, or concepts that appeared mutually exclusive, blended and overlapped into complementary forces. For example, Dewey's educational philosophy was a flexible, constructive endeavor:

> Dewey's educational goals focus on the development of certain habits and dispositions rather than on the acquisition of a fixed body of knowledge or belief. He maintains the world is changing. He calls it "unstable, uncannily unstable" (*Experience and Nature,* Dewey, 1958, p. 38) ... Dewey wants students to develop flexibility or 'intelligence'—the ability to respond to novel situations, access their culture's resources, reshape their plans, and take positive residue from these experiences. Of course this critical and constructive process must be done, if it is to be moral, in cooperation with others. (Fishman & McCarthy, 1996, pp. 346-347)

With a non-foundational approach to education, the context and the individual within the situation were important. In fact, Dewey advocated active learning or a "reconciliation of tensions between the self and its surroundings" (1916, p. 19). In the writing classroom, this meant personal narrative because the personal experience transitioned into a dialogic, social activity as others related and reacted. In the field of composition, proponents of Deweyian philosophy have argued for the effectiveness in using personal narrative writing in the classroom.

Perhaps the most influential proponents of Dewey's theories written in the field of composition were Fishman and McCarthy. They revisited criticisms of expressivism that proclaimed the movement "dead." Fishman defended expressivism against the notion of the isolated writer. He supported Peter Elbow's use of expressivist pedagogy as a means to better understanding one's self and, ultimately, society. Considering expressivism as rooted in German romanticism, Fishman explained that personal experience was not used for isolation but to identify with one another and restructure community. Elbow and the German romanticist Johann Gottfried Herder suggested writing was a social connection. In eighteenth century German romanticism, people sought unity through diversity. The people didn't trust one another and constructed a social contract to ensure protection: the trade of liberty for protection. The contract united the personal and social—Elbow and Herder suggested we write to understand our own thoughts and to communicate with society, continually reshaping and reforming our social worlds (Fishman, McCarthy, 1998, p. 648).

Neo-expressivists or pragmatists such as Thomas Newkirk, Lad Tobin, Karen Paley, and Michelle Payne examined writing and writing pedagogy from a non-foundationalist perspective. They advocated use of the personal narrative for pragmatic reasons, but their focus remained predominantly social. Personal narratives were a pragmatic way to develop writers. Newkirk discussed students' autobiographies, or essays, as narratives of development. Erving Goffman's notion of "presentation of self" supported Newkirk's belief that students strived to formulate their ideas, experiences, and understandings into acceptable form through their writing. As Goffman suggested, "in all public performances … we selectively reveal ourselves in order to match an idealized sense of who we should be" (Tobin, 1993, p. 4). Writing personal narratives was viable, explained Newkirk, because students saw themselves as learners, revised beliefs, learned narrative conventions of literature, celebrated self-discovery, and developed critical thinking skills (quoted in Payne, 200, p. xxi).

Newkirk supported the narrative of development, derived from Montaigne, that was challenging and exploratory, open to inconsistencies that demonstrated critical analysis of the self and world. Personal student writing was criticized for cornering the teacher into the role of counselor, but Newkirk pointed out that students who confess their intimate realities want to share, and through the act of writing they become consoled. Students want to have their experiences treated as normal, and their texts allow them this right. Personal narratives were criticized for their emotionality, but Newkirk affirmed the importance of emotion in real life. While there is a place for emotion in personal narrative, he also addressed the need for reason and ethos. The most persuasive writing stems from personal, emotional concerns that are examined reasonably and presented credibly.

Tobin argued that emotion and relationships were essential in the writing classroom. The most effective pedagogical approach depended upon the students' and their teacher's interactions. A writing teacher is not a counselor, but feelings needn't be omitted from writing because of the fear of role confusion:

> By attempting to edit feelings, unconscious associations, and personal problems out of a writing course, we are fooling ourselves and shortchanging our students. The teaching of writing is about solving problems, personal and public, and I don't think we can have it both ways: we cannot create intensity and deny tension, celebrate the personal and deny the significance of the personalities involved. In my writing courses, I want to meddle with my students' emotional life and I want their writing to meddle with mine. (Tobin, 1993, p. 33)

Tobin addressed the expressivist shift of teacher authority, correcting the faulty assumption that teachers got out of the way so students could just write.

Rather, he argues that teachers were still the center of decentered classrooms and the stakes were even higher with personal narrative and conferencing, which gave the teacher more authority. Tobin suggested the real key for student-teacher success was to develop good relationships.

Like Tobin, Karen Paley worked with elements of expressivism and constructed a philosophy which proved useful for her. Paley called herself a social-expressivist and argued that expressivism included, but was not limited to, narratives in which a writer focused on personal experiences. A writer used first-person and could isolate his or her individual consciousness; however, a writer could use first-person and write about social issues without mention of the individual writer's thoughts and feelings, experiences and understandings. Paley's re-assessment of expressivism justified criticisms of the movement's strictly personal focus. She called her notion of the personal essay "psychosocial" and argued that it could communicate social significance—not that it must or should, but that it could (2001). Paley's pragmatic distinction opened the personal narrative genre to the social, while not forcing the social into it indefinitely. To her, personal narratives often represented gender, class, family, and ethnic group matters. Accordingly, personal issues were social, and social issues were personal.

Picking up on the potential of personal narratives, Michelle Payne examined personal narratives that explored physical pain, and surmised that we "stop seeing emotion, pain, and trauma as threatening, anti-intellectual, and solipsistic, and instead begin to ask how we might, like therapists, feminist theorists, and philosophers, begin to recognize them as ways of knowing" (2000, p. 30). The body, she argued with reference to Foucault, was not only a representation of the personal but a composite of the social. The body was "not our own anymore. Or, at least within the academic discussions of the body. It is more text than substance, more a product of language than a corporeal presence" (Payne, 2000, p. xxi). We did not need to fear personal writing, but, rather (as Foucault argues), we should consider the implications of deviant identity, emotion, power, and discipline suggested by writing about the physical body.

THE ESSAI AND CRITICAL SOCIAL EXPRESSIVISM

I propose teaching writing with the essai, following the above conversation on the development of critical, social expressivism. My conceptualization of the essai extends the various discussions above by drawing together aspects of these effective, pragmatic arguments on using personal writing in the academy. For example, my notion of the essai incorporates Newkirk's narrative of development within which one explores and analyzes one's self and the world (Tobin, 1993, p. 4). Writing an essai, one works from a similar pedagogical impulse as proposed by Newkirk and Tobin who argue that emotion, reason, and ethos inform writing (Tobin, 1993, p. 33). Furthermore, Tobin argues that teaching writing effectively depends upon teacher-student relationships (Tobin, 1993, p. 34). Teaching the essai can foster positive, responsive relationships by the teacher's invitation (by assignment) for students to compose on personally significant and socially relevant topics. Additionally, essai writing can be therapeutic as one realizes that one's personal life relates with others and is, therefore, socially significant. While Paley notes that the personal essay can communicate social significance (2001), so can the essai, even if the tone is highly personal and even intimate. Essai writing can demonstrate an awareness of the body as it moves and thinks within the social situations of life. Furthermore, the act of composing an essai necessitates awareness of the reader. A writer of the essai pays critical attention to how she writes so that another can understand what is personally important to the writer; therefore, it is even more essential for an essai writer to achieve clarity because the message is valuable on both a personal and social level. Additionally, an essai writer evaluates the messages she arrives at from the process of writing and, ultimately, must determine if it is pre-essai writing or personally relevant and socially significant and therefore worth submitting to another.

Within a critical social expressivist pedagogy, using the essai to teach writing in freshman composition is ideal. Essais might bridge the gap between play and rigor in a freshman composition course where students are expected to assimilate within a new academic culture. Using students' own lives as material for inquiry teaches them early on in their academic careers to self-reflect and apply critical thinking to their real lives. However, despite the effectiveness of the essai in drawing together the personal and the social and inviting students to critical reflection, three false assumptions relegate personal narratives to creative writing classrooms: serious writing is void of playfulness; emotion hasn't a place in academic discourse; and private is irrelevant in public institutional settings. However, writing with a spirit of playfulness can motivate the writer. And a challenging intellectual task is to write one's emotions in a controlled and exacting manner. Furthermore, emotion, whether cloaked or exposed, is always a part of communication, as it informs one's positions and leads one to reason in particular ways. When one develops an ethos and reasons alongside emotional claims, one develops an essai.

Though school essays have diverged from essai's original attempt to think critically and construct meanings with personal relevance, scholars such as Graham Badley harken back to Montaigne by his reflective essaying model for higher education. For Badley, as with Montaigne, essai writing is a process where students try out opinions and test responses, reflect on ideas, and develop valuable relationships with others. Badley's reflective essaying model is "the free and serious play of mind on an interesting topic in an attempt to learn" (2009, p. 248). He bases this definition on four assumptions: that there is academic freedom, that the university is a safe place to be serious and playful, that reflection is useful for students and teachers who respond to questions, and that the process of composing an essay is an attempt to learn (Badley, 2009, p. 249). In Badley's model, learning occurs as writers interpret experiences and reconsider previous interpretations. The writer's objective is to convince an audience that his or her reflections are plausible and to convince another that his or her ideas are useful and even valuable (Badley, 2009, p. 251). The reader and writer together determine what constitutes use and value. Badley's model illustrates that essai writing is social and personal because meaning is made by the construction of relationships whereby the student initiates learning and acts upon necessary impulses and needs. Moreover, by clearly seeing the relationship between the personal and the social, students learn to invest in social concerns and mature past solipsistic and immature thinking "only of me." Importantly, the personal and the social are in relationship.

James Zebroski presents Mikhail Bakhtin's argument that many voices inform one's thoughts and this "accentuates the plurality of a text and the push-pull, center-seeking, center-fleeing forces of the word" (1989, p. 35). Because meanings in an essai can be constructed within relationships between readers and writers, my argument lies beyond the debate of personal versus social impetuses for writing. Instead, composing the essai implicates the individual writer with the writer's audience and, thus, "the author gives [ideas] to the world, neither as a work wholly original, nor as a compilation from the writings of others. On every subject contained in them, he has thought for himself" (Blair, *Lectures on Rhetoric and Belles Lettres,* quoted in Ferguson, Carr, and Schultz, 2005, p. 20). Consequently, essai writing can be personal, social, and cognitive.

Some may still argue that my interpretation of the essai's personal, I-voiced, anecdotal narrativist nature belongs with creative writing. But academic and creative writing have the similar objective of clear, concise, and, ultimately, persuasive writing. By composing an essai, students might learn to reason, present emotion, and demonstrate a trustworthy ethos. Of course, a writer learns to write appropriately for a given audience, and a coffee house reading is not the same as a graduate seminar for which one presents an essay. However, there is more benefit in teaching composition students to write essais than funneling them into an academic vacuum within which the five-paragraph essay becomes a formula for thoughtless composition.

At first glance, academic writing may often have different expectations from creative writing. However, as Carini demonstrates through work with children creating art, prisoners writing poems, and student writing, creative acts can be pleasurable, therapeutic, and educational (1994). It is not my intention to define the many genres and objectives for writing. Instead, writing as "verbal habits and dispositions oriented to public effectiveness and virtue" (Fleming, 2003, p. 110) is not a form but a way of perceiving and responding with words. Writing to more carefully consider and reconsider things, including one's own experiences, is academic and real-to-life.

An essai is like creative writing and school essay writing, but can be more than both because it is a way of illustrating one's thoughts by details and scenes, as well as research and representation of others' ideas. Importantly, the writer's response to his or her own life and the writer's response to scholarship is what can set the essai apart from other forms of writing and makes it a form that shows one's thinking. Janet Emig observes: "all student writing emanates from an expressive impulse and that they then bifurcate into two major modes," which she calls "extensive" (interactive, writer and situation) and "reflexive" (contemplative, personal meaning-making) (1967, p. 130). An essai can blend these dichotomies through the vein of writing to show thinking of one's own life as well as of others' lives and social issues pertinent to the writer's time and place. The in-between place of the essai serves as a spine and holds together the extending frame that explores and expresses meaning.

Gregory Light distinguishes between creative writing and essay writing and differentiates between surface understanding where students reproduce conceptions and deeper grasping where students transform conceptions. Light argues that when the essay is essentially about another's argument, and not the student's own, the writing can be unreflective and mechanical (2002, p. 258). The goal of an essai is to move past filler words and borrowed thoughts and to demonstrate understanding in specific, personally relevant ways.

Students often find the jump between high school and college writing intimidating. They seem to understand that more is expected of them, and that "better" writing is supposed to result. However, the expectation in much of college writing seems to be a confident rhetorical sense of self. And yet, one's voice is always changing and being found. Diane Glancy argues that one writes as one is written by "circumstance and environment" to make use of one's self as a "found object" (quoted. in Adrienne Rich, 1993, p. 206). In order to make use of one's self as a found object, one must inquire and rethink the familiar. One learns to examine things near and far, and to believe that in the process of seeking to understand relationships among aspects of life, meanings will emerge.

*

An essai is an attempt to understand and should be used as such. I view it as essentially a process and not a finished product. Carini argues that students are composing a sense of themselves, and, therefore, professionals who use writing in such a way could treat these attempts as "thinking spaces" in which students think through "images, ideas, form and media" (1994, p. 53).

However, after the rigors of drafts, conferences, and peer work, instructors often expect students' essays to be polished. I submit that teachers might shift their focus instead on how well students express what has happened to them personally, information and ideas related to larger societal concerns, and meanings derived from reflecting upon that relationship between one's experience and socially relevant issues. Teachers might evaluate work based on how well students have demonstrated the degree their subject holds personal relevance.

Students entering academe contribute to discourse communities by writing their own cultures into existing frames. Through the more experimental, intuitive processes that go along with the essai, we might convey that intellectual rigor is worthwhile because it transcends the classroom. Using the essai can allow students to connect personally to socially relevant issues, respond with confidence, and speak to society in important ways—beginning with the college writing classroom and reaching past it.

REFERENCES

Badley, G. (2009). A reflective essaying model for higher education. *Education + Training, 51*(4), 248-58.

Carini, P. (1994). Dear sister bess: An essay on standards, judgment and writing. *Assessing Writing, 1*(1), 29-65.

De Montaigne, M. (1580/1958). *Essays.* (J. M. Cohen, Trans.). Harmondsworth, UK: Penguin Books.

Dewey, J. (1916). *Democracy and education.* New York: Macmillan.

Emig, J. (1967). On teaching composition: Some hypotheses as definitions. *Research in the Teaching of English, 1,* 127-135.

Ferguson, S., Carr, L., & Schultz, L. (2005) Archives of instruction: Nineteenth-century rhetorics, readers and composition books in the United States. Carbondale, IL: Southern Illinois University Press.

Fish, S. (1980). *Is there a text in this class?* Cambridge: Harvard University Press.

Fishman, S., & McCarthy, L. (1998). *John Dewey and the challenge of classroom practice.* Urbana, IL: NCTE.

Fishman, S., & McCarthy, L. (1996). Teaching for student change: A Deweyan alternative to radical pedagogy. *College Composition and Communication, 47,* 342-364.

Fleming, D. (2003). The very idea of progymnasmata. *Rhetoric Review, 22,* 105-118.

Light, G. (2002). From the personal to the public: Conceptions of creative writing in higher education. *Higher Education, 43,* 257-276.

Nystrand, M. (1989). A social-interactive model of writing. *Written Communication, 6*(1), 66-85.

Paley, K. S. (2001). *I-writing: The politics and practice of teaching first-person writing.* Carbondale, IL: Southern Illinois University Press.

Payne, M. (2000). *Bodily discourses: When students write about abuse and eating disorders.* Portsmouth, NH: Heinemann.

Rich, Ad. (1993). *What is found there, notebooks on poetry and politics.* New York: W.W. Norton.

Tobin, L. (1993). *Writing relationships: What really happens in the composition class.* Portsmouth, NH: Heinemann.

Zebroski, J. (1989). A hero in the classroom. In B. Lawson, S. Ryan, & R. Winterowd (Eds.), *Encountering student texts: Interpretive issues in reading student writing* (pp. 35-48). Urbana, IL: NCTE.

SECTION TWO:
PERSONAL WRITING
AND SOCIAL CHANGE

COMMUNICATION AS SOCIAL ACTION: CRITICAL EXPRESSIVIST PEDAGOGIES IN THE WRITING CLASSROOM

Patricia Webb Boyd
Arizona State University

In his highly influential essay "Rhetoric and Ideology in the Writing Class," James Berlin positions expressionistic rhetoric as a "romantic recoil from the urban horrors created by nineteenth-century capitalism" (2009, p. 674). In the early twenty-first century, we face a new set of horrors based in a sense of imminent threats from both domestic and global forces along with strident concerns about the influence that our government is having on individual lives. In this time, many feel unable to control their own lives much less effect change in larger society. Academics have responded to the problems of modernity by constructing theories that emphasize the importance of language in constructing reality and the need to critically analyze our social and material conditions. As compositionists have taken up these postmodern goals, they have, as Diane Freedman points out, eschewed expressivism, positioning it as a supposedly "naïve acceptance of the notion of a rational, coherent and unified 'self,' a notion critiqued by postmodernists and thought to inhere in all personal writing" (2001, p. 206). Instead of focusing on the importance of the self as a counter to problematic social conditions, postmodernists argue that the expressivist individual actually "conspire[s] in the replication of a capitalist/consumerist hegemony responsible for various forms of political, social, and economic oppression" (O'Donnell, 1996, p. 423).

How can we imagine creative alternatives where students and teachers can, as Paul Markham suggests, see themselves as active participants in public spheres/discourses who can co-create change rather than be passive consumers waiting for others to "fix things"? Giving importance to individual experiences and beliefs is an important step in this process. Critical expressivism highlights that the individual is not a fixed or unchanging entity, acknowledging the role that culture plays in individuals' identity and identifications. As Sherrie Gradin argues, social expressivism (her version of critical expressivism) "suggests that all subjects negotiate within the system; they act and are acted upon by their environments.

In order to be effective citizens and effective rhetorical beings, student must first learn how to carry out the negotiation between self and world" (1995, p. xv). In order to carry out these connections between the individual and the world, though, "a first step in this negotiation must be to develop a clear sense of one's own beliefs as well as a clear sense of how one's own value system intersects or not with others, and how finally to communicate effectively" (Gradin, 1995, p. xv). So, students need to begin with their own experiences in order to be active participants in the larger society.

Critical expressivism suggests that it is through individual experiences that commitments are made, stances are taken, responsibility is assumed and actions are advanced—not through an ephemeral, relative subject position that can easily be seen as objectified by social structures. The more ephemeral and fragmented we see ourselves, the less ability we feel we to have to transform things. Further, the more fragmented we feel, the less connection we sense to communities around us. Feeling connected to communities is an important aspect of transforming the issues that face us today. Feeling disconnected from the self translates into particular views on the power (or lack thereof) of one's ability to act as well. Too often, people feel disempowered to change any of the problems they see in the world, thinking that the problems are too large and must be changed by someone else.

These feelings are also translated into beliefs about communication. Too often students see discussions and writing as empty exercises that have no ability to change social situations. Critical expressivist practices can help us challenge these views of communication. Instead of seeing communication as empty exercises or as tools to only analyze social texts rather than change society, students can learn to see writing—and social discussions—as social action—i.e., a way of being an agent in public discourses. When students realize their words matter and can have impact on social action (and can even be social action), then they become more aware of how important it is to take responsibility for their words and the work those words do in their communities and the lives of people.

Critical expressivists' emphasis on individual experiences illustrates the importance that those experiences play in one's interactions in the world—including the political and social problems that face us domestically and globally. Instead of seeing the individual as an isolated, monolithic entity whose sole intent is to search for inner truth, critical expressivists demonstrate that the individual is situated within larger social experiences. Eschewing the importance of individual experiences as postmodernism does fails to acknowledge the important work that a fairly stable concept of the individual plays in the beliefs we have; our lived realities of who we are and how we engage with others; and the actions we take and their impact on others. Even as they recognize the durable quality of the individual, critical expressivists are aware (and work to teach students to be aware of as well) that these beliefs and actions are socially situated and constructed over time. Learning how we learned and developed those beliefs and how they have solidified over time is an important step in building public voices that help us become active agents in public arenas, both of which are important practices in critical expressivist classrooms. We need to see both the "stable" self that is somewhat durable across time and recognize how it is constructed to be durable and the consequences of that durability.

In this chapter, I analyze how critical expressivist pedagogies can help students learn to incorporate individual experiences into education in order to create public voices that provide them with agency in public arenas. Critical expressivism focuses on "conditions of language use," not "studying private truths" (O'Donnell, 1996, p. 437). By doing so, critical expressivism can help students learn to situate their own experiences and personal narratives within larger social arenas and take responsibility. Students can become more responsive to their audiences and more responsible for their words so that they can see the ways communication is more than just an empty exercise. Students can "become invested as writers when they realize that being articulate when something is at stake ... is what launches individuals into public life" (Danielewicz, 2008, p. 444). Communication can be social action.

THE IMPORTANCE OF PERSONAL EXPERIENCE AND PERSONAL GENRES

Postmodern critics argue that expressivists define the individual much like the modernist individual: eternal, universal, rational, coherent, unique, and authentic (Judd, 2003, p. 489, Freedman, 2001, p. 206). Berlin argues that for expressivists, reality resides "within the individual subject. While the reality of the material, the social, and the linguistic are never denied, they are considered significant only insofar as they serve the needs of the individual" (Berlin, 2009, p. 674). In Berlin's estimation of expressivism, the external world serves as material for the individual to "understand the self" (2009, p. 674) and "awaken in readers the experience of their selves" (2009, p. 675). He argues that expressivism denies "'the place of intersubjective, social processes in shaping reality. Instead, it always describes groups as sources of distortion of the individual's true vision, and the behavior it recommends in the political and social realms is atomistic, the individual acting alone' (2009, p. 146)" (quoted in Paley, 2001, p. 190). Other critics insist that expressivist rhetoric and pedagogy focus "upon personal growth while ignoring the social setting of the specialized skills and bodies of knowledge," thus emphasizing "a naïve view of the writer ... as possessing innate abilities to discover truth" (Fishman & McCarthy, 1992, p. 648).

This definition of the individual leads to problematic views of the solutions to the world's problems. Berlin argues that for expressivists, the solutions to the problems of a commodified culture are supposedly found through re-experiencing the self. For expressivists, the only hope in a society working to destroy the uniqueness of the individual is for each of us to assert our individuality against the tyranny of the authoritarian corporation, state, and society. Strategies for doing so must of course be left to the individual, each lighting one small candle in order to create a brighter world (Berlin, 2009, p. 676-677).

Donald Judd shares Berlin's critique of expressivist solutions to the current social problems, describing a class project on homelessness that had only minimal success. Although students were awakened to new ways of thinking about homelessness through discussing their personal beliefs on homelessness, Judd claims expressivist practices left students "ignorant of larger social forces which play fundamental roles in the eviction of the homeless" (Judd, 2003, p. 77). Judd argues that because it focuses only on individual's reflections on social issues, expressivist teaching "offers little guidance on how to think more critically about homelessness and many other important social issues" (2003, p. 76). Judd insists that focusing on individual responses to problems—a practice he attributes to expressivism—leaves students floundering to find solutions.

Interestingly enough, although Judd agrees with Berlin on some accounts, he argues that Berlin offers an overly simplified definition of the individual used by expressivism. Countering Berlin's argument that expressivists see the "self as 'universal, eternal, authentic … that beneath all appearances is at one with all other selves'" (Judd, 2003, p. 489), Judd shows how, in actuality, for expressivists "the self goes through changes in its interactions with other selves and with the world. The self is neither universal, eternal, nor autonomous" (Judd, 2003, p. 63); instead expressivists argue that the self is shaped by other people and institutions (2003, p. 71). And he is not alone. Many critics have illustrated that branches of expressivism like critical expressivism draw on an individual that is not "monolithic, centered or rational" (Gradin, 1995, p. xv). In fact Sherrie Gradin argues that the expressivist individual is one who "confronts one's own beliefs and examines her interaction with culture [and] is particularly plural and decentered because the self is constructed differently in various times and in multiple classes and cultures" (1995, p. xv). Critical expressivists highlight the way the individual builds connections with communities in which the individual is situated, valuing both individual experiences and social relationships.

This process of building relationships can be facilitated by genres that have been traditionally labeled "personal" and have been critiqued by postmodernism. These genres can help students become more engaged in the classroom and their worlds because they encourage students to start with their own experiences, and then negotiate between them and different worlds. Freedman writes of "the capacity of personal classroom writing ... to negotiate the divide college students often feel between school and work or school and home, their writing and their caring, their knowing and their being" (2001, p. 199). When students begin with their own experiences, they can feel empowered in institutional settings that can often be alienating, and they can find a public voice that gives them agency. Students begin to see the ways that various institutions and various identities/identifications have shaped their actions (and inactions) and have caused them to feel powerful or powerless in particular situations. Writing about these instances can help students understand the causes behind their actions (or inactions), help them feel passionate about these life experiences, connect them to others through these analyses, and lead them to take different kinds of actions out of those new realizations.

As Freedman insists, "students are unavoidably bringing their personal lives into their academic work, the classroom space, and their conversations with teachers and peers" (2001, p. 200). Drawing on those experiences in both the kind of discussions they have and the kind of writing they do are useful ways for students to learn what is at stake in their communications. Starting with personal experiences and locating them in larger social contexts is a center stone of critical expressivism practices that help students learn they are "supposed to have something at stake" in their learning. As Danielewicz argues, there are two key results of personal writing genres: "students learn that they are supposed to have something at stake in writing an argument, academic or otherwise" (2008, p. 421) and "students who do write when something is at stake are participating in public discourse; they expect something to happen as a result of writing" (2008, p. 421). Both of these benefits highlight why the genres typically denigrated as "personal" hold much value for students and our classrooms.

The next section discusses two examples that illustrate the way critical expressivist pedagogies in the classroom can help students be responsive to audiences and take responsibility for their words and actions. They show the ways that discussions and writing in personal genres can help students start with personal experiences in order to create authoritative public voices that make them active participants in public arenas.

EXAMPLES OF CRITICAL EXPRESSIVISM AT WORK

EXAMPLE 1: CURRICULUM AS CONVERSATION AND DISCUSSION

Class discussions and conversations are one crucial way that students can learn to be responsible language users. Instead of seeing them as "just" discussions, critical expressivist pedagogies can turn class discussions into moments where students take responsibility for their words in a community and learn to place their own experiences within larger social contexts. Once students see how their ideas have been shaped, they realize that their ideas are not "givens" but have been produced and can, thus, be changed and transformed. Classroom discussions and the curriculum the teacher establishes can be a starting point for this kind of change.

The narratives students bring to the classroom should be an important part of the class curriculum. In "What Is Public Narrative," Marshall Ganz argues that we make sense of the world through three types of stories: story of self, story of us, and story of now. The story of self "communicates who I am—my values, my experiences, why I do what I do;" the story of us "communicates who we are—our shared values, our shared experience, and why we do what we do;" and the story of now "transforms the present into a moment of challenge, hope, and choice" (Ganz, 2008, p. 1). All three steps are important in critical expressivist classrooms because the story of us cannot be built without a thorough knowledge of the story of self and the story of now, which leads to civic agency and action, requires both of the other two stories.

Making these stories a central part of the class situates the curriculum as a conversation rather than a merely a presentation of information (Shields & Mohan, 2008, p. 296). Carolyn Shields and Erica Mohan advocate for curriculum as conversation that focuses on "teaching students to ask about other perspectives, and to question, reflect, critique, and challenge" (2008, p. 296). This approach requires that instructors honor "each student's unique experiences in the sense-making conversations of the classroom" (Shields & Mohan, 2008, p. 296) in order to "ensure that a greater range of student experiences is considered valid and valuable as a basis for learning" (2008, p. 296). Thus, classroom conversations should honor students' experiences and situate them in larger social contexts as a way of making sense of what is happening in the world, just as Ganz's three types of stories encourage students to do. Creating the curriculum as a conversation means the students' stories and sense-making are the basis of the class, but these experiences are situated within a questioning of, reflecting on, and challenging of other perspectives—connecting the story of self and story of us, ultimately moving toward a story of now that can be filled with hope and choice.

Thomas O'Donnell's article "Politics and Ordinary Language: A Defense of Expressivist Rhetorics" (1996) provides a good example of how class discussion can use the story of self, story of us, and story of now to create curriculum as conversation that helps raise students' awareness of the way their views are situated within larger social contexts. He describes a class discussion on whether health insurance should pay for alcoholics' rehabilitation treatment—a discussion that, interestingly enough, quickly turned into a debate about what "free will" meant. The discussion pivoted around the question of whether alcoholism was a disease or a choice. If students saw alcoholism as a disease, then they thought that alcoholics should be given treatment, just like any other sick person. If, however, students thought that alcoholism was a "free will" choice that one made, then they did not think that health insurance should pay for that choice. Instead of an abstract discussion of public policy, the class discussion quickly turned to a story of self in which they discussed what "free will" meant to them and where they learned that term; then because they were discussing their perceptions within the classroom, they had to take responsibility for their word use and be responsive to their audience. Through deep engagement with their peers in the classroom discussions which were situated in curriculum as conversation (not curriculum as information transmission), they were participating in the story of us. They began to learn the culture's shared values and shared narratives about "free will." The story of now came into play when students realized those larger cultural narratives of "free will" (in which they played a part) had an impact on the actions taken by public policy makers and health care agencies as well as on those whose lives were directly affected by those decisions. They realized that narratives of "free will" and other such concepts directly shaped people's lives and were not abstract terms that meant little beyond personal opinion. These concepts were based in public narratives that could create despair or could be challenged and questioned to create hope and choice.

O'Donnell's class demonstrates that critical expressivist teaching does offer students help in sorting through public issues, thus challenging critiques like Judd's who argues that students in expressivist classrooms are offered "little guidance on how to think critically" (Judd, 2003, p. 76). Discussions like the one on health care that centered on multiple socially-constructed definitions of "free will" illustrate that "it makes little sense to see the expressivist move to the personal as emerging from an inordinate confidence in the capacity of individuals to apprehend untainted truth" (O'Donnell, 1996, p. 432). The point of the class discussion was not to find the one "true" meaning of "free will" and therefore the "right" policy; instead, the point of the discussion was to explore the impacts of language use and the importance of being responsible for one's language use. In O'Donnell's class, the group helped individuals sort out their assumptions about "free will" and consider the impact on public policy. The conversational nature of the curriculum focused on students' stories of how they learned the terms and shifted those conversations to considering how the community used the various narratives to construct policies and who was served (and not served) by those policies. Knowing what stories they are a part of will help students realize the impact of the public narratives. Realizing this, according to Paul Markham in "You Don't Know Where You're Going until You're on the Way There: Why Public 'Work' Matters," can help them create public narratives—"a discursive process through which individuals, communities, and nations construct their identity, make choices, and inspire actions" (2011, p. 6). Critical expressivist pedagogies that center on the importance of drawing on multiple narratives in class and establishing the curriculum as a conversation can help students take responsibility for their words and to see their communications as actions that have impact—that matter.

O'Donnell's class illustrates that expressivist principles can help students enter into public discourse in a way that makes them engaged and active citizens rather than passive dupes of institutional structures, as Berlin and others want to position them. How students use language and to what effect becomes the main focus in critical expressivist classrooms, not the solipsistic analysis of the self, as critics of expressivism claim. Students in critical expressivist work need to connect to their audiences and to be responsive to and responsible to their audiences for their words to have impact and to create a powerful public voice. Students focus on the communities they are located within, they begin to contextualize their views within difference, and they work to build intercontextual connections to be responsive to and responsible to their communities and audiences.

Example 2: Writing Personal Genres/Creating Public Agency

Critical expressivist pedagogies shape class discussions in ways that teach students about taking responsibility for their language use and studying the impact that use has on the communities in which they are located. Critical expressivist pedagogies can also teach students to achieve similar goals through writing—to help them become "invested as writers" (Danielewicz, 2008, p. 443) and create public voices in their writing. In her article "Personal Genres, Public Voices," Jane Danielewicz advocates for teaching personal genres that have too often been short-sightedly critiqued as "solipsistic indulgent exercise[s]" (2008, p. 439) and "private, confessional discourse[s], personal catharsis" (2008, p. 440). In an analysis of her seminar course called "Reading and Writing Women's Lives," Danielewicz illustrates how students can draw on personal genres to create public voices. In the process of writing personal genres like autobiographies, students can learn the process of being responsive to their audience and being responsible for their words. They can learn to write multiple versions of their stories and multiple tellings of the "I," thus seeing that there is not one true inner "I" revealed through writing, that interactions with their audiences powerfully shape their tellings, and that personal stories are powerful material for creating public agency.

Danielewicz asserts that writing in personal genres does not mean that the self written about is solipsistic, or that the topics written about are only personal. In her class, the first drafts of the personal genres focused on religion, family drama, sexual orientation, cherished hobbies and were written in very writerly-based prose, presenting one version of the "I" and one particular retelling of the experience. While these were "personal" stories, they were also common experiences, ones that contained "issues that concern us all"—"surface[ing] organically," even though public issues were not assigned, and even in their first drafts (2008, p. 443).

As Danielewicz points out "when students write their own autobiographies, a two-way process is at work: first, they identify and articulate their distinctive positions, and second, in writing for a public audience, they come to terms with how to represent themselves and then must contend with how audiences respond" (2008, p. 436). Students begin writing to express their experiences, but through discussing their work in small peer groups and learning about genre conventions, their goals for their work shift to connecting with the audience, wanting the audience to understand the individual's experiences. In order to do so, they have to be responsive to how the audience reacts to the telling of the story and the "I" that is constructed through that telling. The small groups, then, help students locate the individual in larger social contexts and lead to changed motivations for writing. Danielewicz disagrees with critics like Berlin who "reduces the dialectic in expressionist editorial groups to one function: 'to enable the writer to understand the manifestation of her identity in language through considering the reaction of others—not, for example, to begin to understand how meaning is shaped by discourse communities'" (Paley, 2001, p. 191); instead, she found in her class that critical expressivist peer response groups have a significant impact on an individual's understanding of how their identities—their "I's" are individually situated and socially constructed. These kinds of groups help students understand how their representations of themselves impact their audiences and shape their possibilities for agency and effective public voice.

Jackie, one of the women Danielewicz studies in her article, is a good example of how writers can use personal genres to create a public voice that gives them agency and authority in public spheres. More importantly, perhaps, Jackie is a great example of how writing personal genres can help students learn "more effectively than any book they might read the truth of the hard, theoretical claim that identity is constructed by institutions, groups, and other social forces" (Danielewicz, 2008, p. 443). Jackie's first draft of her autobiography expressed strong resentment and anger toward God and toward her family whom she felt pushed religion on her when she was growing up. Through extensive small group peer responses, though, Jackie realized that the way she represented the "I" in her first draft alienated her audience. It was through the small group work and through studying the genre of autobiography that Jackie came to see that in order to connect to her audience, she had to rewrite the outpouring of emotion included in her first draft since her representation of that emotion that was off-putting to her audience. She had to step back—in her thinking and writing—to analyze the original situations she included and rewrite them so that her audiences understood "the origins of 'the outpouring of shocking and offensive rhetoric' or her life as 'a trained monkey,' descriptions that were included in her early draft" (Danielewicz, 2008, p. 430) of her autobiography. In order for her work to be relatable to a larger audience, she needed to understand how her audience responded to her language use and the impact it had on her ability to achieve her goals in her autobiography She had to learn to construct an "I" that was situated in a larger social context. She positioned herself as one writing with "authority, knowledge, convictions, and self-consciousness about issues that concern us all" (Danielewicz, 2008, p. 443) rather than presenting an "I" giving an angry diatribe. As she made these revisions, she clearly felt she had much at stake in writing. "Her portfolio letter states the case with conviction: 'I adore this piece and I hope that the readers I hope that the readers can connect to it as much as I do'" (Danielewicz, 2008, p. 434). Instead of seeing her autobiography as a personal expression of feelings or as an empty exercise, Jackie hoped her writing made a difference to a public audience. She felt her writing made a difference—at least she hoped it did, that it somehow changed her audience. This is a powerful outcome from a class assignment. As Danielewicz asks: "How often do our first-year writers 'adore' an essay? That achievement alone—recognizing and valuing a powerful piece of work—is significant. But I'm most impressed with that Jackie's criteria for success include a consideration of whether or not 'the readers can connect to it'" (2008, p. 434). She truly wanted to make her assertions of "I" relatable to the collective—to make her "I" a "we."

It is clear, then, that Jackie wrote her way into an authoritative, agentive voice that responsibly connected to an audience to help her position her stories within a larger social context, not to better understand her "inner" self but to understand how the self is socially constructed by engagement with others and how one's representation of self is never unmediated or "pure." Her revisions show that voice is not an internal truth but is instead socially constructed, based on responses from and responsibility to audiences. Personal genres as used in critical expressivist pedagogies help students learn more about public issues. Genres like autobiographies can help them understand relationships between self/other/institutions/world (Freedman, 2001, p. 199; Danielewicz, 2008, p. 442). Danielewicz argues "experiments that involve writing different versions of the self lead to growth, to knowledge of public issues, and to authority. Writing about one's own or another person's life makes the stakes personal, therefore immediate, tangible, even urgent" (Danielewicz, 2008, p. 442). In fact, Danielewicz contends "we (and our cultures, communities, families) need such assertions of self, such articulation of differences, as a way to fight against the depersonalization and homogenizing effects of globalization" (2008, p. 439). Instead of conspiring to replicate "a capitalist/consumerist hegemony responsible for various forms of political, social, and economic oppression" (O'Donnell, 1996, p. 423), critical expressivist practices can help students fight oppression by seeing the ways they can take actions in our current cultural moment. Unlike critiques that personal genres are empty exercises (Danielewicz, 2008, p. 442), it is clear that they can help students actively engage with social issues and develop public voices that make them active participants in public arenas. If students realize that something is at stake when they write, they become more invested and may, perhaps, see writing as social action (Danielewicz, 2008, p. 443-4). Drawing on critical pedagogies like these, we can help students learn to be responsible language users in public spheres.

CONCLUDING THOUGHTS/STORY OF THE ARTICLE

Near the beginning of this article, I asked if we could imagine creative alternatives that could help students position themselves as active voices in public discourses. I suggested that an important step in the process is valuing individual experiences and beliefs. Throughout the chapter, I have illustrated some of the ways that critical expressivist pedagogies use individual experiences to help students become more responsible language users in public discourse. So, if we return to that question now, I hope I have presented a few useful ideas.

I recognize the paradoxical nature of this chapter: I am advocating for incorporating individual experience into academic and other kinds of work in both writing and discussion, and yet there is not one bit of evidence of my individual story here. I have also encouraged including personal genres into academic and other kinds of writing, and yet there is not a stitch of autobiography or autoenthography or auto-anything in this article. And to be honest, it didn't even occur to me to include it in the chapter until I was writing the 27th out of the 50th draft of this piece (numbers are approximate)—I was trained well in traditional academia.

In an effort to answer some of the calls I have made in this article, I want to tell some of the stories of this article—to foreground the motivations, beliefs, values, and hopes that drive this article. Ganz's story of self, story of us, and story of now help me do so.

Story of Self

My motivations for writing this piece come from a strong belief: The individual matters! By this, I do not mean to suggest that I am resorting to a "naïve acceptance of the notion of a rational, coherent, and unified self" (Freedman, 2001, p. 206); nor am I suggesting that the individual is "insular, confined or private" (Danielewicz, 2008, p. 440). I am suggesting we need to examine the work that ideas like "self" and "individual" play in people's lives. Many people find it important to have a "ground" to stand on—a sort of foundation that they can rely on in this world, and that ground can come from many places. Yes, it's important to realize that the "ground" changes over time and that we learned that "ground" through social experiences. Nevertheless, a sense of identity—i.e. being an individual—does important work in people's lives. Susan Hekman argues that "selves must necessarily experience themselves as coherent identities, historically located and contingent, but enduring through time" (2010, p. 299). It is the both/and that is appealing to me, that I believe in, and that attracts me to critical expressivism: stablity and contingency.

Just as I passionately argue that the individual matters, I just as passionately insist that pedagogy matters—that composition is a valid and valuable field and that critical expressivism is an important part of teaching. I am disturbed by the divisiveness I sense every time I go to meetings where those who identify themselves loudly as "rhetoricians" work actively to distance themselves from "teaching." Many moons ago, Stephen North said that the field was suffering because the Researchers didn't value the Practitioners, the Philosophers didn't value the Researchers, and so on (1987). All too often I see this same struggles occurring today. My lived experiences in departments that too often feel that rhetoric and theory is privileged over teaching and composition (although I realize that teaching is not the only thing that scholars of composition study). I have lived through many meetings where I alternately felt like sinking in my seat, somehow feeling ashamed to value teaching, or standing up on the table shouting "Teaching matters!" I have lived—and sadly continue to live—a sense of alienation as "the" composition person in an area where Rhetoric is privileged.

My first passion and interest in higher education is teaching and writing about teaching. That's why it was so important to me to contribute to this collection. I believe in students. I believe in studying learning. I believe it's important to study teaching. I believe that the divisiveness in our departments and our own areas is corrosive. I like how Karen Surman Paley puts it: "I am not asking naively, 'Why can't we all just get along?' but rather I am saying, 'Let us look more carefully before we write each other off.'" (2001, p. 197). That is precisely what North urged us to do in 1987. I believe books like this can help move us toward that. These are core personal beliefs I bring with me to the writing of this chapter, to the conversation.

Story of Us

"Our stories of self overlap with our stories of us .... A story of us expresses the values, the experiences, shared by the us we hope to evoke at the time" (Ganz, 2008, p. 12). The "us" being invoked in this collection is the kind of teacher I want to be—the kind of compassionate, critical, thinking, reflective teacher (person) I want to be. It is an "us" I want to use to help shape my story of self because we are collectively constructing a community of values and experiences that help our students, communities, and worlds. The "collective identity" being constructed here across the articles is one I wish to be a part of. The overlap of my story with this collective "us."

"Like the story of self, [the story of us] is built from the choices points—the founding, the choices made, the challenges faced, the outcomes, the lessons learned" (Ganz, 2008, p. 12). I see this book as a story of us, covering all of these ideas (explicitly or implicitly)—beginnings, ongoing choices, perpetually changing outcomes, ever blossoming lessons. It is a story in which I feel welcomed, not isolated. It is a story in which teaching is valued.

Ganz says the story of us requires one key storyteller, "an interpreter of experience" (2008, p. 12), but I suggest that we are all storytellers. We are all serving a critical leadership function in interpreting "the movement's new experience" (Ganz, 2008, p. 12). That is a central part of this book's story seen through the emails we've shared, the engagements across articles, the nature of the "collective" part of the edited "collection."

Story of Now

This is the hardest of the three stories: "A story of now articulates an urgent challenge—or threat—to the values that we share that demands action now. What choices must we make? What is at risk? And where's the hope?" (Ganz, 2008, p. 13).

While I do not think one writing class can change the world, I do believe that one writing class can help students become stronger language users and can learn that language can be an important part of social action. Words have impact; words can make things happen; words do things; words are action. Students can/should take responsibility for their words. Students can/should be responsive to their audiences. Instead of seeing writing assignments as, well, assignments, they should/can see them as actions that matter—as tasks that matter.

But some writing matters more than others. Part of our responsibility as teachers is to make sure the writing we have them do and the discussions we have them participate in matter. It is also our responsibility to help them see how they matter and to realize that they won't matter to every student in the same way. We can't assume that they should see the world the way we do and that they should take the stances we do—i.e. take on our political views or political agendas.

But we do face a collective sort problem—i.e. a view that someone else somewhere else should fix the problems that plague us. In "You Don't Know Where You're Going until You're on the Way There: Why Public 'Work' Matters," Paul Markham summarizes it well. He argues that we must "re-imagine citizenship for the twenty-first century" (2011, p. 4). Challenging the "customer service mentality" where we wait for someone else to serve us and fix our problems "requires more than policy change alone—it requires a cultural change, a new civic imagination. This new kind of everyday politics emphasizes the creative role of citizens and their ability to solve a wide variety of complex public problems" (Markham, 2011, p. 4). That emphasis on "a new civic imagination" and "the creative role of citizens" is something that there is an urgent need for. However, there is certainly not one path to fulfilling that need. And there is definitely not one political agenda that will achieve that goal.

Likewise, there is not one writing method or approach that best prepares students to learn the kind of creative problem solving that sort of citizenship will/does require. Valuing individual experiences and situating them in larger social contexts—larger social narratives—will, however, be a crucial part of it. And critical expresssivism can be an important part of that process, as I have argued. Critical expressivism can, thus, be an important part of the story of now. Ganz writes: "In a story of now, we are the protagonists and it is our choices that shape the outcome" (2008, p. 13). The choice/action does not need to be huge/monumental, but it must be specific and hold a vision. When making choices, Ganz points out, "It can begin by getting that number of people to show up at a meeting that you committed to do. You can win a 'small' victory that shows change is possible. A small victory can become a source of hope if it is interpreted as part of a greater vision" (Ganz, 2008, p. 13).

What we need is small steps and new stories to tell about those steps—exactly what this article has allowed me to do, to consider: what do I want for my students? For our classrooms? For our educational institutions? For our communities? For our nation? While hope may seem like a vague and abstract concept, Ganz insists that "it is a strategy—a credible vision of how to get from here to there" (2008, p. 13). We all have that hope. This collection has allowed me (us?) to make a space for vision and hope in our academic pursuits. The story of now—the hope of critical expressivism.

REFERENCES

Berlin, J. (2009). Rhetoric and ideology in the writing class. In S. Miller (Ed.), *The Norton book of composition studies* (pp. 667-684). New York: W. W. Norton.

Danielewicz, J. (2008). Personal genres, public voices. *College Composition and Communication, 59*(3), 420-450.

Fishman, S., & McCarthy, L. P. (1992). Is expressivism dead? Reconsidering its romantic roots and its relation to social constructivism. *College English, 54*(6), 647-661.

Freedman, D. P. (2001). Life work through teaching and scholarship. In D. Holdstein & D. Bleich (Eds.), *Personal efects: The social character of scholarly writing* (pp. 199-219). Logan, UT: Utah State Press.

Ganz, M. (2008). What is public narrative? Retrieved from New England Grassroots Environmental Fund Web site: http://wearesole.com/What_is_Public_Narrative.pdf

Gradin, S. (1995). *Romancing rhetorics: Social expressivism on the teaching of writing.* Pourtsmouth, NH: Heinemann.

Hekman, S. (2010). Private Selves, public identities: Reconsidering identity politics. Penn State Press.

Judd, D. (2003). *Critical realism and composition theory.* New York: Routledge.

Markham, P. (2011). You don't know where you're going until you're on your way there: Why public "work" matters. *Journal for Civic Commitment, 17,* 1-17.

North, S. (1987). *The making of knowledge in composition: A portrait of an emerging discipline.* Pourtsmouth, NH: Heinemann.

O'Donnell, T. (1996). Politics and ordinary language: A defense of expressivist rhetorics. *College English, 58*(4), 423-439.

Paley, K. S. (2001). The social construction of "expressivist" pedagogy." In D. Holdstein & D. Bleich (Eds.), *Personal effects: The social character of scholarly writing* (pp. 178-198). Logan, UT: Utah State Press.

Shields, C. M. & Mohan, E. J. (2008). High-quality education for all students: Putting social justice at its heart. *Teacher Development, 12*(4), 289-300.

Warnock, T. (2003). Bringing over yonder over here: A personal look at expressivist rhetoric asi action. In T. Enos, K. Miller, & J. McCracken (Eds.), *Beyond postprocess and postmodernism: Essays on the spaciousness of rhetoric* (pp. 203-216). Mahwah, NJ: Lawrence/Erlbaum Press.

FROM THE PERSONAL TO THE SOCIAL

Daniel F. Collins
Manhattan College

> We live, think, and write between baby steps and master theories, where the richness, confusion, tragedy, violence, and joy of life rush at us where we are and await us where we go.
>
> —Robert L. Davis and Mark H. Shadle

"We are all learning to live together." So reads the banner hanging in the prototypical classroom depicted in the graphic introduction to teaching, *To Teach: The Journey, in Comics*, by William Ayers and Ryan Alexander-Tanner. Good teaching prompts students to engage the surrounding world. Such engagement commences by honoring each student in the room, each voice, each person.

*

We are all learning to live together. So evoked President Barack Obama in his January 2011 Tucson speech after the shooting of Congresswoman Gabrielle Giffords and others. "It's important for us to pause for a moment and make sure that we are talking with each other in a way that heals, not a way that wounds," the President advised (2011). Learning to live together, we check our ideas and their expression through others.

*

We are all learning to live together. Mary Rose O'Reilly describes her composition pedagogy in the same intertwining of the personal and the social. O'Reilly asks students to begin writing in the personal, because such a stance honors their voice and provides them an opportunity to write from who they are, what they know, and what they want. Her pedagogy concludes in the social, or the communal, as students write for an audience, and this audience informs what they say and how they say it. Writing to find one's voice, O'Reilly argues, "defines a moment of presence, of being awake, and it involves not only self-understanding, but the ability to transmit that self-understanding to others. Learning to write so that you will be read, therefore, vitalizes both the self and the community" (2009, p. 58). By encouraging writing as the expression of the inner world, O'Reilly escorts students from the idiosyncrasies of the personal to the checks and balances of the social. "It seems important," O'Reilly writes, "that many opposing communities exist in balance, polishing each other up like rocks in a river bed, with the friction of daily contact" (2009, p. 11).

*

We are all learning to live together. This is the feeling and tenor of the writing classroom I try to construct and implement, a classroom set to up to explore writing from personal and social perspectives. This collage—an homage to the writers and teachers that inform my practice—attempts to articulate the ways in which personal and social dimensions of writing are embedded in expressivist thinking. Writing, Sherrie L. Gradin describes,

> is an act of the whole being; it is through reflecting, questioning feeling, experiencing, reasoning, and imagining that writers become writers. While this might seem an ambitious and ideal approach to writing instruction, I would argue that it is such an ideal that we need to hold to fully educate students in a system that often denies the emotive, creative, and imaginative aspects of the intellect. (1995, p. 57)

For Gradin, expressivism has always been an exploration of self and social world, a form of inquiry and discovery; expressivism has always been about the construction of meaning, about the development of self through a concern for voice and lived experience.

*

Robert Yagelski asks writing teachers to uphold writing as an ontological act: "When we write, we enact a sense of ourselves as beings in the world. In this regard, writing both shapes and reflects our sense of who we are in relation to each other and the world around us. Therein lies the transformative power of writing" (2009, p. 8). While Yagleski upholds the act of writing over any product, the transformation of self and world enmeshed in writing as an ontological act mirrors an expressivist impulse to write in two specific ways. First, Yagelski endorses "the capacity of writing to enhance an awareness of ourselves and the world around us, both in the moment and over time" (Yagelski, 2009, p. 16). Second, Yagelski acknowledges the transformative qualities of writing as "it opens up possibilities for awareness, reflection, and inquiry that writing as an act of textual production does not necessarily do" (Yagelski, 2009, p. 7). The act of writing, from Yagelski's perspective, affirms the need to compose one's story in meaningful ways and provides the means through which to develop a need to reckon with the self through the act of writing. Expressivism reinforces these same dimensions.

*

Expressivist writing theory, it seems to me, upholds the idea that to write is to discover oneself amidst an array of others. It honors the importance of the student engaging and making sense out of the world. Expressivism grew from personal uses of language to using language to engage others. "Personal modes of writing," Peter Elbow argues, "help writers take more authority over their writing: not to feel so intimidated by it and not to write so much tangled or uninvested prose or mechanical or empty thinking" (2002, p. 16). Randall R. Freisinger agrees, arguing that an academic neglect of the expressivist function of language impairs the cognitive development of students simply because students remain alienated from writing by a strict emphasis on academic writing (1980, p. 162). Sherrie Gradin seeks to redress this neglect by reminding her readers of these social dimensions of expressivism:

> I envision a social-expressivism where the best of both expressivism and social epistemic theories are practiced: students carry out negotiations between themselves and their culture, and must do this first in order to become effective citizens, imaginative thinkers, and savvy rhetorical beings. Learning to enact these negotiations means first developing a sense of one's own values and social constructions and then examining how these interact or do not interact with others' value systems and cultural constructs." (1995, p. 110)

Freisinger argues that the end result of the expressivist impulse is no less than connecting personal experience and voice to an expansion of the student's conception of the world (1980, p. 164). We are all learning to live together.

*

bell hooks offers a productive definition of voice from a social perspective: "Coming to voice is not just the act of telling one's experience. It is using that telling strategically—to come to voice so that you may also speak freely about other subjects" (1994, p. 148). Part of hooks' instruction here is the direction of student attention to the voices of others. hooks' sense of self-understanding has both personal and social dimensions: "A personal definition of self aids, and is indeed necessary in, the development of an awareness of one's socially defined interactions with others" (1994, p. 166). In other words, writers come to know themselves through their actions as social beings. Without a voice, Gradin argues, students may be unwilling to begin important work: "understanding what their beliefs are and where they come from in terms of their own experiences, so that they can see how their value systems might differ from others'" (1995, p. 119).

*

An expressivist classroom can become a transformative community, one that embeds personal discoveries in social engagement (Fishman & McCarthy, 1992, p. 659).

*

"We believe that all learning is autobiographical and passionate," Robert Davis and Mark Shadle confess (2007, p. 9). Davis and Shadle go to great lengths to paint themselves as composition traditionalists upholding the sanctity of academic projects and academic discourse even as they work to extend (and undo) the purview and parameters of both. "We do not think that being the best of academicians is the end point for students or the most useful manner of being. Instead, we hope that students will be intellectuals pursuing pressing questions and fertile mysteries, who can engage, and change, the rhetorical and actual situations of their lives" (Davis & Shadle, 2007, p. 3). Davis and Shadle offer a useful distinction here: writing from the self versus writing about the self (see, too, Elbow, 2002, p. 18): expressivist writing begins from the self, from the personal experiences and observations of the writer. But the writer is not separate from larger social contexts, and so the writing process does not end until such inquiry is used in the making of meaning for the writer and for others.

*

Peter Elbow considers expressivism as a form of discourse that addresses the ways in which interested parties engage other interested parties, all the while identifying (and checking and modifying) our individual and collective stakes in the matters at hand. Elbow endorses the intellectual tasks of "giving good reasons and evidence yet doing so in a rhetorical fashion which acknowledges an interested position and tries to acknowledge and understand the positions of others" (2002, p. 148). Self in a world of others—we are all learning to live together.

*

Stephen M. Fishman and Lucille Parkinson McCarthy argue that Peter Elbow "hopes to increase our chances for identifying with one another and, as a result, our chances for restructuring community" (1992, p. 649). Expression, then, becomes about both self-discovery and social connection (Fishman & McCarthy, 1992, p. 650). Both goals rest in the clarification of meaning embodied in the act of expression, acts designed to help us engage our sense of selves and of others (Fishman & McCarthy, 1992, pp. 650, 652).

*

Ken Macrorie writes, "All good writers speak in honest voices and tell the truth" (1985, p. 15). Macrorie values writing as truth-telling: "a connection between the things written about, the words used in the writing, and the author's experience in a world she knows well—whether in fact or dream or imagination" (1985, p. 15). Such truth-telling overrides the perceived importance of academic discourse, which rings so false and pretentious to Macrorie that he gives it another name: Engfish. Engfish, according to Macrorie, prevents the telling of truth and promotes the telling of lies (1985, p. 14). Instead of Engfish, Macrorie promotes the use of natural, authentic, alive voices, voices that recount and recreate experiences using concrete facts and details to produce meanings for readers (1985, p. 34).

*

Macrorie identifies three resources at hand for any writer. First, the writer has her experiences from which to draw. These experiences can and should acknowledge the ways in which the thoughts and feelings of others have impacted the writer. Second, the writer has her writing skills, those rhetorical strategies used to speak in an authentic voice to connect with her readers. Third, she has her writing group, this circle of others to be used to hone the writing, the practice of writing (Macrorie, 1985, p. 74). "Good writers meet their readers only at their best," advocates Macrorie, indicating a concern for audience that is generally downplayed in discussions of his work (1985, p. 35). This concern for audience seems fundamental to the ways that Macrorie's work is about the impact of writing on its readers.

*

Robert Yagelski offers three important points relating to the act of writing: "the experience of writing is an experience of our being as inherently social; it is the experience of the interconnectedness of being" (2009, p. 14); writing "is an act of the self becoming more fully present in the world at the moment of writing" (2009, p. 13); and writing can be a profound act of self-awareness, a deepening of understanding of the self as a being in the world (2009, p. 15). "Writing is therapeutic not because it is the catharsis of confessing," argue Davis and Shadle, "but because writing about topics that writers are passionate about can help transform lives" (2007, p. 72). The ontological act of writing favors an expressivist emphasis on imagination, creativity, and process.

*

Mary Rose O'Reilly asks her students to enchant themselves with their writing, through their writing (2009, p. 54). To be enchanted suggests that the work will be engaged, completed, relished. One danger may be that that students simply fall in love with their stories. I don't simply want student narratives, stories about their lives. I want well-written narratives, crafted compositions about who they are and who they want to be. Meaning made by meaning shaped. Ander Monson helps me out here, in a passage I distribute to my students for discussion. Forgive the lengthy quotation:

> But I still don't want to read what most people have to say about themselves if it's just to tell their story. I want it to be art, meaning that I want it transformed, juxtaposed, collaged—worked on like metal sculpture, each sentence hammered, gleaming, honed .... The action of telling is fine: kudos for you and your confession, your therapy, your bravery in releasing your story to the public. But telling is performing, even if it seems effortless .... With years of reflection on that story and how it can be shaped as prose (and how its shape changes from our shaping it, reflecting on it), given audience and agents and editors, rhetoric and workshop and rewriting for maximum emotional punch—given the endless possibilities of the sentence on the page, I expect to see a little fucking craft. I guess I want awareness, a sense that the writer has reckoned with the self, the material, as well as what it means to reveal it, and how secrets are revealed, how stories are told, that it's not just being simply told. In short, it must make something of itself. (Monson, 2010, p. 13)

Yes, writing should move and surprise; it should teach its readers and writers something new.

*

Bristling against the personal narrative, Ander Monson attempts to articulate his concerns: "These writers presume—and doubtlessly been told, perhaps in workshops, perhaps by me—that their stories, finally, matter in themselves. Still, I see something in these also-rans: they might serve to matter if explored further, with style, an angle, some kind of action working as a countermeasure against the desire of the I to confess" (2010, p. 16). Against this backdrop, Monson argues the need "to tell a compelling story, but also to examine that compelling story and the act of storytelling through the prose, to let the sentences get some traction and complexity, to generate friction against what is being told" (2020, p. 17). Yes, through their writing, writers explore their relationship with others and with the social and cultural conditions that inform their writing. And through their writing, students develop a conscious linguistic shaping toward purpose and effect.

*

"I am learning to consider what my students can do with their knowledge," offers Ken Macrorie in his book *A Vulnerable Teacher* (1974, p. 111). Increasingly discouraged about the lack of student engagement in the classroom, Macrorie sought to create ways that students could engage classroom texts through their experiences. Classroom teaching became concerned with the mutual illumination of course texts and student experiences. "When my students and I are learning most powerfully, we are ever remembering where we came from. And so there is some living going on in our learning place" (Macrorie, 2010, "Preface"). No longer bored, Macrorie and his students began to surprise one another, if only because they do not know what others might say aloud to the class. Macrorie's practice becomes an invitation to self-reflection and self-scrutiny in a community of others doing much the same work. With no monopoly on knowledge, students and teachers alike use their experiences to offer insight into course materials and then use course materials to reframe their understandings of the world (Macrorie, 2010, p. 79). Students come to value their own experience and their insights into these experiences.

*

Our courses fail, Macrorie argues, when we deny students their lives (Macrorie, 2010, p. 13). Macrorie's sharp reminder indicates the need to ask students to connect their lives to the classroom. By making actual feelings, thoughts, and experiences significant to the ways in which students and teachers engage each other in the classroom, vulnerability becomes an important ingredient in the construction of knowledge. This is a vulnerability not based on fear and weakness—which would be simply another form of trampling on students (which is probably worse than simply ignoring them)—but a way of exercising their power as thinkers, writers, and people.

REFERENCES

Ayers, W., & Alexander-Tanner, R. (2010). *To teach: The journey, in comics*. New York: Teachers College Press.

Davis, R. L., & Shadle, M. F. (2007). *Teaching multiwriting: Researching and composing with multiple genres, media, disciplines, and cultures*. Carbondale, IL: Southern Illinois University Press.

Elbow, P. (2002). Exploring problems with "personal writing" and "expressivism." *The Selected Works of Peter Elbow*. Retrieved from http://works.bepress.com/peter_elbow/16

Elbow, P. (1991). Reflections on academic discourse: How it relates to freshmen and cColleagues. *College English, 53*(2), 135-155.

Fishman, S. M., & McCarthy, L. P. (1992). Is expressivism dead? Reconsidering its romantic roots and its relation to social constructionism. *College English, 54*(6), 647-661.

Freisinger, R. R. (1980). Cross-disciplinary writing workshops: Theory and practice. *College English, 42*(2), 154-166.

Gradin, S. L. (1995). *Romancing rhetorics: Social expressivist perspectives on the teaching of writing*. Portsmouth, NH: Heinemann.

Harris, J. (2006). *Rewriting: How to do things with exts*. Logan, UT: Utah State University Press.

hooks, b. (1994). *Teaching to transgress: Education as the practice of freedom*. New York: Routledge.

Macrorie, K. (1974). *A vulnerable teacher*. Rochelle Park, NJ: Hayden.

Macrorie, K. (1985). Telling writing (4th ed.). Portsmouth, NH: Heinemann.

Monson, A. (2010). *Vanishing point: Not a memoir*. Minneapolis, MN: Graywolf.

Obama, B. (2011, January 14). *The Washington Post*. Retrieved from http://voices.washingtonpost.com/44/2011/01/obama-in-tucson-full-text-of-p.html

O'Reilly, M. R. (2009). *The peaceable classroom*. Portsmouth, NH: Heinemann.

Yagelski, R. P. (2009). A thousand writers writing: Seeking change through the radical practice of writing as a way of being. *English Education, 42*(1), 6-28.

"IS IT POSSIBLE TO TEACH WRITING SO THAT PEOPLE STOP KILLING EACH OTHER?" NONVIOLENCE, COMPOSITION, AND CRITICAL EXPRESSIVISM

Scott Wagar
Miami University

> Can we say that our pedagogies are not about expressivist writing or about entrance to the academy but about learning how to live?
> —Michael Blitz and C. Mark Hurlbert

> Perhaps what I am encouraging ... is Inner Peace Studies, which asks Who am I? Am I at peace with who I am? Who are these other people? What is the nature of community? What do they believe, and why? Is it possible for us to work together?
> —Mary Rose O'Reilley

A small, quiet movement within composition studies, focusing on connections between nonviolence and the teaching of writing, was arguably established by Mary Rose O'Reilley's 1993 *The Peaceable Classroom*, in which O'Reilley asked "Is it possible to teach English so that people stop killing each other?" In O'Reilley's wake have come works such as Michael Blitz and C. Mark Hurlbert's *Letters for the Living: Teaching Writing in a Violent Age* (1998) and essays by compositionists such as Sara Dalmas Jonsberg and G. Lynn Nelson. Such attempts to link composition and nonviolence have often been characterized by advocacy of what might be termed an expressivist approach to writing pedagogy. And yet a primary element of the notion of nonviolence is, of course, the relationship between self and other. How, then, could expressivist writing, with its focus on the personal, possibly lead to less violent ways of being in society? Below, I attempt to explain this seeming paradox by arguing that attempts at nonviolent composition provide signal examples of critical expressivism (a term I want to embrace, at least in the present context)—an approach foregrounding writing that is simultaneously based on personal experience and intimately connected with how individuals relate to one another.

NONVIOLENCE, THE PERSONAL, AND THE SOCIAL

To locate the origins of nonviolent sympathies within rhetoric and language studies, we might go at least as far back as Kenneth Burke, whose early cold war *Rhetoric of Motives* is offered as a small gesture "to counteract the torrents of ill will" he observed in the world of his time, sentiments that drove him ever more to believe "that books should be written for tolerance and contemplation" (1969, p. xv). Burke takes pains, for instance, to point out the irony of war, "that ultimate disease of cooperation:" a thousand instances of rhetorically induced coordination must occur to make a single destructive martial act possible (1969, p. 22). Elizabeth Ervin argues, meanwhile, for the impact of Wayne C. Booth's World War II experiences on his development as a rhetorical theorist, and quotes a late piece of his writing: "human love, human joining, 'critical understanding' as a loving effort to understand—that has always been at the center [of my endeavors]'" (Booth, as quoted in Ervin, 2003, p. 190). But in the contemporary era of composition and rhetoric, O'Reilley's *The Peaceable Classroom* is probably the best-known work explicitly focused on nonviolent English teaching, and not only because of its very quotable articulation (borrowed from Ihab Hassan, one of O'Reilley's graduate-school professors) of the "Is it possible … ?" question. Much of the book's impact stems from O'Reilley's honesty about her life, about the situatedness of her perspective on nonviolence, and about her failures. Relatable yet provocative, and endlessly quotable—"bad teaching … is soul murder" (1993, p. 47)—the book follows O'Reilley's attempts to enact a pedagogy of nonviolence, from the beginning of her career in the Vietnam era up through the then-recent first gulf war. The primary foundational element of her pedagogy is teaching personal writing (in perhaps all three of the senses articulated by Peter Elbow in this volume) to her students: "First of all, as teachers in the humanities, we encourage students to explore the inner life" (1993, p. 32). But—and this point is crucial in a discussion of critical expressivism—O'Reilley insists that

> our second goal should be to help the student bring his subjective vision into community, checking his insights against those of allies and adversaries, against the subjective vision of the texts he studies, and in general against the history of ideas. The classroom, then, must be a meeting place for both silent meditation and verbal witness, of interplay between interiority and community. (1993, p. 32)

She goes on to write that "finding voice [in writing]—let's be clear—is a political act … it involves not only self-understanding, but the ability to transmit that self-understanding to others. Learning to write so that you will be read, therefore, vitalizes both the self and the community" (1993, p. 58). Preemptively asking the question her reader might be formulating—"What Does This Have to do With Nonviolence?"—O'Reilley argues that "war begins in banality, the suppression of the personal and idiosyncratic" (1993, p. 59) and in linguistic abstractions such as "sacrifice" and "glory" (drawing on terms taken from Hemingway's *A Farewell to Arms*) (1993, p. 60). Abstractions have their place, she notes, "particularly in manipulating broad areas of cultural consensus," but "before we buy into an abstraction, we need to know what *we* think" (1993, p. 60). Here again she writes of the connection between the personal and the communal, but in this case, rather than focusing on how the community must bring the individual vision into check, O'Reilley reverses the argument: socially-constructed, and possibly dangerous, abstractions must be checked against individual perspectives and experiences.

Claims about the importance of the individual viewpoint for nonviolence are also advanced in Michael Blitz and C. Mark Hurlbert's 1998 *Letters for the Living: Teaching Writing in a Violent Age*. Blitz and Hurlbert suggest that their work "is one attempt to peel away some theoretical abstractions so that we might better understand the personal and culture implications of what each student is telling us, the uniqueness of each student, of each life. No one encounters violence or peace in general. The experience of each is always unique" (Blitz & Hurlbert, 1998, p. 21). With Blitz and Hurlbert, unlike in *The Peaceable Classroom*, samples of personal experience-based student texts make up a sizable percentage of the book; it is this direct inclusion of student writing that perhaps most distinguishes *Letters for the Living* as a "composition" work (despite her interest in the teaching of writing, O'Reilley might be said to identify more as a literature scholar and poet than a compositionist). The book, however, is similar to O'Reilley's in a couple of key ways: it foregrounds a writing pedagogy that asks students to bring their subjective experiences into conversation with a community; and it is itself written in a highly personal style, although structured mainly as a chronological transcript of an ongoing email exchange between the co-authors. Blitz and Hurlbert muse about the role of violence—and peace—in their students' lives as well as their own. The three main textual threads running through the book—the authors' messages to each other, their students' writing (mostly embedded in the email message texts), and the jointly-authored commentary in between—add up to a more intense version of the familiar back-and-forth between student writing and researcher commentary often seen in composition studies literature. In some sections, the effect is soothing, as these two friends trade late night messages. But in any given chapter, the reader is never far from a jarring personal account from a student: a neighborhood murder, family violence, a friend's suicide. In this sense, *Letters for the Living* embodies its twin subjects: the violence of students' worlds and the world at large, and the moments of peace that Blitz and Hurlbert maintain are possible to find in our lives as well as in our students' writing and our own.

This focus on peace, not just violence, and on the personal also distinguishes another notable contribution to this conversation about composition's possible relationship with nonviolence: a 2000 special issue of *English Journal*, entitled "A Curriculum of Peace," that emerged in the wake of the 1999 Columbine High School shootings. Though *English Journal* is primarily aimed at secondary school instructors, this issue includes contributions from college compositionists Sara Dalmas Jonsberg, Marsha Lee Holmes, and G. Lynn Nelson, among other university instructors. (Sadly, of course, prominent college shootings such as those at Virginia Tech would soon take place after this issue appeared.)

Nelson insists that a "personal story" must be at the heart of any attempt to work toward peace through teaching writing: "Deny me my stories, as the modern dominant culture does, and I will eventually turn to the language of violence" (2000, p. 43). Indeed, he insists that his writing classes and workshops at all levels are built around variations on the simple injunction, "tell me a story" (2000, p. 45)—but, citing O'Reilley's concept of "deep listening," he also emphasizes the importance of fostering audience attentiveness in those classes. That is, stories do not achieve their full value when they are mere expression; they have to be heard, not just told, and in the classroom this means that a community of listeners must be constructed, including students and the instructor. So the personal cannot be disconnected from the social.

Jonsberg, meanwhile, invokes this connection in her own way, insisting on the importance for nonviolent teaching of respecting what each individual student brings to the classroom and to her or his writing and reading. Respect in this context is

> born of understanding first the source of a reader's unique vision—seeing that there are reasons behind a particular reading of a text, reasons of experience, gender, religion, cultural, and/or linguistic background. With that introspective understanding comes an awareness that others will read differently, out of their experiences and genders and religious training and so on. (2000, p. 30)

The "unique vision" of the individual, then, can be simultaneously honored for its own value and understood as a perspective to which social factors make an absolutely crucial contribution. Further, "introspective understanding" leads not to self-absorption but to knowledge of a commonality with others: other people are different, paradoxically, for the same reasons I am "myself"—because of personal experiences and a mix of socializing elements.

Jonsberg thus follows O'Reilley, Blitz and Hurlbert, and Nelson in arguing for a pedagogy that gives pride of place to the stories and voices of individual students, without in any way discounting the importance of the social (that is, fellow students and the teacher, but also the world at large). Below, I offer pedagogical possibilities in presenting a small toolbox of projects and practices that might aid the composition instructor inspired by nonviolent principles. But first I want to point out another of Jonsberg's arguments that highlights a second key commonality in the work of many compositionists of nonviolence. Jonsberg suggests provocatively that "WHAT we teach doesn't matter half so much as HOW we teach it. WHO we are, what values we model, has far more effect on our students than the words they may read or hear" (2000, p. 28). For Jonsberg, a posture of absolute respect and acceptance on the teacher's part is critical; she strives for a classroom where "all members are welcome in the fullness of their being" (2000, p. 30). Nelson's valuation of deep listening seems to arise from a similar place. O'Reilley bluntly argues that the "adversarial stance" (1993, p. 30) of many traditional teaching methods leads to "academic brutalization" (1993, p. 31), and that the little things we do matter, down to our comments on student papers: "rude and demoralizing labeling of student work" is one example of how students are "insulted, bullied, and turned into objects," planting "seeds of violence. It follows, therefore, that the first step in teaching peace is to examine the ways in which we are already teaching conflict" (O'Reilley, 1993, p. 31).

TEACHERLY REFLECTION

But how can we conduct such an examination? O'Reilley's and Blitz and Hurlbert's longer texts point toward an answer: as teachers we should reflect with seriousness and honesty on our own lives, considering how they connect to and influence what we do in the classroom. Blitz and Hurlbert claim in their introductory chapter that "writing and living and teaching are not separable. As you will see, our lives are in this composition [*Letters for the Living*] as our students' lives are in their compositions" (1998, p. 2). And indeed, even though their book is overwhelmingly focused on their experiences with their writing students, a reader also witnesses the two teachers wrestle with fears for their own children; relate stories of troubled visits to dying hometowns; and recall quiet moments when they sat peacefully as friends, staring into the night. These details are offered not gratuitously but as part and parcel of Blitz and Hurlbert's project of wondering how they might help their composition students navigate violent landscapes; one gets the impression that these teachers are better able to sympathetically encounter their students' writings by reflecting on their own values, goals, and experiences vis-à-vis peace and violence. Their work, then, grows out of a desire to "stop pretending that that our real lives are secondary or irrelevant to the work of teaching" (1998, p. 2). O'Reilley, for her part, has followed up *The Peaceable Classroom* with two similarly personal and candid volumes (1998's *Radical Presence: Teaching as Contemplative Practice* and 2005's *The Garden at Night: Burnout and Breakdown in the Teaching Life*) focusing on teachers' lives as they relate to the classroom. In the view of these compositionists of nonviolence, critical expressivism isn't just for our students; it's for us too. Any teacher who's been unable to banish from her head a negative comment from a student evaluation, or been troubled for days afterward about a testy exchange in the classroom, knows that our teaching hours influence our non-teaching ones. But a moment's thought will reveal that the influence runs in the other direction as well, and the critical expressivism of Blitz and Hurlbert and O'Reilley's own writing helps us consider some of the connections between violence, nonviolence, and what we bring into the classroom from outside it.

Part of what we bring into the classroom, of course, is our personal sense of highest meaning and purpose, of our connection with the rest of the universe and how we might act to deepen that connection: what I will call our spirituality. In considering the history of nonviolence, we do a disservice to figures such as King and Gandhi if we forget how entwined their spiritual ideals were with their commitments to turning the other cheek. Of the compositionists of nonviolence, O'Reilley in particular is unabashed about the influence of her spiritual beliefs and practices, to the point where Peter Elbow, in his foreword to *The Peaceable Classroom*, classifies the book's subfield as spirituality (xi). Earlier, I cited O'Reilley's claim that "finding voice [in writing] ... is a political act"—but here I want to note her parallel claim, given equal weight in the text, that "finding voice is a spiritual event" (61), the province of prophets; and a "prophet, or a prophetic writer, calls us to a higher standard of what we could be. That's simply a prophet's job description" (62). In this view, the spiritual and the political are as tied together as the personal and the political: an individual's spiritual experience—which may be triggered by finding voice in writing—gives rise to a call for the betterment of the community. Certainly, O'Reilley seems to suggest that this pattern holds for her. Each of her books on the teaching life is substantially concerned with her experiences as an eclectic mix of Quaker, Buddhist, and Roman Catholic, and how these traditions motivate her to be a particular kind of person, writer, and teacher (a nonviolent one, among other things). She notes in *The Peaceable Classroom* that her purpose in highlighting her spirituality is not to forward "dogma" but instead to foreground the importance of "discipline: a way of being-in-time that these traditions propose" (73).

"Is it Possible to Teach Writing So That People Stop Killing Each Other?"

Variously referred to by O'Reilley as contemplation, deep listening, presence, mindfulness, or being awake, such discipline—which for O'Reilley is particularly influenced by the teachings of the Vietnamese Zen practitioner Thich Nhat Hanh[1]—helps a teacher to actually be there with students, paying full attention in the given situation: in the classroom, during office hours, while planning class or commenting on papers.

"Spirituality" in this sense, then, involves not so much a set of beliefs as a set of practices and ways of understanding, and relating to, others and the world. For O'Reilley, we know that the frameworks of Buddhism, Quakerism and Catholicism feed these ways of being. Blitz and Hurlbert are quieter about their relation to established spiritual traditions, though Hurlbert occasionally quotes the wisdom of a rabbi neighbor, and fondly remembers the "peace be with you" of the Catholic masses of his childhood. But in any case I think that we can see, in these teachers' deep concern for student well-being and their intense personal reflection, a commitment to the same values that spirituality-in-education proponent Parker J. Palmer approvingly attributes to O'Reilley in his foreword to *Radical Presence*: "seeing one's self without blinking, offering hospitality to the alien other, having compassion for suffering, being present and being real" (ix). When Blitz and Hurlbert ask in *Letters for the Living*, "what if ... peace depends upon a constant, incremental, local, personal vigil?" (1998, p. 56), they seem not far from the mindfulness-based notion of "being peace" forwarded by Thich Nhat Hanh in books such as *Being Peace* and *Peace is Every Step*. And at the same time they hint at why their pedagogy is based on personal writing: the "local, personal vigil" is what they encourage in their students' experience-based compositions, and exemplify in their own prose in *Letters for the Living*.

Nhat Hanh's notion of interbeing also seems worth mentioning here; it's the idea that every seemingly separate thing in the universe is in fact, from a certain perspective, connected in a web of interdependence. For example, the computer keyboard I'm typing on wouldn't exist without the sun and soil that helped grow the food for its designers; or without the ancient creatures whose compressed remains created the raw material for the petroleum-based keys; or without the inventors of the letters represented on those keys; and so on and so on. According to Nhat Hanh, to really understand the theory we have to be able to see its truth at an intuitive level, not just logically. But I think understanding it logically can still be valuable for a project involving composition and nonviolence. As teachers and scholars of language and writing, we have little problem accepting a similar theory about texts: any given book, for instance, is written in an alphabet the author did not create, using a language of words with rich histories and ever-shifting meanings, and indebted to myriad other texts and thinkers—either implicitly or explicitly—in its allusions, quotations, adherence or lack thereof to genre conventions, and so on. So we may be especially well-positioned to accept a theory of interbeing. Our familiarity with Burke's notions of rhetorical identification and consubstantiality may also help us appreciate a perspective highlighting connection. It's important that we not understand interbeing in a manner that denies the existence of difference.[2] Rather, in the Buddhist tradition of embracing paradox, we see that from one perspective things are separate, whereas from another (perhaps more profound) viewpoint they're inextricably connected. My point here is that if one of our operative frameworks—or terministic screens, to use Burke—as teachers is a perspective of interbeing, we may be bolstered in our efforts toward nonviolent teaching: simply speaking, we come to understand that hurting others means, at a fundamental level, hurting ourselves. And it's not hard to see the connection with critical expressivism, if by this term we mean the notion that in writing (from) the self we must inevitably encounter, and consider our relationship with, others and society. As Blitz and Hurlbert suggest, quoting Nel Noddings, "We need to create curricula which include ample 'opportunity to study response, beauty, and almost mystical interdependence'" (1998, p. 83).

The purpose of this discussion of spirituality is not (necessarily) to call for teachers to take up any particular reflective practice (e.g., meditation, contemplation) but to point out spirituality's importance in one of the most frequently cited texts (*The Peaceable Classroom*) among compositionists of nonviolence, as well as to show how certain spiritual perspectives align with both a nonviolent stance and a critical expressivist one. More broadly, my focus on teachers' spirituality is one way of calling attention to the importance compositionists of nonviolence place on the value of deep listening to students and to committed, continuing self-scrutiny on the part of instructors; for those so inclined, a discipline of personal spiritual practice may help support such attentive teaching and honest self-reflection.[3] Those for whom the notion of "spirituality" feels problematic may, of course, draw inspiration from other wells and frame the values underlying their commitment to nonviolence in different terms—"humanist," "feminist," "progressive," or something else.[4] Similarly, in what follows, I include pedagogical suggestions that might be understood as spiritual by some, but simply secular by others.

WORKING TOWARD A COMPOSITION CLASSROOM OF NONVIOLENCE

To this point I've written mainly about the philosophical perspectives informing attempts at nonviolent composition. Here I'd like to talk a bit more practically, discussing possibilities for assignments, activities, and classroom practices drawn from or inspired by the work of compositionists of nonviolence as well as by the notion of critical expressivism. Obviously, composition is taught in a wide variety of contexts, and my suggestions encompass first-year as well as advanced composition courses, themed and non-themed courses. This examination is certainly far from comprehensive and interested readers are, of course, encouraged to consult cited works for further information.

Longer Assignments

If we strive to work toward peace in our teaching of composition, we might ask students to write about violence and nonviolence explicitly, or we might ask them to focus on these issues in less direct ways. In attending to the personal and the local when thinking about where peace, and violence, reside, Blitz and Hurlbert detail a project that asked students to reflect upon and research various aspects of their cities and neighborhoods and compile a collaborative class "book." For the first part of this assignment (the focus of an entire chapter in *Letters for the Living*), Blitz's students, most of them based in New York City, corresponded with Hurlbert's rural Pennsylvania students to describe their respective cities and neighborhoods and their lives there. Blitz and Hurlbert write, "in every case" students reported this letter-writing aspect of the course as their favorite (1998, p. 96). The potential value of such a place-based approach for students' critical rhetorical understanding is articulated by David Seitz elsewhere in this volume. Further, a local approach is in keeping with the work of some writers in ecocomposition, a subdiscipline that seems allied with composition and nonviolence; for instance, Derek Owens offers a "place portrait" assignment (2001, p. 30) designed to help students think about their immediate environments. Ecocompositionist Christian R. Weisser, meanwhile, asks students to write a paper about their "relationships with non-human others" (2001, p. 92), an assignment certainly relevant to present purposes since a robust vision of nonviolence would extend to nonhuman animals as well as the natural world at large.[5]

Compositionist Michael Eckert, author of "Writing for Peace in the Composition Classroom," asks students to think more directly about peace and violence as well as about the role of rhetoric in both when he assigns a paper focusing on "personal argument style" in which "students tell a story about a time when they personally tried to make peace" (Writing for Peace). Marsha Lee Holmes, arguing that meeting violence head on is an effective strategy for understanding and ameliorating it, suggests having students focus on their experiences with violence in popular culture such as music, television, and film. Citing Ann E. Berthoff, Holmes believes that such an approach is pedagogically effective because it "begin[s] with where they are" (as quoted in Holmes, 2000, p. 105), calling on texts with which students are intimately familiar to allow for deeper thought about students' relationships with those materials and with the various kinds of violence they represent (physical violence, to be sure, but also mental violence as well as racism, sexism, homophobia, and the like).

INFORMAL WRITING

Perhaps unsurprisingly, O'Reilley is an unabashed fan of freewriting, which for her specifically means "automatic" writing or writing without stopping or editing, not just informal writing in general. Sometimes calling it "prewriting," O'Reilley (1993) cites the practice as one of the key "tool[s] of nonviolent discipline in the writing class" (p. 43). She goes so far as to suggest that in outlining "what we now think of as a process model of teaching writing," early freewriting proponents "Macrorie, Elbow and their colleagues were laying out, I believe, a pedagogy of nonviolence" (pp. 38-39); in other words, modern composition, with a focus on process almost a given, is in some ways inherently a nonviolentist enterprise. For O'Reilley, freewriting moves students away from being "generic products" formed by years of conformist socialization: "in prewriting ... we begin to listen to voices inside. They may surprise us" (p. 44). So far, so expressivist. But characteristically, O'Reilley goes on to connect interior and exterior: the inner voices accessed through freewriting may also "surprise the world, which badly needs new ideas" (p. 44). However, she does not believe in surprising the world with raw freewriting, preferring to employ some type of intermediate "'focus' exercise that allows the reader to revisit the material, shape, amplify, cut, explain, and edit ... thus, we teach both appropriate sharing and appropriate restraint" (p. 51). Journals, long a mainstay of composition courses, could serve well as a medium for such "sharing" in a course working toward nonviolence, motivating regular writing practice and self-reflection—on the part of teachers as well as students.

READINGS

The appropriate role of writings generated by authors other than the students in the class has long been debated in composition; although it's probably safe to say that most composition classes include outside readings, the issue is worth raising again in the context of a critical expressivist pedagogy of nonviolence, at once concerned with students' personal stories and with an outside "topic" (nonviolence/peace). However, the seeming conflict need not be. Students can certainly respond from experience to outside readings, and these could be texts with or without overt nonviolent perspectives; in fact, the argument could be made that a critical expressivist approach would—or should—by definition put students' own experiences into dialogue and tension with existing texts and cultural conversations. O'Reilley reports that her "peaceable classroom" experiment began with a literature course on War and the Modern Imagination featuring authors such as Hemingway and Vonnegut (1993, p. 20); as mentioned, Holmes calls on familiar texts from students' pop-culture experiences; and Blitz and Hurlbert's Interstate Neighborhood Project occurred in the context of the two teachers' research writing courses, where students were responsible for finding and using outside sources. However, teachers can expect challenges—for instance, Blitz and Hurlbert (1998) report rather glumly on a widespread failure in their students' work that semester to "make connections between the insights they created about their own lives during the letter writing in the first half of the semester and their research" about their neighborhoods detailed in the final class book project (p. 128). Eckert (Writing for Peace), for his part, details two assignments built mainly around outside texts: one asks students to research a "peace hero" (e.g., Jane Addams) and to write a Rogerian-style encomium about that figure for a skeptical audience; while the other requires a comparative-contrastive argument about two literary representations of "nonviolent sentiment." Though these projects lack overt expressivist elements, we can certainly imagine that they might be modified to include experiential input from students, including in accompanying writer's-letter-type reflections.

CLASSROOM PRACTICES AND PERSPECTIVES

What other practices and attitudes might characterize a writing classroom of nonviolence? Another standby of many classrooms, the peer-response group, is likely to be one. O'Reilley (1993) writes:

> I think the writing group—as envisioned by contemporary writing theorists—functions specifically as a peacemaking strategy: it encourages us to listen to each other and figure out ways of criticizing without inflicting terminal injury, and it helps us learn to accept criticism without rancor. The writing group forces us to stake out the terrain between our own and other people's view of reality; hence, it reinforces both personal identity and the sense of relationship to a community. (p. 33)

Blitz and Hurlbert (1998) summarize their teaching style thusly: "A workshop pedagogy: an organic, creative, socially responsible pedagogy" (p. 138). So yet again, in this view, critical expressivism and nonviolent pedagogy are understood as intertwined.

There is also the question—hinted at above in Eckert's "peacemaker" assignment—of how to approach the concepts of rhetoric and argument themselves with students. Although some scholars, such as Sally Miller Gearhart (1979), have provocatively suggested that "any intent to persuade is an act of violence" (p. 195), others, such as Barry Kroll (2008) and Richard Fulkerson (2005), have proposed that we instead re-envision rhetoric in different, more peaceable terms. Kroll, in a 2008 *College Composition and Communiation* article, introduces writing students to possible parallels between the martial art of aikido—which focuses on meeting physical attacks with minimal force and an intention to do no harm—and more harmonious ways of arguing with adversaries; he suggests that taking such a rhetorical approach may be akin to "practicing the art of peace" (p. 468).[6] Fulkerson, meanwhile, surveying feminist critiques of argument, wonders if rhetoric could be reconceptualized as "partnership rather than battle" (and, relevantly for a discussion of critical expressivism, notes that his attempts to encourage students in this direction include requests for personal experience as part of their research-based arguments).[7] Teachers seeking shorter activities along these lines might ask students to play around with metaphor in the vein of M.J. Hardman (1998), who has suggested possible alternatives, drawn from realms such as gardening and cooking, to violent and war-based metaphors; for instance, "This is a battle over principles, not just opinions" can become "This is rooted in principles, not just opinions" (p. 43) and "You can't mount a successful attack if you're afraid to speak up" can be reconceived as "You can't have a gourmet meal if you're afraid to turn on the stove" (p. 45).

Finally, as I've pointed out, many compositionists of nonviolence make persistent cases for the importance of our quality of attention with students, and even mundane pedagogical practices can take on new meaning when viewed through this kind of lens. In her fellow teachers' meetings with students, O'Reilley (1998) witnesses deep presence, respect, and a gift for cultivating students' own understanding of their experiences: "I see my colleagues practicing this patient discernment as seriously as any Zen master, though they may call it simply draft conferencing" (p. 3). I'm enamored of the idea of using a "back-and-forth" attendance-keeping sheet for every student: each class session, the sheets are distributed, and each student signs in on her or his sheet with some kind of very brief note or question to the teacher, either formal or informal. The instructor collects the sheets and writes a very brief response to each student before the next class, when the cycle begins again. The response process can take as little as five minutes per class for the teacher, and a written dialogue between the student and teacher is established for the entire semester, ideally fostering a greater sense of connection.[8] Other daily practices matter too: in *Letters for the Living,* Blitz and

Hurlburt (1998) quote a holiday card from a former student, Jeremy, who shares the good news of a new job as a Youth Division caseworker, noting that in his employment interview he cited Blitz as the teacher who "made the most serious impression" on him during college. Jeremy at first found "weird—almost corny" Blitz's daily practice of greeting the class by saying "I'm glad you're here." But Jeremy "started to admire" the practice because he "could tell [Blitz] meant it," and he emphasizes the practice's importance to other students by recounting the time Blitz forgot to greet the class and was prompted by "that girl in the front" of the room. "So you see," the student concludes, "you made a difference to me and so I want to wish you happy holidays and God bless you" (pp. 65-66). Surely all of us can work at making at least this kind of difference as teachers.

CONCLUSION

> Peace is present right here and now, in ourselves and in everything we do and see. The question is whether or not we are in touch with it.
> —Thich Nhat Hanh

My goal here has been to highlight some of the core claims of compositionists of nonviolence, and in so doing to argue that notions of nonviolence in composition and critical expressivism can be mutually illuminating. Although I agree with much of what these teachers have to say, I don't mean to present their ideas unproblematically. It's worth noting that Blitz and Hurlbert and O'Reilley in particular do not sugarcoat the accounts of their attempts at the peaceable teaching of writing. But for my part, in the limited space of this essay, I've largely played Elbow's believing game, and I've certainly left unaddressed many concerns that might be raised about appropriate goals for teaching writing, politics and religion in the classroom, and issues of terminology raised by Elbow himself in this collection. So too has the lack of space prevented me from sufficiently examining the influence of feminist, virtue, and care theorists on pedagogies of nonviolence. And more activism-oriented critical pedagogues and purist proponents of nonviolence may feel that the approaches discussed here don't go far enough in the direction of social action and explication of nonviolent philosophy. Certainly, these are all points worthy of discussion.

On a more positive note, readers may have noticed that many of the suggestions here don't necessarily lead us very far astray from where we already are in terms of the philosophy and practice of teaching writing. This, then, is another of my goals: to show what we're already doing right, and to hearten writing teachers by suggesting that many mainstay activities of our classrooms can be seen as peaceable (and critical expressvist) if viewed through the kind of lens offered here. I'm pointing out, in other words, that we might consciously reframe our work in nonviolent terms. I want to appeal finally to Jonsberg's notion of a "hidden curriculum of peace" (p. 31) in which there might or might not be overt mention of nonviolence but behind which there's certainly a reflective teacher, searching within—and allowing students to do the same—in order to foster connections without.

NOTES

1. English educators who have read bell hooks' *Teaching to Transgress* will recognize Nhat Hanh's name since she, like O'Reilley, identifies his philosophy as foundational for her, both personally and as an educator.

2. Since I've mentioned Burke here, I'd like to point out (especially in the context of a conversation on nonviolence) that we've been reminded by scholars such as Krista Ratcliffe (2005) of the importance of keeping difference firmly in mind when we invoke notions of identification; if we neglect difference, we may neglect those most marginalized or othered by it. In his essay elsewhere in this collection, Eric Leake similarly considers some of the complexities and paradoxes inherent in concepts of identification and empathy as they relate to self, other, and difference. I also want to acknowledge that contemporary "spirituality" as a construct has come under criticism for reasons related to questions of self and other: individualistic spirituality, increasingly privatized and unmoored from institutions such as churches that have traditionally been concerned with social justice, may breed quietism and narcissism and allow injustice and inequality to grow. In fact, this line of argument—advanced in works such as Jeremy Carrette and Richard King's 2005 *Selling Spirituality*—has definite parallels with some of the most well-known claims against expressivism in composition studies. It's well worth noting here, however, that Carrette and King single out Nhat Hanh as a contemporary spiritual figure who bucks this narcissistic trend, instead advocating a socially-engaged spirituality.

3. Those for whom a discussion of spirituality qua spirituality resonates may wish to investigate the interesting and continuing conversation on this topic within composition and rhetoric. Among the sources I'd recommend would be the edited collections *The Spiritual Side of Writing* (1997), *The Academy and the Possibility of Belief: Essays on Intellectual and Spiritual Life* (2000) and *Presence of Mind: Writing and the Domain Beyond the Cognitive* (1994); *College Composition and Communication* articles by Ann E. Berthoff et al. ("Interchanges: Spiritual Sites of Composing," 1994) and Gesa E. Kirsch ("From Introspection to Action: Connecting Spirituality and Civic Engagement," 2009); and numerous essays from the *Journal for the Assembly of Expanded Perspectives on Learning* (JAEPL), such as Briggs, Schunter, and Melvin's "In the Name of the Spirit" (2000).

4. As scholar Ursula King (2008) notes, "some people may ... reject the language of spirituality, but may nevertheless espouse what one might call spiritual values through commitment in their lives to care and concern for others, or to such values as social justice, work for racial and gender equality, or for peace making in their communities" (p. 111).

5. Weisser (2001) also calls for the development of an "ecological self" (Weisser 86) in scholars' conceptions of identity, suggesting that ecology be taken not just as a metaphor for writing and knowledge but considered literally to include all aspects of our environments. In an assertion easy to link with Nhat Hanh's interbeing, Weisser writes, "ecological selves perceive their interconnection with others and comprehend the degree to which their own identities are inseparable from the non-human world—a recognition that the material world 'out there' is part of our identity 'in here'" (p. 86).

6. Relevant to my earlier arguments here, Kroll (2008) repeatedly notes the importance of spirituality in the development and practice of aikido, finally suggesting in his concluding paragraph that more peaceable ways of arguing are in line with aikido's insistence that "physical goals and ethical/spiritual ideals are enacted simultaneously" (p. 468).

7. Somewhat ironically, however, Fulkerson (2005) is quoted by Chris Warnick elsewhere in this volume referring to arguments against expressivism as "poundings at the cannons of postmodernism" (p. 655, as quoted in Warnick). It's worth pointing out that the article Warnick cites shows that Fulkerson doesn't ally himself philosophically with expressivism despite his advocacy of first-person accounts of personal experience in student argumentative writing.

8. Thanks to C.J. Opperthauser for introducing me to this idea.

REFERENCES

Berthoff, A. E., Daniell, B., Campbell, J., Swearingen, C. J., Moffett, J. (1994). Interchanges: spiritual sites of composing. *College Composition and Communication, 45*(2), 237-263.

Blitz, M., & Hurlbert, C. M. (1998). *Letters for the living: Teaching writing in a violent age.* Urbana, IL: NCTE.

Brand, A. G., & Graves, R. L. (Eds.). (1994). Presence of mind: Writing and the domain behind the cognitive. Portsmouth, NH: Boynton/Cook.

Briggs, L., Schunter, F., & Melvin, R. (2000-2001). In the name of the spirit. *Journal of the Assembly for Expanded Perspectives on Learning, 6,* 20-28.

Buley-Meissner, M. L., Thompson, & Tan, E. B. (2000). *The academy and the possibility of belief: Essays on intellectual and spiritual life. (Critical education and ethics).* Cresskill, NJ: Hampton.

Burke, K. (1969). *A rhetoric of motives*. Berkeley: University of California Press.

Carrette, J. R., & King, R. (2005). *Selling spirituality: The silent takeover of religion*. New York: Routledge.

Eckert, M. (n.d.). *Writing for peace in the composition classroom*. Retrieved from Journal for the Study of Peace and Conflict 1999-2000 Web site: http://jspc.library.wisc.edu/issues/1999-2000/article5.html

Elbow, P. (1993). Foreword. In M. R. O'Reilley, *The peaceable classroom* (pp. ix-xiv). Portsmouth, NH: Boynton/Cook.

Ervin, E. (2003). Rhetoricians at war and peace. In T. Enos, & K. D. Miller (Eds.), *Beyond postprocess and postmodernism: Essays on the spaciousness of rhetoric* (pp. 181-196). Mahwah, NJ: Lawrence Erlbaum.

Foehr, R. P., & Schiller, S. A. (Eds.). (1997). The spiritual side of writing. Portsmouth, NH: Boynton/Cook.

Fulkerson, R. (2005). Composition at the turn of the twenty-first century. *College Composition and Communication, 56*(4), 654-687.

Fulkerson, R. (1996). Transcending our conception of argument in light of feminist critiques. *Argumentation and Advocacy, 32*(4).

Gearhart, S. Miller. (1979). The womanization of rhetoric. *Women's Studies International Quarterly, 2*, 195-201.

Hardman, M. J. (1998). Metaphorical alternatives to violence—Report from a workshop. *Women and Language, 21*(2), 43-47.

Holmes, M. Lee. (2000). "Get real: Violence in popular culture and in English class. *English Journal, 89*(5), 104-110.

hooks, b. (1994). *Teaching to transgress: Education as the practice of freedom*. New York: Routledge.

Jonsberg, S. D. (2000). A place for every student. *English Journal, 89*(5), 27-34.

King, U. (2008). *The search for spirituality: Our global quest for a spiritual life*. New York: Bluebridge.

Kirsch, G. E. (2009). From introspection to action: Connecting spirituality and civic engagement. *College Composition and Communication, 60*(4), W1-W15.

Kroll, B. M. (2008). Arguing with adversaries: Aikido, rhetoric, and the art of peace. *College Composition and Communication, 59*(3), 451-472.

Ratcliffe, K. (2005). *Rhetorical listening: Identification, gender, whiteness. (Studies in rhetorics and feminisms)*. Carbondale: Southern Illinois University Press.

Nelson, G. L. (2000). Warriors with words: Toward a post-Columbine writing curriculum. *English Journal, 89*(5), 42-46.

Nhat Hanh, T. (1987). *Being peace*. Berkeley, CA: Parallax.

Nhat Hanh, T. (1993). *Interbeing: Fourteen guidelines for engaged Buddhism*. Berkeley, CA: Parallax.

Nhat Hanh, T. (1991). *Peace is every step: The path of mindfulness in everyday life.* New York: Bantam.

O'Reilley, M. R. (1998). *Radical presence: Teaching as contemplative practice.* Portsmouth, NH: Boynton/Cook.

O'Reilley, M. R. (2005). *The garden at night: Burnout and breakdown in the teaching life.* Portsmouth, NH: Heinemann.

O'Reilley, M. R. (1993). *The peaceable classroom.* Portsmouth, NH: Boynton/Cook.

Owens, D. (2001). Sustainable composition. In C. R. Weisser, & S. I. Dobrin (Eds.), *Ecocomposition: Theoretical and pedagogical approaches* (pp. 27-37). Albany, NY: SUNY Press.

Palmer, P. J. (1998). Foreword. (1998). In M. R. O'Reilley, *Radical presence: Teaching as contemplative practice.* Portsmouth: Boynton/Cook.

Weisser, C. R. (2001). Ecocomposition and the greening of identity. In C. R. Weisser, & S. I. Dobrin (Eds.), *Ecocomposition: Theoretical and pedagogical approaches* (pp. 81-95). Albany: SUNY Press.

THE (UN)KNOWABLE SELF AND OTHERS: CRITICAL EMPATHY AND EXPRESSIVISM

Eric Leake
Texas State University

The common rap against expressivism is that it is solipsistic, endeavoring to give clear expression to a personal voice speaking an individual truth. In this understanding of expressivism the social and constitutive qualities of language are largely ignored in favor of personal revelation. James Berlin aligns what he calls "expressionistic" rhetorics with Platonism and later also psychoanalysis and depth psychology (1987). I also align expressivism with psychology, but in this case current understandings of empathy from developmental and social psychology. I do so in order to propose an understanding of critical expressivism that builds upon critical empathy to examine personal understanding and identity within a network of social and affective connections.

Any description of expressivism can be problematic because, like current-traditional rhetoric, it is a category created to encompass a constellation of more and less disparate approaches that share some key features. As Peter Elbow notes in this volume, there are relatively few who claim to be expressivists. The label is more commonly placed on others and other approaches in a pejorative sense. The diverse nature of those approaches is recognized by Berlin, who proposes a spectrum of expressionists, with the "anarchists" of a completely uninhibited writing on one end, and on the other "the few that are close to the transactional category—especially to epistemic rhetoric" (1987, pp. 145-146). Those few include Ken Macrorie, Donald Murray, and Elbow. As Berlin describes their brand of expressivism:

> These rhetoricians see reality as arising out of the interaction of the private vision of the individual and the language used to express this vision. In other words, in this view language does not simply record the private vision, but becomes involved in shaping it. The unique inner glimpse of the individual is still primary, but language becomes an element in its nurturing. This brand of expressionistic rhetoric finally falls short of being epistemic ... because it denies the place of

> intersubjective, social processes in shaping reality. (1987, p. 146)

The role of language in this description adds a social element to what is otherwise solipsistic. Language is the "shaping" and "nurturing" element of the private vision of that deeper individual. I am not as certain as Berlin that intersubjective and social processes are not already here in the shaping function of language. Critical empathy offers a way to employ the personal to inform the intersubjective and social. Indeed, the social qualities and questioning of the personal in its assumptions and limitations is vital to the practice of critical empathy. This is what needs to be added to an expressivism as described by Berlin: more awareness and questioning of those social elements and an examination of the relationships between the personal and the social in forming that not-quite-so-private understanding of others as well as oneself.

In this chapter I use theories of perspective-taking and critical empathy to argue for a critical expressivism that moves beyond the limited personal that Berlin identified as common to expressionist rhetorics. Berlin's characterizations are useful in providing a rough map of the historical disciplinary terrain and in providing terminology for discussing topographical differences. But an updated understanding of both critical expressivism and empathy provides a more accurate mapping of the epistemological and rhetorical work of the personal. Some of these features were already inherent in the work of Elbow and others, as Berlin notes. Critical empathy makes clearer the social and affective dimensions of a working critical expressivism. It calls for a critical voice that questions the circumstances of its own speaking. A critical expressivism, rooted here again in psychology and critical empathy, offers a social critique of that otherwise personal voice, its privileges and assumptions, while recognizing that no voice is purely individual, just as no language is a language of one's own. The vital questions asked in a critical empathy concern social relations, power differences, affective connections, and commonalities and differences. Critical expressivism through critical empathy fosters a voice that speaks in order to simultaneously ask these questions. It uses knowledge of oneself—and an ongoing critique of that knowledge—to better understand and communicate with others about one another and the world.

PERCEIVING SELF AND OTHER

I begin with theories of identification and perspective-taking as a way to establish how processes of empathy are always concerned with the tensions and questions of knowing about the self and others. Personal knowledge, in this critical sense, is always more than personal. The tension between self and other in processes of empathy, and the tendency to shift between those perspectives, reminds me of F. Scott Fitzgerald's (1945/1994) notion that "the test of a first-rate intelligence is the ability to hold two opposed ideas in the mind at the same time, and still retain the ability to function" (p. 520). Processes of empathy may attempt to keep both self- and other-centered perspectives in mind at the same time. The relation of these processes, as with definitions of empathy itself, varies according to theorist. Some define empathy to include only other-oriented perspective-taking (Coplan, 2011), while others define empathy more broadly to also include self-oriented perspective-taking (Hoffman, 2001). While I align myself with the broader definition, a review of both types of identification and the tensions between them helps demonstrate how a critical empathy might productively foreground such tensions within a critical expressivist framework.

Developmental psychologist Martin Hoffman defines what he calls "self-focused role-taking" as "when people observe someone in distress [and] they may imagine how they would feel in the same situation" (2001, p. 54). For Hoffman, this involves a similarity in affective experience—essential to his definition of empathy as "an affective response more appropriate to another's situation than one's own" (2001, p. 4)—because "if they can do this vividly enough, they may experience some of the same affect experienced by the victim" (2001, p. 54). Hoffman's emphasis here is on people in distress, but the same process can apply to other situations and affective states. He offers self-focused role-taking as a way to imagine how the self would feel in the other's position. This applies one's own experiences and background, as well as the narratives and interpretations that one carries to another affective state and circumstance. The focus remains throughout on how the self would feel if the self were in that other's position. In contrast, Hoffman's "other-focused role-taking" occurs when "on learning of another's misfortune, people may focus directly on the victim and imagine how he feels; and doing this may result in their feeling something of the victim's feeling" (2001, p. 54). Hoffman allows only that one may feel "something" of another's feelings. Other-focused role-taking is much more limited and more difficult than self-focused role-taking because one can only have partial and largely imagined access to another's affective states and what another makes of those affective states. At the same time, however, other-focused perspective-taking may provide greater insight into the causes and consequences of another's affective state (Matravers, 2011). The limits of knowledge about others is also at the core of philosopher Amy Coplan's emphasis on other-oriented perspective-taking. Self-oriented perspective-taking, she argues, "leads to a type of pseudo-empathy since people often mistakenly believe that it provides them with access to the other's point of view when it does not" (2011, p. 12). It follows that "one of the benefits of drawing attention to the distinction between self-oriented and other-oriented perspective-taking is that perhaps some of us will begin to stop assuming that we 'get' the other's experience, when we do not." (Coplan, 2011, p. 12). While self-oriented perspective-taking may contribute to a stronger affective response, other-oriented perspective-taking requires more active imaginative and affective regulation and results in a stronger differentiation of an otherwise blurry boundary between affective states and knowledge among self and other. Other-focused role-taking can be less susceptible to biases, which are always a risk of empathy, and more amenable to critical processes. This is one of the benefits of a critical empathy, the acknowledgement and questioning of one's own assumptions.

The sometimes blurry and problematic nature of that boundary between self and other in identification and perspective-taking is evident in the many types of biases inherent in processes of empathy. These include egocentric biases, false empathies, and biases of proximity and familiarity. Of particular interest here is Hoffman's notion of "egoistic drift" (2001), which illustrates the slippery nature of empathy and the tendency to slide in empathy toward the more comfortable and familiar. Egoistic drift occurs when within the process of empathy one's attention begins to shift away from an other-focused perspective and more toward one's own affective experience of empathizing. The irony is that the very process of identification that drives empathy can at the same time sever empathy as the observer responds more affectively to his own memories and associated affected states, which are initiated at the observation and perspective-taking of another. Egoistic drift and associated biases demonstrate how empathic identification is constantly in flux, shifting between self and other and among memory, situation, and affect. There is the constant risk of slipping into egoistic drift or, for the sake of avoiding egoistic drift, losing the affective power and accuracy of empathy. Identifying with another is also identifying with oneself and always at risk of slipping further adrift. This is the paradox of trying to see the world of another through one's own eyes. It requires, as Martha Nussbaum argues, "a kind of 'twofold attention,' in which one both imagines what it is like to be in the sufferer's place and, at the same time, retains securely the awareness that one is not in that place" (2003, p. 328). Here again in the idea of a "twofold attention," which Nussbaum borrows from Richard Wollheim, is a reminder of Fitzgerald's notion of a first-rate intelligence as applied to rhetorics of empathy. That twofold attention is exactly the work of a critical expressivism through critical empathy. In acknowledging the implied paradox of identifying simultaneously with self and other, it asks that we see the world with twofold attention. This is an important shift, because in applying a twofold attention one is compelled to ask questions of relation and purpose that may not otherwise be so obvious or demanding. There is a sense, then, that like any paradox, that of empathic identification with self and other points through its seeming contradictions to greater insights into processes of understanding self and other in the work of critical expressivism.

THE PERSONAL AS COMMUNICATION AND BELIEF

Empathy's communicative importance is well established in the work of Carl Rogers. He argues for empathy in contrast to more competitive and judgmental moves in communication. Rogers finds the major barrier to communication to be "this tendency to react to any emotionally meaningful statement by forming an evaluation of it from our own point of view" (1961, p. 331). Without using the word "empathy" here, he proposes a communication strategy that nonetheless is very much grounded in empathy:

> Real communication occurs, and this evaluative tendency is avoided, when we listen with understanding. What does that mean? It means to see the expressed idea and attitude from the other person's point of view, to sense how it feels to him, to achieve his frame of reference in regard to the thing he is talking about. (1961, pp. 331-332)

Rogers' work on empathy is based upon the relationship between therapist and client in a clinical context. Although Rogers is not concerned with the rhetorical use of empathy—and even rejects the role of empathy in the employ of argumentation—he does offer much of use in defining empathy and its communicative and epistemological potential. Rogers focuses on empathy as an emotional perspective, as a means of understanding, and as potentially transformative in how it can change people and their interpersonal relationships. He understands empathy to be a powerful position of listening. Rogers' influence and his attention to empathy have had a significant influence in rhetorical theory. Elbow, for example, similarly offers his believing game as a positive alternative to the traditional doubting game. Elbow has come to see the believing game as the core of his work. He describes it as

> the disciplined practice of trying to be as welcoming or accepting as possible to every idea we encounter: not just listening to views different from our own and holding back from arguing with them; not just trying to restate them without bias; but actually trying to believe them. We are using believing as a tool to scrutinize and test. (2009, p. 1)

Elbow's believing game differs from Rogerian rhetoric in important ways— the reference to "not just trying to restate them without bias" (2009, p. 2) is one of those—but more importantly it includes a process of empathy. The move to not only understand other points of view but to try to believe them is at its heart an exercise in empathy; it is an attempt to enter as fully as possible into another's perspective and even another's experience of holding that perspective. Elbow recognizes that such a move has cognitive, phenomenological, emotional, and physical qualities. In an earlier draft of his contribution to this collection, he advises that one "eat like an owl," which means "just listening and swallowing and even trying to believe their (other's) experiences no matter how odd they seem." He adds that "writers should trust that their organism will automatically let go of what's useless or misleading and benefit from what's useful." The idea that writers should trust their organism is a nod to ways of thinking beyond the purely cognitive to include the emotional and physiological, as empathy pushes people to do. This is not to reduce Elbow's method to purely trusting your gut. Elbow stresses the methodical nature of the believing game as a form of critical inquiry into the value of ideas, all of which is based upon the practice of empathy in a critical expressivist framework.

Empathy occupies a central position in how we imagine and come to understand ourselves and others, and both self- and other-oriented perspective-taking rely upon some degree of personal knowledge. In self-oriented, the empathizer or observer is imagining him or herself in the position of the other and drawing from experiences and emotions analogous to the context and conditions of the observed. In other-oriented perspective-taking, the observer still must draw upon his or her own experiences in attempting to imagine the state of the observed. Philosopher Derek Matravers allows that a person may move beyond personal history to experience empathy even in regard to emotions that he or she has not previously experienced personally by empathizing "face to face with another who is experiencing some strong emotions, or describing some situation with strong emotion" (2011, p. 28). In these cases, emotions in empathy may be recalled from one's past emotions and experiences in self-oriented perspective-taking and may be experienced personally through direct engagement with the emotions of another. In either case, the personal recollection or immediate personal experience of the emotions becomes a necessary part of empathy.

As evident in Rogers, Elbow, Matravers, and elsewhere, empathy uses the personal constructively as a route to knowledge about oneself and others. This incorporation of the personal differs from that characterized as solipsistic. When Berlin describes expressivism as concerned only with self-calibrated truths, private and incommunicable to others, he may be accurately describing some types of personal writing, but seems to be lumping together the merely personal with the possibly critically so. As Elbow argues in this volume, there are many ways that writing may be personal in topic, in language, and in thought. I would add empathy or perspective-taking to Elbow's list of personal ways of thinking and writing. It is an employment of the believing game when one imagines, in self-oriented perspective-taking, "what if I were myself in that other person's situation?" Or, in other-oriented perspective-taking, "what if I were that other person in that other person's situation?" To attempt to experience and know these positions is a cognitive, affective, and bodily move toward belief, understanding, and communication. In these ways and others critical empathy is a personal mode, one that uses personal imagination, experiences, and knowledge in order to arrive at greater understanding of self, others, and society. This is a different use of the personal than inward-gazing self-discovery. And yet empathy as a personal mode remains a liability because of its inherent assumptions and biases, as illustrated in the concept of egoistic drift. This is why a critical empathy, one that questions its own understanding, is such an important component of a critical expressivism.

THE NECESSARY AND CONSTANT CRITIQUE OF EMPATHY

Although scholars in the humanities have recently seized upon empathy as perhaps best representing the hopes, values, and social purposes of a liberal arts education, empathy itself is not without useful academic skepticism and criticism. Amy Shuman calls for a critique of empathy in the circulation and telling of other people's stories. She finds liberatory possibilities via empathy in critiquing dominant narratives, even as "empathy is always open to critique as serving the interests of the empathizer rather than the empathized" (2005, p. 18). Empathy may be a way for some tellers to claim ownership, knowledge, or privilege over another's story. At the same time, Shuman notes that stories need to travel beyond their owners in order to accomplish cultural work. This is part of the paradox, Shuman writes, because: "Empathy is one of the failed promises of narrative, but in that failure, it provides the possibility of critique and counternarrative, providing whatever redemptive, emancipatory, or liberatory possibilities narrative holds" (2005, p. 19). Processes of empathy are both promise and failed promise. But just as the liabilities of empathy can prove to be a productive asset, so can the failed promise allow some redemption through the possibilities of counternarratives. The primary question that needs to be asked, as Theresa Kulbaga has argued, is "empathy to what ends?" (2008, p. 518). This gets to the rhetorical and epistemological purposes of empathy and helps raise further questions about the relationships between empathizers and the empathized. Explaining her idea of a critique of empathy, as well as the possibilities of empathy, Shuman writes

> Empathy offers the possibility of understanding across space
> and time, but it rarely changes the circumstances of those who

> suffer. If it provides inspiration, it is more often for those in the privileged position of empathizer rather than empathized. Storytelling needs a critique of empathy to remain a process of negotiating, rather than defending, meaning. The critique of empathy, and the recognition of the inevitably failed promises of storytelling, avoids an unchallenged shift in the ownership of experience and interpretation to whoever happens to be telling the story and instead insists on obligations between tellers, listeners, and the stories they borrow. (2005, p. 5)

A critique of empathy foregrounds the relationships among those who are involved with the story, its provenance, its telling, and its rhetorical and social application. Shuman's critique of empathy is also a way to guard against the erasure or removal of the other within processes of empathy. The critique of empathy is an attempt to maintain the positive social potential of empathy as a means of understanding and as a mover to action, even while guarding against the liabilities of empathy. In their criticisms of rhetorics of empathy, Kulbaga and Shuman are not discounting empathy but are arguing for a more reflective and responsible understanding and use of rhetorics of empathy.

They are not alone in pushing toward a more critical empathy. Those who advocate for some form of critical empathy do so because of how empathy functions, how it is situated socially and culturally, and how the questions of a critical empathy can themselves help us negotiate larger issues. I borrow the term "critical empathy" from Todd DeStigter, who credits the idea to Jay Robinson. Critical empathy, as DeStigter defines it

> refers to the process of establishing informed and affective connections with other human beings, of thinking and feeling with them at some emotionally, intellectually, and socially significant level, while always remembering that such connections are complicated by sociohistorical forces that hinder the equitable, just relationships that we presumably seek. (1999, p. 240)

DeStigter's definition is notable for being both hopeful and realistic. He, like Shuman, is proposing a form of critical empathy that seeks to fulfill the promise of more just relationships while maintaining awareness of the severe limitations and complications that are always part of that empathic seeking. DeStigter's critical empathy is of additional value because it focuses upon the context of empathy as always situated within sociohistorical forces, just as critical expressivism should always recognize an already social self. This brings attention to the circumstances that inform and limit rhetorics of empathy and the differences in social positions among those involved.

DeStigter defines empathy as a way of thinking and feeling, which is in line with how Nussbaum as well as many psychologists, including Hoffman, define empathy. Such definitions of empathy align with a contemporary understanding of empathy from cognitive neuroscience as including processes of both mirroring (purely affective) and imaginative reconstruction (directed cognitive) (Goldman, 2011). In a similar way, Kristie Fleckenstein argues that the thinking and feeling aspects of empathy uniquely situate empathy for reflective and rhetorical work. Fleckenstein writes, "As a complicated mixture of affect and rationality, empathy lends itself to deliberative discourse—to negotiation, debate, and persuasion—in the public sphere and serves as the foundation for social justice" (2007, p. 707). Fleckenstein is responding here to Matthew Newcomb's essay on compassion in the rhetoric of Hannah Arendt, who defines compassion as purely affective and as creating silences and impeding discourse. Newcomb argues against Arendt that a "Critical compassion can note the issues of appropriating the stories of others and question the need to actually feel like the other" (2007, p. 128). Fleckenstein supports this position in her argument for empathy as already involving thinking; we do not have to rely upon a critical compassion in order to open that rhetorical and evaluative space in empathy. She cites ideas of "realistic empathy" and "critical affirmation" as illustrating the feeling and thinking elements of empathy and the critical roles empathy plays in deliberative discourse. As Fleckenstein writes, "Whether we call it empathy, compassion, realistic empathy, critical affirmation, or critical empathy, the experience of sharing another's suffering is essential to deliberative discourse, to negotiation, and to persuasion in the public sphere" (2007, p. 714). Critical expressivism would be in good company here. A definition of critical empathy such as provided by Fleckenstein better allows one to acknowledge the interplay and tensions that always exist in thinking and feeling with others and the ways those may be used to arrive at judgments and actions.

Employing critical empathy also enables one to better question and acknowledge differences in economic, political, social, and cultural positions. These are elements of the "complicated sociohistorical forces" that DeStigter mentions. Among the greatest liabilities of processes of empathy is how it can enable the elision of these differences as one individual empathizes with another. Kulbaga already has pointed to this problem in rhetorics of empathy in the case of relatively more privileged Western readers enjoying identification with less privileged others without also reflecting upon the significant differences in experiences and positions. Min-Zhan Lu proposes "critical affirmation," a term she borrows from Cornel West, as a form of literacy in which reading and writing are employed for the following goals:

(1) To end oppression rather than to empower a particular

> form of self, group, or culture; (2) To grapple with one's privileges as well as one's experience of exclusion; (3) To approach more respectfully and responsibly those histories and experiences which appear different from what one calls one's own; and (4) To affirm a yearning for individual agency shared by individuals across social divisions without losing sight of the different material circumstances which shape this shared yearning and the different circumstances against which each of us must struggle when enacting such a yearning. (1999, p. 173)

Lu proposes these critical affirmation practices in response to how the personal is abused politically. Hers is a reflective approach that allows acknowledgment and revision of one's own affective responses. Critical affirmation is affirmative, hopeful, and politically progressive in the ways in which it allows the building of coalitions based upon the shared yearning for individual agency. And, crucially, Lu's critical affirmation is critical because it is always keeping affirmation—or empathy—from overreaching by foregrounding historical, material, and situational differences. Critical affirmation is most applicable to how we read and write one another's stories, which serve as our sites for empathy and as exercises in critical expressivism. Perhaps it is most critical in how we read and write our own stories. As Lu writes, "I join others to mark writing, especially personal narratives, as a site for reflecting on and revising one's sense of self, one's relations with others, and the conditions of one's life" (1999, p. 173). Lu is arguing for critical affirmation as literate and rhetorical practices that bring one's life and relationships continually into reflection and potential revision. This reads to me as the best possible critical expressivist work, similar to that proposed in this collection by Nancy Mack in her idea of the "critical memoir." I add to these practices rhetorical questions, posed by Kulbaga and Shuman, best represented by the question of empathy to what ends? Likewise, we might ask in the practice of critical expressivism, expressivism to what ends? By foregrounding questions of social positions, differences, and the ends of empathy, a critical empathy guards against risks of appropriating the experiences of others, especially to validate or serve one's own interests.

The tensions in empathy and expressivism require critical practice because of the inherent instability of any moves to empathy or understanding and expression of self. Critical practices necessitate questions about the limits of knowledge and differences in experiences and situations; how empathy and personal writing, often in the form of stories, are positioned, how they function, and what their results are; how emotions, reflections, and evaluations interact; and what the personal and social effects of these processes are. These are fundamentally epistemological and rhetorical questions that deal with our relations to one another. Because critical empathy demands such questions, these inherent liabilities can be seen as an asset. Critical empathy and critical expressivism push us to ask the questions that we already should be asking. I draw here from the argument of Dennis Lynch, who contends that the necessary move to a critical reflection is among the best reasons to return to the study of rhetorics of empathy. As Lynch writes, "I do not wish to treat empathy as the master concept of rhetoric, nor will I defend empathy against the serious questions that have been raised about it as a practice. I will argue instead that empathy is rhetorically productive not in spite of but because of the dangers to which it is prone" (1998, p. 7). Those dangers push us toward employing a critical empathy that in turns requires us to be more reflective generally of personal questions of epistemology, differences, and relations. A critical empathy continually reminds us that any knowledge of self and others is always at best a careful and purposeful approximation of perspectives, situations, and experiences through the lens of the self.

REFERENCES

Berlin, J. (1987). *Rhetoric and reality: Writing instruction in American colleges, 1900-1985*. Carbondale, IL: Southern Illinois University Press.

Coplan, A. (2011). Understanding empathy: Its features and effects. In A. Coplan, & P. Goldie (Eds.), *Empathy: Philosophical and psychological perspectives* (pp. 3-18). New York: Oxford University Press.

DeStigter, T. (1999). Public displays of affection: Political community through critical empathy. *Research in the Teaching of English, 33*, 235-244.

Elbow, P (2009). The believing game ormethodological believing. *The Selected Works of Peter Elbow*. Retrieved from http://works.bepress.com/peter_elbow/41/

Fitzgerald, F. S. (1994). The crack-up. In P. Lopate (Ed.), *The art of the personal essay* (pp. 520-532). New York: Anchor. (Original work published 1945)

Fleckenstein, K. (2007). Once again with feeling: Empathy in deliberative discourse. *JAC, 27*(3/4), 701-716.

Goldman, A. I. (2011). Two routes to empathy: Insights from cognitive neuroscience. In A. Coplan & P. Goldie (Eds.), *Empathy: Philosophical and psychological perspectives* (pp. 31-44). New York: Oxford University Press.

Hoffman, M. L. (2001). *Empathy and moral development: Implications for caring and justice*. New York: Cambridge University Press.

Kulbaga, T. A. (2008). Pleasurable pedagogies: Reading Lolita in Tehran and the rhetoric of empathy. *College English, 70*(5), 506-21.

Lu, M.-Z. (1999). Redefining the literate self: The politics of critical affirmation. *College Composition and Communication, 51*(2), 172-194.

Lynch, D. A. (1998). Rhetorics of proximity: Empathy in Temple Grandin and Cornel West. *Rhetoric Society Quarterly, 28*(1), 5-23.

Matravers, D. (2011). Empathy as a route to knowledge. In A. Coplan, & P. Goldie (Eds.), *Empathy: Philosophical and psychological perspectives* (19-30). New York: Oxford University Press.

Newcomb, M. (2007). Totalized compassion: The (im)possibilities for acting out of compassion and the rhetoric of Hannah Arendt. *JAC, 27*(1/2), 105-133.

Nussbaum, M. (2003). *Upheavals of thought: The intelligence of emotions.* New York: Cambridge University Press.

Rogers, C. (1961). *On becoming a person.* New York: Houghton Mifflin.

Shuman, A. (2005). *Other people's stories: Entitlement caims and the critique of empathy.* Champaign, IL: University of Illinois Press.

SECTION 3: HISTORIES

JOHN WATSON IS TO INTROSPECTIONISM AS JAMES BERLIN IS TO EXPRESSIVISM (AND OTHER ANALOGIES YOU WON'T FIND ON THE SAT)

Maja Wilson

I was in the Yale archives for the first time, reading the correspondence of early behaviorists John B. Watson and Robert M. Yerkes, and I couldn't stop sneezing. A venerable looking scholar next to me, inspecting ancient manuscripts with a magnifying glass, moved to the back of the room. Apparently, I was allergic to history.

My very present problems had brought me to the archives: as a high school teacher, I had felt oppressed by the system of high stakes standardized testing mandated by No Child Left Behind (NCLB). The stated intent of NCLB was to promote equity, but the effects of testing seemed to be quite the opposite. Despite the modern rhetoric of equity associated with testing, I wondered if the original intent behind the creation of standardized tests foreshadowed the disastrous effects I saw playing out in schools.

I knew that the first large scale standardized test in the United States—the Army Alpha Test (AAT)—had been created by eugenicists and used to promote their causes. Robert M. Yerkes, an avowed eugenicist, had helped create and administer the AAT during both World Wars. His assistant, Carl Brigham, published *A Study of American Intelligence* in 1923, in which he argued for "selective breeding" to preserve the integrity of the "Nordic race." The AAT had revealed, according to Brigham, that southern and eastern Europeans had scored lowest on the test.

Brigham's book fueled growing anti-immigrant sentiment in the United States, and was used by Harry Laughlin, appointed by a House committee as an "expert eugenics agent," to propose and pass the Immigration Restriction Act of 1924, which targeted eastern and southern Europeans. While Brigham renounced his position in the 1930s, he helped to transform the AAT into the Scholastic Aptitude Test (SAT).

The troubling origins of standardized testing were well known. I was at the Yale archives because I suspected there was more dirt to be dug up. I had a hunch: Besides creating inequity, it seemed to me that standardized tests were oblivious to (or disrespectful of) the experience of teachers and students. I had seen that dismissal of teachers' experience in the rationale for the "research-based" educational agenda that went along with the tests (see Institution of Education Sciences) and I wondered if I would see evidence of this dismissal of individual experience in Yerkes' theoretical orientation toward his work.

There were over 200 boxes of Yerkes' papers, manuscripts, and notes, so I thought I'd look first in the correspondence between Yerkes and his friend and colleague Robert B. Watson, the father of behaviorism. In my view, Watson's work with infants couldn't have been undertaken if he took infants' experiences seriously.

Watson was famous for his research on primates but also for his popular child-rearing book, *The Psychological Care of Infant and Child*, in which he argued that, "mother love is a dangerous instrument" (1928, p. 87). The book, written in 1928 "with the assistance" of his wife, Rosalie (she was not given a proper byline), was based on Watson's infant experiments. Watson was interested, among other things, in knowing if he could condition fear in infants. He systematically conditioned his young test subject, an eight-month-old boy ("Little Albert") naturally unafraid of any animal, to be afraid of a fuzzy bunny, and, by association, a fur muff and a furry-faced Santa Claus (1928, pp. 23-30). He proudly presented this research in *The Psychological Care of Infant and Child* as proof that parents (and, specifically, mothers) are to blame for children's fears, laziness, and neurosis; furthermore, in Watson's estimation, no parent knows how to be a good parent, and his work in behaviorism was the answer.

How could Watson live with himself as he systematically instilled fear in Little Albert? Was this simply the case of a researcher's natural enthusiasm in the days before International Review Boards? Or was there something particular about Watson's mindset, assumptions, or theoretical orientation that engendered callousness? Had Watson spoken of these experiments to Yerkes? Did Yerkes share Watson's mindset or assumptions? I felt that Yerkes, imposing standardized testing on hundreds of thousands of soldiers and then generations of schoolchildren, was somehow akin to Watson, instilling fear in a baby—at least in the sense that I suspected each man of a certain blindness to his test subjects' experiences.

As I paged through letter after letter, I found myself slipping—like a traumatized infant myself—into the world of early twentieth century American psychology, a world of artifacts and conversations that bewildered me: descriptions of rat mazes; blueprints for a stimulus boxes large enough for dogs and monkeys

(Letter to Robert Yerkes, October 17, 1912); Watson's description of his experimental work with babies (Letter to Robert Yerkes, October 12, 1916); Yerkes' repeated attempts to get Watson to leave the advertising work he did at J. Walter Thompson Company in the 30's and return to the laboratory; Watson's request in 1919 for Yerkes to send three hundred blank Army Alpha test booklets and blanks to The Gilman School, at which his youngest son was a student (Letter to Robert Yerkes, March 29, 1919); Watson's objection to Yerkes' use of the multiple choice test in his primate research (Letter to Robert Yerkes, May 12, 1916); and a debate about the battle between the behaviorists and introspectionists (Watson, J., Letters to Robert Yerkes, April 7, 1913; October 27, 1915; November 1, 1915; October 24, 1916). I suspected that my sneezes weren't just a physiological reaction to the dusty pages I was leafing through, but a fear of becoming lost in this historical rat maze.

I knew nothing of primate research, nothing of introspectionism, and I was beginning to forget why I had come to the archives in the first place. Finally, it was Watson's mention of Edward Titchener that reoriented me. But instead of returning me to the problems that had sent me to the archives in the first place,[1] Watson's full-fledged behavioristic ire at Titchener and the introspectionists led me to a problem that had plagued me as a student of composition studies: James Berlin's full-fledged social epistemic ire at Peter Elbow and the "expressionists."

JOHN B. WATSON'S BATTLE AGAINST TITCHENER AND INTROSPECTIONISM

I first caught on to Watson's battle against Titchener in a letter from Watson to Yerkes in 1916. In this letter, Watson refers to a slight disagreement he is having with Yerkes regarding the future of behaviorism. Watson summarizes Yerkes' position: that psychology should continue on its current track, as defined by Titchener and the introspectionists, and Yerkes and Watson's shared interest in behavior should be absorbed into physiology or biology. Watson strenuously objects to this separation, asserting his unwillingness to leave psychology in Titchener's hands.

To understand these disagreements—between Watson and Yerkes and between Watson and Titchener—I needed to understand Titchener's view of psychology, which had preceded Watson's. I turned to Titchener's 1898 *A Primer of Psychology*, which begins with a definition of psychology.

> The Meaning of 'Psychology.'—The word 'psychology' comes from the two Greek words psyche, 'mind,' and logos, 'word.'

> Psychology therefore means, by derivation, 'words' or 'talk about mind.' (1898, p. 1)

Titchener defined mind not as an object inside the body that either holds or does things to thoughts and feelings, but as "the sum" (1898, p. 5) of thoughts and feelings. In Titchener's view, "we must not say that mind 'has' thoughts and feelings; but that mind is thoughts and feelings" (1898, p. 6). If mind is thoughts and feelings, not an object, then the only way to study mind, the only method of the psychologist, is to look inward and talk about thoughts and feelings—introspection. To Titchener, then, psychology's subject was mind and its method was introspection.

The method of introspection had been used by Titchener's teacher, the German philosopher Willhelm Wundt, who had had created one of the world's first psychology laboratories in 1879. Because Titchener himself was interested in distinguishing psychology from philosophy and from the work of his teacher, he went to great lengths to make introspection an objective process that took several years of training: "only by looking inward can we gain knowledge of mental processes; only by looking inward under standard conditions can we make our knowledge scientific" (1898, p. 32).

But introspective psychology still depended on an individual's description of his private experience, an admittedly subjective basis for a field that Titchener claimed should be more objective and scientific. Titchener's approach to this problem began with implementing rigorous training for each introspector—he called them "Observers"—consisting of a series of standardized introspection exercises: For example, observers in training were instructed to describe what they experienced when listening to certain tones or when exposed to various lights. Titchener invented several instruments for standardizing these exercises himself, including a "sound cage," a mesh of wires surrounding the head connected to a telephone receiver designed to give each Observer practice in pinpointing the exact location of an auditory stimuli. In *Class Experiments and Demonstration Apparatus*, Titchener proposed a standard set of instruments for all psychology classrooms:

> whenever possible, we should call on the class to do psychology for themselves. The demonstration apparatus which I have in mind are, then, apparatus which shall subserve this latter purpose: apparatus that shall standardise the conditions for such introspections as the lecture-room and the lecture-hour allow. (1903, p. 440)

Titchener considered Observers themselves to be highly trained scientific instruments, and he bemoaned psychology's great disadvantage in its ability to share results and instruments across space and time. In the external sciences, scientists could easily ship specimens and the conclusions of their experiments to other interested scientists. But to facilitate the sharing of results and specimens in psychology, the inner science, Observers themselves would have to be shipped at great expense and inconvenience (1909, p. 278).

Still, the knowledge gained by Titchener's Observers was not scientific, objective, or standard enough for John Watson. Other philosophers and psychologists had critiqued Titchener's methods and aims—including the philosopher John Dewey, under whom Watson had studied at the University of Chicago at the turn of the century—but on far different grounds than Watson would. In his 1891 textbook, *Psychology*, Dewey outlined a transactional objection to introspection:

> When introspective analysis begins, the anger ceases. It is well understood that external observation is not a passive process ... We shall see hereafter that there is no such thing as pure observation in the sense of a fact being known without assimilation and interpretation through ideas, already in the mind. This is as true of the observation of the facts of consciousness as of perceiving physical facts. (1891, pp. 8-9)

Dewey took no issue with introspection as a psychological method, but simply pointed out that observation is never objective. Watson, however, claimed to find Dewey's ideas altogether incomprehensible, proclaiming in 1936 that, "'I never knew what he was talking about then, and unfortunately for me, I still don't know'" (Watson, quotedin Cheney & Pierce, 2004, p. 14). We can imagine Watson pausing and winking at his audience—unfortunately for me. After living with almost a century's accumulation of behaviorist influence in everything from advertising to educational policy, we can, of course, wink back—unfortunately for us.

Dewey's colleague, the psychologist William James, also took issue with some of Titchener's ideas. He didn't discredit introspection as an appropriate method for accumulating psychological knowledge, but he disagreed with Titchener's assumption that mind was composed of elementary mental processes and that the goal of introspection was to discover and describe them. In "On Some Omissions of Introspective Psychology," James objects to "mental atomism," which he refers to here as "the traditional psychology":

> The traditional psychology talks like one who should say a river consists of nothing but pailsful, spoonsful, quartpotsful, barrelsful and other moulded forms of water. Even were the pails and pots all actually standing in the stream, still between

> them the free water would continue to flow. It is just this free water of consciousness that psychologists resolutely overlook. Every definite image in the mind is steeped and dyed in the free water that flows around it. With it goes the sense of its relations, near and remote, the dying echo of whence it came to us, the dawning sense of whither it is to lead. (1884, pp. 16-17)

But Watson wasn't interested in Dewey's inherently subjective observations or James' "free water of consciousness." While James' objection to Titchener's mental atomism led to a conception of experience that influenced Husserl and other phenomenologists (Schuetz, 1941, p. 442), Watson's objections would extend to the very concept of consciousness itself—along with purpose, value, and meaning.

Watson had come to believe that mind or consciousness was a religious, medieval construct, unworthy of scientific inquiry. In a private disagreement about the topic with Watson in 1915, Yerkes suggests that perhaps "there should be encouragement given those who are willing to make use of it [introspectionism]" even as they continued their own behaviorist project. Watson counters two days later with what at first seems like a mild, conciliatory reply, suggesting that the two men, in fact, disagreed about very little (Letter to Robert Yerkes, November 1, 1915). But, as Watson points out in his next breath, the small area of disagreement that remains is actually the crux of the matter: introspection depends on the concept of consciousness, which is no more a scientific concept than the soul.

In other words, Watson didn't just disagree with the method of introspection, but with the very construct on which the method was based—consciousness itself. He thought it best to leave the soul and its secular counterpoint, consciousness, to religion; if philosophy wanted to take it up, then psychology must separate wholly from philosophy and study behavior alone. In fact, "religion," along with "mediaeval tradition" and "philosophy," headed the list of insults that Watson was most likely to employ in putting down Titchener and his introspective philosophy. Consider how he uses these terms in the opening four sentences of *Psychology from the Standpoint of the Behaviorist*, published nine years after Watson's small disagreement with Yerkes:

> Mediaeval Tradition Has Kept Psychology From Becoming a Science.—Psychology, up to very recent times, has been held so rigidly under the dominance both of traditional religion and of philosophy—the two great bulwarks of mediaevalism—that it has never been able to free itself and become a

natural science. Chemistry and physics have freed themselves. Zoology and physiology are now in the process of becoming emancipated. (1924b, p. 1)

In the following six pages of the book, Watson characterizes psychology's concern with mind and consciousness with these phrases:

The Old Psychology of Mind and Consciousness

... deistic idol already fashioned and worshipped (vii) ... crude dualism ... theological mysticism ... mediaeval tradition ... religion ... philosophy ... mediaevalism ... soul ... so-called states of consciousness ... phenomena of spiritualism ... not objectively verifiable ... no community of data ... mental curiosities ... introspection ... serious bar to progress ... failed to become a science ... deplorably failed ... it would not bury its past ... hang onto tradition ... will not bury their 'medicine men' ... subjective subject matter ... (1898, pp. vii-3)

For all of his emphasis on objectivity, Watson presented his own ideas in an emotionally charged narrative. In Watson's story, psychological medicine men such as Titchener had been sacrificing science and truth on the altar of mediaeval philosophers. His stimulus-response experiments would arm psychologists with objectively verifiable data that would bury these psychological medicine men, emancipating psychology once and for all. Freed from the hocus pocus of mind and consciousness, Watson would help Man—including the military, parents, advertisers, and teachers—finally get control of his actions. (Or, rather, the actions of others.)

For those who cut their teeth on Freudian psychology, it might be tempting to note here that Watson had chafed under the rearing of a strict fundamentalist mother who expected him to become a southern Baptist minister (Buckley, 1989, p. 5). We might see his string of associations—from mind ("a concept as unscientific as the soul") to religion (a "serious bar to progress") to mother love ("a dangerous instrument")—and understand his disposal of the first two as his own attempt to "become emancipated" from his mother. But that would be to put Watson on Freud's couch, a place he would never voluntarily lay his own head (not to be confused with his mind!).

Instead, Watson's definition of psychology—its subject, its methods, and its goals—is inextricable from his rejection of Titchener's. In the first lines of the article in Psychological Review (which would later be referred to as the Behaviorist Manifesto) Watson sets his definition directly in opposition to Titchener's:

> Psychology as the behaviorist views it is a purely objective experimental branch of natural science. Its theoretical goal is the prediction and control of behavior. Introspection forms no essential part of its methods ... the behaviorist ... recognizes no dividing line between man and brute. The behavior of man, with all of its refinement and complexity, forms only a part of the behaviorists' total scheme of investigation. (1913, p. 158)

Everything about Titchner's psychology is dismissed here in one fell paragraph: introspection has no place; behavior is all that matters; and since both man and beast exhibit behavior, the study of animal behavior belongs with the study of human behavior.

To psychologists who believed in the study of mind or consciousness, two major assumptions made the study of animals irrelevant to the study of humans. First, animal mind or consciousness, if it existed at all, was too different from human consciousness to be of use. Second, introspection was the only method of studying mind; introspection involved speaking or writing, and animals couldn't speak or write. (They could, however, as Yerkes would try to prove, take multiple-choice tests!) But in rejecting consciousness, Watson disposes of the first major assumption separating human and animal study. In rejecting introspection as a method, he disposes of the second: animals (or humans, for that matter!) need not talk at all to be of interest to psychologists, who should only be concerned with behavior.

In redirecting psychology's gaze from mind to behavior, Watson didn't just open the door to animal studies—which is why he met Yerkes, who studied primates—but he also redefined psychology's application and goals. In Titchener's psychology, an understanding of an individual's thoughts and feelings had a crucial role to play in ethics, and he went so far as to assert, "Psychology is the foundation of ethics" (1898, p. 296). Titchener saw ethics as general laws that must be determined from the particular "facts of life" (1898, p. 296). He recognized that these facts of life are different in different societies, not to mention different for different individuals, so ethics must be sensitive to these differences. One way to assure such sensitivity was to use the insights of psychology—drawn from the experience of individuals—as an ethical check on the laws of ethics.

The same concern for individual differences in relation to generalizable laws is evident in Titchener's discussion of the application of psychology to pedagogy:

> The problem of pedagogy is to lay down rules or norms of education ... the abstract "child" of psychology does not exist for education, not "the child," but real children, Katie Jones and Tommy Smith. Psychology cannot deal with Jones-ness

and Smith-ness, but only with child-ness. Science, indeed, can
never be "applied" offhand. (1898, pp. 298-299)

While Titchener acknowledged that psychology is a science that generalizes, the method of his science—the description of an individual's thoughts or feelings—led to his concern for the interaction of generalizations and individual experience. In other words, a science that made experience its special province had a special interest in how the application of that science affected individual experience.

The reverse was true in Watson's science: a psychology that dismisses mind, thoughts, feelings, and consciousness as central constructs showed little interest in the effects of its application on individual (human) experience. Watson's views on the application of psychology to education show none of the caution and respect for individual experience we see in Titchner's discussion of "Smith-ness" and "Jones-ness." To Watson, learning was a change in behavior in response to a stimulus, a process that is the same for Katie Jones as it would be for John Smith as it would be for a rat. Later, B. F. Skinner would take Watson's position on the connection between rats and humans even further, leading Arthur Koestler to write in 1964 that, "for the anthropomorphic view of the rat, American psychology has substituted the rattomorphic view of man" (pp. 560).

Without an introspectionist's grounding in the experience of the individual, Watson had no qualms about proclaiming the goal and application of psychology as the "control of behavior," which very quickly came to mean, in practice, the control of individuals. While early critics of behaviorism attacked Watson's lack of attention to states of mind or consciousness on moral grounds, they perhaps underestimated the potential power of behaviorism to do what Watson says it would: to control behavior.

In 1929, Watson and William MacDougall, a British psychologist, published their debate about behaviorism in *The Battle of Behaviorism*. MacDougall wasn't opposed to behavioral studies: As he reminded Watson at the outset of their debate, MacDougall himself had been calling for psychologists to attend to behavior a full ten years before Watson began his first behavioral studies of infants. In fact, MacDougall called himself "The Arch-Behaviorist." But MacDougall objected to Watson's focus on behavior to the exclusion of concepts such as "'incentive,' 'motive,' 'purpose,' 'intention,' 'goal,' 'desire,' 'valuing,' 'striving,' 'willing,' 'hoping,' and 'responsibility'" (1929, p. 69). He worried about the effects of a psychology that ignored such terms:

> I submit to you the proposition that any psychology which
> accepts this mechanistic dogma and shapes itself accordingly
> is useless, save for certain very limited purposes, because it

is incapable of recognizing and of taking into account of the most fundamental facts of human behavior ... If all men believed the teaching of the mechanical psychology (and only beliefs that govern action are real beliefs) no man would raise a finger in the effort to prevent war, to achieve peace or to realize any other idea. So I say that the mechanical psychology is useless and far worse than useless; it is paralyzing to human effort. (1929, pp. 69-72)

On one level, MacDougall was strikingly wrong: the application of behaviorism (the control of behavior through the use of conditioning was immediate and widespread. On another level he was strikingly right: behaviorism was most famously used to not to further individual human interests, but to control individual humans in the interests of political and economic power.

The application of behaviorism for the purpose of controlling individuals to further the interests of political and economic power played out most distressingly through Yerkes' involvement in the war effort and Watson's involvement in advertising.

In April of 1918, Yerkes was called to an "Informal Conference on Morale" with the Assistant Secretary of War and the Chief of Intelligence to apply the work of psychology in creating a "systematic plan for stimulating and sustaining morale of troops" (Report of Informal Conference on Morale, 1918). It is worth noting that, in general contemporary usage, morale connotes a happy (or unhappy) individual emotional state. But in the first half of the twentieth century, the military definition of morale emphasized collective action (behavior): "the psychological forces within a combat group that compel its members to get into the fight" (Grinker & Spiegel, quoted in Manning, 1994). In this formulation, "psychological forces" may or may not have anything to do with emotions, much less happiness. What matters is group behavior: if the group is compelled to action, its morale, by definition is high. If it hesitates or refuses to get into the fight, its morale is low.

Of course, as MacDougall might point out, the experience of the soldier whose morale is in question matters greatly. MacDougall had treated victims of "shell shock" in the British army during World War I. Unlike some of his colleagues who used "disciplinary" treatments, which were "behavioural"—"electric shocks, shouted commands, isolation and restricted diet"—MacDougall's treatments followed "psychotherapeutic lines," emphasizing recalling the traumatic experience and discovering its individual meaning to the patient (Howorth, 2000, p. 226). This treatment wouldn't just help the soldier get "back into the fight," but would also help society figure out if the war is worth its experiential and psychological toll. But that toll—for instance, the years of depression, anxiety, and nightmares that my grandfather suffered after serving in WWII—would mean nothing in the behaviorist's schema of morale, since my grandfather was able to "get back into the fight" shortly following several injuries and a Purple Heart.

Yerkes' behaviorist influence on the American military's discussion of morale could be seen a month after the first meeting of the Conference on Morale when the group met a second time. The title of the group changed slightly: "Conference on *Control* of Morale" (emphasis added). Yerkes' report on the "Scope of the Problem," frames the problem in behaviorist terms, citing a "great variety and complications of *conditions* affecting morale" (emphasis added), asserting that "the problems are in the main those of human behavior" and so the appropriate person to study such problems is one "who has the ability alike to *predict* reactions and to properly relate methods of *control* to military requirements and needs" (emphasis added). In other words, Yerkes framed the problem of morale as a behavioral one, offering the behaviorist psychologist as its solution.

The group consciously drew on the German system of propaganda as a model for their recommendations, viewing morale as a lifelong process of patriotic conditioning. Approvingly reporting the Germans' use of school as a tool of propaganda and their use of "furloughs and rewards" (positive reinforcements) with soldiers, the group began to plot a comprehensive system to control of morale from the ground up. Yerkes credited his work with this group, and the multiple-choice test he devised to sort and reward recruits with promotion, with helping to win the war (Gould, 1981, p. 224).

Yerkes' application of behaviorism to the military may have helped to win the war, but MacDougall implied that "human effort" would involve the effort to end war. Even if the majority agrees that the war is a good cause, the experiences of those actually participating in the war cannot be dismissed unless, as Watson's behaviorists held, their behavior is all that matters. If it can actually be attributed to him, Yerkes' success in controlling soldiers' morale by focusing solely on their behavior and the conditions shaping that behavior likely confirmed MacDougall's fear: behaviorism at the expense of mind and consciousness is paralyzing to human effort.

Ten years later, Watson would leave the imprint of behavioral psychology on advertising (and generations of consumers) through his work for the J. Walter Thompson Company. In *Mechanical Man: John Broadus Watson and the Beginnings of Behaviorism*, Kerry Buckley argues that before 1910, advertisements emphasized rational appeals to consumers (1989, p. 138). Watson used his behaviorist techniques to condition consumers to associate products with emotions:

> Advertisers, [Watson] cautioned, must always keep in mind that they are selling "more than a product." There are "idea[s]

> to sell—prestige to sell—economy to sell ... It is never so much as dry, solid, or liquid matter" ... in one carefully controlled experiment funded by the J. Walter Thompson agency, Watson found that smokers with definite brand preferences could not distinguish one brand of cigarettes from another. This reinforced Watson's conviction that the marketing of goods depended not on an appeal to reason but upon the stimulation of desire. (139-41)

Watson's large-scale experimental test on consumers (i.e. advertising campaigns) was just an extension of his test on eight-month old "Little Albert." Just as he conditioned Albert to associate the rabbit with a loud noise, Watson encouraged advertisers to condition consumers to associate the product with prestige and love, or to associate the lack of a product with fear and rage. While Watson claimed to have been capable of reconditioning Little Albert back to a state of fearlessness (his mother removed him from the study before he could do so), there would be no attempt to "recondition" the public back to their senses. The application of behaviorism to advertising, which took place after MacDougall's debate with Watson, would confirm MacDougall's fears that the application of behaviorism would be useless in terms of serving "human purposes."

THE RESEARCHER PAUSES TO DAYDREAM ...

Several battles had indeed been fought in those archived letters and texts, and the corpses of human purpose, mind, and consciousness littered the dusty pages. It was a heartbreaking spectacle to witness, and my vantage point of nearly a century didn't make it much easier to bear. I began seeing the behaviorists' initials on everything about my life I felt to be lonely or controlling. Standardized tests? R. M. Yerkes. Consumer culture? J. B. Watson. Computer grading programs? R.M.Yerkes + J.B.Watson 4-Ever.

Though I had found some of Titchner's work amusing, and agreed with Dewey's point that introspection changed the emotional state under observation, I felt a kinship with the introspectionists. I mourned the loss of Titchner's respect for "Smith-ness" and "Jones-ness" and the influence of behavioristic systems of standardized testing and educational research that had come to shape schools. I had a new explanation for my sense of alienation as a teacher; I had descended from the losers of Watson's war.

A lost cause always drives me to desperate mental (if not behavioral) measures. I imagined calling for a National Day of Introspection. Individuals all over the country would stand up and introspect—rising from wheelchairs in nursing homes, climbing on top of desks in schoolrooms, walking out of cubicles in office buildings, stepping from cars in the rat maze of suburban sprawl—all of us standing to boldly speaking the sum of our thoughts and feelings, our consciousness, our mind. The fact that no one would listen would be irrelevant. We would be rising from the carnage, asserting that Watson had won the battle but not the war, that we would not be controlled, that mind mattered.

I knew the image teetered on the edge of insanity, but it made me feel better, so I let it linger. I was looking around me, wondering if the gentleman at the table next to me, texting with one hand and tapping the mouse of his computer with the other hand, would be willing to introspect as a subversive act. I suspected not. Who would join me? I ran through my list of family and friends. As a graduate student, I had so few friends left that I skipped directly to leading figures in the field of composition studies I'd been living with for the past years. Peter Elbow? Definitely. Donald Murray? To be sure. Jane Emig? Hell, yeah! James Berlin? Pshaw. Never in a million years.

That's when it hit me—my thesis, the result of my hours of scholarly research: James Berlin was a behaviorist. James Berlin was a behaviorist? The words were so entirely absurd that they couldn't possibly have come from me. They must have infected me from without, and the only way to rid myself of them was to figure out what they meant. It was either that, or start embroidering National Day of Introspection t-shirts.

THE "EXPRESSIONISTS" AS INTROSPECTIONISTS

I was proceeding with a working thesis—James Berlin was a behaviorist—which I almost completely rejected. Without a doubt, James Berlin would have shared Professor MacDougall's distress at the exercise of power at the expense of human interest. Ira Shor's pedagogy, which Berlin admiringly describes in "Rhetoric and Ideology in the Writing Class" (1988), is based in a rejection of the consumerist culture that Watson helped create through his work in advertising. Berlin's work is suffused with an ethical sensibility completely lacking from Watson's.

Still, something felt true about my fantastical thesis. I backed up to the most reasonable image in my research-induced fantasy: the picture of Elbow, Murray, and Emig, publicly and subversively introspecting with me. This part of my daydream proved both simple and supportable: Elbow, Murray, and Emig were, in some important way, like Titchener. The comparison held up when I placed a passage from Titchener's psychologoy textbook next to a passage from Murray's 1970 article, "The Interior View: One Writer's View of Composition":

> A mental process is a process which can form part of the experience of one
>
> person only ... Not only does the mental process go on inside of you, it is so entirely inside of you that you are the only person who can ever get at it and observe it. (Titchener, 1989, pp. 9-10)

And,

> At the moment of writing the writer has a fundamental aloneness ... I have found that at the center of the process I am alone with the blank page, struggling to discover what I know so that I can know what to say" (Murray, 1970, p. 22)

Each man put the experiences of an individual at the center of his work. In fact, as I re-examined the works of Murray and Elbow, I realized that they, along with other leaders of the writing process movement, had built an entire theory and practice around introspection—their own, and their students'.

The fact that Murray, a columnist for the Boston Globe, would write about his writing in 1970 was not entirely remarkable. Writers had written about their experiences of writing long before he did, and his published work is peppered with their insights: in The Interior View alone, Murray quotes no less than 10 authors who write about their writing, including Goethe, Spender, and William Carlos Williams. What was remarkable, perhaps, was that Murray was not just writing as a writer, but as a writing teacher, and he was beginning to construct a theory of how we compose and how we could teach composition from his introspection and the collected introspection of generations of great writers.

Surely, as Tom Newkirk points out, some of the practices Murray advocated—conferencing, regular discussion of student writing, daily writing—had been practiced by Barrett Wendell in the late 1800's (Newkirk, 1994, pp. 88-89). But Wendell's theory of composition was not grounded in his observations of his own writing practice; instead, he describes "elastic general principles" that are "observed by thoroughly effective writers" (Wendell, 1891, pp. 2-3). While he does focus on thought and emotion, asserting that they are "the substance of what style expresses" (1891, p. 4), he never describes how a writer manages to compose from those thoughts and emotions.

Wendell is perhaps more comfortable introspecting—observing and narrating his thoughts and feelings—as he reads an example of good style; his discussion of style includes a lengthy (and quite moving) description of how Robert Browning's style in "Grammarian's Funeral" (1891, pp. 8-11) affects him. He builds a theory of composition, in a sense, around his observations of himself as a reader: I observe coherence when I read x, a great poem, and therefore, that poet must have observed the principle of coherence. His advice to writers, then, is to observe the principle of coherence, and his job as a writing teacher is, in part, to describe the principle of coherence and its effects on a reader.

Murray calls this approach the "exterior view of writing, principally examining what has been written or studying patterns which have evolved by the analysis of what has been published" (1970, p. 21). He doesn't dismiss this view as useless, but explains his own view differently: "I do not see writing from the exterior view but from within my own mind and my own emotions as I try to write every single day of my life" (1970, p. 21). Murray's attention to his own experience—like Titchener's almost a century earlier—leads him for a concern of the experiences of his students as individuals:

> There is no one way to write and there is no one way for the student to learn to write. We must accept the individual student and appreciate his individualness .... ultimately he [the student] has to learn the process for himself. (1970, pp. 24-25)

Three years later, Peter Elbow would publish *Writing Without Teachers*, in which he warned readers that his advice to writers is based on his own experience:

> Though much or all of this may be in other books—some of which I have probably read—it seems to me my main source is my own experience. I admit to making universal generalizations upon a sample of one. Consider yourself warned. (1973, p. 16)

Elbow's generalizations are the product of his introspection about his writing process. He describes how he came to the practice of freewriting: when he got stuck while writing, he would,

> ... take out a fresh sheet of paper and simply try to collect evidence: babble everything I felt, when it started, and what kind of writing and mood and weather had been going on. (1973, p. 18)

Similarly, when Elbow successfully broke through his writing block,

> I would often stop and try to say afterwards what I thought happened. I recommend this practice. If you keep your own data, you may be able to build your own theory of how you can succeed in writing since my theory of how I can succeed may not work for you. (1973, p. 18)

Elbow didn't just introspect in order to arrive at the principles that student writers must observe: he proposed a form of introspection as the means by which each individual student writer might "learn the process for himself" (1973, p. 15).

Ten years after Elbow's *Writing Without Teachers*, Murray would suggest in *Teaching the Other Self: The Writer's First Reader* that the point of the writing conference was not to examine the student text, but to interact with the introspecting student—the "other self" created by the student's introspection. Murray claimed that the writer must be his own reader, and that in reading his own writing, he forms two distinct selves: the first self who writes; and the "other self" who reads, counsels, advises, and navigates the territory mapped out by the writing for the first self. The other self also introspects: "the other self articulates the process of writing" (Murray, 1982, p. 142).

Lest we confuse an articulation of the process of writing with a purely behavioral description of what the writer does, Murray assured us that the teacher must first acknowledge and respond to the writer's descriptions of his feelings as he writes (1982, p. 145). The writer needs this other self to develop and grow, and the teacher can help make this growth possible simply by encouraging, expecting, and listening to the other self speak.

FROM INTROSPECTION TO FREUD: LAYERS OF SELF

Despite my fear that Watson had littered the pages of history with the corpses of mind and consciousness, introspection was clearly alive and well in the 1970s and 1980s, at least in composition studies. Introspection might have fallen out of vogue in the wake of behaviorism, but the "interior view" of the introspectionists had survived and been nurtured elsewhere while it waited for Elbow and Murray to surface anew as spokespersons. While writing process movement founders such as Murray, Elbow, and Emig never drew directly on Titchener's work or mention the method of introspection, they drew consciously on Freud's work. Three years after Murray proposed nurturing the student writer's "other self," Janet Emig described the multiple selves—or multiple layers of self—that must be attended to by the writing teacher. Her version of Murray's "other self" had a Freudian twist: the writing teacher must nurture the student's unconscious self.

Rather than dividing the writer into two separate selves as Murray did, she divided the self into layers. These layers first take the form of skin in her opening startling and wonderful image of the writer who has dutifully produced "the conscious student theme" (1983, p. 46):

the theme seems to have been written from one layer of the self—the ectoderm only, with student involvement with his own thought and language moving down an unhappy scale from sporadic engagement to abject diffidence. (Emig, 1983, p. 46)

Emig quickly drops the skin analogy—we hear nothing further about the ectoderm or endoderm—but in this line, she vividly plants the idea of the layered self, some of the layers exposed on the surface, and some submerged underneath. It was a small leap to Freud's concept of the conscious and unconscious self, and the related (though not strictly interchangeable) constructs: the id, ego, and super-ego.

Freud never viewed the conscious or unconscious as having different locations within the body in any literal sense. But popular imagination did. Even now we talk of "uncovering" our unconscious thoughts, of "peeling the onion" of our selves in therapy, of repressed or recovered memories which implies a place where the forgotten memories have been stored, held under the surface, hidden from our conscious self, which lies at the surface. Emig was not a Freudian scholar, and did not cite Freud in "The Uses of the Unconscious in Composing" (1964) so she was likely working with this popular understanding of the spatial division of the conscious and unconscious selves.

Like Murray, who wanted to see a shift from the "exterior view" of composition to the "interior view," Emig argued that traditional writing instruction doesn't allow the student to "consult this [unconscious] part of the self" and "conspires against his inwardly attending" (1983, p. 46). She discusses how author Rudyard Kipling personified the "unconscious part of the writing self into daemons" (1983, p. 49) and how Amy Lowell described dropping a simple topic for a poem "into the subconscious much as one drops a letter into the mailbox. Six months later ... the poem ... was 'there'" (Lowell quoted in Emig, 1983, p. 52). Writing teachers needed to encourage inward attending—journeys to the unconscious—if students were to write papers that went beyond (or below) the "surface scrapings" produced by a traditional overemphasis on the surface of the self—the control of the conscious mind.

Five years after Emig's "The Uses of the Unconscious in Composing," Murray would make his plea for the role of procrastination in composing on the grounds that procrastination allowed the subconscious to do its work. In *Write Before Writing*, he describes why writers procrastinate:

> They sharpen well-pointed pencils and go out to buy more blank paper, rearrange offices, wander through libraries and bookstores, chop wood, walk, drive, make unnecessary calls,

> nap, daydream, and try not 'consciously' to think about what they are going to write so they can think subconsciously about it. (1978, p. 376)

To Murray, Elbow, and Emig, one legitimate subject of composition studies was the writing self, and that self was divided: into the writing self and the other self; into the unconscious or subconscious and conscious; or into the id, ego, and super-ego. Emig and Murray emphasized the subconscious mind, unconscious mind, or the id as a corrective to the overemphasis in traditional writing instruction on the conscious mind. Just as the concept of self (or "selves," or "layers of the self") was central to the work of early writing process pioneers such as Murray, Elbow and Emig, consciousness (not in the Freudian sense), or mind had been central to the work of introspectionists such as Titchener. And this comparison provided me the bridge to my otherwise absurd claim that James Berlin was a behaviorist. To use an analogy that would never show up on the SAT: John B. Waston is to Titchener as James Berlin is to Murray, Elbow, and Emig.

Like Watson, who rejected the concept of consciousness and thus the central concepts of introspectionists like Titchener, James Berlin would reject the self at the center of Murray, Elbow, and Emig's version of composition studies. Berlin's criticism of the self in the late 1980s boils down to his view that the self—as a private space—does not exist, and the self that does exist cannot be trusted in the way that Elbow, Murray, and Emig trust it.

Berlin's critique of this private self begins with a discussion of the concept that Berlin would put at the center of his composition theory and practice: ideology. Drawing from Theborn's interpretation of Althusser's definition of ideology, Berlin establishes his working definition of ideology as "economic, social, and political arrangements" (1987, p. 667), which privilege certain groups and their interactions with each other and the material world. He "situates rhetoric within ideology" (1987, p. 667), which means that he sees rhetoric as advancing instead of mediating various ideologies.

Berlin labels the rhetoric of Elbow and Murray as "subjective" or "expressionistic." He labels Emig's work in *The Composing Process of Twelfth Graders* as "cognitive rhetoric," but ignores her "Uses of the Unconscious in Composing," which would probably have qualified her for membership as an expressionist. In *Rhetoric and Reality*, he identifies the focus of Elbow's expressionistic rhetoric:

> His emphasis, like that of all the expressionists considered in this section, is on the "I," on defining the self so as to secure an authentic identity and voice. This type of expressionistic rhetoric focuses on a dialectic between the individual and

analogy as a means of getting in touch with the self. (1987, p. 153)

While Berlin acknowledges that Elbow and Murray's version of expressionistic rhetoric was actually a protest against the dominant political and pedagogical ideology and practice of the mid-twentieth century, he asserts that their focus on the individual perpetuates a naïve understanding of the self that undermines its own potential for changing dominant political and economic inequalities.

Berlin claims that expressivism's focus on discovery of the self is problematic in two ways: it doesn't acknowledge the ways in which the self has been formed by ideological forces, so it often replicates dominant oppressive ideologies; and a focus on individual self-expression can be appropriated by the dominant ideology because it leads to only individual resistance (1987, p. 676). Individual resistance is impotent; a rhetoric that doesn't lead to collective action, in Berlin's mind, supports hegemony.

Here to save the day is social epistemic rhetoric. In Berlin's description of social epistemic rhetoric, knowledge results from the dialectic between a person, the social group in which the person is acting, and the "material conditions of existence," all of which depend on language because they are "verbal constructs" (1987, p. 678). Furthermore, language—in which all three elements of this dialectic are grounded—is itself the result of social construction in discourse communities, so the individual is never really an individual. In essence, the "self" or knowledge or idea that the student in an expressivist classroom is discovering and expressing is actually the product of social construction and ideology. According to Berlin, ideology is inescapable but "must be continually challenged" so as to reveal its economic and political consequences for individuals ... (1987, p. 679). In Berlin's opinion, the only rhetoric prepared to continually challenge and reveal ideology is the social epistemic.

Pedagogy based in a social epistemic rhetoric, then, starts by showing students the ways in which they have been constructed by their social, economic, and political realities in ways that make them feel powerless. Then, it attempts to help them work towards "a social order supporting the student's "full humanity" (Berlin, 1987, p. 680). Berlin describes Ira Shor's interdisciplinary study of the hamburger as an example of social epistemic pedagogy. Shor's class used economics, history, health sciences, sociology, English, and philosophy in order to analyze the modern rise of the hamburger and its effects on students' lives. According to Shor, the only goal worth considering in a classroom is the goal of "liberated consciousness" (Berlin, 1987, p. 682).

Berlin's critique of expressivism is curious, on many levels. None of the expressivists he critiques would oppose several of his main assertions: that language is social; that different teaching practices express different ideologies; that one of the goals of writing instruction is liberation. But despite these major areas of agreement, there is something incredibly aggressive about Berlin's treatment of the expressivists. Like Watson's Battle of Behaviorism, in which Watson is determined to advance behaviorism at the expense of introspectionism, Berlin is engaging in an act of warfare against the expressionists. This is hard to see, at first, since Berlin's writing comes across as completely rational, academic, and disinterested.

But his attitude is revealed in the one metaphor that manages to invade his otherwise sterile prose. Held up next to the writing of the expressionists, Berlin's writing is almost completely stripped of metaphor and analogy—no surprise, since he associates metaphor and analogy with the expressionists. But one recurrent metaphor stretches throughout Berlin's Rhetoric and Ideology, a more polemic essay than his (relatively) descriptive categorization of various influences on writing instruction in *Rhetoric and Reality*. The metaphor, embedded in the word "camp," is undeveloped in the text but central to Berlin's attitude in the text: the image of a battle between Berlin and the expressionists belies Berlin's academic, rational, reasonable tone. Berlin's "camps" are not separate but happily co-existing summer camps on opposite sides of the same lake, with expressionists sunbathing on one shore and social epistemics drinking bug juice on the other. Instead, they are the camps of opposing armies, bunkered down and strategizing against one another. Or, at least, Berlin is bunkered down and strategizing against the expressionists; he is looking to defeat them.

Berlin's aggression seems contraindicated. In an ethnographic study of expressivist writing classrooms conducted in 1994 at Boston College, Karen Surman Paley (2001) found how the writing in these classes resists the divisive categories imposed by Berlin. The "expressivist" instructors she studied invariably moved students beyond the personal in ways envisioned by the social epistemics. Furthermore, Paley visited the class of Patricia Bizzell, whom Berlin labels a social epistemic, and describes the ways in which Bizzell's focus on the social led to personal, autobiographical writing (2001). In other words, the focus on the individual Berlin ascribes to the expressivists and the focus on the social that Berlin ascribes to the social epistemics do not work against each other in practice, although he set them apart in theory.

Furthermore, Emig, Murray, Elbow, and Berlin ultimately have the same goal—to escape manipulation of the dominant ideology when that ideology works against the "human purposes" MacDougall so eloquently defended against Watson's focus on behavior. But Berlin's ire at the expressionist is perhaps not rational, and may be rooted in an unconscious reaction to the unconscious self, the very construct he derides in the expressionists' work. Thus, my absurd sub-thesis: Berlin is a man uncomfortable with the unconscious. Yet, for all his attempts at consciousness and control, he cannot escape the unconscious: his ire at the expressionists is as much a gut reaction against their embrace of the unconscious as a conscious criticism of their theory or pedagogy.

While Emig never cited Freud, it may be useful to examine his description of the id in *New Introductory Lectures in Psychoanalysis* when trying to understand Berlin's response to the unconscious:

> we call it a chaos, a cauldron full of seething excitations ....
> It is filled with energy reaching it from the instincts, but it
> has no organisation, produces no collective will, but only a
> striving to bring about the satisfaction of the instinctual needs
> subject to the observance of the pleasure principle. (1989, p.
> 91)

The beginning of Berlin's discomfort is the preverbal nature of the unconscious. The unconscious is beyond and before language, in Freud's formulation, and we can describe it only by analogy. We know it only through its metaphoric manifestation through our dreams and in our feelings—our non-verbal reactions to events and people. But Berlin wants to believe that knowledge doesn't exist without rhetoric—"there is no knowledge without language."

In Emig's view, the unconscious, or id, knows things, not necessarily knowledge that comes through or from language, and in using the unconscious in composing, students can find a site of invention—a place to generate or discover knowledge. For example, my daydream—the image of Elbow, Murray, and Emig's participation in my National Day of Introspection—was an example of my subconscious invention. To mix Amy Lowell's unconscious mailbox analogy with Elbow's cooking metaphor, I dropped my research on Watson and the introspectionists into the mailslot, let it mix around and simmer with my previous discomfort about Berlin's attitude toward the expressionists, presto! Out came my daydream, the image of Murray introspecting and Berlin refusing, which was a preverbal thesis of sorts. That preverbal knowing, or image-knowledge, quickly turned to words when I meditated on it.

But Berlin's second, more urgent point of contention is with the idea that the id "produces no collective will" (1987). The collective will that interests Berlin, of course, is a collective resistance to the dominant ideology. However, Berlin forgets that Freud's complementary concept—the super-ego—could be viewed as the individual's internalization of the dominant ideology. Emig is just as interested as Berlin in overcoming the damaging aspects of the super-ego, or dominant ideology, but, unlike Berlin, she sees the id as immensely useful in this quest.

In Emig's view, the super-ego does damage on two fronts, and the use of the id can be used to correct both. First, the super-ego speaks in stale, flat, cliché. The id can provide fresh image and language to counteract these dead expressions. Secondly, and more to Berlin's point, access of the id can point to differences between the values of the dominant ideology internalized by the super-ego and the needs of an individual human being which are contained in the id. Let's consider an example from the Vietnam War, which played a major role in shaping Murray, Emig, and Elbow's views of on the role of authority in the classroom. A male student's super-ego may have internalized all forms of societal authority, including the authority of the draft. But, in an expressionist classroom, that student might be invited to listen to his unconscious, in a journal, or through freewriting, perhaps. He might find that his id is uncomfortable with the war. He might move to Canada or become a Quaker or even become an activist. Listening to your unconscious, then, for the expressionists, can be the first step in political action—individual or collective action.

But Emig's use of the id to escape ideology is frightening to Berlin, who views the presence of "desire" in the id as problematic. In Althusser's work, which Berlin relies on quite a bit, desire cannot be trusted, since ideology creates and structures desire. Thus, desire itself and all inner life is unreliable and cannot be trusted. While the expressionists and Berlin both want to escape manipulation of the ideological forces that abuse power, Berlin's distrust of the unconscious makes him suspicious of the expressivists. Emig sees the unconscious as a means of escaping the dominant ideology, but Berlin actually sees Emig's means of escape as a trap door. The only alternative, then, is for Berlin to consciously escape manipulation. There is nothing to trust, in Berlin's world, except social epistemic rhetoric, which helps him escape himself. He has consciously divorced himself from his id, and divorces himself from anyone who hasn't. The expressivists' acceptance and use of the id is not only naive, but dangerous, a trap door.

Berlin's criticism of the expressivists for failing to privilege collective over private action is the most distressing part of his critique. Elbow, Emig, and others protested Berlin's critique on the grounds that they are, quite obviously, interested in political action. But what concerns me most in Berlin's emphasis on collective action is what it reveals about his own attitude toward individual experience: in dismissing the value of an individual act of conscience, he expresses a disregard for the value of that individual's experience.

Berlin's dismissal of private acts of conscience points to a similarity between Berlin and Watson. Watson rejected consciousness, mind, and individual experience, and his dismissal of experience as a theoretical construct made him callous to the experience of the people whose behavior he would try to control—including Little Albert and generations of consumers. In a surprisingly similar way, Berlin's dismissal of the value of the private self on theoretical grounds makes him callous to the experiences of those who take private stands against the dominant ideology. While the conscientious objector who moves to Canada instead of organizing a protest on Washington doesn't make any discernable difference in the dominant ideology, his private act of conscience certainly makes a difference in his own experience of his life, and this difference matters—to him, and to the people who love him. Berlin's inability to concede that private experience matters is disturbing, given his ethical stand on matters of ideology.

In the end, my absurd, unconsciously constructed thesis both collapses and stands. Berlin was never a behaviorist. But there are startling similarities between his battle with the expressivists and Watson's battle with the introspectionists. Berlin's ideological critique of the expressivists, for all its ethical posturing, suffers from the same problem that plagues Watson's critique of the introspectionists: his dismissal of the value of an individual's private experience—perhaps grounded in his own unconscious discomfort with the unconscious—leads him to dubious ethical territory. As Titchener reminded us, ethics must be based in a concern for the experience of an individual. Berlin's social epistemic theory cannot be ethically grounded if it wages war on expressivism; the two "camps" need to make love, not war.

NOTES

1. I eventually returned to this dismissal of experience in my dissertation: *Writing Assessment's "Debilitating Inheritance": Behaviorism's Dismissal of Experience.* (Doctoral dissertation). ProQuest Dissertations and Theses.

REFERENCES

Berlin, J. A. (1987). *Rhetoric and reality: Writing instruction in American colleges, 1900-1985.* Carbondale, IL: Southern Illinois University Press.

Berlin, J. A. (1988). Rhetoric and ideology in the writing class. *College English* 50(5), 477-494.

Brigham, C. (1923). *A study of American intelligence.* Princeton University Press. Retrieved from http://archive.org/stream/studyofamericani00briguoft/studyofamericani00briguoft_djvu.txt

Buckley, K. (1989). *Mechanical man: John B. Watson and the beginnings of behaviorism.* New York: The Guilford Press.

Cheney, C., & Pierce, D. (2004). *Behavior analysis and learning.* Mahwah, NJ: Lawrence Erlbaum Associates.

Dewey, J. (1891). Psychology. New York: American Book Company. Retrieved from http://books.google.com/books?id=3mJ9AAAAMAAJ&pg=PR1&dq=Dewey+Psychology+1891&hl=en&sa=X&ei=9MrrU56wOqvgsASU0IDgCQ&ved=0CDcQ6AEwAA#v=onepage&q=Dewey%20Psychology%201891&f=false

Elbow, P. (1973). *Writing without teachers*. New York: Oxford University Press.

Emig, J. (1964). The uses of the unconscious in composing. *College Composition and Communication, 15,* 6-11.

Emig, J. (1983). *The web of meaning: Essays on writing, teaching, learning, and thinking.* Upper Montclair, NJ: Boynton Cook.

Freud, S. (1989). *New introductory lectures on psycho-analysis.* New York: W. W. Norton.

Gould, S. J. (1981). *The mismeasure of man.* New York: W. W. Norton and Company.

Howorth, P. (2000). The treatment of shell-shock: Cognitive therapy before its time. *Psychiatrist Bulletin, 24,* 225-227.

Institute of Education Sciences. (2008). *Funding opportunities.* Retrieved from National Center for Education Research, U.S. Department of Education Web site: http://ies.ed.gov/funding/overview.asp

James, W. (1884). On some omissions of introspective psychology. Oxford University Press.

Koestler, A. (1964). *The act of creation.* New York: Arkana.

Manning, F. (1994). Morale and cohesion in military psychiatry." In F. D. Jones (Ed.), *Military psychiatry: Preparing for peace in war.* Retrieved from Washington, DC: Office of the Surgeon General Borden Institute Web site: https://ke.army.mil/bordeninstitute/published_volumes/military_psychiatry/MPch1.pdf

Murray, D. (1970). The interior view of composing: One writer's philosophy of composition. *College Composition and Communication, 21,* 21-26.

Murray, D. (1982). Teaching the other self: The writer's first reader. *College Composition and Communication, 33,* 140-147.

Murray, D. (1978). Write before writing. *College Composition and Communication, 29,* 375-381.

Newkirk, T. (1994). The politics of intimacy: The defeat of Barrett Wendell at Harvard. In T. Newkirk, & L. Tobin (Eds.), *Taking stock: The writing process movement in the '90s* (pp. 115-132). Portsmouth, NH: Heinemann.

Paley, K.S. (2001). *I-Writing: The politics and practice of teaching first-person writing.* Carbondale: Southern Illinois University.

Report of Informal Conference on Morale. (1918, April 13). Yale University Archives (Robert Mearns Yerkes papers, Box 92, Folder 1752), New Haven, CT.

Report of Second Conference on Control of Morale. (1918, May 15). Yale University Archives (Robert Mearns Yerkes papers, Box 92, Folder 1752), New Haven, CT.
Schuetz, A. (1941). "William James's concept of the stream of consciousness." *Philosphy and Phenomenological Research, 1,* 442-452.
Titchener, E. (1898). *A primer of psychology.* Norwood, MA: Norwood Press.
Titchener, E. (1903). Class experiments and demonstration apparatus. *American Journal of Psychology, 24,* 439-455.
Titchener, E. (1909). *Lectures on the experimental psychology of the thought-processes.* New York: Macmillan. Retrieved from https://archive.org/details/lecturesonexper00goog.
Watson, J. (1912, October 17). [Letter to Robert Yerkes]. Yale University Archives (Robert Mearns Yerkes papers, Box 51, Folder 982), New Haven, CT.
Watson, J. (1912, February 21). [Letter to Robert Yerkes]. Yale University Archives (Robert Mearns Yerkes papers, Box 51, Folder 982), New Haven, CT.
Watson, J. (1912, May 21). [Letter to Robert Yerkes]. Yale University Archives (Robert Mearns Yerkes papers, Box 51, Folder 982), New Haven, CT.
Watson, J. (1913, April 7). [Letter to Robert Yerkes]. Yale University Archives (Robert Mearns Yerkes papers, Box 51, Folder 984, New Haven, CT.
Watson, J. (1913). Psychology as the behaviorist views it. *Psychological Review, 20,* 158-177.
Watson, J. (1915, October 27). [Letter to Robert Yerkes]. Yale University Archives (Robert Mearns Yerkes papers, Box 51, Folder 986), New Haven, CT.
Watson, J. (1915, November 1). [Letter to Robert Yerkes]. Yale University Archives (Robert Mearns Yerkes papers, Box 51, Folder 986), New Haven, CT.
Watson, J. (1915, November 9). [Letter to Robert Yerkes]. Yale University Archives (Robert Mearns Yerkes papers, Box 51, Folder 986), New Haven, CT.
Watson, J. (1916, October 12). [Letter to Robert Yerkes]. Yale University Archives (Robert Means Yerkes papers, Box 51, Folder 987), New Haven, CT.
Watson, J. (1916, October 24). [Letter to Robert Yerkes]. Yale University Archives (Robert Mearns Yerkes papers, Box 51, Folder 987), New Haven, CT.
Watson, J. (1916, March 31). [Letter to Robert Yerkes]. Yale University Archives (Robert Mearns Yerkes papers, Box 51, Folder 987), New Haven, CT.
Watson, J. (1916, May 12). [Letter to Robert Yerkes]. Yale University Archives (Robert Mearns Yerkes papers, Box 51, Folder 987), New Haven, CT.
Watson, J. (1919, March 29). [Letter to Robert Yerkes]. Yale University Archives (Robert Mearns Yerkes papers, Box 51, Folder 988), New Haven, CT.
Watson, J. (1924a). *Behaviorism.* New York: W.W. Norton and Company.
Watson, J. (1924b). *Psychology from the standpoint of a behaviorist* (2nd ed.). Philadelphia: J. B. Lippincott Company.

Watson, J. (I) (1928). *The psychological care of infant and child.* New York: W.W. Norton.

Watson, J, & MacDougall, W. (1929). *The battle of behaviorism.* New York: W.W. Norton.

Wendell, B. (1891). *English composition: Eight lectures given at the Lowell Institute.* New York: Charles Scribner's Sons.

Yerkes, R. [Letter to John. B. Watson.] Yale University Archives (Robert Mearns Yerkes papers, Box 51, Folder 986), New Haven, CT.

EXPRESSIVE PEDAGOGIES IN THE UNIVERSITY OF PITTSBURGH'S ALTERNATIVE CURRICULUM PROGRAM, 1973-1979

Chris Warnick
College of Charleston

James Berlin's account of 1960s-era expressive pedagogy is over twenty years old, but it continues to inform scholarship in composition and rhetoric. Despite the critical reappraisal of Berlin's histories in the wake of the field's archival turn, some scholars continue to cite Berlin's taxonomy of rhetoric and pedagogy, and the place of expressive pedagogy within it, to analyze the field's history and future. In describing what he sees as a dearth of archival histories on twentieth century writing instruction, David R. Russell observes that Berlin's "book remains the most-cited treatment of the 20th century" (2006, p. 258). Richard Fulkerson draws extensively on Berlin's tripartite classification of the field in "Composition at the Turn of the Twenty-First Century. Using overblown rhetoric similar to that Maja Wilson observes in Berlin's critique of expressivism (see her contribution in this volume), Fulkerson concludes "that expressivism, despite numerous poundings by the cannons of postmodernism and resulting eulogies, is, in fact, quietly expanding its region of command" (2005, p. 655). But as Karen Surman Paley and others have pointed out, Berlin's conclusions about expressivism rest on evidence found in textbooks and published research and ignore actual classroom practice. According to Paley

> it is unfortunate that Berlin ... does not seem to have tested his theoretical conclusions against actual "expressionist" classroom practice. If he had, he might have seen a range of pedagogies, some more overtly sociopolitical than others, depending on the comfort level and belief system of the teacher. (2001, p. 22)

This essay takes up Paley's call to research "actual 'expressionist' classroom practice" by examining materials from an experimental first-year program at the University of Pittsburgh known as the Alternative Curriculum, which ran from 1973 to 1979.[1] While the Alternative Curriculum archive provides an incomplete picture of classroom practices, syllabi, student papers, newsletters, and other program documents upset the generalizations of expressivism made by Berlin and others. Specifically, program documents reveal that teachers and students adopted personal writing strategies for purposes other than self-knowledge. Students, for example, engaged in personal writing activities to experiment with alternative writing styles, to build a group identity as members of the program, and to critique American higher education and its marginalization of alternative learning programs such as the Alternative Curriculum. The purpose of journal writing within the program was not always "to capture one's unique, personal response to experience," as Berlin contends (1987, p. 152); instead, students practiced journaling to complete writing activities that stressed audience, revision, and genre. Perhaps most importantly, teachers in the program who drew from expressivist theory—especially economist David Bramhall, who taught a journal writing course that used a chapter from Ken Macrorie's *telling writing*—led courses that in practice challenged expressivist assumptions about personal writing.

THE ALTERNATIVE CURRICULUM PROGRAM

The Alternative Curriculum, a first-year program that eventually accepted sophomores as well, was part of a larger general education reform package at Pitt that itself was a response to student and faculty unrest (see "Arts"; Levenson; Marbury; Tiernan). A letter sent to new students in 1975, signed by AC core faculty as well as graduate and undergraduate assistants, identifies ten objectives of the program, among which are a "self-designed curriculum," "learning from the inside-out and by practice," an "open environment; learning outside the classroom," and "finding one's own purpose for learning." After several failed attempts to start the program, the AC opened its doors in 1973, enrolling 150 students, 130 of whom were selected through a lottery process with another 20 selected based on interviews with faculty (Kambic, 1974, p. 2). Program announcements indicate that students were assigned to "core groups" consisting of fifteen students and one faculty member. During the first weeks of the semester, groups met to reflect on the nature of education and to discuss their learning goals. According to letters sent to prospective students, there were assigned readings for these group meetings, which included popular texts on alternative education—including *How Children Fail* and *Freedom and Beyond*, by John Holt, and *Summerhill*, by A.S. Neill. Students were also expected to attend what were called "offerings," lectures given by faculty and community members who spoke on their area of interest or expertise. These offerings, which covered such topics as "Black Autobiography and the Liberal Experience," "The Physics of Music,"

"A Revolution in Catholicism," and "Change in Education and the Social Order," were intended to raise questions, issues, and methods that students could pursue in their work throughout the term.

After this initial period, students were responsible for completing four "learning projects" each semester, and these projects could take the form of a group workshop (led by either a faculty member or another student), an independent study, or fieldwork. Students did fieldwork at local public radio stations, area hospitals, and daycare centers; they conducted independent studies on "Labor History," "Basic Calculus," and "Drawing and Design;" they undertook workshops addressing prison reform, children's literature, and writing. Students did not receive letter grades for these learning projects; instead, by enrolling in the program students agreed to take a block of up to fifteen credits each semester on a "credit/no entry" basis. In consultation with a faculty member, students drew up a learning contract in which they outlined the purpose and shape of their particular learning project, and the corresponding faculty member would comment on the strengths and weaknesses of the project.

Former AC faculty member Dan Tannacito characterized the program's overall goal this way: "one could say that the program set out to let students define how to envision an alternative way of life within but opposed to the dominant cultural and educational model." Writing played a vital role in students' attempts to imagine the "alternative way of life" spoken of by Tannacito. According to Tannacito, "students wanted to learn how literature and writing were an asset in their lives. They had experienced them as an imposition, via schooling." Students in the program did not write themes, as they might be expected to do in other first-year writing courses, but they did learn traditional genres of academic writing, such as lab reports, research papers and literary criticism. However, faculty in the program also allowed students room to explore alternative forms of writing. Tannactio explained, for instance, how he regularly assigned forms of writing other than the essay. "The main forms of writing that I asked of students," he told me, "were journaling, note-taking, and creative writing. Sometimes, we asked people to write letters and arguments related to public issues that were being debated or in the local news. There were also community-based writing tasks."

Tannacito's comments suggest that at least some AC faculty had a lot in common with expressivists. They, too, wanted students to learn how writing could play a meaningful role in their lives as thinkers and citizens, and they imagined that one way to reach this goal was to teach personal, reflective forms of writing. More importantly, though, Tannacito's comments reveal that expressive practices such as journaling and creative writing assignments sometimes took place alongside or as part of public and politically-oriented writing projects, which runs counter to Berlin's claim that expressivist classrooms encourage students to find their voice "not through the happening or the political confrontation" (1987, p. 152), but through private reflection.

EXPRESSIVIST PRACTICES IN THE ALTERNATIVE CURRICULUM

Expressive practices and values surfaced in the AC in a variety of ways that both uphold and resist common generalizations made about expressivist theory. Syllabi, workshop announcements, evaluations, and other documents illustrate that students practiced journaling, freewriting, drafting, and revision. Writing courses were run as workshops, with students sharing and evaluating one another's writing. Students compiled portfolios to document the work they did to complete a workshop or fieldwork project and wrote reflective papers describing what they learned from this process. Some of the program's writing courses taught texts and methods directly associated with expressivism. For example, a fall 1976 program newsletter advertises a workshop based on Peter Elbow's *Writing Without Teachers*. According to the advertisement, the workshop

> is geared towards strengthening the ability to write, even when you're "not in the mood," and learning to constructively criticize the works of others and hopefully your own. *Writing Without Teachers* by Peter Elbow is used as a guideline. Each workshop session is started off with ten minutes of free writing, after which the group is broken into smaller groups to read and discuss what people have written that week. All types of writing are encouraged.

As the text of this advertisement illustrates, students were encouraged to approach peer review, an important aspect of expressive pedagogy, as a critical and rhetorical practice. Students are prompted to "constructively criticize" each others' work, not simply "check for the inauthentic in the writer's response," which Berlin describes as the purpose peer review serves in expressivist classrooms (1987, p. 152).

While it remains unclear how important peer review was in the program as a whole, journaling appears to have been a widespread practice. Documents in the archive suggest that the purpose of journaling wasn't always "to capture one's unique, personal response to experience," as Berlin argues was the case in expressivist classrooms (1987, p. 152)—although this type of writing did take place. For example, a September 1974 handout written by physics professor John Townsend titled "Learning Strategies and Tactics: A guide and discussion promoter for students in the Alternative Curriculum" recommends journal writing as an effective learning strategy: "Keep a journal. Because the AC is not tied to specific courses, keeping a journal helped students last year to provide a continuity and a record of events that was valuable to have at year's end. It also gives you practice in expressing yourself by writing." A document listing projects completed during the 1973-1974 academic year corroborates Townsend's comment. Among the projects listed are "Self-evaluation; discussions, journals and essay," "Working for the University Times; a journal and essay," "Apprentice movie projectionist; a journal," and "Becoming a volunteer fireman; a journal and essay." Townsend's advice and projects such as these suggest that one function journals served in the program was for students to document their experiences and to generate ideas for more finalized projects that weren't necessarily personal in nature.

Instead of earning letter grades, students received descriptive comments from an AC faculty member who was responsible for overseeing the project. As part of the evaluation process, students wrote brief descriptions of the projects they completed. These descriptions sometimes took on the shape of reflective personal essays in which the student described what they learned from this project. One such example is an activity description by an unnamed student discussing her writing workshop. Stating that she "found a number of outlets for exploring the uses of writing," the student lists the different writing activities she completed, which included "a description of AC for the University Course Selection Bulletin," "an introductory letter to AC for high school seniors," and "articles for the AC newsletter." She goes on to describe how, alongside these projects, she also wrote a journal:

> I've been keeping a journal, for no one but myself to "get at" my confusions, to clarify my idea(L)s, and to record the changes within me in an outward form. I read Dave Bramhall's packet on "Keeping a Journal" with great fervor. Re-reading excerpts from my journal I now realize that my life is disintegrated; the experiences each day, the forces which are playing important roles in my life, and my real-imaginary wishes all blend into one whole. Writing is becoming more of a natural expression for me. I am choosing it and using it in many ways and I now see why I always will.

The type of journal writing the student describes here is intensely personal. According to her, the journal is "for no one but myself" and it serves to capture the writer's complex self, its contradictions, beliefs, and changes. At the same time, though, the student claims the process of keeping a journal was among a set of writing activities that helped her understand the rhetorical nature of writing. By stating that "I am choosing it [writing] and using it in many ways," this student seems to have an emerging awareness of "how meaning is shaped by discourse communities," knowledge Berlin claims expressive pedagogy ignores (1987, p. 153).

There were occasions where journal writing within the program took on more of a social dimension. An article in the October 1974 issue of the program's newsletter, which was designed and written by students, discusses students' plans for an Alternative Curriculum magazine. The article indicates that there was some debate about what shape this magazine should take and one "idea calls for a community journal in which people, workshops, offering presenters can contribute on a day to day level. We may choose to keep the journal in epic form (a continuous "poem" or story of experiences)." The author of the article appears to prefer this option because she argues that a collective journal would enable students to better process their coursework: "We would begin to use retrospection. So very much is happening all the time. If we take some time out to write/think about it, somehow it all begins to make sense."

It's unclear how this debate was resolved or whether a magazine was ever produced; no copies exist in the archive and individuals I interviewed didn't recall it. However, students and faculty who participated in a field trip to New England-area experimental learning programs in the spring of 1975 did compose a collective journal that sounds similar to the one described in the program newsletter. According to a memo written that same year to Robert Marshall, the Dean of the College of Arts and Sciences, Tannacito and Bramhall proposed that interested faculty and students visit the Inner College at the University of Connecticut, Goddard College in Vermont, and other institutions. They hoped to consult with John Holt, Jonathan Kozol, and other educational activists. Estimating a total budget of roughly $3,000, Tannacito and Bramhall state the trip would result in a 30-minute film and journal recording the fieldwork. No record of the film exists, but a copy of the journal, titled *Total Bus*, does survive. The journal includes over thirty anonymous entries that range from one-paragraph personal reflections to three-page reports that explain the history, structure, and purposes of organizations the group visited. An example of the latter is this excerpt from an entry on the New Haven Women's Liberation Center:

> The center has been in existence for about 5 years. It is not a Yale organization and most women that come to the center now are not Yale students. "The New Haven Women's Liberation Center developed out of small meetings between friends working on political issues in New Haven in 1968-69. These

meetings soon grew and attracted 30-60 women every Sunday
evening, including a number of Yale graduate and undergraduate women." (NHWLC) The center is funded by donations
monthly pledges [sic], $5.00 fees from women joining the
Connecticut Feminist Federal Credit Union and a current
$2,000 NIMH grant.

Passages like this one, which cites the group's research, suggest the group imagined the journal to serve public, as well as private, needs. The research trip members conducted and wrote about in the journal could be used by leaders in the Alternative Curriculum and other institutions across the campus, especially Pitt's Women's Center, to evaluate their organizations and generate new ideas. Journal entries such as this one further complicate the characterization of expressive writing as merely personal or at best quasi-public.

AN ECONOMIST TEACHES KEN MACRORIE

The course documents I examine in this section dramatize what happens when any set of pedagogical theories—be they expressivist, current-tradition-al, or social-epistemic—gets deployed by specific teachers in specific classrooms with specific students: elements of these theories are accepted and followed while others are ignored, misread, challenged, or revised. David Bramhall, a political economist who helped found the AC and often served as the public face of the program, led a workshop in the first two years of the program entitled "On Keeping a Journal," which included among its readings a chapter on journal writing from Macrorie's telling writing.[2] Bramhall's course is concrete evidence that expressivism influenced the work of faculty across the curriculum. This influence can't be described in simple terms, however. The course syllabus and sample student journals suggest that Bramhall appropriated certain aspects of Macrorie's pedagogy while disagreeing with or misreading others. Specifically, Bramhall's advice to students about journal writing echoes what Macrorie states about the importance of "oppositions," but Bramhall, who imagines the purpose of journaling differently than Macrorie does, also seems to misread Macrorie's point about "telling facts."

The course syllabus contains only one sentence that references Macrorie directly, but other passages in the document allude to points Macrorie makes in telling writing. For example, the course description ends with this paragraph that touches on, without naming specifically, Macrorie's idea of "oppositions:"

> So, try it. Don't feel you have to write every day, but when
> you have an idea, an impression, an experience, a new way of

seeing something (or yourself), write it down in a real paragraph so you can recapture it later. Argue with yourself when you feel yourself divided about something. You can always rethink and write new feelings about a past entry—you're not committed forever to a first impression. But let go some, be honest with yourself, and have fun with it!

Macrorie begins an earlier chapter on "oppositions" with this definition:

Strong writers bring together oppositions of one kind or another. Kitchen language and elevated language, long and short sentences, fast and slow rhythms. And what they choose to present from life—whether it be object, act, or idea—is frequently the negative and the positive, one thing and its opposite, two ideas that antagonize each other. (1970, p. 71)

According to Macrorie's definition, opposition may be created through style or content, the latter of which seems to be more important to Bramhall. His advice to "Argue with yourself when you feel yourself divided about something" sounds similar to Macrorie's idea of opposition being created by "two ideas that antagonize each other" (1970, p. 89).

The only direct reference Bramhall makes to Macrorie in the syllabus is this summary of the chapter on journal writing: "I guess the main thing stressed in the MacCrorie [sic] chapter included here ["keeping a journal"] is to write concretely—and to write thoughts and feelings rather than mainly a record of actions." Here Bramhall seems to be alluding to what Macrorie calls "telling facts," concrete images and details that portray a writer's realization of a feeling or idea. Macrorie recommends the following steps for creating "telling facts":

when you have to mention anything in order to tell a story or make a point, force yourself to put down the name of that thing if it has a name, or to show it in its particular setting or doing its thing particularly. Don't say you pushed the throttle and the motorbike did its thing. Give the name of that thing and the sound and fell or smell, or whatever you can. (1970, p. 35)

For Macrorie, "telling facts" are important to journal writing for an additional reason: they allow the writer to get meaning from their journal entries upon subsequent re-readings (1970, pp. 122-123). It's interesting to note, however, that Bramhall appears to distill this concept down to the commonplace advice "to write concretely," which doesn't capture the imagistic nature of Macrorie's "telling facts." Additional evidence in this passage—Bramhall's phrase "I guess the main thing stressed in the ... chapter" suggests Bramhall is uncertain about his reading of Macrorie, understandable given his professional training is in economics, not writing.

The most significant point at which Bramhall's syllabus diverges from Macrorie's approach is when Bramhall explains the purpose of journaling. Unlike Macrorie, who argues that "all good journals observe one fundamental: they do not speak privately" (1970, p. 123), Bramhall tells students they can share their journals with others after the fact, but they'll have more success keeping a journal if they think of it as private. (See Daniel Collins' essay in this collection for a further explanation of the social dimension behind Macrorie's pedagogy.) The journal, according to the course description, "is your continuing dialogue with yourself—that's the purpose and you won't make it if you try to write it for anyone else—a teacher, posterity, or even a loved one." It remains unclear whether this disagreement with Macrorie was conscious on Bramhall's part. Especially given his summary of Macrorie's chapter, it could be that Bramhall overlooked or misunderstood this part of Macrorie's argument, and/or it could be that this sense of the journal as an engine of private reflection better fit Bramhall's teaching philosophy, which was described in a profile of Bramhall that appeared in the fall 1974 issue of the AC Newsletter. An important aspect of Bramhall's pedagogy, according to the unnamed student writer, is reflection: "Finally there is reflectiveness. Dave feels we must keep looking at the process of learning, and at what is happening to human relations." Even though the latter part this comment suggests that there was a social dimension to Bramhall's teaching, it appears that an even more important goal of Bramhall's teaching was to have students better understand themselves as learners, which could help explain the syllabus' definition of the journal as a "continuing dialogue with yourself."

The course file also contains model student journals that Bramhall distributed to the class, and these texts further reveal the complex manner in which Bramhall appropriated Macrorie's work. This is especially the case with the first journal in the file, which was written by an unnamed young woman enrolled in the program during its first semester. The journal consists of a handful of entries, all of which focus on the writer's attempt to figure out who she is. One particular entry discusses the writer's realization that she has no discernible self:

> I want to write something about myself but I don't know
> what because I don't know myself. I'm not even sure I have
> a "myself" any more at this point. Right before I went home
> for Thanksgiving I felt as though I really had things straight in
> my mind and that I was happy with me. Maybe I was justified

in feeling like that for a few days because I really did think I had my head together. But now I know I'm wrong. There is no "me." "Me" is a lot of other people's ideas, opinions and gestures. I am what I want other people want me to be.

A later entry from the journal shows the writer expressing more self confidence, although it remains unclear whether she's come to any greater understanding of who she is, other than that she wants to be happy: "I am fighting. Sometimes I think the other side is getting the better of me, but I won't lose. I can't. Because if I don't win, I'll die. And I don't want to die. A dead person cannot be happy. I want to be happy and I will. Today is the first day I'm going to be alive."

Absent from this writer's journal, or at least those excerpts Bramhall shared with the class, are any "telling facts." Instead of recording images, descriptions, or quotes that capture her self-doubt, these passages present a string of declarative sentences that simply state the writer's predicament ("There is no 'me.'" "I want to be happy and I will."). And even though these passages follow Bramhall's advice "to write thoughts and feeling rather than mainly a record of actions," they don't follow his suggestion "to write concretely." The reasons behind the writer's self-doubt remain unclear, and nowhere does she explain why she has a new understanding of herself or what she will do exactly "to be alive." Bramhall's syllabus suggests that this writer's journal, along with the others he distributed to the class, serves as a model for students. "They help to show how different journal styles may be," he writes. But this student's journal doesn't always seem to match up with Bramhall's own approach to journal writing.

My intention in pointing out this inconsistency is not to criticize Bramhall or the unnamed student writer. Instead, I cite these examples because they illustrate my larger point that we are unable to fully determine the exact pedagogical practices that emerge from expressivist theory—or any theory, for that matter. If we are to understand the myriad ways an important pedagogical theory (or rather, set of theories) like expressivism informed classroom practice, more archival research needs to be done on 1960s-era classrooms and programs, including those, like the Alternative Curriculum, that existed separately from English departments.

NOTES

1. In his essay included in this collection, Peter Elbow similarly claims that historians of the field "need to find more accurate ways to describe the views of the people [expressivism] was pinned on." I agree with Elbow, and this essay attempts to answer his call. I am aware that my reliance on the terms "expressive," "expressivist," and "expresivism" in this essay could be read as problematic because they potentially

re-inscribe the simplistic attitude toward expressivism I seek to contest. However, I use these terms because they frame the field's long-standing debate about pedagogies involving personal writing (another term Elbow complicates in useful ways). In analyzing the complexities involved whenever any theory is adapted to classroom practices, this essay can be read as a first step toward Elbow's goal of eliminating the word "expressivism"—and the assumptions that surround it—from our historical lexicon.

2. Other readings included excerpts from Henry David Thoreau's and Simone de Beauvoir's journals; The Education of Kate Haracz: Journal of an Undergraduate, which was originally printed in a 1970 issue of Change magazine; and a chapter from Barrett Mandel's Literature and the English Department that examines students' journal writing in an Honors drama course. Mandel had previously taught at Pitt and had worked alongside Bramhall on curriculum reform.

REFERENCES

Alternative Curriculum Records. (1973-1979). University of Pittsburgh Archives, Archives Service Center, University Archives, Pittsburgh, PA.

Arts and sciences review committee reports open hearing findings. (1970, January 19). *The Pitt News* Microfilm.

Berlin, J. A. (1987). *Rhetoric and reality: Writing instruction in American colleges, 1900-1985*. Carbondale: Southern Illinois University Press.

Fulkerson, R. (2005). Composition at the turn of the twenty-first century. *College Composition and Communication, 56*(4), 654-687.

Haracz, K. (1970). The education of Kate Haracz: Journal of an undergraduate. *Change in Higher Education, 2*(3), 12-26.

Holt, J. C. (1972). *Freedom and beyond*. New York: E.P. Dutton.

Holt, J. C. (1964). *How children fail*. New York: Pitman.

Kambic, M. (1974, March 4). Unusual class prepares frosh. *The Pitt News* Microfilm.

Levenson. (1969, May 27). Bramhall talks course review. *The Pitt News* Microfilm.

Macrorie, K. (1970). *Telling writing*. Rochelle Park, NJ: Hayden.

Mandel, B. J. (1970). *Literature and the English department*. Champaign, Il: National Council of Teachers of English.

Marbury, D. (1969, October 22). ASRC: Curriculum innovation. *The Pitt News* Microfilm.

Neill, A. S. (1977). *Summerhill: A radical approach to child rearing*. New York: Simon and Schuster.

Paley, K. S. (2001). *I-writing: The politics and practice of teaching first-person writing*. Carbondale, IL: Southern Illinois University Press.

Russell, D. R. (2006). Historical Studies of Composition. In P. Smagorinsky (Ed.), *Research in Composition: Multiple Perspectives on Two Decades of Change*. New York: Teachers College Press.

Tiernan, D. (1969, June 10). Houston, four others join Bramhall, ASCRC. *The Pitt News* Microfilm.

REREADING ROMANTICISM, REREADING EXPRESSIVISM: REVISING "VOICE" THROUGH WORDSWORTH'S PREFACES

Hannah J. Rule
University of South Carolina

To take up the idea of critical expressivism is to insist upon complexity, contradiction, revision, and expansion, rather than reduction, dismissal, and simplification. Being critically expressivist too then involves a stance toward how we shape disciplinary histories. Current-traditional, expressivist, social constructionist—these are meant to signal broad and sure shifts in the foundations of writing pedagogy and disciplinarity. While these camps might render a telos or progress narrative, they at the same time inevitably diminish practice and concepts. There is imprecision in monolithic terms—expressivism, social constructionism, the personal, the social, romanticism—because, as Peter Elbow writes in this volume, these broad terms conceal their multiplicity. Equally unproductive, the terms are often wielded as weapons, as instruments of reduction and dismissal. As this essay works to point out, pedagogies and rhetorics are deemed untenable because they are labeled romantic or expressivist, or romantic-expressivist. This essay works to complicate these alliances.

Over time, composition scholars have found both resonance and dissonance with romanticism. While some have found romantic influence a reason to dismiss certain practices or pedagogies, still others have drawn upon the romantic period to invigorate our conceptions of expressivism. Finding the British romantic period a productive historical site, in this essay I suggest that nuance can be brought to understanding how expressivism, through romanticism, might understand language as "personal." Through the canonical text on language in the Romantic period, Wordsworth's *Prefaces to Lyrical Ballads* and theories of language circulating in the romantic period, I offer a means of seeing romantic—and by extension, expressive—language and expression in a novel way. Establishing connections between Wordsworth's *Prefaces* and the work of Peter Elbow make it possible to understand that language emanates not from the radically isolated individual (as the most familiar cultural understandings of romanticism would have it), but from immersion in the physical world. Understanding romantic-expressivist language in this way illuminates under-theorized aspects of language in the expressivist tradition, including the role of the physical body in writing, as well as the role of sense experience, presence, and physical location. Most significantly perhaps, this rereading complicates the field's often obsessive disavowals of the idea of voice in writing. Finally, this reimagined romantic conception of language brings productive complication to the most familiar and over-simplified divides between expressivism and constructionism, a goal of many contributors in this volume.

READING ROMANTICISM FOR COMPOSITION STUDIES

Since its disciplinary beginnings, composition studies has forged curious links to romanticism. Linda Flower, for example, in her textbook *Problem-Solving Strategies for Writers*, defines her problem-solving view of writing in opposition to what she deems a particularly romantic version of invention. The romantic model of writing, exemplified by Coleridge's "Kubla Kahn," she suggests, posits writing as effortless, mysterious, and as the domain of genius. Wanting to emphasize "learnability," Flower defines her rational, problem solving approach as the only reasonable alternative to Coleridge's (and by extension, romanticism's) seeming creative mysticism, its "myth of inspiration" (Flower, 1989, p.41). Accepting Coleridge's conception of writing, after all, would mean the writer isn't able to learn to write at all. For Flower, Coleridge, and romanticism more broadly, is big trouble for invention and big trouble for writing instruction.

Tethered to familiar romantic cultural tropes of original genius, mysticism, and inspiration, Coleridge, and more generally familiar "romantic" conceptions of writing, have become sites against which some compositionists have defined our disciplinary pursuits. Among the most familiar of these voices include Richard E. Young, who works to separate rhetoric's pursuits from a particularly resonant word on theories of Romantic invention, vitalism. "Vitalist assumptions, inherited from the Romantics," Young matter-of-factly states,

> with [their] stress on the natural powers of the mind and the uniqueness of the creative act, leads to a repudiation of the possibility of teaching the composing process, hence the tendency of current-traditional rhetoric to become a critical study of the products of composing and an art of editing. Vitalist assumptions become most apparent when we consider what is excluded from the present discipline that had earlier been included, the most obvious and significant exclusion being the art of invention. (2009, p. 398)

Vitalist influence for Young is then simultaneously romantic and detrimental to rhetoric's pursuits. Both Flower and Young offer shorthand conceptions of romantic ideas that they assume endure in culture, influencing writing students and teachers of writing. Moreover, they define this romantic influence antithetically to the pursuits of composition studies. From this viewpoint, to purport pedagogies or rhetorics inflected with romantic assumptions is to be backward—as Young says, romantic-vitalist assumptions put focus on products and take us back to the debunked, product-centered days of current-traditionalism. Indeed, as Hawk points out, composition scholars have most often used romanticism as "a category … in the discipline for identifying and excluding particular rhetorical practices" (Hawk, 2007, p. 1). Quickly naming a concept in composition studies "romantic" has then, on one hand, become shorthand in composition studies for dismissal and obsoletism.

On the other hand, though, and often working to problematize these quick links, many compositionists have conversely found the romantic period a fruitful site for contextualizing and expanding some of our disciplinary concerns. Berlin, Hawk, Fishman and McCarthy, and Gradin, to name a few, bring complexity and dimension to the relationship between composition and romanticism primarily through close readings of primary romantic texts and figures. James Berlin, for example, in "The Rhetoric of Romanticism" questions the grounds on which Young and others have made "Romanticism—and, by implication Coleridge—responsible for the erosion of rhetoric as a discipline" (1980, p. 62). Berlin close reads the primary texts of Coleridge to arrive at the conclusion that "many of the objections made to Coleridge's view of rhetoric would be rendered nugatory if those making them would realize that Coleridge does not demean rhetorical activity in favor of the poetic" (1980, p. 72). The close reading of primary romantic texts and figures reveals productive insights on the nuance of Coleridge's considerations of rhetoric and poetic. Byron Hawk performs similar, sustained close readings in order to understand differently the traditionally romantic concept of vitalism. Though he includes Coleridge on the way, Hawk reworks romantic influence by contextualizing vitalism in a history much longer than just the romantic period, extending it toward complexity theory (2007, p. 259). His book complicates the often-easy ways romanticism gets linked to composition. The result of these "closer looks" at romantic texts and ideas is a more nuanced understanding romantic writers and cultural ideals and an invigorated concept in composition. For Hawk, a more nuanced conception of vitalism opens space for him to reimagine pedagogy that fits "our current electronic context and the complex ecologies in which students write and think and situates these practices within a contemporary vitalist paradigm of complexity" (2007, p. 10). While there has been a habit of using romanticism to undermine certain schools of composition thought, romanticism can be equally generative, bringing new light to pervasive questions or conventional composition wisdoms. In the broadest sense, in this essay, I continue this productive act of looking back to romanticism to question the tacit ways in which expressivism has been tenuously linked to certain thin versions of romanticism.

Like vitalism, expressivism has garnered strong connections between composition and romanticism; naming expressivism "romantic," scholars have attempted to make it out of time, untenable, and passé. Lester Faigley, for example, implicitly weaves expressivism with romanticism in "Competing Theories of Process: A Critique and a Proposal." Faigley describes expressivism exclusively in romantic terms: expressivist and romantic figures become advocates of the other, such that romantic figures somehow anticipate and embody tenets of expressivist pedagogy. Faigley narrates these implicit connections by first naming Rohman and Wlecke "instigators of a 'neo-Romantic' view of process;" Peter Elbow is described as subscribing to the romantic theory "that 'good' writing does not follow the rules but reflects the processes of creative imagination" (1986, p. 530). And paradigmatic romantic figures make arguments about expressivism: "at times Wordsworth and to a lesser extent Coleridge seem to argue that expressivism precludes all intentionality" (1986, p. 530). In this way, Faigley's description of expressivist rhetoric doesn't argue for its romantic inflections, but makes this connection implicit. In his later work (Faigley, 1992) questions expressivism especially on its theorization of subjectivity,[1] finding it out of sync with the reign of postmodern subjectivity which, like other social constructivist-leaning compositionists, pushes him toward seeing language as shared social material rather than the domain of the individual. Here, yoking expressivism to romanticism ultimately becomes, as it did for Flower and Young, a means of undermining expressivist rhetorics.

Faigley finds the romantic-expressivist notion of selfhood problematic and ultimately finds ground for favoring social constructionist formulations of self and language. As Chris Burnham writes, "Faigley argues that expressivism's romantic view of the self is philosophically and politically retrograde, making it ineffectual in postmodern times. Further, expressivism's concern with the individual and authentic voice directs students away from social and political problems in the material world" (2001, p. 28). Burnham encapsulates how expressivism is most often defined against social constructionism. Expressivism, this broad juxtaposition tends to go, constructs a coherent self with a radically unique voice, while constructionism recognizes fragmented subjectivity and the sociality of language.

The link of expressivism to romanticism is, I suggest, in part from where this oversimplified binary emanates. Theories of language and selfhood tend to sharply divide constructionism from expressivism on the basis of expressivism's implicit links to versions of romantic theories of language and expression. Berlin—in spite of the nuanced way he understands romanticism and rhetoric—illustrates these connections; Gradin notes that Berlin is "almost single-handedly responsible" (1995, p. 2) for the divisions observed in contemporary rhetorics of expressivism, social constructionism, and cognitivism. As Berlin categorizes rhetorics and their histories in *Rhetoric and Reality*, he first links "expressionist rhetoric" emergent in the era of progressive education with "Brahminical romanticism" (1987, p. 73), a rhetoric devoted uniquely to the individual. From this perspective, in romantic-expressionistic rhetorics "the writer is trying to express—the content of knowledge—is the product of a private and personal vision that cannot be expressed in normal, everyday language" (1987, p. 74). In this description, romanticism, expressivism, and the idea of private language are consolidated. Later in his history Berlin writes that expressionistic rhetoric, or what he calls the "subjective rhetoric" of the 1960s and 70s," held the

> conviction that reality is a personal and private construct. For the expressionist, truth is always discovered within, through an internal glimpse, an examination of the private inner world. In this view the material world is only lifeless matter. The social world is even more suspect because it attempts to coerce individuals into engaging in thoughtless conformity. (1987, p. 145)

Berlin again emphasizes that in expressivist rhetorics, language and expression are thought to emanate from within the individual. Expression is deemed to be radically individual, unique and avoiding (or ignoring) influence from both the material and, by extension, social world. Berlin, ultimately an advocate of social constructionism, is quick then to explain how this inward-turned paradigm "denies the place of intersubjective, social processes in shaping language" (1987, p. 146). Put more plainly, social constructionists accuse expressivism of understanding language as individual, a private language that is supposed to be true and radically unique. Social constructionists, by contrast, see language as the province of the social group and thus there can be no purely personal truth or unique expression.

Taken together, Faigley and Berlin are constructionists who define themselves against expressivism on the issue of from "where" language emanates. Patricia Bizzell too echoes this distinction when she discusses the difference between outer and inner directed theorists:

> one theoretical camp sees writing as primarily inner-directed, and so is interested more in the structure of language-learning

and thinking processes in their earliest state, prior to social influence. The other main theoretical camp sees writing as primarily outer-directed, and so is more interested in the social processes whereby language-learning and thinking capacities are shaped and used in particular communities. (1992, p. 77)

Associating expressivism with romanticism enhances this divide. In the next section, I reread romanticism to complicate our sense of romantic expression.

REREADING ROMANTICISM: WORDSWORTH'S PREFACES TO LYRICAL BALLADS

This essay argues that romanticism can be an illuminating historical period for composition studies, laden as it is with theories of creativity, language, and subjectivity. In particular, as some compositionists have already demonstrated, taking a closer look at romantic texts complicates the dichotomy between expressivism and social constructionism. Steve Fishman, for example, aligns the writings of Elbow and German Romantic philosopher Johann Gottfried Herder, suggesting ultimately that "it was the social reform dimension of German romanticism that inspired expressivism" (1992, p. 647). This revised lineage provides a means of understanding expressivism's relation to the social. Fishman suggests that Herder and Elbow "stress the integration of personal life and public expression," understand expression as "the start of our dialogue with others," and are "critical of the exclusionary quality of academic discourse" (1992, p. 651). Fishman's comparative reading of Elbow and Herder leads him to understand both romanticism as a movement and Elbow as an expressivist figure in a new light: neither romanticism nor expressivism should be seen as asocial; instead, the emphasis on the individual's relation to the broader political and social community. In this way then, Fishman eases the dichotomy between expressivism and constructionism, understanding the focus on the personal as implicitly a focus on the social.

So too does Gradin, in her book-length second look at romanticism, seek ways to ease the divides between expressivism, feminism, and social constructionism. To accomplish this, like Fishman, Gradin revisits romantic primary texts primarily to see within romantic philosophies an investment in the social. Unlike Fishman however, she turns to highly visible figures from the English tradition, particularly Wordsworth and Coleridge, as she suggests that these figures "were much more directly influential on American educational thought that were the Germans" (Gradin, 1995, p. xvii). Overall, Gradin finds a productive thread running from romanticism to expressivism especially in the romantic theories of imagination (1995, p. 38) and in the ways romantics theorized education ("the importance of the individual; the importance of personal experience; and an emphasis on activity as opposed to passivity" (1995, p. 36)). Like Gradin, I turn back to a familiar romantic, William Wordsworth, but with a different goal. In theories of language from the period and from the pinnacle statement on language in the period, Wordsworth's *Preface*(s) and Appendix to *Lyrical Ballads*, I question the easy assumption that romantic-expressivist language is thought to emanate from the interior of the unique, isolated individual. Instead, the *Prefaces* suggest that language and meaning is found in of the sensuous world of physical experience. Following Fishman and Berlin's reading of Coleridge, depth and insight can come from careful micro-focused reading.

In order to glean from Wordsworth's *Prefaces* a novel way of understanding romantic expression, it's helpful to contextualize his work in conversations about language's origins popular in this period. In the eighteenth century, language became a philosophical "problem." Inquiries into the nature and the origin of language, including the relationship of physical, worldly things to language, accumulated. According to Hans Aarsleff, "language study" in this period "even when called philology," was not merely a matter of knowing the forms, syntax, phonology, historical relationships, and other aspects of particular languages. It involved questions of wider significance. What, for instance, was the origin of thought? Did the mind have a material basis? Did mankind have a single origin? (1967, p. 4). Considerations of language in the romantic period were also an opportunity to consider mind, thought, being, and knowledge. In these theories, many hypothesized a physical, embodied basis for language in early human interactions and interactions with the physical environment.[2] This broad sense that language has physical and material bases, provides the central premise of the work of Horne Tooke, the most important and popular language theorist in the period, to advance what would become a popular (Aarsleff, 1967, p. 73), provoking, lightning-rod text.

Tooke's *Diversions of Purley* published first in 1786, reissued in 1798 and released with a second volume in 1805 (dates which correspond with Romanticism's heyday) posits the most simplified version of language which argues that both language's origins and contemporary language systems are based in the material world. Completely undermining arbitrariness and fully embracing empiricist sensation, Tooke's "linguistic materialism" (McKusick, 1986, p. 12) deploys elaborate etymologies to show how words are immediately the signs of material things and concepts or what he calls "abbreviations" of them. Says Aarsleff, "Naming is the essence of language as Tooke had shown by tracing all words via etymology to the names of sensible objects" (1967, p. 94). Etymological analysis shows how parts in words correspond to the way we associate our physical experience with these things in the world; for example, Tooke offers "bar" as example meaning "defence," and then goes on to explain that a 'barn' is a covered enclosure, a 'baron,' a powerful man, 'barge,' a strong boat, etc. (Tooke, 1847). This simple idea that "all words can be reduced to names of sensations" was quite popular and tapped into some of the major concerns of the moment. In claiming that language is implicitly connected to physical experience in the world, Tooke's pervasive and popular thoughts on language carried many implications for romantic thought. One such implication is language's relationship to education. If language is out there in the material world, and not the domain of mind and education, rationality is dislodged from its centrality in matters of thinking and speaking. Olivia Smith helps articulate this implication for education as she states, "if sensation and feeling are the basis of vocabulary and all modes of thought, then experience and perception become reputable forms of knowledge and can no longer be described as essentially different from rationality and abstraction" (1984, p. 213).

Taking up the popular interest in language, Wordsworth's famous poetic experiment, *Lyrical Ballads*, with its explanatory prefaces and appendix, founds Romanticism as a movement. As is commonly remembered, recited in fact, Wordsworth's Advertisement to the 1798 *Lyrical Ballads* describes the poetry collection as an experiment as to "how far the language of conversation in the middle and lower classes of society is adapted to the purposes of poetic pleasure." And thus, language becomes central, but not so central, to Romanticism as a literary movement. I say, "not-so" as an acknowledgement to the fact that while language is the experiment so touted, it is not what is often considered "revolutionary" about this text. Rather in more conventional readings of Romanticism, feeling seems to overshadow language's sensuousness. However, especially in light of Tooke's theory—published and republished as it was just before Wordsworth's first publication of *Lyrical Ballads* in 1798—Wordsworth's *Prefaces* participate in the origin of language debates by arguing that expression suited to poetry should be saturated not with the unique emanations of the genius poet, as is often thought, but instead this expression should reveal the physical, inhabited world of the speaker.

One place to see Hooke's theory of language reflected is in Wordsworth's articulation of his experiment in the 1802 preface. Here Wordsworth shifts the terms of his language revolution to "a selection of the real language of men in a state of vivid sensation" and "a selection of language really used by men" (Preface to 1802). I want to here really lean on that new phrase "vivid sensation" and link it to Tooke's theory of language. Wordsworth advocates for language that emerges in relation to physical, material, natural encounters. Rather than language being abstract, poetical language should emerge from context, sensation, and feeling.

Moreover, as Gradin's work details, Wordsworth had particular liberatory ideas about education and the social classes. For his poetic experiment, he focuses on "low and rustic life" as the subject and speakers of many of his poems. Wordsworth focuses on the lives of the "rustics" as a poetic ideal because, he writes, "in that condition, the essential passions of the heart find a better soil in which they can attain their maturity, are less under restraint, and speak a plainer more emphatic language" and because "such men hourly communicate with the best objects from which the best part of language is originally derived" (Preface to 1802). Like Tooke, Wordsworth believes that expression should not be trained, rational, and abstract; which is to say in another way that poetry should no longer follow neoclassical rules. Instead, expression should emerge from lived experience; facility with language and expression comes best from those who can "hourly communicate" with the physical world.

The Appendix to the 1802 *Lyrical Ballads* too dramatizes Wordsworth's theory of romantic expression. To begin, Wordsworth thinks back to the origins of poetry first stating, "The earliest Poets of all nations generally wrote from passion excited by real events; they wrote naturally, and as men" (Appendix to 1802). By contrast, he sees in his immediate predecessors the mechanization of poetic language. These poets produce language without the influence of sense experience:

> desirous of producing the same effect, without having the same animating passion, set themselves to a mechanical adoption of those figures of speech, and made use of them, sometimes with propriety, but much more frequently applied them to feelings and ideas with which they had no natural connection whatsoever. A language was thus insensibly produced, differing materially from the real language of men in any situation. (Appendix to 1802.)

Wordsworth's poetic experiment is in this way a critique of poetic expression that fails to rely on physical sensation and physical experience with the world. He wants poets to express language having a "natural connection" to one's real, lived experience in the world. He is against "a language ... thus insensibly produced" (Appendix to 1802), against language that's hollow and abstracted. This phrase—"insensibly produced" language—echoes Tooke's theory of language. Wordsworth aligns with Tooke by understanding language as emergent from the world of experience, sense, and feeling. Wordsworth's "rustics," close to nature and "hourly communicat[ing] with the best objects from which the best part of language originally derived" (Preface to 1802) become the expressive ideal. This theory of romantic language and expression, as shaped by close readings of Wordsworth and Tooke, sees words as fundamentally "out there," accessed through physiological sensation and feeling. Rather than assuming that romantic expression as isolated and inward-looking, this second look at the most canonical of Wordsworth's thinking shows instead that expressive-romantic expression looks decidedly outwardly, toward first-person, embodied, sense experience, as if writers were "standing in a landscape of language" (Smith, 1984, p. 215).

REREADING EXPRESSIVISM: ANOTHER LENS FOR "VOICE" IN WRITING

By taking this second look at romantic theories of language, the "expression" in expressivism can look substantially different. By expanding on the tacit link that Berlin and others have made between expressivism and romanticism through close reading of a canonical romantic text, some of Berlin's foundational and lasting assertions about expressivism denying the social and valuing the inwardness of unique expression could be challenged. For one, this rereading of Wordsworth goes some distance in undoing certainty about the supposed inwardness of language in romantic philosophies. It is useful also to cut through these binary impulses more directly by applying Wordsworth's romantic theory of language directly to a still percolating debate about the idea of voice in writing. I want to expand the possibilities for understanding language and voice, and ultimately then, expand our senses of the "expressivist tradition."

There are few more vexed concepts in composition, and in expressivism more specifically, than voice. Linked to this concept are debates about subjectivity and selfhood, structures of power, and theories of language. Most stable about this concept seems to be its unrelenting persistence and imprecision. As Peter Elbow writes in *Voice in Writing Again: Embracing Contraries*, critiques of voice "seem valid, yet voice stays alive, even in the most "naïve" forms that have been the most powerfully critiqued" (2007, p. 3). Darcie Bowden, among the most vociferous critics of the voice metaphor, echoes this ambivalence: "the permutations and varying conceptions of voice, especially during the 1970s and 1980s, make voice difficult to completely support or to completely reject as a useful metaphor for textual analysis or for pedagogy" (1999, p. vii). Voice has become a key site for debate in liberatory, feminist, expressivist, and multicultural rhetorics, as "voice is a pivotal metaphor in composition and rhetoric studies [as it] focuses attention on authorship, on identity, on narrative, and on power" (Bowden, 1999, p. viii). While voice in general endures as a concept, there are nonetheless voices in the field that, like Faigley, understand voice as matter-of-factly untenable in our current postmodernist, poststructuralist framework. Mimi Orner, for example, scrutinizes the idea of voice in liberatory education rhetorics, claiming plainly that "calls for 'authentic student voice' contain realist and essentialist epistemological positions regarding subjectivity which are neither acknowledged specifically nor developed theoretically" (1992, p. 75). Voice, under this critique, implies stable identity and personal language. Writes Orner, "discourses on student voice are premised on the assumption of a fully conscious, fully speaking, 'unique, fixed, and coherent' self" (Orner, 1992, p. 79). Bowden, on similar theoretical grounds, argues that voice has lived past its usefulness as her whole book rests on the "assumption that that there can be no such thing as voice, that it was a metaphor of particular historical moment, and that that moment has passed" (1999, p. viii). The idea of voice in writing becomes most vigorously critiqued when voice is said to reveal a unique individual and when language is thought to reveal the self, each accusations leveled at expressivist voice in general.

Keeping Wordsworth's desire for expression to be saturated with experience in mind, we can understand Peter Elbow's concern with voice as a concern with physical reality and experience; that is, voice in Elbow and more broadly across expressivist thinking, can be understood not as transcendent personal truth or unique expression, but instead as alive, embodied language that sounds like a real human person is speaking. Using Wordsworth's romantic theory of language as a backdrop highlights Elbow's concern with the physical body, the spoken voice, and attention to contexts for speaking.

To begin seeing this physical nuance in expressivist voice, I look back to Elbow's 1968 essay "A Method for Teaching Writing." This essay describes Elbow's experience helping conscientious objectors writing petitions to avoid the draft. Much of how Elbow talks about voice and expression in this essay is echoed in how Wordsworth talks about poetic language in his *Prefaces*. Central to this essay is Elbow's concern for writing that is "alive" (1968, p. 122). Evidence of life in written language is, for Elbow, "when words carry the sound of a person" (1968, p. 122). Like Wordsworth, then, Elbow emphasizes the importance of language sounding true to one's lived experience, the words uttered in the experienced world—or as Wordsworth might say, the "real language of men in any situation" (Appendix to 1802). Moreover, Elbow explicitly values language connected to experience, explaining that "everyone does have a 'word-hoard': a collection of words that are connected to his strong and primary experiences in the world—as opposed to words which (putting it inexactly) are only connected to other words" (1968, p. 120). With a focus on language relating to physical experience in the material world, Elbow here cites Vygotsky's *Thought and Language* on the difference between spontaneous and scientific concepts. Just as Elbow briefly explains, spontaneous or "everyday" concepts "are the meanings of words of everyday language, which a child uses in everyday life/interaction, while scientific concepts are the ones the child masters during systematic instruction of basic knowledge" (Temina-Kingsolver, 2008). Implicit then in Elbow's suggestion of writer's "word-hoards" is the idea that language has an explicit connection to worldly experience, aligning with the romantic-expressivist conception of language as having a material, physical basis.

There is much made about how expressivism falsely supposes that one can access through language a transcendent self or personal truth. Mimi Orner, writing on voice in liberatory rhetorics, argues that "calls for student voice in education presume students, voices, and identities to be singular, unchanging and unaffected by the context in which the speaking occurs" (1992, p. 80). In "A Method for Teaching Writing," an essay that could be categorized under liberatory rhetorics, Elbow moves away from this side of the voice concept, explaining again more of a concern with physical bodies in the real world. Elbow writes:

> but I am not talking about intimate, autobiographical "self-exposure" when I talk of "revealing a self in words." Writing in words which "reveal the self" has nothing necessarily to do with exposing intimacies—undressing. For I am talking about the sound or feel of a believable person simply in the fabric of the words ... the most impersonal reasoning—in lean, laconic, "unrevealing" prose—can nevertheless be alive and infused with the presence of a person or a self. (1968, p. 123)

Elbow here is very clear that he's not interested in personal truths or confessions, but with getting words on the page that are saturated with experience, words that come out of the body, not ones conceived of in a purely intellectual way, not from that tissue of words only connected to other words.

There is certainly more to say about Elbow's takes on voice across his work but in this 1968 essay it becomes very clear that voice has fundamentally to do with the body and sense experience. But this embodied basis for voice is somewhat under-theorized in Elbow's own considerations and the more general ways voice circulates as a concept in our field. In his most recent, extensive consideration of physical voice too, *Vernacular Eloquence,* Elbow only seems to narrowly suggest that his interest in the speaking voice and the natural pacing of intonation units has something to do with the body and with language being connected to the physical world. Sounding a lot like Wordsworth in the *Prefaces*, Elbow's mission in the book is to shift the paradigm of literate culture: "our culture of literacy functions as though it were a plot against the spoken voice, the human body, vernacular language, and those without privilege" (2012, p. 7). But only in one section does Elbow attempt to consider the implications of embodiment theory. Occasionally, he will make mention of the embodied nature of language, such as, "our longest and usually deepest experience of how words carry meaning involves felt bodily experience, not just intellectual understanding" (2012, p. 252). Beyond this though, the voice in expressivism has remained mostly disembodied. Putting new focus on romantic primary texts reveals a way to understand romantic expression as experiential and physical. Rereading romanticism in this way helps us disrupt the sticky sense that expressivism is about radically unique self-expression and even that language is the domain of each individual. Rather, another version of romantic expressivist version of voice only really asks that writer's "put their body where their words are" (Elbow, 2012, p. 253).

Elbow has tirelessly reexamined voice in his own thinking, as well as in the thinking of his critics. This view of voice as seen above encapsulates Elbow's most recent emphasis on voice as spoken, lived, and embodied. And this embodied dimension of voice seems to be something Bowden can agree with Elbow on. Bowden takes a whole chapter of her book to "detach the literal voice from the metaphorical one" (1999, p. 82) and demonstrate the usefulness of this to reading practices: "the only useful application of voice may stem from an understanding of how the literal voice operates in reading" (Bowden, 1999, p. 83). Bowden's chapter in support of literal voice has her sounding very much like Elbow in her recommendations to enlist the spoken voice for interpretation and revision. Bowden writes: "reading aloud helps writers and readers tap into their aural imaging, and understand at a visceral level the rhythms, contours, and tones of a written text" (1999, p. 97). Amidst the restless ground of voice then, Bowden, Elbow, and Wordsworth find a common ground in the idea that written expression has a basis in the embodied and physical voice.

A rereading of romanticism highlights a way of conceptualizing voice and language in the expressivist tradition in a way that emphasizes its physicality, rather than its inwardness. This in turn complicates the easy ways expressivism is divided from social constructionism. Romantic theories of language value first-person experience, but experiential and sense experience instead of uniqueness or transcendence. Moreover, looking back to romanticism provides another, under-theorized way of considering language that can also disrupt the expressivism/constructionism binary.

The romantics conceived of language and meaning as fundamentally embodied and material. Wordsworth and Tooke's romantic theories of language create an under-theorized connection from romanticism to composition. This emphasis can be linked to current work in composition. For example, Sondra Perl's conception of felt sense would be a site at which language is understood as a physical act. Working from the philosophies of Eugene Gendlin, Perl's conception of felt sense "calls attention to what is just on the edge of our thinking but not yet articulated in words" (2004, p. xiii), a view that there is meaning, located in the body, prior to and informing of language. Perl suggests "that language and meaning are connected to inchoate, bodily intuitions" (2004, p. xvii). Perl ends up nodding to an expressivist tradition here too, positing the physical body as a site of fresh and "true" expression. Tapping into felt sense in this way echoes expressivist practice in which the body's "natural" rhythms might resonate with lived experience. This embodied view of language is further elaborated in the work of Lakoff and Johnson. *Metaphors We Live By* kicks off their exploration of the embodied foundations of language, demonstrating that metaphors aren't specialized language but have implicit physical dimensions. Johnson, in his book *The Meaning of the Body: Aesthetics of Human Understanding*, writes "an embodied view of meaning looks for the origins and structures of meaning in the organic activities of embodied creatures in interaction with their changing environments" (2007, p. 11). Much more than a cognitive engagement with language, Johnson suggests, "meaning reaches deep down into our corporeal encounter with our environment" (2007, p. 25). Johnson here echoes Wordsworth's concern for "hourly communicating" with the physical world. If we see language as having a physical basis, the product of embodied human beings inhabiting a material world, how might we understand voice, expression, identity, and authorship differently?

CONCLUSION: REVISING THE DIVIDES

If composition studies can be neatly divided into camps, paradigms, and pedagogies, there certainly will be some generalizing that doesn't hold true in all cases. Expressivism, a historical time period and a set of informing orientations, certainly takes its fair share of overgeneralizing. As a complement to these broad disciplinary stories, we also engage in work on the micro-level, calling into question the way these broad camps divide us. As Hawk says, "counter-histories can always be drawn, and new groupings of texts, events, and practices can always be articulated. The goal of such a historiography is not simply to arrive at a more accurate image of the past but to create a particular affect in the present" (Hawk, 2007, p. 11). Looking back to romantic theories of language brings another more complex dimension to voice, expression, and the mythos of personal language that often sticks to conceptions of expressivism. While the broadest strokes tend to come from critics of expressivism, this revisionary move can even shift the grounds that expressivist advocates may stake for it. Chris Burnham for example describes "expressivism's strength" as "its insistence that all concerns, whether individual, social, or political, must originate in personal experience and be documented in the student's own language" (Burnham, 2001, p. 31). This is a familiar refrain about expressivism. But in the context of Wordsworth, how we understand "personal experience" and the "student's own language"—some of the most essential ways we have to talk generally about what expressivism is—is different. Personal experience, then, is not necessarily personal writing or self-expression, but writing infused with physical experience out in the world—first person experience, in other words, that doesn't lead necessarily to one's own singular language. Rather than seeing expressivist language as personal, unique, and transcendent, romantic texts make available a way of seeing language and expression as having fundamentally a material and embodied basis.

If language can be conceived as neither the domain of the individual or purely the social group, then some of the deepest divisions between constructionism and expressivism are eased. Especially as constructionism has branched off in our current moment to a focus on networks, location, situatedness, and material systems in ecological, post-process, and spatial theories, a revised sense of romantic-expressive language as material and embodied draws attention to a writer's always shifting physical location and relation with the world.

NOTES

1. In *Fragments of Rationality: Postmodernity and the Subject of Composition*, Faigley "questions the existence of a rational, coherent self and the ability of the self to have privileged insight into its own process" (1992, p. 111).

2. Three essayists who considered the origins of language were Thomas Reid, Lord Monboddo, and Condillac. Thomas Reid thought that in language there are artificial as well as natural signs, and "particularly that the thoughts purposes, and dispositions of the mind have their natural signs in the face, the modulation of the voice, and motion and attitude of the body" (McKusick, 1986, p. 11) and without this natural meaning located in the body, "language could never have been established among men" (McKusick, 1986, p. 11). For Lord Monboddo, the process of language learning should begin with the natural, embodied signs and meanings and "only by means of them can the learner become oriented within the much larger class of conventional signs" (McKusick, 1986, p. 12). Condillac, by contrast, pushes the origins of language out in to the physical world. These thinkers' explanations of language's relationship to sense experience demonstrate the pervasiveness of this embodied, experiential view in the romantic period.

REFERENCES

Aarsleff, H. (1967). *The study of language in England: 1780-1860*. Princeton, NJ: Princeton University Press.

Berlin, J. A. (1980). The rhetoric of romanticism: The case for Coleridge. *Rhetoric Society Quarterly, 10*(2), 62-74.

Berlin, J. A. (1987). *Rhetoric and reality: Writing instruction in American colleges, 1900-1985*. Carbondale, IL: Southern Illinois University Press.

Bizzell, P. (1992). *Academic discourse and critical consciousness*. Pittsburgh, PA: University of Pittsburgh Press.

Bowden, D. (1999). *The mythology of voice*. Portsmouth: Boynton/Cook.

Burnham, C. (2001). Expressive pedagogy: Practice/theory, theory/practice. In G. Tate, A, Rupiper, & K. Schick (Eds.), *A guide to composition pedagogies* (pp. 19-35). New York: Oxford University Press.

Elbow, P. (1968). A method for teaching writing. *College English, 30*(2), 115-125.

Elbow, P. (2007). Voice in writing again: Embracing contraries. *College English, 70*(2), 168-188. *Selected Works of Peter Elbow*. Retrieved from http://works.bepress.com/peter_elbow/23/

Elbow, P. (2012). *Vernacular eloquence: What speech can bring to writing*. New York: Oxford.

Faigley, L. (1986). Competing theories of process: A critique and a proposal. *College English, 48*(6), 527-542.

Faigley, L. (1992). *Fragments of rationality: Postmodernity and the subject of composition*. Pittsburgh, PA: University of Pittsburgh Press.

Fishman, S. M. & McCarthy, L. P. (1992). Is expressivism dead? Reconsidering its romantic roots and its relation to social constructionism. *College English, 54*(6), 647-661.

Flower, L. (1989). *Problem-solving strategies for writing* (3rd ed.). San Diego, CA: Hartcourt Brace Jovanovich.

Gradin, S. L. (1995). *Social expressivist perspectives on the teaching of writing*. Portsmouth: Boynton/Cook.

Hawk, B. (2007). *A counter-history of composition: Toward methodologies of complexity*. Pittsburgh: University of Pittsburgh Press.

Johnson, M. (2007). *The meaning of the body: Aesthetics of human understanding*. Chicago: University of Chicago Press.

Lakoff, G., & Johnson, M. (1980). *Metaphors we live by*. Chicago: University of Chicago Press.

McKusick, J. C. (1986). *Coleridge's philosophy of language*. New Haven, CT: Yale University Press.

Orner, M. (1992). Interrupting the calls for student voice in "liberatory" education: A feminist poststructuralist perspective. In C. Luke, & J. Gore (Eds.), *Feminisms and critical pedagogy* (pp. 74-89). New York: Routledge.

Perl, S. (2004). *Felt sense: Writing with the body*. Portsmouth, NH: Heinemann.

Smith, O. (1984). *The politics of language, 1791-1819*. Oxford: Oxford University Press.

Temina-Kingsolver, V. (2008). Scientific v. spontaneous concepts: A Vygotskian perspective. *Languageavenue.com*. Retrieved from http://languageavenue.com/psycholinguistics/language-and-thought/scientific-vs-spontaneous-concepts-vygotskian-perspective/distinctive-characteristics

Tooke, J.H. (1857). *Diversions of Purley*. London: William Tegg. Retrieved from https://play.google.com/books/reader?printsec=frontcover&output=reader&id=izYOAAAAMAAJ&pg=GBS.PA436

Wordsworth, W. (1798). Advertisement to lyrical ballads. Retrieved from University of Pennsylvania Department of English Web site: http://www.english.upenn.edu/~mgamer/Etexts/lbprose.html#advertisement

Wordsworth, W. (1802a). Appendix to the preface to lyrical ballads: By what is usually called Poetic Diction. Retrieved from University of Pennsylvania Department of English Web site: http://www.english.upenn.edu/~mgamer/Etexts/lbprose.html#advertisement

Wordsworth, W. (1802b). Preface to lyrical ballads. Retrieved from University of Pennsylvania Department of English Web site: http://www.english.upenn.edu/~mgamer/Etexts/lbprose.html#advertisement

Young, R. (2009). Paradigms and problems: Needed research in rhetorical invention. In S. Miller (Ed.), *The Norton book of composition studies* (pp. 397-415). New York: W.W. Norton.

EMERSON'S PRAGMATIC CALL FOR CRITICAL CONSCIENCE: DOUBLE CONSCIOUSNESS, COGNITION, AND HUMAN NATURE

Anthony Petruzzi *
University of Massahussetts Boston

Ralph Waldo Emerson, William James and John Dewey, in various keys, develop a philosophy of pragmatic naturalism that articulates the continuity and inter-animation between human experience and nature. By the time Darwin published *Origin of the Species* in 1855, Emerson's work as a natural philosopher had already led him to a general understanding of the evolutionary continuity between simple and complex forms of life: "the fossil strata show us that Nature began with rudimentary forms, and rose to the more complex, as fast as the earth was fit for their dwelling place; and that the lower perish, as the higher appear" (1983, p. 1033; also pp. 175-176; 668-669; 945). James and Dewey both started their work by focusing on psychology and evolution—exploring the ways that mental activity is connected to our physical nervous system. They argued that the brain is continuous with the body as part of their critique of the traditional philosophical dualism between body and soul. Hephzibah Roskelly and Kate Ronald note, "Emerson foreshadows not only the pragmatism of Peirce, James and Dewey, and others, but the studies of cognition and literacy that have influenced composition studies so profoundly in the last thirty years" (1998, p. 56).[1]

Joan Richardson places pragmatism's studies of cognition in a Darwinian context: "the signal, if implicit, motive of pragmatism is the realization of thinking as a life form, subject to the same processes of growth and change as all other life forms" (p. 1). Human cognition is located in our animal nature; our minds are embodied (Lakoff & Johnson, 1999, pp. 16-44; Unger, 2007, pp. 136-137; Herrnstein Smith, 1997, pp. 46-47). As Richardson notes, "James learned from Darwin and from Emerson to consider not only language but thinking, too, as a life form constantly undergoing adaption and mutation" (p. 8). For Emerson, the brain is continually expressing these adaptions and transformations. Some, like Descartes, claim our minds are eternal "souls" and our brains are merely mechanical (Doidge, 2007, pp. 213). Others such as

Emerson and the classical pragmatists claim that "because the history of nature is characterized in" the brain (1983, p. 548; also see Pierce, 1955, p. 359) our mind/soul must be understood in terms of natural science: the evolutionary and cognitive patterns of instincts, habits, beliefs, affects, attention, moods, classifications, and imaginations constitute various historically sedimented and yet evolving cognitive abilities.

For Emerson and the classical pragmatists, persuasion must understand, explore, and use cognitive patterns to effectively alter others' beliefs. In order to understand the materiality of persuasion, Emerson identifies two patterns in the human mind—two evolutionary forces or instincts, one centripetal and the other centrifugal. They form our double consciousness, one private and one public, which are locked into an "irreconcilable antagonism" (Emerson, 1983, p. 174). The inter-animation of these "two poles of nature" (Emerson, 1983, p. 173) provides "a certain self-regulated motion, or change" (Emerson, 1983, p. 457). The human conscience is constituted in the space between the centripetal and centrifugal forces that inter-animate one's double consciousness of private and public mind. The two evolved cognitive tendencies are survival instincts: self-protection, a conservative, centripetal force;[2] and self-projection, an expansive, innovative, centrifugal force.[3] The call to conscience emerges and sways between the two poles of nature, between the two instincts, where a social and individual psychology emerges with the same biological and cultural plasticity and ameliorative properties as the rest of nature.[4]

Emerson articulates the two primary forces of nature's self-regulation—self-protection and self-projection—which occur in the human brain as two contrary instincts more persistently and clearly than the other classical pragmatists. "No [hu]man" Emerson states, "can continue to exist in whom both of these elements do not work" (1983, p. 176). However, he admits, to establish a "harmony of the centrifugal and centripetal forces" (1983, pp. 174; 549; 628) would make "an impossible whole." In The Conservative, Emerson identifies this "primal antagonism" as "the two parties that divide the state, the party of Conservatism and that of Innovation" (1983, p. 173). Human politics, throughout civic history, demonstrates how we strive to hold society together in "an impossible whole" (Emerson, 1983, p. 175). Self-protection is the centripetal force that conserves tradition, "the actual state of things" (Emerson, 1983, p. 174) and the individual's everyday public understanding of one's world. In the self-protecting mode, one's discourse and understanding is embodied, limited, partial; while it does have some truth value, it also has false values; but it remains useful because in this mode of being-in-the-world, we are conditioned to operate in the known limits of the state of things (Emerson, 1983, p. 176-177). This "existing world is not a dream ... but it is the ground on which [we] stand, it is the mother of whom [we] are born" (Emerson, 1983, p. 177). We are thrown into the existing world and it provides a conditioned ground for us to thrive. As Emerson states: "we are encamped in nature, not domesticated" (1983, p. 552).

Self-projection is the centrifugal force that pushes us from our center, our grounding in endoxa (everyday public knowledge), opening an individual's understanding to different understandings of one's world. In the self-projecting mode, one's discourse and understanding is incarnate, expansive, and ecstatic; its force pushes us up from the ground of the actual so that the private mind emerges from self-protective modes of thinking imposed on it by public embodied discourse to imagine new possibilities for being-in-the-world. Neither feature of double consciousness, the private or the public, is otherworldly; rather, they exist in a transitive network down to the molecular level: "All things are in contact; every atom has a sphere of repulsion" (Emerson, 1983, p. 585). The sphere of attraction and repulsion, of closing one's self off from possible threats to one's being and opening one's self up to new possibilities for being, is at the heart of the undomesticated antagonism.

Self-protection is the centripetal adaptive instinct to defend tradition and the status quo—to conserve the beliefs and knowledge of the present order. It does not domesticate us because it is compensated by self-projecting instinct to change and transform ourselves and our relations to the environing world. These "strange alternation[s] of attraction and repulsion" (Emerson, 1983, p. 503) are tendencies or patterns of nature nurturing; they sway between the withdrawing (self-protection) and arrival (self-projection) to disclose the partiality of truths, which are not calculable, not measureable. The polarities are always already embodied in human discourse, cognition, and experience, and, for Emerson, indicative of how the brain/mind physically operates according to tendencies of human nature. The self "can not live without a world" (1983, p. 254), Emerson claims, because it is a necessary platform that resists our instinct to expand outwards, to be self-reliant, to imagine and project ameliorations for one's future.

One's imagination emerges in the gravitational force that sways between the private and public minds or selves—what Dewey calls the "inner and outer vision," when "possibilities are embodied … that are not elsewhere actualized" (1980, p. 268). Imagination is not isolated from the environing world, nor is it a faculty of mind, self-contained and separate from history; it is a cognitive and communicative act: "Expression of experience is public and communicating because the experiences expressed are what they are because of experiences of the living and dead that have shaped them" (Dewey, 1980, p. 270). Self-expression is a most human behavior, opening our habituated public self to "an influx of the ever new, ever sanative conscience" (Emerson, 1983, p. 256). The call of conscience emerges in the inter-animation of private integrity—"nothing at last is sacred but the integrity of your own mind" (Emerson, 1983, p. 261)—and public care for one's world. Conscience calls the private mind from submersion in the public mind, and recalls our desire for self-reliance—to imagine, project, and innovate towards a better state of things (Emerson, 1983, p. 174; Dewey, 1922, pp. 106ff). Self-projection is the imaginative reformation of the self and existing reality.

Contrary to Richard Rorty and Stanley Fish's claims—that there is no conception of critical self-awareness or self-consciousness that is not "at once impossible and superfluous" (Fish, 1989, pp. 463-464; also see Rorty, 1991b, pp. 211ff), I argue that the "axis" upon which a classical pragmatist theory of persuasion turns is a "call to conscience," which discloses critical self-awareness as a cognitive event that is directed by care and attention, imagined by thinking and disclosed by action that is ameliorative. Emerson and the classical pragmatists—James, Pierce, and Dewey—are important interlocutors for the field of rhetoric and composition, even though in most classification schemas of the field, their work has not been fully explored. I focus on three cognitive features that Emerson and the classical pragmatists describe—classification, imagination, and the plasticity of the mind—that are particularly useful for understanding how classical pragmatism is affiliated with rhetoric and composition. On the one hand, we will see how critical conscience is the way human beings interact with their environment at specific moments, not a faculty of mind, or a permanent state of critical awareness. And, on the other hand, I propose an interpretation of pragmatist rhetoric that has substantial differences from what Steven Mailloux calls, "a rhetoricized version of contemporary neo-pragmatism" (1998, p. 56). Rather than focusing on conventions and beliefs, as do the neo-pragmatists, the classical pragmatists focus on why affective reasoning and imagination are both persuasive and expresses truth: as Dewey notes, reasoning "must fall back upon imagination—upon the embodiment of ideas in emotionally charged sense" (1980, p. 33). My claim focuses on three aspects of human expressivity—classification, imagination, and plasticity—explicated by pragmatism's cognitive science; which can lead rhetoric and composition to a less antagonistic relationship with critical discourse—legitimating research that focuses on individuality, self-expression, and mindful being-in-the-world.

COGNITION AND CLASSIFICATION

Classical pragmatists were at the forefront of cognitive psychology to contextualize the continuities between humans, as beings embodied in the world, and nature. The continuities include, but are not limited to, these three cognitive features—classification, imagination, and plasticity—which offer us useful, albeit narrow, examples that contribute generally to pedagogy, and specifically to rhetoric and composition, so, as James puts it, we can "make our nervous systems our ally instead of our enemy" (1992, p. 140). For James, classification is a feature of "our organic mental structure" that was produced accidentally by evolutionary variation, "then transmitted as fixed [a] feature" (1955, p. 851). As George Lakoff and Mark Johnson note, "every living being categorizes ... food, predators, possible mates, members of their own species, and so on" (1999, p. 17). Culturally and socially, classification is central to organization of human institutions, particularly education and generally to the organization of intellectual history. As Mike Rose aptly notes, classification schemes both "sharpen [our] own abilities to systematize what [we] study, and to develop a critical awareness of the limitations of classification schemes" that we are submerged in (1989, p. 139).

From a rhetorical point of view, classification starts as an invention strategy divisio, the division into categories or classes and then becomes dispositio, the effective arrangement of ideas that structure an argument. As Frank J. D'Angelo argues, rhetorical topics are "differentiations of basic mental processes that have evolved over thousands of years" (Judd, 2005, p. 81. From a cognitive point of view, classification is a phenomenological/hermeneutical act that psychologically is both private and public: we understand everything in term of its structure. We understand it as a danger, as a food source, as something that matters or not, as something to care for, or not. According to Patricia Smith Churchland, "pre-scientifically, we classify things on the basis of their gross physical and behavioral similarity, or on the basis of the relevance to our particular needs and interests." (2002, p. 124). In a scientific context, classification schemes order "the reality behind appearances" according to specific principles that "have an effect on perceptual recognition" (Churchland, 2002, p. 129). In either case, classification structures how the brain understands something as-something: we must know something as-something before we can understand or make statements about it (Heidegger, 1996, pp. 139ff). What one perceives depends upon either one's needs and interests or one's sense that there is a pattern that organizes what is perceived.

Classification, in the public sense, is the process of surveying a field of objects to discern and thematize patterns, to identify and distinguish and therefore to define or redefine the topic. This is useful for cognition because it frames and structures one's argument in relation to the categories created by the topographical map. In the public mind,[5] the classification becomes part of social and institutional power—i.e. in higher education, it is used to control what and how a subject is taught.[6] How does one teach composition in the university? Is there one theory of composition that works most effectively? Should pedagogy focus on the product or on the writing process? Questions like these exist because our minds are embodied; cognitive operations like classifying are structured by how bodies/minds have evolved, therefore structuring our everyday understanding of the order of things.

Emerson was fascinated by natural science, especially how the cognitive ability of the human brain uses classification schemes to advance factual knowledge.[7] Emerson intends to give an "account, which the human mind gives to itself of the constitution of the world" (1983, p. 634). Emerson's knowledge of neural networks was up to date for his time; he was aware of Galvani's discovery that nerves operate on electrical energy and he hypothesized that the mind uses electrical, and therefore physical, force to shape and animate the mind. The interaction of a brain/mind shapes both the mind and world: "Every solid in the universe is ready to become fluid on the approach of the mind, and the power to flux it is the measure of the mind .... The whole world is the flux of matter over the wires of thought to the poles or points where it would build" (Emerson, Essays 1983, p. 964-965).

Classification is closely related to imaginative cognition that is necessary in the natural sciences, as well as the humanities: "Science does not know its debt to imagination" (Emerson, 1929, vol. 8, p. 10). Emerson argues that classification is a cognitive activity, a "tyrannical instinct of the mind" (1972, vol. 2, p. 23): "it is the perpetual effort of the mind to seek relations between the multitude of facts under its eye, by means of which it can reduce them to some order" (1972, vol. 2, p. 22). Emerson identifies classification both as an instinct and as one of "the actions of the intellect" (1972, vol. 2, p. 25) because it discloses unexpected resemblances and common origins between things that, at first, appear unrelated (1972, vol. 2, p. 27).

For Emerson, classification creates a vocabulary that becomes part of the private and public mind, an antagonistic discourse within our double consciousness. The instinct to classify is natural and useful; yet, it has a double edge because as it becomes commonplace knowledge of the public mind, we lose sight of the fact that we are part and partial of an organic system that continually changes:

> A nomenclature, a classification used by the scholar as a help to the memory, or a bare illustration of his present perception of the law of nature, the memorandum only of his last lesson, and, in the face of it, merely a makeshift; merely momentary; a landing place on the staircase, a bivouac for a night, and implying a march, a progress [that] becomes, through the indolence or absence of mind, a barrack, a stronghold, an obstacle; in which the man settles down immoveable, insane, obstinate,

mistaking his means for his ends ... and requires your respect to this whimsy as to truth itself. (1972, vol. 3, pp. 129-130)

Emerson and the classical pragmatists describe classification in a way that is useful to argumentation, persuasion, and pedagogy of composition because it is based on understanding our human nature—how our brain/mind actually works. For classical pragmatists, every time one classifies, one encounters the sway of "doubleness" between its usefulness for the private mind and its dangers for the public mind.

Dewey agrees with Emerson, classification is one of the various instinctual organizational tendencies that circumscribe all mental activity:

> To classify is, indeed, as useful as it is natural. The indefinite multitude of particular and changing events is met by the mind with acts of defining, inventorying, and listing, reducing to common heads and tying up in bunches. [These acts] are performed for a purpose. [But we often lose sight of the purpose] to facilitate our dealings with individuals and changing events. Our thought [becomes] hard where facts are mobile; bunched and chunky, where events are fluid and dissolving. The tendency to forget the office of distinctions and classifications, and to take them as marking things in themselves, is a fallacy. (1992, p. 131)

Dewey's stipulation that classification does not represent things in themselves echoes Emerson's description of how self-protection works to turn contingent classifications into fixed truths.

Our environment forces us to pay attention to an array of "indefinite multitude of particular and changing events" (James, 1992, p. 227); also, we use systems of classification to assess the amount of attention we need to spend on a given object. In other words, in order to create opportunities to self-project, to take advantage of changing events, decisive classification is necessary. As Herrnstein Smith notes

> human beings have evolved as distinctly opportunistic creatures and that our survival, both as individuals and as a species, continues to be enhanced by our ability and inclination to reclassify objects and to "realize" and "appreciate" novel and alternate functions for them—which is also to misuse them and to fail to respect their presumed purposes and conventional generic classifications. (1988, pp. 32-33 also see pp. 122-123)

Lakoff and Johnson give a concrete biological example of how classification allows us to function in the world opportunistically:

> Each human eye has 100 million light-sensing cells, but only about 1 million fibers leading to the brain. Each incoming image must therefore be reduced in complexity by a factor of 100. That is, information in each fiber constitutes a "categorization" of the information from about 100 cells. Neural categorization of this sort exists throughout the brain. (1999, p. 18)

Most of our cognitive categorizations come from how our bodies function in our environment. These are mostly unconscious and when we are in stable environments, we tend to rely on them to speed decision making processes; however, in environments that are unstable we tend to more carefully examine objects, sometimes creating new classifications.

Elizabeth Flynn argues that the received view of romanticism/expressivism is a form of "anti-modern" discourse or rhetoric: "Since individuals are unique and since perceptions of reality are entirely subjective, scientific knowledge has very limited authority, and the ability of scientific projects to lead to valid or reliable truth claims is questioned" (1997, p. 542). Flynn is correct that romantics and expressivists, like classical pragmatists, critique the modernist drive to calculation and commodification of nature. Yet, while romantic writers are generally considered to be reacting against the modernist quest for certainty, for objective truth typified by modern science, these critiques do not mean that every expressivist rejects natural science tout court. Many expressivists—Goethe, Thoreau, and Emerson, to name a few—actually embrace the useful applications of new facts that natural sciences disclose. Emerson notes that the human brain becomes impatient when confronted with

> a multitude of facts; it aims to find some pattern or reasoning to set them in some order. Classification is one of the main actions of the intellect .... every theory of science, every argument of the barrister, is a classification, and gives the mind the sense of power in proportion to the truth or centrality of the traits by which it arranges. (,1972, vol. 2, p. 25.).

IMAGINATION, USE, AND THE CONDUCT OF LIFE

> The endless passing of one element into new forms ... explains the rank which the imagination holds in our catalogue of mental powers. The imagination is the reader of these forms.
>
> —Emerson

Descartes' claim—that our minds are disembodied, not physical and that our brains are material objects, merely things—has a dramatic effect on how imagination has been classified in modernity. He claims imagination does not produce "entirely certain and indubitable" knowledge (1968, p. 95). Therefore he rejects imagination (and emotion) as essential components of rationality or human nature (1968, pp. 151-152). Rhetoricians tend to agree with Descartes that the expression of affect and imagination is not a cognitive activity, and while they are not separate from the mind, they are separate from the social realm: "key terms [of Romantic rhetoric] are solitude, spontaneity, expression of feeling and imagination—all quite opposed to the rhetorician's concern for society, planned discourse, communication, and moving the will through reason and passion"; the received view reduces "expressivism" to a "soliloquy, not an argument, and ... reflection not action" (Bizzell & Herzberg, 2001, p. 995).

The received view claims that "expression of feeling and imagination" is opposed to the rhetorical goals of "reason and passion;" however, pragmatists do not make the foundation lists move by appealing to "reason" because that implies the imagination is an innate faculty like reason and passion. Neither the idea of antecedent thought nor the social constructionist denial of our biological human nature explains how our experiences of the world are inseparable from our conceptualization of the world (Lakoff & Johnson, 1999, p. 509). As Lakoff and Johnson argue, the metaphoricity of language is fundamental to the "sensorimotor inferences" that minds use to perpetually search for relations in order to classify things, to describe emotions, concepts, and percepts in terms of similitude (1999, p. 555). Classical pragmatists understand imagination as a natural part of our cognitive network. "Imagination uses an organic classification" (Emerson, 1929, vol. 8, p. 29) that is part of our self-projecting instinct: "imagination expands and exalts us" (Emerson, 1929, vol. 8, p. 29). Imagination moves us from the embodied realm of self-protection; it brings us to new ways of living in the world; "imagination animates" (Emerson, 1929, vol.8, p. 29).

Imagination is not a solitary or quietist concept for the classical pragmatists: "Our modes of living are not agreeable to our imagination" (Emerson, 1929, vol.1, p. 271). Neo-pragmatists Rorty and Unger argue that pragmatism and romanticism are not opposed because both give priority to the imagination rather than to reason (Rorty, 2007, pp. 105ff).[8] "Imagination," says Unger, "does the work of crisis without crisis [showing] us how we can turn what we have into something else" (2007, pp. 61-62). Emerson, like Dewey notes, "imagination [is] a perception and affirming of a real relation between a thought and some material fact" (1929, vol. 8, p. 29).[9] The imagination is not a discrete faculty of a static brain; rather, it is the use of materiality, the transformation the material world to ameliorate environing conditions. The power of eloquence is that one uses the materiality of language "to report the inner man adequately to the multitudes of men, and [to] bring one man's character to bear on all others" (Emerson, 1972, vol. 3, p. 349).

While many assume that Emerson's first work, *Nature*, announces a uniquely American iteration of romantic idealism which is monological, others understand the book's lasting contribution as being the first to articulate a pragmatic "doctrine of Use."[10] The imagination is important to Emerson; yet, in terms of priority, he emphasizes use over either imagination or reason: "the imagination may be defined to be, the use which the Reason makes of the material world" (1983, p. 34).[11] Emerson's "doctrine of Use" is a central principle shared by pragmatists, "neo" or classical. He analyzes the materiality of "brute nature," and how nature educates the brain/mind "in the doctrine of Use, namely, that a thing is good," and has being only so far as it serves "the production of an end" (1983, p. 29).

For Emerson, the doctrine of use is "the axis on which the frame of things turns" (1983, p. 747). As Emerson and Unger note, sudden moments of crisis force humans into revising their commonplace beliefs (Emerson, 1929, vol. 7, p. 92). The imagination, according to Unger, "does the work of crisis without crisis" (2007, p. 61). As in moments of crisis, imagination provokes the self-protection instinct, and releases energy that powers our imaginative performances and our conduct in implementing them as caring acts in the world. Emerson argues that nature does not serve any single or multiple ends; nature follows an ecstatic structure of circular movement that tends to produce redundancy and excess, focused on momentary ends that are always superseded by new ends, and therefore open to modification and transformation (Herrnstein Smith, 1997, pp. 38, 46, 49). The imagination expresses possible new ends and communicates its fundamentally social dimensions: "the heart of language is not 'expression' of something antecedent, much less expression of antecedent thought. It is communication; the establishment of cooperation in an activity in which there are partners, and in which the activity of each is modified and regulated by partnership" (Dewey, 1958, p. 179).

Rorty is correct that pragmatists explicate the universal dispositions and tendencies of human minds in terms of the exigencies of the existential context. As Emerson notes, the exigency of each generation resolves "itself into a practical question of the conduct of life" (1983, p. 943). These dispositions and tendencies provide the means for a "comprehensive and persisting ... standardization of habit" that orders all "social interaction" (Dewey, 1958, p. 190). For Emerson, the "worst feature of this double consciousness is, that the two lives, of the understanding and of the soul, which we lead, really show very little relation to each other, never meet and measure each other" (1983, pp. 205-206).

Concrete understanding of the environing world—which attunes to its use and takes protective care of it—is human conduct based on the desire for stability and consistency. The individual mind (self), which uses imagination and reason to self-project, to create, and to communicate new possibilities in the world, renews habituation and the conduct of life. Renewal happens because nature has various forms of compensation to maintain the balance between self-protection and self-projection. If society privileges the concept of materialism, then idealism emerges as compensation, and so it is with concepts like the one and the many, reality and imagination, identity and difference, stasis and change, reform and conservation, or, subjective and objective. In the run of everyday life, the double consciousness shows little relation to each other. It is, as we see below, the call of conscience that connects the private mind and the public mind.

Compensatory behavior does not emerge from "a single and all-at-once beginning," but from the natural evolutionary pattern of fits and starts, composition and decomposition, and from an excess of ends, the ecstatic culminations of "incessant beginnings and endings," which animate nature (Dewey, 1958, p. 97-98; Emerson, 1983, pp. 120-121; Poirier, 1992, p. 54-55). The human brain/mind reflects nature's propensity for "calculated profusion": "the craft with which the world is made, runs also into mind and character of" human beings (Emerson, 1983, p. 550). Peirce calls the brain/mind "organized heterogeneity"—which, nonetheless, has "extreme complexity and instability. It has acquired in a remarkable degree of a habit taking and laying aside habits" The laws of the brain/mind are "so fluid a character as to simulate divergence from law" (Peirce, 1955, p. 359-360).

The brain/mind is, as Pinker says, a complex and interactive media that is attuned to the world. It uses all of its unpredictability in order to adapt to and reorganize the world; evolution produces a basic design for relatively stable habits of mind (1997, p. 32). In other words, the innate aspects of human nature are "what all minds have in common, and how minds can differ" (Pinker, 1997, p. 34). The mind has various organizational tendencies that circumscribe species-wide mental activity: "Simple logic says that there can be no learning without innate mechanisms to do the learning. Those mechanisms must be powerful enough to account for all kinds of learning that humans accomplish" (Pinker, 1997, p. 101). But these mechanisms are not, a priori, knowledge: "Saying that the different ways of knowing are innate is different from saying that knowledge is innate" (Pinker, 1997, p. 315). The claim that the human brain has sets of habits, or internalized adaptations, characterized by reflexive actions or instinctual reflexes, should not be confounded with claims that human nature has an unalterable or essential nature, or biological determinism, as is crudely articulated by Social Darwinism or by the more modern notions like genetic determinism, or that the brain is a modular and 'hard-wired' computer-like machine (Unger, 2007, pp. 131-133).

There is continuity between nature and the dispositions acquired that have evolved into brain/mind (Dewey, 1980, p. 29). Some neo-pragmatists, like Rorty, claim the lack of intrinsic, genetic or evolutionary human nature does not make human existence a relativistic "abyss." The traditional interpretation of Emerson, which often acknowledges his repeated claim, "there are no fixtures in nature. The universe is fluid and volatile" (1983, p. 403), is coterminous with Rorty's non-foundation position. The only way it would not be synonymous is if one erroneously assumes "abyss" somehow implies a bipolar, other-worldly ideal or stable universal, which Dewey disputes: Emerson "finds truth in the highway ... in the unexpected idea .... His ideas are not fixed upon any Reality that is beyond or behind or in any way apart" (1980, pp. 27-28) from the natural world. Rorty's argument, however—that there is an "absence of an intrinsic human nature"—is not supported by evidence from contemporary cognitive and biological science (1991a, p. 132). All mental development or learning depends upon the deconstruction of useless neurons and reconstruction of useful neural networks. Current neutral studies show that each human brain has "100 billion neurons and 100 trillion synaptic connections" (Ratey, 2002, p. 18). Many unused connections die during a development stage called 'pruning' and "new connections grow, again depending on which are used and which are not" (Ratey, 2002, pp. 34-47). Therefore, a) the concept of innateness can only hold meaning in terms of potentialities, and b) the tabula rasa theory can only hold meaning in terms of reconstructing what we are born with, not simply inscription on a blank slate by experience. As Lakoff and Johnson state, "the traditional innateness versus learned dichotomy is simply an inaccurate way of characterizing human development, including linguistic development" (1999, pp. 507-508).

Dewey clarifies how human nature contains "regularity" without resorting to static universals:

> Since nothing in nature is exclusively final, rationality is always means as well as end. The doctrine of the universality and necessity of rational ends can be validated only when those in whom the good is actualized employ it as a means to modify conditions so that others may also participate in it, and its universality exist in the course of affairs. (1958, p. 120)

Dewey, like James and Emerson, argues, "nothing in nature is exclusively final" (1958, p. 120), including things like the brain/mind, which were thought to be static and unchanging, like truth or the self (James, 1992, p. 287). Imagination and classification are cognitive behaviors adapted from the plasticity of nature; both cognitive behaviors are useful insofar as they "incarnate themselves in action." Thinking is for use; it frames, animates, alters, and ameliorates both the private or public mind; Emerson, 1929, vol. 12, pp. 18-19).

PLASTICITY AND HUMAN NATURE

> Whilst we converse with truths as thoughts, they exist also as plastic forces.
> —Emerson

The third cognitive disposition that Emerson and the classical pragmatists analyze, which makes humans capable of experiencing moments of critical conscience, is an inherent evolutionary plasticity both in the human brain/mind and in nature. Darwin's evolutionary discovery—that species have no foundational point of origin but emerge, reconstructing themselves and in effect deconstructing those that cannot or do not change—is fundamental to pragmatic naturalism. This structure of "continual decomposition and recomposition" (Emerson, 1983, p. 656; 1929, vol. 8, p. 213) is fundamental to the ways classical pragmatists think about the world—not as a telos intended to culminate in stable fixed object with a predetermined origin and end—but as an endless creative production of infinite ends. All organisms in nature change without logical end or goal; evolutionary changes emerge randomly and yet conservatively. Usefulness is the architect of the human mind. If a structure in the brain is not useful, it wastes away; yet, if it is useful, it is maintained even if new structures get added to face later challenges. As Wolf Singer notes, "the architectures of brains evolved according to the same principles of trial, error, and selection as all other components of organisms. Organisms endowed with brains whose architecture permitted realization of functions that increased their fitness survived and the genes specifying these architectures were preserved" (2011, p. 98).

As James argues, "our fundamental ways of thinking about things are discoveries of exceedingly remote ancestors, which have been able to preserve themselves throughout the experience of all subsequent time" (1975, p. 83). Our most primitive ways of thinking can be traced back the reptilian brain, or the paleo-mammalian brain which maintains the old structures but adds the limbic system, memory and emotion, and the neo-mammalian brain, which maintains both and adds abstract thinking and planning abilities.[12] Taken together, we have a triune brain (Ratey, 2002, p. 10), what James calls an "additive constitution" (1975, pp. 82-83). The cognitive and physical changes in the brain follow the evolutionary process. Plasticity works both at the historical/evolutionary scale and the contingent individual scale: "changing your pattern of thinking also changes the brain's structure.... Activities that challenge your brain actually expand the number and strength of neural connections devoted to the skill" (Ratey, 2002, pp. 36-37). Cognitive science now understands the brain can repair certain injuries, rewire itself by relearning, for example, how to speak after a stroke. We now know that the act of learning can rewire certain parts of the human brain; sustained and mindful learning causes neurons to link and then fire at the same time (Doidge, 2007, p. 63). After the neurons wire together and fire together the brain becomes more efficient (Doidge, 2007, p. 67); the more we learn (an essential survival trait) and the faster we think, act, and react to environing conditions.

As Pinker notes, "neural plasticity is not a magical protean power of the brain but a set of tools" that indicates the complexity of human nature (1997, p. 100). Some parts of the brain are not plastic, and even in childhood, our most plastic developmental period, plasticity has real limits. However, plasticity also explains why persuasive discourse must focus on habits, moods, and beliefs (rather than logic and evidence)—because the brain/mind can learn to change how it thinks, but generally only adapts to change by gradually retuning its disposition to a topic or issue. The self-protecting instinct conserves so that change is resisted: "we keep unaltered as much of our old knowledge, as many of our old prejudices and beliefs as we can" (James, 1975, p. 83). James states

> the moment one tries to define what habit is, one is led to the fundamental properties of matter .... Organic matter, especially of nervous tissue, seems endowed with a very extraordinary degree of plasticity ... so that we may, without hesitation, lay down as our first proposition the following, that the phenomena of habit in living beings are due to the plasticity of the organic materials of which their bodies are composed. (1955, p. 68)

Plasticity is the brain's ability to change according to environmental conditions, circumstances, and experiences. It is essential for learning and developmental processes, and for recovery from injuries. While the most active period of plasticity is between the ages of three and ten, the brain maintains a level of plasticity throughout its existence (Ratey, 2002, pp. 35-47). New changes are carried forward through the variety of useful adaptations and transformations (Lakoff & Johnson, 1999, p. 43). Evolution discloses that the human brain is "far from being a freely instructable tabula rasa" (Singer, 2011, p. 100). As Dewey argues, "reformers, following John Locke, were inclined to minimize the significance" of instincts and dispositions in order to emphasize "the possibilities inherent in practice and habit acquisition" (1922, p. 106).[13] While Locke attempts to describe a more plastic vision of humanity by arguing that all human brains are potentially and equally unlimited—depending upon the social or phenomenal experience inscribed upon them—it has left us a legacy that ignores how human nature develops from important interactions between biology, instincts, and the environment. Wilson, in *On Human Nature*, argues: "the human mind is not a tabula rasa, a clean slate on which experience draws intricate patterns … The accumulation of old choices, the memory of them, the reflection on those to come, the re-experiencing of emotions by which they are engendered, all constitute the mind" (Wilson, 1979. pp. 67). Like Pinker, Wilson argues that Locke's description of human nature as a tabula rasa misrepresents human nature and excludes biological evolution, which has thoroughly integrated into the human organism sets of instinctual, reflexive, and innate behaviors, some of which are interactional, some socially determined, and some that are determined by genetics. For Pinker, the "blank slate" is only partially true: in some cases, social experience does inscribe and construct human practices in a purely situational and contingent manner. His objection centers on their denial of biological and evolutionary forces, some of which are intrinsic to all species and some of which emerge in specific interactions with the environing world.

Some neo-pragmatists, like Rorty, argue there is no such thing as human nature because any description offered is either another set of justifications or another effort to reinscribe metaphysical dualisms and create a foundation outside of a human life-world through a non-linguistic access. According to Rorty, "Dewey spent half his time debunking the very idea of 'human nature'" (1991b, p. 211). However, other neo-pragmatists, like Herrnstein Smith and Unger, agree with the classical pragmatists' understanding that common tendencies can shape the brain, mind, and cognition, without over-determined universalism. Unger argues that innate human nature does not require metaphysical foundations or dualisms: "we associate innateness with constraint. However, our most significant innate faculty is a structure for out-reaching and rebuilding all structures" (2007, p. 132). Unger identifies the recursive process of the brain as the fundamental habit of mind that powers the imagination—the instinct of surprise and to invent. To survive, the mind must be able to make cognitive moves that it has never made before (Unger, 2007, p. 68). The call to conscience is an instinctual care for one's world—conduct attempts to create ameliorating and imaginative reconstructions.

Herrnstein Smith and Unger agree with the classical pragmatists that human nature exists and includes innate components—while guarding against the "first generation" of cognitivist claims (Lakoff & Johnson, 1999, p. 75-76)—which claims the brain works like a computer, has an innate modular structure, and is "hardwired," stable, unchanging (Unger, 2007, p. 131). As Unger notes, the brain is an open system "subject to the enrichments and transpositions resulting from the plasticity of the brain" (2007, pp. 131-132). This openness includes rethinking the way innate aspects of the mind actually produce the ability to self-project. The brain's plasticity, they argue, allows for constant adaptation and reorganization—connecting the contingent existential conditions to how we know and what we do (Dewey, 1966, pp. 336-338).

Herrnstein Smith notes, "plasticity of belief is obviously advantageous and indeed necessary for any creature that survives, as humans do, by learning …. the countertendency—that is, mechanisms that foster the *stability and persistence* of beliefs—would, under a broad range of conditions, also be necessary and advantageous. We are, it seems, congenitally both docile and stubborn" (1997, pp. 50-51). These two instinctual tendencies, stability and plasticity, provide us with cognitive power to imagine new or ameliorating possibilities that can arise either in moments of crisis (Unger, 2007, pp. 61, 112, 130, 132) or in moments of imaginative self-projection. On the other hand, they provide us with "cognitive conservatism," the instinctual act of self-protection—both individual and social.[14] Herrnstein Smith notes, it "is not merely the tendency to hold fast to one's beliefs but to incorporate into them whatever comes along and, often enough … to turn what might otherwise be seen evidence against one's beliefs into evidence for them" (1997, p. 51). Human nature, like nature itself, grows not from "a single and all-at-once beginning" but ecstatic culminations of "incessant beginnings and endings" (Dewey, 1958, pp. 97-98; Emerson, 1983, pp. 120-121).

The classical pragmatists (and neo-pragmatists Herrnstein Smith and Unger) apply evolutionary adaptions to deconstruct the Mind/Body binary, arguing that human nature exists as shared, evolved tendencies to certain temperaments, habits, and dispositions. They understand science as a method of inquiry into nature's regularities and tendencies—without claiming that human nature is a static essence operating from discrete and static faculties of mind. Human nature is configured by the species' interactions in the environing world. As beings-in-nature we produce culture and the arts, including eloquence and argumentation (Dewey, 1922, p. 16), through ecstatic moments of imagination that allow an individual to momentarily step out from habituation. Moments of critical conscience and nonconformity to social conventions are both possible and necessary.

THE CALL TO CRITICAL CONSCIENCE

> The failure of critical consciousness is a failure without consequences since everything it would achieve—change, the undoing of the status quo, the redistribution of power and authority, the emergence of new forms of action—is

already achieved by the ordinary and everyday efforts by which, in innumerable situations, large and small, each of us attempts to alter the beliefs of another.

—Stanley Fish

We only insist that the man meliorate, and that the plant grow upward, and convert the base into the better nature.

—Emerson

The call to conscience reaches across both social realms of preserving and transforming society; it operates on the level of individual citizens whose best thought allows for democratic and ameliorative cultural critique. As James describes it, social evolution is caused by the interaction of the individual, who bears "the power of initiative and origination" of change, and the public or social environment that has the "power of adopting or rejecting" original ideas to reform and change society. The self-projecting instinct is necessary to balance the self-protecting instinct, which tends to conformity, passivity, and fixity of a public everyday understanding of one's world: "the community stagnates without the impulse of the individual. The impulse [to change] dies away without the sympathy of the community" (James, 1992, pp. 629-630).

Both Fish and Rorty argue against a form of critical consciousness that leads to emancipation or freedom (Fish, 1989, p. 332; Rorty, 1991b, p. 211ff). For Rorty, a pragmatist utopia should be based on "narratives of increasing cosmopolitanism, though not narratives of emancipation." Rorty's utopia is "not one in which human nature has been unshackled …. [t]here is no human nature which was once, or still is, in chains" (1991b, p. 213). Unfortunately, Rorty frames emancipation or freedom in terms of over-determined universalism. Dewey makes a different claim, arguing that emancipation "designates a mental attitude rather than external unconstraint of movements" (1966, p. 305). Dewey does not claim to free individuals from human nature, but rather to develop democratic societies that promote intellectual freedom.

While Fish and Rorty deny that "critical consciousness" is possible because they deny that human nature exists, classical pragmatists articulate a melioristic call to conscience framed around democratic political processes that provide a context for cultural critique. The "human condition," Emerson states, is tied up in "old knots of fate, freedom, and foreknowledge;" the way to untie the knots is to propound double consciousness: the oscillation between the public and private mind (1983, p. 966). Critical thinking extends the narrow understanding of existing conditions by projecting into the truly practical realm of the unknown. For Emerson, the public mind of everyday understanding is "a comatose tendency in the brain" (1929, vol. 11, p. 300). As Dewey states it:

> men [sic] must at least have enough interest in thinking
> for the sake of thinking to escape the limits of routine and
> custom. Interest in knowledge for the sake of knowledge, in
> thinking for the sake of the free play of thought, is necessary
> then to the emancipation of practical life—to make it rich
> and progressive. (as quoted in Brinkmann, 2013, p.96).

Critical conscience, according to Unger, shortens "the distance between the ordinary moves" we make in everyday life, which are unconscious and operate within established habits and limits, and "the exceptional moves by which we redefine these limits" (2007, p. 57). We can ameliorate and liberate "individuals from entrenched social division and hierarchy" (2007, p. 56) shrinking the distance "from context-preserving and context-transforming activities" (2007, p. 57). The power of thought to transform the world—the "choosing and acting" of the mind—provides the context for what Dewey calls emancipation. Emerson states it this way: "so far as a [hu]man thinks, he is free" (1983, p. 953). Thinking that is self-projecting is based on futurity. Thinking ends in ameliorative action: it is "an actual alteration of a physically antecedent situation in those details or respects which called for thought in order to do away with some evil" (Dewey, 1916, p. 31).

For West and Rorty, Emerson's style of writing is "culture criticism" (Rorty, 1982, p. xl; West, 1989, p. 36).[15] Cultural criticism is not a discrete analysis or evaluation of literature, intellectual history, moral philosophy, epistemology, or social problems; rather, "all these things mingled together into a new genre" (Rorty, 1982, p. 66) defy "disciplinary classification" (West, 1989, p. 9). Emerson's position outside of academic institutions allows him to evade and "strip the profession of philosophy of its pretense, disclose its affiliations with structures of powers (both rhetorical and philosophical) rooted in the past, and enact intellectual practices, i.e., produce texts of various sorts and styles, that invigorate and unsettle one's culture and society" (West, 1989, p. 37).

James and Dewey both refer to the same passage in *Nature*: while "crossing a bare common" Emerson experiences an ecstatic union with nature in which he emerges from the public conventional external way of understanding, to a living incarnate sense that humanity's "life currents" are given by the material world (James, 1992, p. 856). As Dewey states, "every individual has grown up, and always must grow up, in a social medium …. He lives and acts in a medium of accepted meanings and values" (1966, p. 295). These values are embodied beliefs that shape his mind; therefore the idea that a mind is isolated and singular is impossible: a "self achieves mind in the degree in which knowledge of things is incarnate in the life about him, the self is not a separate mind building up knowledge anew on its own account" (Dewey, 1966, p. 295).

Persuasion is a form of cultural criticism that "flourishes in free countries" (Emerson, 1929, vol. 8, p. 112) and is most noticeable during moments of social crisis (Emerson, 1929, vol. 8, p. 119). Unger argues that imagination transfers to moments of everyday life the call to conscience that emerges in social crisis. If the call to conscience can be heard in everyday practices then a critical inquiry can occur in every "account which the human mind gives to itself of the constitution of the world" (Emerson, 1983, p. 634). It therefore becomes the duty of each individual to become more fully free; concomitantly, each individual has a public duty to make "laws just and humane ... and with the simple and sublime purpose of carrying out in private and public action the desire and need of mankind" (Emerson, 1929, vol. 11, p. 538). Finally, the pragmatic theory of "double consciousness" represents the "incessant" role that human nature plays in "the formation of the speculative man or scholar" (Emerson, 1983, p. 747). As Emerson notes, in the United States, the power of eloquence to persuade and suddenly expand the public mind is privileged:

> here is room for every degree of it, on every one of its ascending stages, —that of useful speech, in our commercial, manufacturing, railroad and educational conventions; that of political advice and persuasion on the grandest theatre, reaching ... into a vast future, and so compelling the best thought and noblest administrative ability that the citizen can offer. (1929, vol. 8, p. 132)

By focusing on Emerson's psychological and cognitive understanding of "double consciousness ... of [our] private and public nature" (1983, p. 966), I offer a counter-history to the received view about Emerson's pragmatic understanding of eloquence. His focus on biological and cognitive aspects of the brain/mind leads us to recognize his affiliations with James and Dewey, and to see that pragmatism has an inherent call to critical conscience, which is embedded in the hopeful sense that continual democratic cultural critique brings with it amelioration and social change. For Emerson and other pragmatists, eloquence is a means to provoke ameliorating social action in a democracy. Democratic persuasion, as a call to conscience, describes the sway between personal and public as the space where self-reliant behavior demonstrates that critique is a form of attending to one's world with care. Change entails persuasion directed at the private duty of each individual to care for what Emerson calls the "secular ... evolution of man" (1929, vol. 11, p. 299). Care is a demonstration of our duty to use new knowledge practically, for the purpose of becoming more fully free, and our public duty to make "laws just and humane ... and with the simple and sublime purpose of carrying out in private and public action the desire and need of mankind" (Emerson, 1929, vol. 11, p. 538).

EXPRESSIVISM

The field of composition and rhetoric is arguably dominated by "social constructionist" interpretations, which, as Steven Pinker argues in *The Blank Slate*, have become hegemonic in social sciences and humanities (2002, p. 6). As Xin Liu Gale notes, social constructionists base much of their theory on neo-pragmatist philosophers (1996, p. 18), especially the work of Richard Rorty. Typically compositionists assume that Rorty's philosophy articulates a "social constructionist" position. Olson is startled because "Rorty does not recognize the term social constructionism as referring to any intellectual movement that he is aware of" (1988, p. 1). In another context, Rorty aptly argues the claim that everything that is socially constructed is "hopelessly misleading" (2007, p. 115). Rorty claims classifying all objects as "social constructs" detracts from the debate over "the utility of alternative constructs" (1999, p. 86).

Berlin traces expressive rhetoric "to Emerson and the Transcendentalists, and its ultimate source is to be found in Plato" (1987 p. 71).[16] Emerson, like Peter Elbow and others, is categorized by social constructionist taxonomies, like James A. Berlin's, as an expressivist.[17] Berlin's position simply recapitulates the received literary view of Emerson, what Thomas G. O'Donnell calls "expressivist bashing" (1996, p.423), or what Michael Lopez calls the "anti-Emerson tradition (1996)," epitomized by W. Ross Winterowd's "Emerson and the Death of Pathos" (1996).[18] In the received view, Romantic rhetoric based on Kantian or neo-Platonist idealism is committed to "an epistemology that locates all truth within a personal construct arising from one's unique selfhood [and] prevents these expressionists from becoming genuinely epistemic in their approach" (Berlin, 1987, p. 153). While there have been many articles that have defended Elbow against what O'Donnell calls the "common but false assumptions about expressivist epistemological orientations" (1996, p. 424); also see Donald C. Jones, Sherrie Gradin, Stephen Fishman and Lucille Parkinson McCarthy (1992 and 1995), Kathleen O'Brien, Philip P. Marzluf, and Kristi Yager), only Hephzibah Roskelly and Kate Ronald defend Emerson's position in this dispute, which is particularly odd given the resurgent interest in literary and philosophical studies in Emerson's contributions to pragmatism[19] and the emergence of a neo-pragmatist "school" of rhetoric.

Yet Emerson argues that knowing is not a subjective state of mind; rather it is an activity, an event in service of use: "my metaphysics are to the end of use …. There is something surgical in metaphysics as we treat it" (1929, vol. 12, p. 13). Imaginative discourse is useful and social because it releases and increases the interactions between interlocutors and the agency of individuals. Emerson's description of the uses of eloquence and argumentation appropriately integrates the social and personal process in which individuals participate in coming-to-know truth and work to apply those truths to provoke political change.

NOTES

* Editors' Note: Anthony Petruzzi passed away while writing this chapter. We are grateful to his family and friends for making sure his work was able to be included here.

1. Mark Bauerlein also argues that the classical pragmatists develop their ideas around a conception of mind: "in the writings of Emerson, James, and Peirce [there is] a close relation between method and mind" and their pragmatic 'method' develops from "a sophisticated model of cognition" (1997, p. 5).

2. James says, "We find this mode of protecting the Self by exclusion and denial very common ... All narrow people entrench their Me, they retract it, from the region of what they cannot securely possess" (1955, p. 201).

3. Self-projection is what James calls self-seeking, one "of our fundamental instinctive impulses": "by self-seeking we mean the providing for the future as distinguished from maintaining the present" (1955, p. 198).

4. As a discipline, Psychology separates from Philosophy in the mid-19th century. Robert Danisch aptly notes, in *Pragmatism, Democracy, and the Necessity of Rhetoric*, that James and Dewey both wrote key texts and played significant "roles in the burgeoning science of psychology" (2007, p. 5). Current discussions of pragmatic rhetoric exclude Emerson, who, of the three, is the only practicing rhetorician; Crick and Danisch's recent books suggest that pragmatism helps us to retrieve a sophistic, proteagorian, rhetoric for the 21st century. Neither book distinguishes classical pragmatists from neo-pragmatists, who tenuously claim that pragmatism is postmodern sophistry (Mailloux, 1998, pp. 1ff; Smith, 1988, p. 86; Crick, 2010, pp. 14 and 22ff; Danisch, 2007, pp. 7ff).

5. Emerson has several terms for what I am calling the "public mind"; he refers to it as "the universal mind," "the mind of humanity," and "the absolute mind" (or what Dewey would call the continuity that interanimates nature's power and "the constitution of things."

6. Carol Synder puts it this way:

> all too frequently students merely rehearse categories and repeat standard distinctions. The absence of argument in these papers suggests that students typically misunderstand the provisional status of classifications and their dependence on disciplinary con-

> ventions, tending to regard them as though they were as reliably permanent .... What such writers need, it seems clear, is a more challenging introduction to division and classification, one that can at once spur the interest that makes for engaged, purposeful writing and promote a better understanding of division and classification as scholarly tools. (1984, p. 209)

7. Classical pragmatists understand that the brain, consciousness (or mind), and language are evolutionary adaptions; they have what Pierce calls "the scientific attitude" (1955, p. 42ff); evolutionary science is a method they use to define pragmatism as a new form of philosophical cultural criticism (Dewey, 1958, p. xvi). The classical pragmatists all considered themselves, as Pierce states, driven by the "impulse to penetrate into the reason of things" (1955, p. 42) through scientific inquiry; however, they want alternatives to modernist claims, which creates a dualism between subject-object, that truth is only valid when disclosed objectively by a neutral and impartial observer.

8. For Rorty, Emerson and the classical pragmatists are also strongly linked together because of their emphasis on self-reliance and their support a uniquely American form of social democracy (Rorty, 1991a, p. 2).

9. Emerson continuously emphasizes the importance of seeing relationships:

> A [hu]man does not see ... that relation and connection are not somewhere and sometimes, but everywhere and always; no miscellany, no exemption, no anomaly, but method, and an even web; and what comes out was put in .... In the human mind, this tie of fate is made alive. The law is the basis of the human mind. (1983, p. 1065)

10. Lopez notes, "in essay after essay Emerson further elaborates and refines his fundamental perception of a universe in which all varieties of relationships ... may be defined in terms of our capacity to use or be used" (1996, p. 57). For Lopez, Emerson's most mature exposition of his "new gospel of pragmatism" is most clearly articulated by the final sentence of Representative Men: human beings can continue to evolve and realize life "first, last, midst, and without end, to honor every truth by use" (1983, p. 761).

11. Contrary to the received view, it is hard to reconcile statements like this and claim that Emerson is a romantic exponent of solipsistic self-expression and asocial political action.

12. Both human consciousness and language are relatively new evolutionary adaptations, generally thought to have developed between 50,000 to 100,000 years ago. Language is an innate or fixed action (not taught) mechanism; for example, speech is a universal human instinct, while literacy, whether reading or writing, universally

needs to be taught to each individual. Speech is important for the survival of the species; it is specialized practice that gives an advantage to the species. Through the continuity of thousands of generations, the species undergoes an adaptation that became instinctual, but language demonstrates not just continuity but wherever the species is found we find a random plurality of diverse, contextual, contingent variations practiced. It is this unity within plurality that is central to pragmatist ontology.

13. Locke's original intent was, probably, to challenge the political structure of his day, which was based on the notion that human nature was unalterable and the political order, the divine right of kings, was based on this foundational principle.

14. Similarly, Pinker argues that an ethic of morality runs across all human emotions to provide stability and plasticity. He claims there are two streams of morality: an ethic of autonomy, which frames judgments about individuality, their interests and cares, and an ethic of community, which frames judgments about following social conventions, deferring to authority, and duty towards tribe, nationality, or political affiliation (2002, p. 271).

15. For Cavell, Emerson prefigures post-modern positions:

> We are by now too aware of the philosophical attacks on system or theory to place the emphasis in defining philosophy on a product of philosophy rather than on the process of philosophizing. We are more prepared to understand as philosophy a mode of thought that undertakes to bring philosophy to an end, as, say, Nietzsche, and Wittgenstein attempt to do, not to mention, in their various ways, Bacon, Montaigne, Descartes, Pascal, Marx, Kierkegaard, Carnap, Heidegger, or Austin .... Ending philosophy looks to be a commitment of each of the major modern philosophers" (1991, pp. 129-130).

16. To Berlin's credit, in Writing Instruction in Nineteenth-Century American Colleges, he reverses his interpretation of Emerson. Berlin rejects the received view that Emerson is a neo-Platonist who claims that truth is a "private vision" (1988, p. 15). Berlin states, "I am convinced that those who find in Emerson a rhetoric of self-expression are mistaken, even though this reading may be used in support of modern expressionist rhetoric" (1987, p. 55). However, Berlin's later of Emerson's work has been ignored because his argument that Emerson is a "post-Kantian" (1987, p. 48), who finds the "ground of reality is the ideal" (1987, p. 46), does little to counter the clichés that frame Emerson as a Romantic.

17. Lopez states

> I am not suggesting that the familiar features of the Transcendentalist Emerson are not there or that are merely critical constructions imposed on him. They are *there* .... The problem is ...

> this way of approaching him leaves out radically contradictory tendencies, tendencies that seem to me not only equal but ultimately greater in extent and importance. (p. 9)

For Patterson, "Emerson's writings exhibit a consistent pattern of contradiction that is fundamental to his critical reassessment of democratic values" (p. 5).

18. Roskelly and Ronald aptly describe Ross Winterowd, as a typical critic of Emerson and romanticism; his response, in general, is "less well articulated and more stereotypical" than received view: "He defines romanticism in predictably traditional ways" (1998, p. 36). They reinterpret and defend Expressivism and Romanticism from the oversimplifications of the social constructionists.

19. By 1988, Michael Lopez, who does an excellent job of summarizing previous scholarly interpretations of Emerson (1996, pp. 19-52), states that the "major, current trend in" Emerson scholarship is "de-transcendentalizing" his work (p. 77).

REFERENCES

Bauerlein, M. (1997). *The pragmatic mind: Explorations in the pyschology of belief.* Durham, NC: Duke University Press.

Bercovitch, S. (1993), Rites of Assent. New York: Routledge, Chapman, and Hall.

Berlin, J. A. (1984). *Writing instruction in nineteenth-century American colleges.* Carbondale, IL: Southern Illinois University Press.

Berlin, J. (1987). *Rhetoric and reality: Writing instruction in American colleges, 1900-1985.* Carbondale, IL: Southern Illinois University Press.

Berlin, J. (1988). Contemporary compostion: The major pedagogical theories. In G. Tate & E. Corbett (Eds.), *Writing teachers sourcebook* (pp. 47-59). New York: Oxford University Press,.

Bizzell, P., & Herzberg, B (2001). The rhetorical tradition: Readings form clasical times to the present. New York: Bedford/St. Martin's.

Brinkmann, S. (2013). *John dewey: Science for a changing world.* NJ: Transaction Press.

Cavell, S. (Winter, 19991). Aversive thinking: Emersonian representations in Heidegger and Nietzsche. *New Literary History, 22*(1), 129-160.

Churchland, P. S. (2002). *Brain-wise: Studies in neurophilosophy.* Cambridge, MA: MIT University Press.

Crick, N. (2010). *Democray and rhetoric: John Dewey on the arts of becoming.* University of South Caroline Press.

Danisch, R. (2007). *Pragmatism, democracy, and the necessity of rhetoric.* University of South Carolina Press.

Dauber, K. (1994). On not being able to read Emerson, or 'Representative man.' *boundary 2, 21*(2), 220-242.

Decartes, R. (1968). *Discourse on method and the meditations* (F.E. Sutcliffe, Trans.). New York: Penguin.

Dewey, J. (1916). *Essays in experimental logic*. New York: Dover.

Dewey, J. (1922). *Human nature and conduct: An introduction to social psychology*. New York: Modern Library.

Dewey, J. (1958). *Experience and nature*. New York: Dover.

Dewey, J. (1966), *Democracy and education: An introduction to the philosophy of education*. New York: The Free Press.

Dewey, J. (1980). *Art as experience*. New York: Perigee.

Doidge, N. (2007). *The brain that changes itself.* New York: Penguin.

Emerson, R. W. (1929). *Thecollected works of Ralph Waldo Emerson* (12 vols.). New York: Wise and Co.

Emerson, R. W. (1972). *The early lectures of Ralph Waldo Emerson* (S. E. Whicher, R. Spiller, & W. E. Williams.) (3 vols.). Cambridge, MA: Harvard University Press.

Emerson, R. W. (1983). *Essays and lectures* (J. Porte, Ed.). New York: Library of America.

Faigley, L. (2009). Competing theories of process: A critique and a proposal. In S. Miller (Ed.) *The Norton book of composition studies* (pp. 652-666). New York: Norton.

Fish, S. (1989). *Doing what comes naturally: Change, rhetoric, and the practice of theory in literary and legal studies*. Durham, NC: Duke University Press.

Fishman, S., & McCarthy, L. P. (1995). Community in the expressivist classroom: Juggling liberal and communitarian visions. *College English, 57*(1), 62-81.

Fishman, S., & McCarthy, L. P. (1992). Is expressivism dead? Reconsidering its romantic roots and its relation to social constructivsim. *College English, 54*(6), 647-661.

Flynn, E. A. (1997). Rescuing postmodernism. *College Composition and Communication, 48*(4), 540-555.

Fulkerson, R. (2009). Four philosophies of composition. In S. Miller (Ed.), *The Norton book of composition studies* (pp. 430-435). New York: Norton.

Gale, X. L. (1996). *Teachers, discourses, and authority in the postmodern composition classroom*. Albany, NY: SUNY Press.

Gradin, S. (1995). *Romancing rhetorics: Social expressivst perspectives on the teaching of writing*. Portsmouth, NH: Boynton Cook Heinemann.

Heidegger, M. (1996). *Being and time: A translation of sein und zeit* (J. Stambaugh, Trans.). Albany, NY: SUNY Press.

James, W. (1955). *The principles of pyschology* (R. M. Hutchins, Ed.) (Vol. 53.). Chicago: Encyclopaedia Brittannica.

James, W. (1975). *Pragmatism: A new name for some old ways of thinking*. Cambridge, MA: Harvard University Press.

James, W. (1992). *Writings: 1878-1899* (G. E. Meyers, Ed.). New York: Library of America.

Jones, D. C. (2002). John Dewey and Peter Elbow: A pragmatist revision of social theory and practice. *Rhetoric Review, 21*(3), 264-281.

Judd, D. (2005). *Critical realism and composition theory*. New York: Routledge.

Lakoff, G., & Johnson, M. (1999). *Philosophy in the flesh: The embodied mind and its challenge to western thought*. New York: Basic.

Lakoff, G. (2010, December). Untellable truths. *Truthout.org*. Retrieved from http://truth-out.org/archive/component/k2/item/93342:untellable-truths

Lopez, M. (1996). *Emerson and Power: Creative antagonism in the nineteenth century*. Dekalb: Northern Illinois University Press.

Mailloux, S. (1998). *Reception histories: Rhetoric, pragmatism, and American cultural politics*. Ithaca, NY: Cornell University Press.

Marzluf, P. P. (2006). Diversity Writing: Natural Languages, Authentic Voices. *College Composition and Communication, 57*(3), 503-522.

O'Brien, K. (2000). Romantism and rhetoric: A question of audience. *Rhetoric Society Quarterly, 30*(2), 77-91.

O'Donnell, T. G. (1996). Politics and ordinary language: A defense of expressivist rhetorics. *College English, 58*(4), 423-439.

Olson, G. A. (1988.May). Social construction and composition theory: A conversation with Richard Rorty. *JAC Online*. Retrieved from http://www.jaconlinejournal.com/archives/vol9/olson-social.pdf

Patterson, A.H. (1997). *From Emerson to King: Democracy, race, and the politics of protest*. Oxford University Press.

Peirce, C. S. (1955). *Philosophical writings of Peirce* (J. Buchler, Ed.). New York: Dover.

Petruzzi, A. P. (1996). Rereading Plato's rhetoric. *Rhetoric Review, 15*(1), 5-25.

Petruzzi, A. P. (1999). The effects of the hegemony of the idea upon the understanding of Plato's rhetoric. *Philosophy and Rhetoric, 32*(4), 368-380.

Pinker, S. (1997). *How the mind works*. New York: Norton.

Pinker, S. (2002). *The blank slate: The modern denial of human nature*. New York: Viking.

Poirier, R. (1992). *Poetry and pragmatism*. Cambridge, MA: Harvard University Press.

Ratey, J. J. (2002). *A user's guide to the brain: Perception, attention, and the four theatres of the brain*. New York: Vintage.

Richardson, J. (2007). *A natural history of pragmatism: The fact of feeling from Jonathan Edwards to Gertrude Stein.* New York: Cambridge University Press.
Rorty, R. (1979). *Philosphy and the mirror of nature.* Princeton, NJ: Princeton University Press.
Rorty, R. (1982). *Consequences of pragmatism: Essays 1972-80.* Minneapolis, MN: Minnesota University Press.
Rorty, R. (1991a). *Essays on Heidegger and others: Philosophical papers* (Vol. 2.). New York: Cambridge University Press.
Rorty, R. (1991b). *Objectivity, relativism, and truth: Philosophical papers* (Vol. 1.). New York: Cambridge University Press.
Rorty, R. (1999). *Philosophy and social hope.* New York: Penguin.
Rorty, R. (2007). *Philosophy as cultural politics: Philosophical papers* (Vol. 4.). New York: Cambrdge University Press.
Rose, M. (1989). *Lives on the boundary.* New York: Penguin.
Roskelly, H., & Ronald, K. (1998). *Reason to believe: Romanticism, pragmatism, and the possibility of teaching.* Albany, NY: SUNY University Press.
Singer, W. (2011). Epigenesis and brain plasicity in ducation. In A. M. Battro, K. W. Fisher, & P. J. Lena (Eds.) *The educated brain: Essays in neuroeducation* (pp. 97-109). Cambridge, UK: Cambridge University Press.
Smith, B. H. (1997). *Belief and resistance: Dynamics of contemporary intellectual controversy.* Cambridge, MA: Harvard University Press.
Smith, B. H. (1988). *Contingencies of value: Alternative perspectives for critical theory.* Cambridge, MA: Harvard University Press.
Snyder, C. (1984). Analyzing classifications: Foucault for advanced writing. *College Composition and Communication, 35*(2), 209-216.
Unger, M. R. (2007). *The self awakened: Pragmatism unbound.* Cambridge, UK: Cambridge University Press.
West, C. (1989). *The American evasion of philosophy: A genealogy of pragmatism.* Madison, WI: Wisconsin University Press. *JAC 16,* 27-40.
Wilson, E.O. (1979). *On human nature.* Cambridge, MA: Harvard University Press.
Winterowd, W. R. (1996). Emerson and the death of pathos. *JAC 16*(1), 27-40.
Yager, K. (1996). Romantic resonances in the rhetor of Peter Elbow's writing without teachers. *Composition Studies/Freshman English News, 24*(2), 144-159.

SECTION FOUR:
PEDAGOGIES

PLACE-BASED GENRE WRITING AS CRITICAL EXPRESSIVIST PRACTICE

David Seitz
Wright State University

In response to students' changing literacy practices within the digital age in contrast to the traditional expectations of academic print literacy, many first year writing programs have rejected expressivist approaches to teaching academic reading and writing. Instead, these programs tend to emphasize rhetorical analyses of written and visual texts, especially in the first course of an academic writing sequence. As economist Robert Reich pointed out, our global knowledge economy requires this focus on analysis. He identified the need for symbolic analysts who "wield equations, formulae, analogies, models, and construct categories and metaphors in order to create possibilities for reinterpreting and rearranging" the deluge of textual and visual data (quoted in Johnson-Eilola, 2004, p. 229).

Yet too often conventional rhetorical analysis relies more on having students consume academic texts (or public criticism in the form of op-ed pages) and only reproduce their discourse and generic forms. Rarely do these approaches aim to mediate the culture and languages from students' communities as a major pedagogical goal. So most often students remain alienated from an academic identity and purpose in these courses. As a graduate professor on the periphery of our official writing program, I hear from frustrated new graduate student teachers who wisely come to identify this problem with the program's suggested assignments. The first course in our program focuses more on analyzing advertisements and commentary pieces. Yet the program's most inexperienced teachers, unequipped with a more expansive pedagogical toolkit, inevitably revert to teaching conventional academic forms rather than creative critical inquiry.

As an alternative to these conventions of textual analysis, another smaller group of teacher-scholars have stressed rhetorical approaches through multigenre projects. As Tom Romano, Nancy Mack, Cheryl Johnson and Jayne Moneysmith, and Robert Davis and Mark Shadle have shown, multigenre pedagogy can definitely foster students' creative inquiry. While I admire much of these multigenre approaches, particularly the work of Romano and Mack, they tend to use genres to help students understand complexities of research writing (Romano, Mack, Davis and Shadle) or argumentation (Johnson and Moneysmith). In contrast, I wanted to draw on genre pedagogy to focus on analysis to meet our writing program's outcomes for the first semester writing course in ways that might be more internally persuasive to our students. In my upper-level undergraduate rhetoric course, students learned to analyze discourse by rewriting political commentaries in other genres and then analyzing the rhetorical effects of their choices (see Seitz "Mocking Discourse"). Now I wanted to create a similar approach to analysis that could motivate and engage most first year writing students.

In this chapter, I will show how the genre writings project in my first year writing course, supported by principles of place-based education and theories of genre as textual sites of social action, helps create a more inductive approach to rhetorical analysis focused on students' languages and values. In contrast to conventional rhetorical analysis of a text, the students analyze the rhetorical choices they make when they compose in diverse genres that respond to the rhetorical situations of local place and community. I believe this approach can help open up a dialectical space through a process of "purposeful mediation" between academic rhetoric and collective rhetorics of local place. Through this approach, students often invest more in the process of their analysis, analyzing what they have accomplished rhetorically through their genre writings.

GOALS, ASSIGNMENTS, AND INTERVIEWS FROM A PLACE-BASED WRITING COURSE

To better show my motives for the rhetorical moves within this project, what follows are the key goals of this course which I designed in accordance with a place-based genre writing pedagogy, an overview of the assignment sequences, and a look at genre connections drawn from interviews.

COURSE GOALS

Students were expected to foster and articulate critical analyses of everyday rhetoric within social and historical contexts. They were also expected to gain awareness of how any place could be analyzed in relation to three conditions: community bonds, local history, and global influences. And I wanted students to understand how written, oral, and visual genres help enact, respond to, and complicate these three connections.

SEQUENCE OF ASSIGNMENTS

Throughout the course students were required to research and write an "Interview Analysis Paper." I wanted them to identify connections between place and community, and develop a genre writing for each of these connections (i.e. community bonds, local history, and global influences). Finally, they were to analyze rhetorical situations of their genre writings and their connections.

In my course, students conducted ethnographic interviews about how a place or community has responded to change. The students' choice of place could be a neighborhood, town, or workplace. I borrowed this emphasis on change from Julie Lindquist's own writing course on place, which helped inspire my own. By emphasizing change, the interviews tended to focus on how the interviewee drew upon the collective rhetorics of the place and community to respond to physical and historical forces as well as the changing rhetorical influences on the place and people. These forces and influences might come from outside groups and institutions, such as the decision to move NCR (National Cash Register, a home industry in Dayton Ohio), to Atlanta. Or they might have come from smaller groups inside the larger community, such as efforts of rural towns to revitalize their downtowns during the recession in a global economy. But the project also allowed for students to demonstrate when the place and community had not changed and how, why, and to what effects. In this manner the project left open the possibility of social affirmation and critique (see Seitz, 2004). We cannot assume before ethnographic research how the interviewee and others in the community view change and stability within this place. Through the work of the interview analysis paper, students then locate three connections from their interviews that respectively address community bonds, local history, and global influences related to this place or community.

GENRE CONNECTIONS DRAWN FROM INTERVIEWS

With regard to community bonds, some of the possible connections could be specific actions people conducted in order to create ties or social networks; specific common traditions, values, and beliefs that brought individuals together; or issues that related directly to the well-being of the local place and its residents. As for the local history of the place and community, these might be major events taking place in the community or place during a specific period and which resulted in some change. These could be political, economic, newsworthy (at least, in the eyes of the community members), or historical—that is, referencing the history of particular groups within the community. And where global influence was concerned (whether considered from state, national, or international perspectives), students were encouraged to explore the political, economic, technological, or cultural influences on the place and community.

For instance, Chelsea Presson interviewed her uncle, one of 15 remaining employees at NCR (which he describes now as a ghost office). From her interviews and analysis paper, she identified the community bonds of strong employee relationships that NCR once nurtured through company programs and abandoned over ten years before the decision to move the company. For the local history, she emphasized the deterioration of NCR's long-standing support of Dayton's communities and small businesses. And for the global influences, she focused on the impact of the national economy that acted as the backdrop for NCR's decision to move. This analysis encourages an historical and global perspective toward the local place. Moreover, rather than the course providing pre-packaged issues, most students come to see that any place or institution is both sustained and impacted by these three connections.

Then for each connection they have identified from their analysis, the students write a text in a non-academic genre that responds to a local rhetorical situation they learned about in their interview research. This approach helps develop greater rhetorical facility (one of the main Writing Program Administrators' outcomes) expanding beyond academic genres in the larger knowledge economy. I provide the students with a vast list of possible genres to choose from, but also suggest they consider what genres community members would more likely write, read, and watch as well as what genres outsiders (state, national, international) whose actions affect this place would write, read, and watch. Through in-class activities, I get them to consider how their genre choices can help show something about each of their three connections. In this way, the activity gets students thinking about how genres enact the social roles and situated action tied to their three genre connections. Students need to also consider the rhetorical situation (considerations of audience, purpose, stance, genre, and medium/design), as defined by Richard Bullock's *Norton Field Guide to Writing* (2009) for each genre connection. When they must consider the fit of the genre choice to rhetorical situation, they begin to analyze the affordances of each possible genre choice.

So for community bonds, Chelsey composed an email dialogue between a surviving Dayton NCR employee and one who moved to the new Atlanta office, elaborating in detail on their past exploits in better company times. For the local history, she took on the voice of a Dayton restaurant owner in the city paper, addressing concerns of small business bankruptcies in Dayton since the pulling out of NCR and General Motors (supported by data drawn from secondary sources). And for the global influences connection, she took on the sunny authoritative tone of NCR CEO Bill Nuti in a slickly designed company newsletter assuring employees that the economy was turning around compared to previous recessions.

The students also had to incorporate secondary sources in the text and footnotes of their genre writings to help them relate the local situations they enacted to similar concerns of other communities (or workplaces) and larger issues at the state, national or international level. For teaching strategies of incorporating research from secondary sources in genre writings, I have learned much from Nancy Mack's scholarship and pedagogy. Finally, as a metacognitive reflection, the students analyze and articulate all these rhetorical choices in an extensive cover letter.

When I designed this course, I knew I wanted students to address place as a generative theme, but I hadn't read much on theories of place-based pedagogy, which is mostly a rural K-12 movement. Now I look back at the students' projects over four years of classes and see how much these theories support my approach.

PREMISES OF A CRITICAL PLACE-BASED WRITING PEDAGOGY

> Illuminate the concept of Intradependence (of place, community, and self).
> —Paul Theobauld

> Support sustainability of civic life at local levels (not migratory culture and rhetoric).
> —Robert Brooke

> Examine, celebrate, and critique the literacy practices that create local knowledge, culture, and public memory.
> —Charlotte Hogg

> Foreground connections to global, national, and regional development trends that impact local places.
> —David Gruenwald

Robert Brooke has asserted pedagogical approaches of place-based education share common ground with the tradition of expressivist pedagogies that explore self and society (2003). As defined and articulated by Paul Theobauld, place-based education should illuminate the concept of intradependence, the connected relationship of place, community and self. To seek intradependence means to "exist by virtue of necessary relations 'within a place'" (quoted in Brooke, 2003, p. 7). Brooke claims "Theobauld wants an education that immerses learners into the life of human communities while they are still in school, thereby teaching the practice of civic involvement" (2003, p. 6).

Most of the students who work on this project in my class begin to practice forms of intradependence when they choose to interview their grandparents about the losses of a viable, walkable downtown life; their parents about the relationship of their workplaces to their home communities; people with institutional roles in the town, such as teachers, coaches, or ministers, about the local effects of demographic shifts; or people in professions that motivated some students, such as law enforcement and nursing, where they learn about the positive and negative impact of new technologies on employee interaction in these workplaces.

Brooke rightly maintains that writing classes which emphasize rhetorical forms and argumentative strategies regardless of local cultures and community issues encourage a migratory culture that disconnects the self from place and does not support sustainability of civic life at local levels. "As educators," Brooke writes, "all of us are implicated in the destruction of small communities" 2006, p. 147). Most American education now serves to create an "identity not linked to a specific place, community, or region but instead to the identity of the skilled laborer, equipped with the general cultural and disciplinary knowledge that will enable the person to work wherever those skills are required"; paraphrasing the naturalist writer Wallace Stegner, Brooke stresses how this kind of migratory living can lead to "harsh exploitation of natural and cultural resources—if you don't plan to live somewhere more than a decade, it doesn't matter in what condition you leave it in" (2003, p. 2).

Instead, Brooke, along with other place-based educators, calls for imagining an education that fosters regional identity of "civic leadership, knowledge of heritage, and stewardship" (2006, p. 153). "It is at the local level where we are most able to act, and at the local level where we are most able to affect and improve community" (Brooke, 2003, p. 4). While the place-based genre writing project in my class doesn't lead to immediate civic action, it does make students think more about establishing a regional, rather than solely migratory, identity within their acts of writing.

But as Charlotte Hogg's scholarship on rural literacies suggests, along with that of her colleagues Kim Donehower and Eileen Schell, place-based education needs to critique as well as celebrate local narratives of place. Hogg's research of Nebraskan women's roles as informal town historians highlights alternative narratives in contrast to the more patriarchal models of the agrarian movement which emphasize the self and the land and tend to neglect the everyday practices of towns that sustain local community. Hogg reminds us the goal is better models of cultural sustainability rather than preservation of a particular version of the past: "local narratives are not static artifacts for preservation, but openings for delving into questions of power and representation" (2007, p. 131). Moreover, the project in my course supports David Gruenwald's call for a teaching approach that is "attuned to the particularities of where people actually live, and that is connected to global development trends that impact local places" (quoted in Hogg, 2007, p. 129).

In the course of this project, the interview analysis activities help most students move toward the kind of analytical complexity suggested by Hogg, Gruenwald, and other scholars of critical pedagogies of place. The scaffolding of the interview analysis activities, along with other analysis activities using readings and movie clips, encourages students to discern social patterns and tensions from their interviews related to a community's cultural values and responses to change.

For example, Zachary Rapp comes from a working class town in southern Ohio. As a proud high school athlete, he wanted to interview his basketball coach. In the course of his analysis, Zach zeroed in on an unexpected tension within the school and town community. Zach's coach explained specific ways this working class community deeply supported the athletics programs as a source of community pride. But he also referred to the teachers' frustration over poor funding and repeated failed levies. In his interview analysis paper and then his genre writings, Zach had to wrestle with another side of this multifaceted story that he had not encountered before. As he began to question the commitment of his neighbors to the full education of the town's children, he certainly considered issues of the town's greater sustainability and the larger national issue of funding for education. But he also recognized, and wanted to explain the daily sacrifices that families made for the children's athletics, and he wanted to celebrate that story, especially in contrast to the attitude of outsiders that his town was a wasted dangerous place which he claimed was part of its local history from the viewpoint of neighboring towns with greater wealth.

In this regard, Zach took up the dialectical positions that Charlotte Hogg encourages—to both celebrate and critique the literacy practices that make up public memory of small town life. While the interview analysis paper gave Zach a genre form to address the significance of both perspectives within an academic frame, the genre writings gave him the opportunity to isolate and emphasize the voices and genres that both supported and challenged the cultural values that made up these aspects of the town's civic life. So Zach writes in the voice of an injured local college athlete in a college application essay to show the community bonds forged at the town football games. He addresses the local history of rumors perpetuated by neighboring towns through a series of email exchanges between a prospective resident who asks a longtime volunteer booster about the town's darker reputation. The booster's replies speak to the town's working class pride. But Zach also writes in the voice of a newspaper editor from a neighboring city paper that urges this local community to put as much emphasis on academic funding in their public schools as they do athletics.

So when students' rhetorical choices of genres (and their purposes and audiences) derive from the ethnographic analysis of these three connections to a local place or community, the students tend to better understand genre as situated social action. As with the place-based pedagogy, I had not read deeply into rhetorical theories of genre when I designed the project. Now I see how these theories support a view of students inhabiting roles and situations they have researched first hand from their interviews.

PREMISES OF RHETORICALLY-BASED THEORIES OF GENRE

> Genres serve as keys to understanding how to participate in the actions of a community
>
> —Carolyn R. Miller

The work of Carolyn Miller, Charles Bazerman, Catherine Schryer, Amy Devitt, and Anis Bawarshi, among others, reminds us that genres work to perform situated social actions and relations, enact social roles, frame social realities, and mediate textual and social ways of knowing and being. When we learn genres, we learn to inhabit "interactionally produced worlds" and social relationships, recognize situations in particular ways, and orient ourselves to particular goals, values, and assumptions.

Apart from the genre pedagogy created by Devitt, Bawarshi and Reiff (2004), many teachers emphasize genre as forms, rather than situating the writing of various non-academic genres within the study of place and community. Rhetorical genre theorists instead view genres, such as a community newsletter or a company brochure, as "sites of social and ideological action" (Schreyer, 1993, p. 208). As Bawarshi sums up the importance of genres, "they embody and help us enact social motives, which we negotiate in relation to our individual motives; they are dynamically tied to the situations of their use; and they help coordinate the performance of social realities, interactions and identities" (2004, p. 77). Devitt, Bawarshi, and Reiff have stated that the term "discourse community" and the relationship of subjectivity to discourse community remain too vague. Instead, along with Miller, Bazerman, and others, they argue that it is the process of genres (within various modalities) that "organize and generate discourse communities" (2003, p. 550) and shape strategies of social action within these rhetorical situations.

In my course project, the interview process and the three connections help to physically situate the cognition required to know what genres might be appropriate at what points in time and space within the local rhetorical situation. Because students encounter the use of various written genres in their interviews and in actual community contexts, they are exposed to genres not only as individual forms but as what rhetorical genre theorists call systems of genre sets. As a result, they must consider what affordances particular genres might offer within the range of appropriate genres in a given system that can best demonstrate the perspective of each chosen connection. As Anne Freadman and other rhetorical genre theorists have argued, the acquisition of genre knowledge includes "uptake"—knowing which genre to use based upon the rhetorical moves of earlier genres in a given system. While my first-year writing students do not explicitly study this genre knowledge or truly embed themselves in the practices of a community's genre systems in ways that lead to full acquisition of genre knowledge, through this project they are more likely to see genres as more than just forms and conventions, and as the "lived textualities" that enact relationships and power relations within community bonds, local histories, and global influences.

Katie Shroyer came to understand these intersections of power relations and genre knowledge over the course of her project. Katie interviewed her mother, a pastor of a local branch of the Christian Family Fellowship Ministry. To show the connection of local history, Katie composed a eulogy for John Shroyer, her grandfather, the founder of the local ministry. In this text, the speaker recounts the specific ways John Shroyer helped build the social environment of the congregation over forty years. What strikes me here is how much her purpose resembles the rhetorical view of epideictic rhetoric—that is, the speech itself is meant to develop identification and persuasion to the values of the larger congregation. To address the connection of community bonds, she took on the voice of her mother in the Ministry newsletter which is distributed to numerous communities. The article addresses the growing movement advocating for home fellowships in small groups compared to the greater anonymity of megachurch models. In her cover letter, Katie claims that this particular genre of the newsletter serves "as a bonding agent" to these different communities, developing a series of "mini support systems."

To examine global influences, Katie refers to a conflict between her mother and the leader of the Fellowship within a semi-formal business letter. As the church has expanded since the days of her grandfather, it has pursued international outreach. To encourage this national and global outreach, the leader has encouraged the production and distribution of service teachings on CDs. Katie's mother repeatedly challenges what she sees as the impersonality of this approach and instead argues for the necessity of physical interpersonal relations in fellowship. Taking on the role of a Congregationalist in Bristol, England, Katie writes a letter to persuade Pastor Shroyer, her mother, to visit their fellowship, so they can gain much more than they can with her CDs. Now, to some composition scholars, this may not seem a strong critical rhetorical move, but to me it does suggest efforts to consider sustainability of the fellowship in the midst of global and technological change. I would also suggest that because the project allowed Katie to demonstrate the strengths of this fellowship community, she was probably more willing to reveal dissent in the church with regard to change as well. Moreover, Katie clearly chooses these genres, in her words, "to serve as keys to participate in the actions of a community," and she analyzes these rhetorical choices very well in her cover letter.

Finally, I believe this teaching approach follows in an expressive tradition because it's about mediating identity and addressing places as communities, however flawed, and recognizing a range of agency within these communities. This pedagogy also draws on assumptions of critical teaching in that students must examine power relations within local communities and their relations to larger global influences.

Genre writings can mediate academic and public rhetorics tied to place and community, thereby creating a dialectical space. The students' interview papers mediated an academic analysis with the interviewee's voice, which spoke from a collective rhetoric of place and community often tied to the student's sense of self. The students' genre writings translated academic insights of cultural, historical and socio-economic analysis into genres and voices of public rhetorics, often situated in place and community. And finally, their cover letters translated the implicit rhetorical analysis behind the creation of their genre writings into explicit demonstrations of analytical choices and use of secondary sources.

In these ways, genre writings can act as a mediating force between the cultures and communities outside and within academe as students analyze place and change from academic perspectives, and then re-integrate those perspectives into the language and genres of public communities. In this sense, my use of the term "translate" is only partially accurate because when we move between these public and academic rhetorics, there is no direct correspondence of meanings—just as when I plug in a French phrase into a digital translator, I will not receive an absolutely English equivalent. So while I do see the process as a kind of partially accurate set of translations, the term mediation suggests a more dynamic fluidity that often takes place. In the process of this project, students gained experience mediating identities, communities, genres, and rhetorical assumptions and strategies—rhetorical experience that can hopefully serve them well in their communications outside the classroom, in their dealings with academic writing, and possibly well into their future lives.

REFERENCES

Bawarshi, A., & Reiff, M. J. (2010). *Genre: An introduction to history, theory, research, and pedagogy.* West Lafayette, IN: Parlor Press and Fort Collins, CO:

The WAC Clearinghouse.
Bazerman, C. (1997). The life of genre, the life in the classroom. In W. Bishop & H. Ostrom (Eds.), *Genre and writing: Issues, arguments, alternatives* (pp. 19-26). Portsmouth NH: Boynton,.
Brooke, R. (2006). Migratory and regional identity. In B. Williams (Ed.*) Identity papers: Literacy and power in higher education* (pp. 141-153). Logan, UT. Utah State University Press.
Brooke, R. (2003). Introduction. In R. Brooke (Ed.). *Rural voices: Place conscious education and the teaching of writing* (pp. 1-20). New York: Teachers College Press.
Bullock, Ri. (2009). *Norton field guide to writing*. New York: W.W. Norton.
Davis, R. L. & Shadle, M. (2007). *Teaching multiwriting: Researching and composing with multiple genres, media, disciplines and cultures*. Carbondale, IL: Southern Illinois University Press.
Devitt, A., Bawarshi, A., & Reiff, M. J. (2004). *Scenes of writing: Strategies for composing with genres*. New York: Longman.
Devitt, A., Bawarshi, A., & Reiff, M. J. (2003). Materiality and Genre in the Study of Discourse Communities. *College English, 65*(5), 541-558.
Freadman, A. (2002). Uptake. In R. Coe, L. Lingard, & T. Teslenko (Eds.), *The rhetoric and ideology of genre: Strategies of stability and change* (pp. 39-53). Cresskill, NJ: Hampton.
Gruenwald, D. (2003). The best of both worlds: A critical pedagogy of place. *Educational Researcher, 32*(4), 3-12.
Hogg, C. (2007). Beyond agrarianism: Toward a critical pedagogy of place. In K. Donehower, C. Hogg, & E. Schell (Eds.), *Rural literacies* (pp. 120-154). Carbondale, IL: Southern Illinois Press.
Johnson-Eilola, J. (2004). The database and the essay: Understanding composition as articulation. In A. Wysocki (Ed.), *Writing new media. Theory and applications for expanding the teaching of composition* (pp. 199-236). Logan, UT: Utah State University Press.
Johnson, C. & Moneysmith, J. (2005). *Multiple genres, multiple voices: Teaching argument in composition and literature*. Portsmouth, NH.
Lindquist, J. (2006). *ATL 150: Mapping community spaces*. Retrieved from Michigan State University Web site: https://www.koofers.com/michigan-state-university-msu/atl/150/
Mack, N. (2006). Ethical representation of working-class lives: Multiple genres, voices, and identities. *Pedagogy, 6,* 53-78.
Mack, N. (2002). The ins, outs, and in-betweens of multigenre writing. *English Journal, 92*(2), 91-98.
Miller, C. R. (1994). Genre as social action. In A. Freedman & P. Medway

(Eds.), *Genre and the new rhetoric* (pp. 23-42). Bristol, PA: Taylor and Francis.

Presson, C. (2009). *Genre writing project*. Unpublished manuscript, Department of English, Wright State University, Fairborn, Ohio.

Rapp, Z. (2010). *Genre writing project*. Unpublished manuscript, Department of English, Wright State University, Fairborn, Ohio.

Romano, T. (2007). *Blending genre, altering style: Writing multigenre papers*. Portsmouth, NH: Boynton.

Schryer, C. (1993). Records as genre. *Written Communication, 10,* 200-234.

Seitz, D. (2011). Mocking discourse: Parody as pedagogy. *Pedagogy, 11*(2), 371-394.

Seitz, D. (2004). *Social affirmation alongside social critique. Who can afford critical consciousness?: Practicing a pedagogy of humility*. Cresskill, NJ: Hampton Press.

Shroyer, K. (2010). *Genre writing project*. Unpublished manuscript, Department of English, Wright State University, Fairborn, Ohio.

Theobauld, P. (1997). *Teaching the commons: Place, pride, and the renewal of community*. Boulder, CO: Westview Press.

MULTICULTURAL CRITICAL PEDAGOGY IN THE COMMUNITY-BASED CLASSROOM: A MOTIVATION FOR FOREGROUNDING THE PERSONAL

Kim M. Davis
Oakland Community College

Composition is a complex, ever-changing field of study that owes its existence and continued growth to its link to the writing courses that almost all students must take as they enter the academy. Because of how these required courses are situated in the academy, theories and practices about student writing are constantly re-evaluated, causing multiple areas of focus. According to Richard Fulkerson in his article "Composition at the Turn of the Twenty-First Century" (2005), the current work in the field revolves around the following axiologies (or theories of value): (1) critical/cultural studies, (2) expressivism, and (3) procedural rhetoric.

The critical/cultural studies axiology is a major movement in the field marked by attention to cultural issues and/or the sociopolitical critique of critical pedagogy, which Fulkerson claims can supplant attention to the teaching of writing (2005, p. 659-660). In this approach, "the course aim is not 'improved writing' but 'liberation' from dominant discourse" (Fulkerson, 2005, p. 660). The expressivism axiology is about consciousness-raising and coming-to-voice, with a focus on more personal writing in which "many of the traditional features of academic writing, such as having a clear argumentative thesis and backing it up to convince a reader, are put on the back burner" (Fulkerson, 2005, p. 666). The axiology that pertains to the more traditional features of academic writing is procedural rhetoric, which includes focus on argument and students' adoption of academic discourse (Fulkerson, 2005, p. 670).

Although Fulkerson's axiologies are important for understanding current theoretical and pedagogical controversies in composition studies, I take somewhat of a departure in terms of how he has set aside the discussion of personal writing versus academic writing. I contend that the rise of critical/cultural goals actually reconfigures this debate in certain contexts. In particular, much contemporary interest in personal writing versus academic writing can be tied to community-based writing courses, also referred to as service learning courses. This chapter explores how community-based courses, when linked to critical pedagogy and multicultural goals, raise questions about the type of writing students should be asked to produce, personal or academic (Herzberg, 1997; Rhoads, 1997).

The intersection of community-based learning and critical pedagogy is an example of Fulkerson's claim that the field has embraced a focus on critical studies. This convergence is viewed as an optimal strategy for promoting students' engagement with critical course objectives because real-life experiences serve as catalysts for learning. As Cynthia Rosenberger in "Beyond Empathy" claims, "consensus exists in the literature that service learning is action and reflection integrated with academic curriculum to enhance student learning and to meet community needs" (2000, p. 24). In particular, Rosenberger argues community-based learning resonates with Freire's problem-posing concept of education; she contends that problem posing education "has the potential to help students construct knowledge about economic and social complexities, and with this knowledge, to begin to entertain alternatives to the present reality" (2000, pp. 41-42). In this way—if the context of the community-based classroom is used inductively to help students explore alternative ways of knowing—critical pedagogy can be introduced without reinstating the banking model of education that Freire denounces by setting up an "I know" and "you don't know" binary (Dobrin, 1997, p. 141). In *Constructing Knowledge*, Sidney Dobrin argues that "like most of the theories that come to composition, Freire's theory of radical pedagogy creates tensions when converted from theory to practice" (1997, p. 139). More specifically, Dobrin questions applications of critical pedagogy where "teachers seem to appropriate the very agency they claim to wish to return to students by prescribing a particular set of values as to what and how students should think 'critically'" (1997, p. 141). Instead, Dobrin encourages attention to the context in which teaching takes place, encouraging a more culturally-centered form of writing instruction (1997, p. 145).

Combining context and content as a pedagogical strategy, Robert Rhoads argues for a cultural studies approach to community-based learning to promote the postmodernist charge to foster dialogue across difference, which exemplifies Fulkerson's claim that the field has turned to cultural studies. Rhoads calls for students to develop an ethic of care that results from an exploration of the self in relationship to diverse others. He argues that "fostering a sense of self grounded in an ethic of care is a necessity as our society becomes increasingly diverse and diffuse" (1997, p. 2). This approach falls under what Thomas Deans argues is the reigning "social perspective" in the field of composition students and which provides the theoretical reasoning for the growth of community-based programs

(2000, p. 9). It is a perspective which, according to Cy Knoblauch and Lil Brannon, "presumes that American citizens should understand, accept and live amicably amidst the realities of cultural diversity—along axes of gender, race, class, and ethnicity" (1993, p. 6). More specifically, according to Gregory Jay in "Service Learning, Multiculturalism and the Pedagogies of Difference,"

> service learning reinforces the necessity that students analyze their own ethnoracial and cultural identity formation, becoming consciously aware of how their identity affects others and how their perception of others is shaped by their identities. The experiences of cross-cultural collaboration promoted by service learning encourage such reflection, which is done formally in directive writing assignments and online postings or through a variety of student-centered projects. (2008, p. 260-261).

Students' reflexive writing, informed through a Freirean lens situating action and reflection as praxis, is, as Jay contends, at the heart of community-based initiatives because it provides students with opportunities to think critically about them/us binaries and other culturally specific issues they encounter in their community contexts. However, questions about the type of reflexive writing students should be asked to produce in community-based writing classroom is why I maintain that the context calls for a renewed discussion about personal writing versus academic writing.

Three theorists whose work raises question about the type of writing students should be asked to produce in the community-based writing classroom—personal or academic—are Robert Rhoads, Bruce Herzberg, and Linda Flower. On opposite sides are Rhoads and Herzberg. Rhoads advocates a theoretical lens that involves personal reflection and explores the self and the self in relationship to the social (1997, p. 4). Herzberg, on the other hand, argues that the use of more traditional, abstract academic writing in lieu of personal, reflexive writing is necessary to promote students' critical thinking about sociopolitical issues (1997, p. 58). However, it is Flower's work that suggests a more nuanced approach. Her noted research mentions students' assignments based on hybrid genres that include personal, academic, and community discourses. Although the focus in the field on her work has primarily been regarding hybrid texts that university students produce collaboratively with community members (Flower, 2003; Flower, 1997; Deans, 2000, p. 132), her scholarship hints at a type of student writing that is both reflexive and critical in ways that address the claims of both Rhoads and Herzberg.

While I do not dispute the value of having students produce more traditional academic writing, I do believe Herzberg's movement away from the personal in students' writing in connection with community-based learning limits the possibilities of critical pedagogy by not taking into account changing definitions of academic writing. First, a movement away from the personal in the experience and a return to the abstraction of academic discourse (Bizzell, 2002) could minimize an important claim about the impact of community-based learning; i.e., it promotes an understanding and critique of the self in relationship to a larger community (Flower, 1997; Rhoads, 1997). Secondly, the type of writing Herzberg describes as academic discourse, particularly when it is defined as working with the works of others (Bartholomae 2003), can be produced without the exclusion of the personal. Peter Elbow opens this collection with a discussion of the complexity—and dare I say expansiveness—of what is considered personal writing. According to Elbow, there is a continuum associated with personal writing in which the "topic can be personal or not; the language can be personal or not; and the thinking can be personal or not." In Elbow's claims, I hear the openness of Deans' assertion about community-based writing classrooms. According to Deans, the "options available for writing about the community are almost without limit, ranging from the personal/affective to the social/analytical" (2000, p. 104).

The following sections in this chapter are based on a larger study that explores the efficacy of using an expanded notion of personal writing—one that foregrounds the personal yet contains elements of more traditional academic texts—in four sections of a community-based classroom with a multicultural approach to critical pedagogy (henceforth referred to "multicultural critical pedagogy"). The progression of writing assignments throughout each term prepared students to produce end-of-term projects that reflected personal yet academic writing. Using Elbow as an inspiration, sudents initially wrote personal "thinking" texts in which they explored their reactions to the site; shifting to a more Bartholomae-inspired approach, they then produced more traditional academic texts about the works of others before moving to the creation of the hybrid texts that were both personal and academic. I undertook a study of the students' texts as artifacts of the type of work that gets done in the writing classroom and to support the claim that writing that foregrounds the personal is essential for providing students with opportunities to work through the emotional issues of border crossing.

I focus on students' texts because, according to Susan Wells in *Sweet Reason*, pedagogy can be understood as the production of particular texts; "what students write provides us with a way to think about the knowledge that we are creating with them" (1996, p. 219-20). To set the groundwork for my study, I collected and coded four semesters' worth of students' papers, although I ultimately focus on two semesters since external factors at the community site for the other two semesters fundamentally changed the overall scope of my classroom and context. Nevertheless, to get a sense of what all students wrote for all key assignments before honing in on just two terms, I entered extended excerpts from 266 student essays so that I could sort and review the content of their texts by assignment. I then created coding categories based on Thomas Newkirk's work on performative responses, and Rochelle Harris' concept of inductive "emergent moments;" I then noted all references to race as this was central to my sense of a multicultural critical pedagogy. I subsequently re-analyzed student essays to look for specific features in these areas and entered information into 342 new data fields.

I touch upon the specifics of this intense process of data coding and analysis because of two driving rationales that underlie my study. First, I wanted to conduct an analysis that went beyond a theoretical debate about the efficacy of personal writing versus academic writing, especially as it relates to the multicultural course goal. Secondly, I wanted to look at the impact of an enactment of critical pedagogy given what instructors actually have at the end of the term—students' writing—against the temporality of a college semester. It might not be possible over the course of a fifteen-week term to see the emergence of a student version of a Nelson Mandela or César Chávez. What is more likely to occur is social change at the incremental level as "small, fleeting, [and] local" moments" that represent the tinkering of progress in the lives of both teachers and students (Gallagher, 2002, p. 87).

Given the site of my study—the Greater Detroit area—I recognized that the exploration of issues of race and place issues could not be fully unpacked within the scope of a single semester. The narratives of negativity about Detroit and its African-American residents are deeply entrenched, and it was not easy for students to discard ingrained messages. Still, the process of constructing personal texts about such prevailing negative sentiments opened up the possibility of incremental changes in the students' perceptions of the other. I contend that their racialized narratives allowed the students to create critical distances between themselves and their constructed beliefs in such a way that those beliefs became open for investigation and potential change. As Patricia Web Boyd claims in her chapter in this collection, "students need to begin with their own experiences in order to be active participants in the larger society." Their experiential, personal texts provided them with opportunities "to see how the personal already intersects with and is embedded within cultural narratives, to study how their texts write them as they write the texts, and to understand how they name the world around them" (Harris, 2004, p. 405). As an assent to the Freirean claim that the world must be named before it can be changed (2003, p. 88), the study in this chapter investigates how personal writing helped students name their struggles with border crossing as part of the community-based program.

BEFORE THE STUDY: A QUESTION OF ETHICS

Before moving to the specifics of this study about a multicultural enactment of critical pedagogy in a community-based classroom, I think it is necessary to address an ethical question tied to such an initiative: is it ethical to take students to communities they may otherwise not wish to enter under the guise that doing so might eventually help them become more civic minded? Because the Greater Detroit region in which my study was conducted is highly segregated, why should White university students be forced to interact with African-American middle schools students? University students might have a vested interest in maintaining the status quo (Bickford, 2002; Trainor, 2002)—the racial distance separating them from the African-American students and also marked by economic disparity. And what about the middle school students? Should they be forced to interact with university students who may view them as charity cases, individuals who are sub par by virtue of their race and economic standing (Bickford, 2002; Himley, 2004)? According to Beverly Tatum, a psychologist who explores racialized identify development, African-American youth can display hostility toward Whites in response to their growing awareness of racial inequalities (1997, p. 60). Thus, should either of the student groups be placed in a setting in which any group could be hostile toward the other? As Deans asserts, "Many teachers are wary, and rightly so, of the dangers of community service, and in particular the habit of casting individuals and communities in the uneven roles of 'server' and 'served'" (2000, p. 21).

Answers to these questions are important and reflect that community-based learning always entails risk. While focusing on the answers to these difficult questions via exhaustive theoretical and philosophical deliberation could "ultimately lead to intellectual detachment, fatalism, or paralysis" (Deans, 2000, pp. 23; 24), I nevertheless believe that ethical issues should be considered and addressed on a case-by-case basis with the understanding that "perfect balance, perfect dialectic, perfect consideration will ever be elusive" (Deans, 2000,p. 24). Yet, I also believe any possible ethical issues regarding the project explored in this study should be subsumed under compelling reasons for implementing community-based learning within the context, a highly segregated region of the country. As Tatum and Thomas Sugrue both claim, segregation is costly, and any effort to address its effects is worth pursuing. Tatum makes the following statements about the impact of racial distances on White individuals in general:

> When I ask White men and women how racism hurts them, they frequently talk about their fears of people of color, the social incompetence they feel in racially mixed situations, the alienation they have experienced between parents and

children when a child marries into a family of color, and the interracial friendships they had as children that were lost in adolescence or young adulthood without their ever understanding why. (Sugrue, 2005, p. 14)

While Tatum calls attention to these general intangible costs, Sugrue, a native Detroiter and historian, focuses on the more identifiable impacts of racial segregation in the greater Detroit area. He argues the distance between Whites, African Americans, and other racial groups translates into separate but not equal school systems and "limits the access of many minorities to employment opportunities, particularly in predominantly White areas (largely rural and suburban areas) that have experienced rapid development and economic growth over the last half century" (1999, p. 6). Given these costs of segregation, community-based initiatives are important programs because of their attempts to help collapse them/us binaries between university students and community members. Although these programs cannot completely eradicate a history of separation and inequality that is reflected in the lives and minds of both groups, they represent a small and positive step toward a more socially just society. Additionally, the pedagogical cost of possibly grappling with a few ethical issues in a community-based classroom pales in comparison to the cost of doing nothing. In the context of pervasive regional segregation, the primary question of ethics should not be about issues that arise within the community-based classroom; the primary concern should be whether or not it is ethical to do nothing to address this social problem although doing so can be emotionally taxing.

A STUDY ABOUT PERSONAL WRITING AND BORDER CROSSING

In the context of a qualitative, ethnographic research study I conducted in Detroit, Michigan—where racial segregation is the norm—personal writing became the vehicle to help bridge the connection between students' lived realities regarding race and place and the critical pedagogy goal of multiculturalism. For two and a half years that began in January 2002, I participated in a community-based initiative in which intermediate writing students worked with Detroit middle school students as part of an after-school program. For my first term in the site, I was merely as a participant observer, studying the dynamics in preparation to teach and looking for possible areas of research. When I began teaching in the site, the community-based school was a charter institution associated with the university. During my last two terms, the school underwent a change in location, administration, and student population as its classification shifted from that of a charter institution to a Detroit public school. Because of this shift, which created a fundamentally different community site, my research focuses on my last two semesters, Fall 2003 and Winter 2004.

The writing that university students produced was tied to a semester-long ethnographic project that included a range of assignments that began with personal writing, moved to more traditional academic writing, and ended with a hybrid genre which included elements of both academic writing and personal writing but foregrounded the personal. David Seitz presents this type of ethnographic student research as particularly effective when using a multicultural critical pedagogy in urban settings. According to Seitz

> many critical writing teachers in urban schools design their teaching practices on a process of "defamiliarizing the familiar," making the familiar strange, urging students to look at experience through sociological or anthropological lenses. This approach can be persuasive especially for urban students who have experienced various forms of sociocultural conflict. (2004, p. 67)

The text used to help the university students conduct their research, H. L. Goodall's *Writing the New Ethnography* (2000), presents a type of ethnographic work that foregrounds critical thinking about one's own positioning—i.e., gender, race, ethnicity, social class, regional particularities, etc.—and how that positioning affected interpretations of various cultures and contexts.

Because my ethnographic study centers on students' texts as a key data source for artifacts of the pedagogy, I relied on the work of Charles Bazerman, Thomas Newkirk, and Rochelle Harris to inform my methodology. To better understand the efficacy of instruction in critical pedagogy along with personal writing and academic writing, I synthesized their approaches so that I could evaluate students' texts in terms of how the moves in those texts represented possible changes in thinking and how those moves correlate to the type of writing students produced, both personal and academic. Bazerman's work was useful for viewing pedagogical strategies and texts as exerting influence upon students' writing. Newkirk's and Harris' scholarship was useful for investigating elements within students' texts that reflected, or did not reflect, pedagogical goals.

In particular, I used Bazerman's concepts of genre systems and genre sets that he outlines in *What Writing Does and How It Does It* (2004). Within the ethnographic research of a classroom, Bazerman claims analyses of genre systems (pedagogical practices and the flow of course documents) and genre sets (the specific course documents) can help one see "the range and variety of the writing work"; "how individuals writing any new text are intertextually situated within a system and how their writing is directed by genre expectations and supported by systemic systems"; "the effectiveness of the total systems and the appropriateness of each of the genred documents in carrying forward that work"; and "whether any change in any of the documents, distribution, sequence, or flow might improve the total activity system." (2004, p. 326). Regarding the work in this study, the combining of Bazerman's concepts of the genre system and the genre set of a classroom were used as a method to analyze how the differences between pedagogical texts and practices and the contexts of the writing classrooms and the community-based setting impacted students' writing.

While Bazerman's work was useful for analyzing the systemic factors of the classroom on students' writing, I used Newkirk's and Harris' work to investigate what took place within students' writing to hint at how they grappled with the course's multicultural goal of border crossing. Newkirk's work in *The Performance of Self in Student Writing* (1997) was used to analyze the choices students made in their writing that reflected the critical pedagogy aim of multiculturalism. Confronting issues of race, ethnicity, etc., can be an emotionally loaded undertaking in the writing classroom (hooks, 1994; Jay, 2008; Trainor, 2002), and it has been argued that personal writing allows students to make the emotional connections necessary to reflect upon and process moments of border crossing (Kamler, 2001; Micciche, 2007; Rhoads, 1997).

Newkirk, a proponent of personal writing, identifies performative responses in students' texts that reflect the possibility of progressive movement or personal development (1997, p. 22), which in the case of this research, is movement toward a more critical, multicultural worldview. He identifies several performances of the self frequently present in students' personal writing: the "turns," also known as before-and-after conversion narratives; expressions of emotion; student optimism; heroes and antiheroes, or testimonials (for the living) and eulogies (for the dead); and pleasure, or more specifically, hedonism. Of the performances that Newkirk identifies, it is two—the "turns" and optimism—that are relevant to this investigation. Turns are before-and-after conversion narratives that show "the writer as someone open to the potentially transforming effect of a life sensitively encountered" (Newkirk, 1997, p. 13). Optimism is a youthful belief in the "ability to transform the disagreeable" (Newkirk, 1997, p. 42). I coded student essays looking for these turns as part of a critical pedagogy aimed at student movement toward more multicultural awareness and border crossing. Although these turns in students' writing might otherwise be easily dismissed (Newkirk, 1997, p. 10), a reading of students' texts through the lens of critical pedagogy counters such a stance.

To investigate students' texts for the critical pedagogy goal of movement toward critical consciousness, I used Harris' concept of "emergent moments."

The term "emergent moments" "names the point at which the personal, the critical, and the rhetorical intersect in a text, a point at which the student can hold multiple perspectives simultaneously and reflexively," "allowing them to become authors of their own experiences, to resist or revise cultural narratives, and to see opportunities to critique and transform themselves and the cultural systems around them" (Harris, 2004, p. 403). Or stated another way, it is at that textual moment when students consider themes and/or see issues as part of larger cultural realities. I analyzed students' texts for the "emergent moments" that represented responses to the pedagogical goal of critical consciousness as critique of issues tied to the community site.

The story of the community that constitutes the setting of the course is one of segregation. The Detroit metropolitan area is one of the most segregated areas of the country, and as a result, many individuals live in isolated pockets of racial groups. Regarding the community-based writing course, this segregated region 1) affected who entered the writing classroom and, in particular, the lived experiences of those students in relationship to the curricular goal of critical pedagogy, and 2) was central to the systemic issues embedded in the course design, i.e., the selection of the site, course readings, and course assignments.

Often, these community-based experiences represented the first time many of the university students had sustained contact with individuals who were African American. Although Wayne State University is located within the city of Detroit, which has a large African-American population, its student body does not reflect the demographics of the city (about 80% of Detroit's population is African American, but over 70% of Wayne State's student population is not (U.S. Census Bureau, 2008; WSU Student Profile, 2006). Many of the students who attend the university come from surrounding counties that are predominantly White. Or in a few cases, they come from communities that are non-White but also non-African-American; for example, the greater Detroit area includes enclaves of racially segregated communities of Middle Eastern and Hispanic peoples.

This racial segregation is exacerbated by a prevailing sentiment portrayed repeatedly in local media: Detroit is a "bad place to be" and its African-American residents are to be feared. Because of this, it was advantageous to enact a cultural studies approach to critical pedagogy that provided writing students with an opportunity to address these emotional commonplaces. About 74% of the student participants, or 17 out of 23, included negative statements about Detroit in their beginning-of-the-term assignment in which they explored their initial reactions to the community site. The six students who did not do so included four of the six African-American students, all Detroit residents, and two other students who attended European schools during their middle school years. The following comments made by a White male student in a beginning-of-the-term assignment exemplifies the impact of anti-Detroit messages that are a part of the daily realities of regional residents:

> I thought, there was no way I was going to a public school, and especially in downtown Detroit. That's where all the black people live. I had heard many stories about the danger in such urban neighborhoods, and I wasn't about to put myself in any situation like that. Not only that, but I didn't have anything in common with these people. Even the color of our skin wasn't the same. I don't listen to hip-hop music and I can't even understand the idioms they use, or their slang. I had heard many stories where black people were considered illiterate and lazy. Most of them were thought to be involved in criminal activities and don't value family, honesty and respect. Women are viewed as objects of sexual satisfaction and are often abused. As I was told, the neighborhoods that these people live in, after a while, would turn into slums or ghettos. In their families, in quite a few instances, children don't even know their fathers. Even their style is different from what I am used to. They like flashy gold or platinum chains, bright color clothing and like to wear hats and have different hairstyles. As some White people believe, they are supposed to be inferior to them and, as in the past, they should be restricted to a separate territory, in order to be controlled.

This excerpt may seem like an exaggeration to anyone who is not familiar with the greater Detroit area, and those who are teachers of college writing might immediately want to question the student's sweeping generalizations regarding African Americans. However, few who live in the region would discount the reality that many, if not all, of the perceptions or misconceptions that this student holds are expressed by many individuals who live in and around the city of Detroit. While I do call attention to this phenomenon as it relates to students' comments in their essays, I am not doing so to reify the dichotomies, or the them/us barriers, between students and community members. Community-based initiatives are designed to challenge and ideally change such dichotomies (Rhoads, 1997; Trainor, 2002). Rather, I underscore students' statements about Detroit in recognition that the pervasiveness of the perceived dichotomies between the city and its suburbs impacted what students wrote about the community-based experience.

Harris claims critical work can occur in such personal texts about topics and issues that are significant to individuals because "the texts we choose to write are important sites to understand the self, the world, and culture" (2004, p. 402). She focuses on the "composing and recomposing of reality and the self through language that happens in personal essays, autobiographies, and memoirs—to name a few genres" as critical work necessary for developing Freirean praxis (Harris, 2004, pp. 402; 405). From Harris' perspective, critical pedagogy is implicitly personal because "a person has first to move to a knowledge of the world being named for him or her and then do the intellectual and emotional work necessary to rename his or her world" (2004, p. 405). In the critical classroom, then, storytelling becomes a medium for change (Harris, 2004, p. 407). Because of the widespread negative sentiments associated with place and race—inner city Detroit and its African-American citizens—students' established beliefs and/or emotional responses were not overlooked but elicited, regardless of whether the responses were positive or negative.

Without opportunities to explore negative emotional responses, Jennifer Seibel Trainor claims that white students in particular might resist a multicultural-based critical pedagogy where whiteness is essentialized in discussions of racism and class. White students are presented with a worldview that situates them, solely by virtue of birth, "as perpetrators of injustice who must be taught to disavow whiteness" (Trainor, 2002, p. 634). In such instances, Trainor argues, many students will "read multicultural texts about difference in essentialist and, thus, defensive terms" (2002, p. 642). Instead, educators should be critically aware of this unintended outgrowth—e.g., essentialized whiteness and an "angry white identity"—and provide space for discourse that allows white students to structure identities outside of a limited rhetorical framing (2002, p. 647).

The progression of writing assignments throughout the term, from personal to academic to hybrid, which included elements of both but foregrounded the personal, was essential to providing students with opportunities to work through the emotional issues of border crossing. It was necessary for students to begin at the personal juncture of emotion as a route to engagement with the site and the course content related to the multicultural course aim because, as Mary Helen Immordino-Yang and Antonio Damasio claim in "We Feel, Therefore We Learn: The Relevance of Affective and Social Neuroscience to Education," minimizing the emotional aspects would have been "encouraging students to develop the sorts of knowledge that inherently do not transfer well to real-world situations" (2007, p. 9).

The move to more traditional academic writing (i.e., article summaries and annotated bibliographies) as an exploration of issues that grew out of students' ethnographic investigation of the community-based context was key to helping students develop broader worldviews regarding sociocultural issues. It gave them practice with what David Bartholomae identifies as academic writing, i.e., the ability to "work with the past, with key texts ... with others' terms ... with problems of quotation, citation, and paraphrase" (1995, p. 66). Bartholomae argues that producing such writing helps students adopt an insider stance that reflects "the peculiar ways of knowing, selecting, evaluating, reporting, concluding, and arguing that define the discourse" of the academic community (2003, p. 623). While having students write both personal and more traditional essays were central to carrying forward the work of the term as part of the classroom genre system (Bazerman, 2004), it was the hybrid genre that students used in their final project that most helped them consider the complex work of border crossing that was embedded in the multicultural, critical pedagogy course goal.

In my analysis of students' final projects, I used Harris' identification of "emergent moments" of critical praxis, reflection and action (Freire, 2003, p. 79). I looked at that textual moment when students consider themes, see issues in their texts as part of larger cultural issues but with recognition that the "emergent moment "cannot be imposed (although it certainly can be facilitated)" (Harris, 2004, pp. 403; 413)—an important claim given the inductive process of ethnographic writing and meaning making. Sometimes they were brief glimpses of students' critical thinking embedded in longer narratives. However, these moments are worthy of analysis and consideration as part of a progressive process of change; they reflected Newkirk's "optimistic turns" that hinted at possible steps toward change. As Chris Gallagher claims, mainstream critical pedagogy calls for grand, sweeping gestures of change, but this is not the stuff of everyday writing classrooms (2002, p. 87). In "the unpredictable and messy terrain of pedagogy, we are not likely to find many grand moments of social transformation, but we are likely to find important (though small, fleeting, and decidedly local) moments" (Gallagher, 2002, p. 87). Thus, I looked at the students' essays for "emergent moments" of critical thinking as a way to investigate the efficacy of a multicultural critical pedagogy.

From my analysis of students' essays from the Winter 2004 term, I focus in this chapter on the essay of 47-year-old Eva. Her entire essay is about the interpersonal connections made, and not made, during the term as she explores the distance and hostility between the university students and the middle school students and the ways in which she believed university students contributed to the environment.

Eva wrote two distinct drafts of her final project because she was initially hesitant about whether she had the license to write about the emotionally charged atmosphere she perceived in the community-based site. Eva stopped me after one class session and asked if she could write about the problematic, interpersonal dynamics of the after-school class. I recorded some of our conversation in my fieldnotes for the day:

> Eva wanted to write about the racial divide that had occurred this term between the middle school students and the non-African-American Wayne Students. We had talked the previous week about the topic. I communicated to her that she had an excellent topic; she just needed to go ahead and make the analysis she alluded to in her first draft.
>
> She was hesitant to set up the dichotomy between her and the other non-African-American university students. It was as if doing so, even in her paper, would be politically incorrect ... Why did she feel silenced in her desire to express this racially-related dynamic? Had she previously been silenced? Was she oppressed (Freire)? Had she not had the experience of presenting her own voice in text?
>
> Because Eva had difficulty putting her positionality in the beginning of her paper, the text was choppy and disconnected. It seemed as if she felt compelled to maintain a distance from the issue, from the text.

I talked to Eva about the discussions we had earlier in the term about positionality and the ethics of ethnography versus what could be considered the more traditional, anthropological telling of the other. "You have to put yourself on the page. If you talk about your positionality, your age, your race, how they affected what you saw and how you reacted to the setting, then I think it will be easier for you to move into what you really want to talk about," I stated.

"You mean I can go there?" she grinned, tilted her head.

"Yes, you can." I smiled in reply.

"Alright!" Eva smiled ecstatically, "You told me I could, so I'm going there."

Eva's response to my statement that she could write about what she felt was problematic affirms Barbara Kamler's claim that "to be authorized by the academy to write about one's life is a powerful and often startling experience for university students" (2001, p. 157). Her initial hesitancy about addressing a sensitive topic reflects that, given her age, Eva more than likely attended school at a time when academic writing comprised a constructed worldview that spoke "through an academic persona who is objective, trying to prevent any emotions or prejudices from influencing the ideas in the writing" (Bizzell, 2002, p. 2). Nevertheless, Eva did revise her essay to take a more personal and ethnographic stance. Following is an extended excerpt from her text:

> I have been privileged to mentor in the [after-school program] with several bright enthusiastic African-American middle school students ... I intend to investigate information on the mentor/students relationships that I observed at [the middle school] .... There are four African-American female mentors. Our ages range from 20-47. We all seem to be straight-forward, generous, and thoughtful. These three characteristics impacted our roles as mentors and we seem to have a good rapport with the students. The students like us. There are several male/female White mentors. While listening to their conversations, it seemed evident that they all live outside of the city of Detroit. They reside in the Tri-county area, namely the suburbs. There is one mentor who is always making some negative comment about Detroit and the people that they see on their way to UPS. He is a White male mentor who always seems to have the right answer and is occasionally humorous. He would talk quietly and could draw other White mentors into his conversations. However, when a Black mentor intervened, he would draw up and be quiet. I threw a flag up in my mind and I thought, "He needs to be watched."
>
> I spend a lot of time tutoring urban Black students. I am very much attuned to the interaction between the young middle school students and the mentors .... The middle school students ... need to be monitored by their mentors; otherwise I've noticed that the whole time spent in the session [the middle school students] will be playing games and listening to, or watching, videos on the computers .... As I observed throughout the room, some [middle] students, especially some male students, were isolating themselves from their mentors, mostly by being preoccupied on the computers.
>
> I overheard this conversation with two male middle school students as they were waiting for their mentors ... "I know he does not like me. I don't know why we have to do this. I could probably show him more about the computer than he

can show me. He never does anything. They don't even talk to us. He probably doesn't even know my name."... As I turned to observe the mentor that they were discussing, it was the White male mentor, the White male that always had the right answer and was occasionally humorous. And then my flag went up. Maybe, I thought all parties involved were having a culture shock reaction ...

I believe the students felt the mentor's communication skills represented a problem. As I observed the mentor, the mentor never approached the students with a "hello." He always waited for the instructor to tell everyone to group up with [their] mentees ... Although, there were no African-American male mentors, I believe they would have settled for one of us. Maybe the students thought the mentor was not willing to work and was afraid to ask questions because they were Black. Maybe the students thought that he was going to make it hard for them and try to set them up to fail. When I looked at the mentor, I thought, "Where was his sense of humor, the I'm the man kind of attitude?" His facial expression was like, "I really don't want to be here."... I noticed a vicious cycle had taken place that had pitted the two male students against their mentor. It seemed like they were never going to resolve their differences. I believe that until the mentor begins to see his problem and seek out a solution, he will continue to engage in a struggle interacting with Black students.

Many problems attributed to "Children of Color" are actually the result of miscommunication at school and other people's children struggle with the imbalance of power and the dynamics of inequality plaguing our system (Delpit, 1995) .... The person in the role of a mentor, especially if the person is from another ethnic and cultural background, must be keenly aware of the miscommunication that can result from cultural diversity. Every effort must be made to keep communication open and free from prejudice .... I made a promise to myself to share this information with the White mentor especially if he planned to teach in a predominantly Black school district.

This excerpt from Eva's essay shows her attempts to make sense out of the hostility and distance between university and middle school students that persisted throughout the term. Her reasoning explores the reality of the racially segregated region in which the university and middle school students reside. Her essay also demonstrates the course's pedagogical goal of having students produce texts that could be called hybrid, including elements of the personal and the academic. Eva cites Lisa Delpit and others in her argument about ways to create connections with African-American youth. Throughout Eva's essay is the theme that the interpersonal distance between university and middle students was problematic for her, particularly given the reason why she had returned to academia: to become a teacher.

Eva's move to critical consciousness—echoing Freire's praxis, "the action and reflection of men and women upon their world in order to transform it" (2003, p. 79), or the "emergent moment,"—happens at the end of her essay when she claims, "I made a promise to myself to share this information with the White mentor especially if he planned to teach in a predominantly Black school district." In this claim to action is praxis; she has seen the impact of the interpersonal and often hostile distance and is willing to take action against it if faced with a similar situation. What Eva produced is an essay in which she immerses herself in ways that clearly foreground her personal connection to the middle school students. For example, she begins her essay by recounting what she believes are the personal characteristics that she and the other three African-American university students possess: "We all seem to be straight-forward, generous, and thoughtful." She then spends the bulk of her essay explicating why she and the other females were liked by the middle school students and some of the White university students were not. Eva's essay demonstrates a central claim regarding enactments of critical pedagogy: emotions matter. As Laura Micciche reminds us, "emotion matters drive motives for action, speech, judgment, and decision-making" (2007, p. 105), important elements given a pedagogical goal of student movement towards a consciousness that leads to change. The absence of emotional connections can lead to objectified analyses of critical issues that are more intellectual games than potential steps toward individual or collective action (Barnett, 2006, p. 361).

Given these assertions about emotion driving action (Micciche, 2007; Barnett, 2006), it is not surprising that Eva's essay ends with a claim to individual action. She maintains she will take future action against "miscommunication that can result from cultural diversity." I believe this action was arrived at inductively because Eva was able to establish an emotional connection to her essay topic. Because Eva felt strongly about what she had observed, she was willing to take the writerly risk to tell her story, one that I believe was aided by the fact that students throughout the term were invited to write in a genre that foregrounded the personal. As Jane Danielwicz claims in her essay, Personal Genres, Public Voices, "writing in personal genres fights alienation (common to academic pursuits from the student's point of view) and instead promotes connectivity: 'You are a part of this world'" (2008, p. 443). Eva took the risk to express her desire to be a change agent because of her experiences in the community-based course in which multicultural critical pedagogy had been enacted. Her response hinted at ways in which she could promote border crossing in diverse settings.

A FEW FINAL WORDS

Emotions matter in general regarding all learning but are particularly central when course content asks students to do the socially complex work of border crossing. As Immordino-Yang and Damasio claim, "emotion-related processes are required for skills and knowledge to be transferred from the structured school environment to real-world decision making because they provide an emotional rudder to guide judgment and action" (2007, p. 3). Thus, in a community-based-writing classroom or any writing classroom in which multicultural critical pedagogy is implemented, students must be given an opportunity to write in ways that allow them to be emotional. Reflexive, personal writing allows students to emote about their experiences of border crossing and construct themselves as influencing, and being influenced by, contexts. When elements of academic writing are added in such texts where the personal is foregrounded, the end result is a hybrid text where emotions meet critical concepts and students are given an opportunity to move from having knowledge about difference to making real-world, incremental steps toward embracing difference.

REFERENCES

Barnett, T. (2006). Politicizing the person: Frederick Douglass, Richard Wright, and some thoughts on the limits of critical literacy. *College English, 68*(4), 356-381.

Bartholomae, D. (2003). Inventing the university. In V. Villanueva (Ed.), *Cross-Talk in Comp Theory* (2nd ed., pp. 623-654). Urbana, IL: NCTE.

Bartholomae, D. (1995). Writing with teachers: A conversation with Peter Elbow. *College Composition and Communication, 46*(1), 62-71.

Bazerman, C. (2004). Speech acts, genres, and activity systems: How texts organize activity and people. In C. Bazerman & P. Prior (Eds.), *What Writing Does and How It Does It: An Introduction to Analyzing Texts and Textual Practices* (pp. 309-339). Mahway, NJ: Lawrence Erlbaum.

Bickford, D. M., & Reynolds, N. (2002). Activism and service learning: Reframing volunteerism as acts of dissent. *Pedagogy: Critical Approaches to Teaching Literature, Language, Composition, and Culture, 2*(2), 229-252. Retrieved from Duke University Press Web site: http://pedagogy.dukejournals.org/content/2/2/229.citation

Bizzell, P. (2002). The intellectual work of "mixed" forms of academic discourses. In C. Schroeder, H. Fox, & P. Bizzell (Eds.), *Alt Dis: Alternative Discourses and the Academy* (pp. 1-10). Portsmouth, NH: Boynton Cook Heinemann.

Danielwicz, J. (2008). Personal genres, public voices. *College Composition and Communication, 59*(3), 420-450.

Deans, T. (2000). *Writing partnerships: Service learning in composition.* Urbana, IL: NCTE.

Delpit, L. (1995). *Other people's children: Cultural conflict in the classroom.* New York: New Press.

Dobrin, S. (1997). *Constructing knowledge: The politics of theory building and pedagogy in composition.* Albany, NY: SUNY Press.

Flower L. (1997). Partners in inquiry: A logic for community outreach. In L. Adler-Kassner, R. Crooks, & A. Waters (Eds.), *Writing the Community: Concepts and Models for Service Learning in Composition* (pp. 95-117). Urbana, IL: NCTE/AAHE, 1997.

Flower L. (2003). Talking across difference: Intercultural rhetoric and the search for situated knowledge. *College Composition and Communication, 55*(1), 38-68.

Freire, P. (2003). *Pedagogy of the Oppressed.* (M. B. Ramos, Trans.). New York: Continuum.

Fulkerson, R. (2005). Composition at the turn of the twenty-first century. *College Composition and Communication, 56*(4), 654-687.

Gallagher, C. (2002). *Radical departures: Composition and progressive pedagogy.* Urbana, IL: NCTE.

Goodall, H. L. (Bud). (2000). *Writing the new ethnography.* Lanham, MD: Rowman and Littlefield.

Harris, R. (2004). Encouraging emergent moments: The personal, critical, and rhetorical in the writing classroom. *Pedagogy: Critical Approaches to Teaching Literature, Language, Composition and Culture, 4*(3), 401-418. Retrieved from Duke University Press Web site: http://pedagogy.dukejournals.org/content/4/3/401.citation

Herzberg, B. (1997) Community service and critical teaching. In L. Adler-Kassner, R. Crooks, & A. Waters (Eds.), *Writing the community: Concepts and models for service learning in composition* (pp. 57-69). Urbana, IL: NCTE/AAHE.

Himley, M. (2004). Facing (up to) "the stranger" in community service learning. *College Composition and Communication, 55*(3), 416-438.

hooks, b. (1994). *Teaching to transgress: Education as the practice of freedom.* New York: Routledge.

Immordino-Yang, M. H., & Damasio, A. (2007). We feel, therefore we learn: The relevance of affective and social neuroscience to education. *Mind, Brain and Education, 1*(1), 3-10.

Jay, G. (2008). Service learning, multiculturalism, and the pedagogies of difference. *Pedagogy: Critical Approaches to Teaching Literature, Language, Composition and Culture, 8*(2), 255-281. Retrieved from Duke University Press Web site: http://pedagogy.dukejournals.org/content/8/2/255.abstract

Kamler, B. (2001). *Relocating the personal: A critical writing pedagogy.* New York: SUNY Press.

Knoblach, C. H., & Brannon, L. (1993). *Critical teaching and the idea of literacy.* Portsmouth, NH: Boynton/Cook.

Mead, S. (2006). Maintenance required: Charter schooling in Michigan. *Education Sector Reports,* 2006.

Micciche, L. R. (2007). *Doing emotion: Rhetoric, writing, teaching.* Portsmouth, NH: Boynton Cook.

Newkirk, T. (1997). *The performance of self in student writing.* Portsmouth, NH: Boynton/Cook-Heinemann.

Rhoads, R. A. (1997). *Community service and higher learning: Explorations of the caring self.* Albany, NY: SUNY Press.

Rosenberger, C. (2000). Beyond empathy: Developing critical consciousness through service learning. In C. R. O'Grady (Ed.), *Integrating Service Learning and Multicultural Education in Colleges and Universities* (pp. 23-44). Mahway, NJ: Lawrence Erlbaum.

Seitz, D. (2004). *Who can afford critical consciousness? Practicing a pedagogy of humility.* Cresskill, NJ: Hampton Press.

Sugrue, T. J. (1999). Expert report of Thomas J. Sugrue; Gratz, et al. v. Bollinger, et al. No. 97-75321 Eastern District of Michigan and Grutter, et al. v. Bollinger, et al. No. 97-75928 (Eastern District of Michigan, January 1999). Retrieved from University of Michigan Web site: http://www.vpcomm.umich.edu/admissions/legal/expert/sugrutoc.html

Sugrue, T. J. (2005). *The origins of the urban crisis: Race and inequality in postwar Detroit.* Princeton University Press.

Tatum, B. (1997). *Why are all the black kids sitting together in the cafeteria? And other conversations about race.* New York, Basic Books.

Trainor, J. Seibel. (2002). Critical pedagogy's "other": Constructions of whiteness in education for social change. *College Composition and Communication, 53*(4), 631-50.

U.S. Census Bureau: State and County Quick Facts. (2008). *Michigan.* Retrieved from http://quickfacts.census.gov/qfd/states/26000.html

Wells, S. (1996). *Sweet reason: Rhetoric and the discourses of modernity.* Chicago: University of Chicago Press.

WSU Student Profile. (2006). Retrieved from Wayne State University Web site: http://about.wsu.edu/about/facts.aspx

THE ECONOMY OF EXPRESSIVISM AND ITS LEGACY OF LOW/NO-STAKES WRITING

Sheri Rysdam
Utah Valley University

Nothing makes evident the inextricable link between writing and the social quite like teaching college writing. The ways in which differences in expectations and outcomes can sometimes be attributed to social class are often easily ignored by educators and administrators. Used purposefully, however, expressivism can be a pedagogical approach that helps support poor and working class students who otherwise are often told that they are "underprepared" or not ready to fully participate in college. Though the popularity of expressivist composition pedagogy as an overarching pedagogical theory has been out of favor by some for well over a decade, the value of an important component of expressivist pedagogy—the practice of low-stakes freewriting—remains. Consequently expressivist pedagogy can help struggling students find success in the writing classroom.

That expressivism has the potential to help support poor and working class students might come as a surprise to some, given the predominant arguments against it—namely that it is classist, favoring an upper and middle class aesthetic. Linda Adler-Kassner, for example, writes that expressivism is about "the achievement of individual success and satisfaction" (1998, p. 211). She continues, stating that "expressivists implied that writing would help students unearth their genuine selves" and could "fulfill their own needs and desires for self-understanding" (1998, p. 218). However, Adler-Kassner also admits that expressivism risks taking for granted a familiarity with what we might describe as middle class academic discourses where students are commonly afforded the luxury of experimenting with self-exploration and discovery. Students who are not already familiar with such educational environments may not feel they can afford to "find" themselves. For them, finding a job might be more important that finding one's "self." Nevertheless, done well, expressivism has the potential to forge intellectual connections between the personal, political, and economic.

To invoke an economic metaphor, we might imagine that expressivism has a certain *laissez-faire* quality to it. In a more conventional, current-traditional classroom, teacher intervention might be compared to government regulation, and the proliferation of student writing seen as equivalent to capital gain. But in an expressivist approach, student writing is less regulated by the instructor, just as the capital gained in a *laissez-faire economic model is usually unregulated by the government.* What I wish to do now is illustrate several examples of more prescriptive, current-traditional approaches that resemble the former, followed by contrasting expressivist examples that illustrate the latter.

*

Using economic metaphors to describe educational models is not novel. Paulo Freire did it most notably, reminding us that an educational experience is an economic experience, both literally and metaphorically. Indeed, it is impossible to engage the concepts of literacy and deficit thinking in education without evoking Paulo Freire's apt metaphor for traditional education as a "banking" model of instruction. In Freire's metaphor, the teacher makes a deposit of information into the student, who is then richer for having received it. In *Pedagogy of the Oppressed*, Freire claims that the "banking" concept works like this: "the teacher issues communiqués and makes deposits which the students patiently receive, memorize, and repeat. This is the 'banking' concept of education, in which the scope of action allowed to the students extends only as far as receiving, filing, and storing the deposits" (1993, p. 53). In this model, students are not taught critical analysis, but are instead taught to memorize and regurgitate.

Although compositionists have significantly revised the outcomes of the composition classroom, in many current-traditional writing classes there is still an emphasis on grammar and form at the cost of relevance and meaning for the writer. While critical literacy and inclusion are often valued in the field of composition in theory, the practice does not always play out. A deficit approach to writing pedagogy still abounds. Freire writes, "the capability of banking education to minimize or annul the students' creative power and to stimulate their credulity serves the interests of the oppressors, who care neither to have the world revealed nor to see it transformed" (1993, p. 54). He continues, "the banking concept of education, which serves the interest of oppression, is also necrophilic. Based on a mechanistic, static, naturalistic, spatialized view of consciousness, it transforms students into receiving objects" (1993, p. 58). Freire reminds us that while education has incredible emancipatory potential, students can also be oppressed in educational institutions. Current-traditional modes of composition pedagogy all too often resemble the "banking concept" Freire describes.

Mina Shaughnessy was not the first scholar to argue for pedagogies of inclusion that seek to help students not acclimated to academic writing, particularly those from poor and working class backgrounds. Shaughnessy's work paved the way for recognizing that the voices in diverse student populations belong in and enrich the classroom environment. In Diving In: An Introduction to Basic

Writing, Shaughnessy concludes by stating, "teaching [students] to write well is not only suitable but challenging work for those who would be teachers and scholars in a democracy" (2003, p. 317). Yet as much as Shaughnessy's work fueled an interest in basic writers, and critiqued practices that exclude certain populations, her work is not unproblematic. In a critique of Shaughnessy's approach to basic writing, Joseph Harris points out the seeming contradictions between her practice and her theory (1996). For example, in *Errors and Expectations* (1977), Shaughnessy actually recreates many of the practices of exclusion that she otherwise condemns; five of her eight book chapters are focused on traditional conventions: "Handwriting and Punctuation, Syntax, Common Errors, Spelling, and Vocabulary." Despite her introduction, which makes it very clear that Shaughnessy is writing about students who are very new to higher education, much of the book reinforces dated "skills and drills" notions of teaching writing. Harris claims that "*Errors and Expectations* … argues for a new sort of student but not a new sort of intellectual practice. It says that basic writers can also do the kind of work that mainstream students have long been expected to do; it doesn't suggest that work be changed in any significant ways" (Harris, 1996, p. 79). So while Shaughnessy argues for inclusion, she does not make the crucial move to inclusive pedagogical strategies associated with critical literacy, alternative discourse, or appeals to the student's right to her own language.

Nor are such inconsistencies relegated to the past. Deficit thinking is still a prominent part of current-traditionalist pedagogy. For example, a popular textbook used for introductory composition courses, *They Say/I Say: The Moves that Matter in Academic Writing* (Graff, G., & C. Birkenstein, 2009), follows a deficit approach to writing instruction. Gerald Graff and Cathy Birkenstein send the message that academic writing is a mysterious process that many students do not already know, one that must be taught to the student because their current way of writing is unacceptable. They provide fill-in-the-blank templates for academic writing, like the following model:

> In discussions of X, one controversial issue has been _____.
> On the one hand, _____ argues _____. On the other hand, _____ contends _____. Others even maintain _____. My own view is _____. (2009, p. 222)

Graff and Birkenstein's templates include some of the most common rhetorical moves made in academic arguments. In the introduction, Graff and Birkenstein write, "often without consciously realizing it, accomplished writers routinely rely on a stock of established moves that are crucial for communicating sophisticated ideas" (2009, p. 1). Later they write, "less experienced writers, by contrast, are often unfamiliar with these basic moves and unsure how to make them in their own writing" (2009, p. 1). As a result they seek to convince student writers that they lack the proper knowledge to make these rhetorical patterns found in academic writing, thus likely making students distrustful of their own writing processes. And since many of the students Graff and Birkenstein have in mind might be from diverse populations, their current-traditionalist model seeks to naturalize and homogenize student writing. The negative effects of their claim that college writing is mysterious, and that new college students are underprepared, hardly seems worth the potential benefits.

*

In contrast to these current-traditional perspectives, Peter Elbow claims that the composition classroom should be a place where students get comfortable with the processes of writing. He wants students to experience writing for its empowering potential, which is how he experiences writing. Elbow writes, "I get deep satisfaction from discovering meanings by writing—figuring out what I think and feel through putting down words; I naturally turn to writing when I am perplexed—even when I am just sad or happy; I love to explore and communicate with others through writing; writing is an important part of my life" (1995, p. 489). From this one can glean that teaching conventional form and grammar is not necessarily as high on Elbow's list of pedagogical priorities as sharing and communication. In one of his discourses with David Bartholomae, he tells him, "I simply want to intervene much less than you do" (Elbow, P., & Bartholomae, D., 1997, p. 507). Elbow wants to intervene less in students' writing as a way to empower and encourage. In my experience, intervention unfortunately often comes in the form of finding errors and making and heavy-handed corrections—teacherly activities that can do very little to encourage and inspire thinking and writing. Elbow explains how he encourages students, writing that "the most precious thing I can do is provide spaces where I don't also do their thinking for them" (Elbow, P., & Bartholomae, D., 1997, p.508). Elbow continues: "students easily distrust their experience, and we do harm if we try to 'correct' them about their own experience" (Elbow, P., & Bartholomae, D., 1997, p.509). Elbow wants students to learn to trust their knowledge and experience. And it has been my experience, both personally and professionally, that students who are new to academia are particularly vulnerable to distrusting their own experiences, their writing, and even their way of speaking.

Ultimately, what I find most valuable about Elbow's expressivism as a counter to deficit thinking is that his pedagogy does not assume students, especially those who are new to academia, are empty receptacles for knowledge or too unprepared for college writing. In this way, Elbow's contribution to the field provides us with potentially revolutionary possibilities, and has potential emancipatory power for students. The message of a pedagogy of freewriting asks students to begin writing and believes that all students can make valuable contributions, wherever they are, in their lives and educational journeys. Elbow's approach is more about helping students express themselves through writing and not about teaching them about how bad their writing is and how much they need to change.

For those who are concerned with the inclusion of diverse student populations, Elbow's argument is appealing. Clearly, Elbow gets satisfaction from writing and that resonates with many teachers of writing. However, Elbow's approach is not without limits. While it can be especially inclusive for poor and working class student populations in that it allows these students to enter the academic conversation sooner, some argue that it actually favors middle and upper-class students who are already competent at reflection and generating ideas and writing. Not only has Elbow argued for low-stakes writing, he actively argues that being a "writer" and being an "academic writer" are not only two different things, but that they are also at odds with each other. Here is what he admits: "I choose the goal of writer over that of academic" (1995, p. 490). He writes, "If my goal is to get them [students] to take on the role of academic, I should get them to distrust language" (1995, p. 495). It is clear that Elbow resists traditional, academic modes of writing, but he makes many compelling points that provide practical approaches to being more inclusive.

Because freewriting asks students to start writing immediately, they can never be too "underprepared" to begin. Students begin writing—*now*. Not only can expressivism be used as a means for understanding social class as it plays out in college-level writing, but it can work to address the corporate, capitalist economic models that are increasingly at play in today's educational systems. Since finding pedagogical ways to support diverse student populations is crucial for a democratic educational model, I argue that there is still something to be learned from a critical expressivist pedagogy. Expressivist pedagogies can provide models that allow for the academic success of diverse student populations, offering a counter to the deficit models found in current-traditional practices. Expressivism is less obsessed with how "underprepared" students are for college (especially students from diverse, nonacademic backgrounds) and is more concerned with the idea of facilitating writing, as well as intellectual liberation, for all students.

*

Concepts taken from expressivist practices—like freewriting, as well as much of the emancipatory language of expressivist rhetoric in general—continue to flourish in composition instruction today. Self-discovery, personal voice, and expression are all tropes one finds circulating in the discourse of expressivist pedagogy. In expressivism, the practice of writing can be viewed as a metacognitive process that allows students to think through ideas, change their minds, and think about process. Like other methods of writing instruction, expressivism promotes a reflective and recursive approach.

Admittedly, in many expressivist pedagogies, attention to an audience can be de-emphasized; students use writing for their own means, as a way to understand their own thinking. A critical expressivist model cannot ignore the economic realities of the educational institution, and perhaps more importantly, the educational realities of students' lives. Victor Villanueva writes that students may rightly be interested in "literacy of the kind that leads to certification, access to high school, maybe to college, the middle class" (1997, p. 633). As much as enlightenment and self-discovery might be the personal pedagogical goal for some teachers, in the end, those teachers are always still constrained by the institution or "the demands of the local chair, or university president" (Villanueva, 1997, p. 635). Students, especially those who are new to college culture, are often still interested in writing, thinking, and speaking in a way that might provide the opportunity for upward mobility if they should so choose to climb. While teaching form and academic literacy cannot be ignored, some aspects of expressivism, like low-stakes writing, can meet the demand for increasing students' academic literacy, while simultaneously valuing the multiple discourses and knowledge they bring to the classroom. This is especially important for those students who do not already have the kinds of literacy that may be conducive to class mobility and success in college.

After all, the personal, the academic, and the economic are always simultaneously at work in the composition classroom. In James Ray Watkins' book, *A Taste for Language: Literacy, Class, and English Studies* (2009), he argues that the evolution of a student's "sensibility" is a sensibility that can be taught, and the writing classroom is one place where that can occur. Watkins writes, "students come to college, the cliché goes, to get a well-paying, secure job; professors teach, in contrast, in order to create critical thinkers and effective democratic citizens" (2009, p. 116). For some students, economic concerns of class mobility and employment are unavoidable realities to their academic experience. Other students might not have the luxury of a time-consuming contemplation and reflection traditionally associated with higher education. Either way, the experience is always also an economic one. If institutions of higher education are unable to achieve change, and "if we do not begin to confront the dominance of economics over democracy," then Watkins argues that "we will increasingly find only the most middle-class students in our classroom" (2009, p. 164). Without some awareness of the status models that are formed in English studies, poor, working class, and first generation students will likely be further alienated in the classroom.

Today's expressivism is not about ignoring the economic, the academic, nor the audience. While it can be about discovering the personal through the act of writing, it is not only about emphasizing self-expression of emotions. Instead, it can be a way to teach students how to use writing as a tool for thinking and a way for students to learn how to generate writing and familiarize themselves with acts of writing. A new expressivist approach to writing instruction might require teachers to develop strategies that allow a lot of classroom space for low-stakes writing and give students opportunities to get used to the process of writing, which can be especially important for poor and working class students. This is not to neglect form altogether. In fact, as teachers allow this process of expression in class, they can also begin to provide feedback to students and begin to teach form and genre and other rhetorical moves that will be conducive to the academic success of a diverse student population beyond the first-year composition classroom. This occurs while some elements of form (those necessary for learning the kinds of literacies that might lead to future success) are still taught in the classroom. That way, even if a student is not already familiar with the various modes of academic rhetoric, they can still experience success producing writing and improving writing through practice and exposure to academic texts.

An expressivist position in writing instruction is all about a desire to encourage students to trust themselves and get comfortable with writing. In this model of writing instruction, students learn to trust the writing process and trust that it can be a useful way to develop their thoughts. Expressivists like myself might see the *They Say/I Say* model as perpetuating student fears that their writing is not already good enough, that they are unprepared, and that there are secret templates that must be mastered for success in college writing. If students learn to distrust their writing, or "distrust language" in Elbow's words (1995, p. 495), then they might be less likely to turn to writing as a mode of communication, developing thoughts, or as a creative outlet. This potential injury to students' relationship to writing is not conducive to perpetuating student comfort with writing or the ability to turn to writing as a safe place to work through thoughts.

Ultimately, the field of composition employs a diverse population of teachers, with their diverse approaches to pedagogy and theory. I like that diversity. It allows individual teachers to teach to their strengths, while considering the goals and political climates of their institutions. In that regard, no one prescriptive "how to" works for all teachers of composition. Though it has problematic interpretations, expressivism ought not be thrown out. In my own teaching, I emphasize the kind of low-stakes writing that Elbow promotes, where students are able to generate writing—to get familiar with and used to writing as a mode of creative and intellectual expression.

Some students come to college for the improved job possibilities, some to climb the social ladder, and some to stay for the life-changing process of receiving a higher education. Deficit thinking, which sees students as empty receptacles that must be filled with the ideologies of the teacher, administrator, institution, and culture of higher education, surely disempowers students and fails to value different ways of writing, thinking, and approaching problems. At the same time as a teacher I want to be careful to work toward empowering my students, especially poor, first-generation, and working class students. I want to teach a kind of critical literacy, while simultaneously teaching some traditional approaches to composition that seem to be in accord with students' educational goals—whether those happen to be personal enlightenment, or having a successful career beyond higher education.

REFERENCES

Adler-Kassner, L. (1998). Ownership revisited: An exploration in progressive era and expressivist composition scholarship. *College Composition and Communication, 49*(2), 208-233.

Elbow, P. (1995). Being a writer vs. being an academic: A conflict in goals. *College Composition and Communication, 46*(1), 72-83.

Elbow, P., & Bartholomae, D. (1997). Interchanges: Responses to Bartholomae and Elbow. In V. Villanueva (Ed.), *Cross-talk in comp theory* (1st ed., pp. 501-509). Urbana, IL: NCTE.

Freire, P. (1993). *Pedagogy of the oppressed.* (M. B. Ramos, Trans.). New York: Continuum.

Graff, G., & Birkenstein, C. (2009). *They say/I say: The moves that matter in academic writing* (2nd ed.). New York: W. W. Norton.

Harris, J. (1996). *A teaching subject: Composition since 1966.* Upper Saddle River, NJ: Prentice Hall.

National Council of Teachers of English. (1974). The students' right to their own language. *College Composition and Communication,* Fall, XXV, (n.p.). Retrieved from http://www.ncte.org/library/nctefiles/groups/cccc/newsrtol.pdf

Shaughnessy, M. P. (2003). Diving in: An introduction to basic writing. In V. Villanueva (Ed.), *Cross-talk in comp theory.* (2nd ed., pp. 311-317). Urbana, IL: NCTE.

Shaughnessy, M. P. (1977). *Errors and expectations: A guide for the teacher of basic writing.* New York: Oxford University Press.

Villanueva, V. (1997). Considerations for American Freireistas. In V. Villanueva (Ed.), *Cross-talk in comp theory* (1st ed., pp. 621-637). Urbana, IL: NCTE.

Watkins Jr., J. R. (2009). *A taste for language: Literacy, class, and English studies.* Carbondale, IL: Southern Illinois University Press.

REVISITING RADICAL REVISION

Jeff Sommers
West Chester University and Miami University

> Although various aspects of the writing process have been studied extensively of late, research on revision has been notably absent.
> —Nancy Sommers

> In my high school days we wrote papers once and handed them in once.
> —Carmen, first-year writing student

> Even as post-process theorists charge process pedagogy with ignoring context, erasing social differences and social forces, their own research similarly effaces writers and scenes of writing ... [and they] don't mention revision practices.
> —Nancy Welch

> I asked them [my students] about revision, and they were stumped ...
> —Nancy DeJoy

> I never appreciated revising because in my past experiences I didn't revise. There was only editing ...
> —Bart, first-year writing student

REVISION OVER THE DECADES

Over the years, I have told many students that "there is no great writing, only great rewriting," and I decided to begin this essay with that quotation, wishing to give it the proper attribution. What I have discovered, however, is that it is not entirely clear whose words these are. The leading contender seems to be Justice Louis Brandeis, but my most recent search uncovered variations on the theme of the primacy of revising ascribed to Nabokov, Tolstoy, Oates, Michener, Dahl, Crichton, et al. This next citation, however, is accurate: "Teaching writing is teaching re-writing" (Fulwiler, 1992, p. 190).

The need to teach revision to student writers has not lessened over the years as the epigraphs to this essay, drawn from three decades, suggest. Nancy Sommers' study described student revision practices of the time as "scratching out," "marking out," and "slashing" (1980, pp. 380-381). Toby Fulwiler described his students' revision practices at that same time in terms similar to Sommers'.

> All too often, students in first-year composition and fourth-year literature alike believed that revision meant shuffling around a few commas on last night's paper before handing it in. While this generalization does disservice to serious students writers, it remains true for many who completed our classes with far less language proficiency that we had hoped for. (1982, p. 100)

I was in the composition classroom during that same period of time. Thanks to the expressivist theorists of the 1970s and 1980s, I had become convinced that teaching revision was vital, given that my students, by and large, seemed unfamiliar with that stage of the writing process. As the 1990s began, Donald Murray made the observation that

> "Revise," we command, and our students change some of the punctuation, often trading new grammatical errors for old; choose a couple of long words they don't really know from Roget to "profound it up" as one of my students said; misspell a number of words in a more innovative way; catch a few typos; and pass back essentially the same paper. It is all they know. (1991, p. vii)

In the mid-1990s I was in my fifteenth year of full-time teaching at Miami University Middletown (Ohio) and had been emphasizing revision in my writing courses as part of a portfolio approach to writing instruction. I decided to find out whether the emphasis on revision in my first-year writing courses had had any impact, so I compiled a list of 85 former students who had taken my first-year writing course anywhere from four to fourteen years earlier to survey them about their experiences and recollections. My list was not random: I deliberately chose memorable students, the ones whom I felt had "gotten it." I received a 29% response rate: twenty-five students completed my survey. The fourth survey question read, "What specific activities in which you participated as a student in freshman composition stand out in your memory? Why?" Despite the open-ended nature of the question, 36% (9) students identified revision as a memorable feature of the course. Their comments were intriguing in that they did not describe their revision process so much as their affective reaction to revising. One student commented, "of the various writing habits I acquired ... the habit of revising my work has proven to be the most valuable," and then she discussed how the habits she had developed persisted after graduation. Another student wrote that the course

> made me feel okay about rewriting ... For some reason I had

this other mistaken belief that people should be able to write perfectly, and that all writers had this inherent talent to choose words. Never once did you make me feel stupid ... You simply suggested a better way. Sometimes I agreed and sometime I didn't, but no matter what, it was okay either way.

A third student wrote that, "the positive experience I received from freshman comp was the ability to learn how to revise. Also, I became extremely confident in my writing." Another student, however, one who later became an English teacher herself, made a telling comment when she wrote, "I like the fact that we used THE WRITING PROCESS and were guided through each phase, rather than rushed. Re-vision was seeing the writing's meaning come to life."

The conclusion I draw from this survey, in retrospect, is that some students who had come of age in the 1980s and early 1990s were receptive to an emphasis on revision as a complex and vital activity because they had previously had, as Sommers, Fulwiler, and Murray assert, a very limited sense of what revision could be. By the end of the 1990s, Nancy Welch was advocating that the process movement's methodology itself for teaching revision was in need of revising. She too looked back to the 1970s and 1980s and noted that there was not much research done into revision. She also observed, however, that while post-process theorists leveled a critique at process pedagogy for "ignoring context, erasing social differences and social forces, their own research similarly effaces specific writers and scenes of writing." In sum, these post-process theorists, she pointed out, "don't mention revision practices" (1997, p. 24).

And, indeed, throughout the next decade of the 2000s, commentary continued to suggest that revision, if taught and studied at all, was not presented as a complex and vital activity but more as a mechanical cleaning up of faulty prose. Lisa Costello has recently reviewed revision articles of the decade and reports that research appears to focus on collaboration, on contrastive studies with experienced writers, and on ESL and tutoring. She concludes that "a survey of recent literature on revision ... suggests that teaching individual revision might still remain an 'afterthought' except as it applies to remedial or struggling writers" (2011, p. 154).

The difference between the discussion of revision and writing in the most recent decade and the discussion of the 1980s and 1990s may be that the new "millennial generation" of college students itself has come under fire. Mark Bauerlein points the finger at students who rely upon electronic chat and no longer care about capitalization and spelling, who do not expect writing to be clearly composed and coherent, and who spend more time playing video games than reading books (2008). While I find Bauerlein's jeremiad unconvincing thanks to its shrill exaggerations, I also note that his observation that the millennial generation of students brings a new set of challenges to the writing classroom is worth considering: contemporary students may not, in fact, have a limited conception of revision so much as a limited interest in it. In a quite different take from Bauerlein's, Andrea Lunsford argues that college students now may, in fact, be writing more and with a greater awareness of audience than the students in the previous decades, thanks to social networking and electronic media. However, she also reports that college students' writing errors have not changed over the past twenty-five years. The inference I draw is that the majority of the "life-writing," in Lunsford's phrase (Haven, 2009), that contemporary students are doing does not necessarily have as its goal the kind of complex and polished final texts expected in the academy. Notably, Lunsford does not say anything about revision and what role it might play in the "life-writing" of the students in the Stanford study.

Nancy DeJoy's research also tends to confirm that revision, for many students in the 2000s, was not even on the radar. DeJoy analyzed more than 600 student placement essays in response to this prompt:

> The faculty of our first-year writing program is busy preparing for your arrival, and you can help by writing an essay in which you explain your strengths as a reader and writer. Conclude by stating both what you will contribute to your first-semester Critical Writing, Reading and Researching class and what you hope to gain from that class. (2004, p. 26)

DeJoy listed two dozen responses in the essays that explored what the students hoped to contribute (2004, p. 33) and 546 responses to what they hoped to gain from the course (2004, p. 35). Not a single student referred to revision by name as either a potential contribution or a hoped-for gain.

The silence about revision continues. Rebecca S. Nowacek's 2011 study of transfer of learning concludes that "good writing is not a skill that can be extracted from the complex social contexts for writing and applied unproblematically. Rather, writing knowledge is actually a complex constellation of knowledges and abilities linked together by a writer's understanding of genre" (p. 100). She continues by discussing "writing processes and analytical approaches" that the students she studied had learned and transferred into other situations, "most often to their invention process" (2011, p. 100). This section of the book does not refer to revision. Nowacek refers to invention on six other occasions in her book, offering several examples. By contrast, according to the book's index, revision is not mentioned once in the study.

A NEW PATH: RECONCILING POST-PROCESS AND PROCESS PEDAGOGY

The larger question may be where does that leave process pedagogy? Lad Tobin's take is that the fundamental beliefs of the writing process movement included the idea that "a premature emphasis on correctness can be counterproductive" (1994, p. 7). And Fulwiler, a decade after his earlier observations, argued in the 1990s that after twenty years of both teaching writing and writing professionally himself, "I have come to believe that knowing when, where, and how to revise is the greatest difference between my own good and bad writing as well as between the practices of experienced and inexperienced writers" (1993, p. 133). But by the end of the 1990s, a post-process approach to teaching composition had begun to hold sway. Robert Yagelski's view, however, is that process and post-process approaches are not "entirely incompatible" and that teachers "still routinely speak of planning, drafting, and revising—terms that suggest individual agency—in our conversations about writing and teaching writing" (1994, p. 204). He explains why this language is still useful because "the idea of composing as a process is a powerful way to understand what writers actually do." The composing process, he continues, "makes simple the complicated activity of writing. It allows us to talk about, study, and teach writing in ways that make the complexity of the act manageable" (1994, p. 205). Of course, post-process theorists' criticism of process pedagogy suggests that it offers too simplistic a view of a complex set of processes, but Yagelski, I believe, has something valuable to contribute in his final sentence—process provides tools to make discussions of writing "manageable."

Nancy Welch agrees that process pedagogy offers something of value in that it presents revision through the concept of dissonance that provides the starting point for revision. She objects, however, to a view of dissonance as a "problem to be corrected" (1997, p. 30) and confesses to being "troubled by constructions of revision that emphasize craft, technique, tidying up, and fitting in" (1997, p. 6), later defining the form of revision to which she objects as "the systematic suppression of all complexity and contradiction" (1997, p. 135). In other words, she wants to find a pedagogy that encourages dissonance, feeling that process approaches do not. In such a critique, Welch echoes James A. Reither's earlier concerns that "composition studies does not seriously attend to the ways writers know what other people know or to the ways mutual knowing motivates writing—does not seriously attend, that is, to the knowing without which cognitive dissonance is impossible" (1985, p. 622). These are powerful—and persuasive—arguments. But the recent history of teaching writing/rewriting is rooted in process pedagogy, and to be more specific, in what has come to be known as expressivism, and expressivist pedagogy has long offered an approach to teaching revision that requires dissonance rather than attempting to squelch it.

Post-process critiques of process, Yagelski says, "problematize the notion of 'individual' or 'subject' as often conceived in expressivist discussions … ," but he concludes that "these critiques of expressivism have less to say about the composing process per se than about the political implications of particular 'expressivist' approaches to teaching that process" (1994, p. 207). To Nancy DeJoy the shift that James Berlin's groundbreaking work encouraged was a "methodological move" away from teaching writing "mastery" to teaching "analysis" (2004, p. 51). DeJoy sketches out an ambitious and exciting pedagogy that involves her writing students in rethinking the composing process, in a sense redefining invention, drafting, and revising into rich, complex acts. However, by emphasizing analysis over mastery, her approach does not offer concrete, usable strategies for less experienced writers so that they might engage in productive revision of their drafts in progress.

Yagelski, Welch, and DeJoy work diligently to find a path that does not set up process and post-process as antagonistic models of writing instruction. Welch and DeJoy in particular seek to offer enriched approaches to understanding and teaching revision in opposition to the spare and underdeveloped models familiar to many students. But, as I hope to show, some "expressivist" approaches to teaching revision are entirely compatible with postmodern notions of the writing process and do indeed offer a rich conception of revising, one that emphasizes the value of dissonance.

A NEW FAMILIAR PATH: PROVOKING REVISION

Nancy Welch's concept of "getting restless" is also designed to promote a complex, complicated, and problematized form of revision, but the voices of expressivist teachers had also been advocating a richer conception of the role of revision, before Welch's book was published in 1997. Kim Korn, in an essay that appeared in the same year as Welch's book, advocated teaching revision as "an act of invention rather than editing" (1997, p. 88) through the use of "strategies that encourage us to step out of our writing comfort zones" (1997, p. 89). Years earlier, Donald Murray had asserted that "Writers are born at the moment they write what they do not expect and find a potential significance in what is on the page" (1991, p. ix), and both Toby Fulwiler and Wendy Bishop were advocating revision pedagogies designed to shake up student writers. Fulwiler's Provocative Revision (1992) and Bishop's edited collection *Elements of Alternate Style: Essays on Writing and Revision*, which presents her concept of "radical revision" (1997), offered an expressivist-derived approach that encouraged students to work toward mastery of revision by unsettling their more routinized approaches to rewriting as editing.[1]

What Fulwiler and Bishop present is an assignment that calls upon students to revisit a completed essay, requiring them to reconceive of the piece by revising it in a major way. Fulwiler outlines four processes that might be employed to provoke a new text related to but different from a previously-completed text; he terms them "adding" (expanding the scope of the piece), "limiting" (narrowing the focus of the piece), "switching" (finding a new perspective for the piece, e.g. switching from first to third person), and "transforming" (changing the genre of the piece, e.g. transforming a narrative into an argumentative essay). Bishop requires her students to produce a "radical revision" of a completed text, accompanied by a reflective commentary on the experience of revising the draft. Her assignment suggests that students consider changes in voice/tone, syntax, genre, audience, time, physical layout/typography, or even medium as a means of producing a radical revision.

I have found Fulwiler's and Bishop's presentations convincing and have been using them, on and off, ever since first learning about them. Most recently, I have used the radical revision assignment in the early part of my semester[2] to conclude a unit of the course that focuses on teachers. We read about teachers, we brainstorm lists of the qualities of good teachers, we analyze video clips of teachers at work in fictional films. The students then write a paper about a memorable "teacher" (as they define the term) in their own lives. I use the topic because first-year students are experts when it comes to this subject, having had a lifetime of experience in dealing with teachers. Once this paper has been completed, the course shifts into a discussion of revision, wherein the students become self-consciously aware of the process of revision through assigned readings.

In a similar fashion, Nancy DeJoy designs her first-year writing course to invite students into the discussion of the writing process that has been ongoing in the composition field. At one point, she observes that in focusing on the role of audience, there are key essays in the field that the students ought to read (2004, p. 29). Although she does not make a similar claim about revision essays, I want to make that assertion. So my classes begin a discussion of revision by reading Nancy Sommers' study contrasting the revision practices of experienced and student writers (1980) and discussing the students' own backgrounds in revision in contrast to the student writers and experienced writers in Sommers' study. I then assign the radical revision and present an overview of possibilities by sharing Fulwiler's four processes with examples. Like Bishop, I include several reflective pieces in conjunction with this process, and I would like to focus on those reflections as a means of making a point about what the students gain from engaging in a radical revision assignment.

At the end of the semester, the students produce a final letter to me in which they are invited to reflect on the activities and experiences during the course that they found meaningful. In the last three semesters in which I taught first-year writing, 190 students completed this letter. I find it striking that eighty-three of them (44%) chose to discuss the radical revision as a key experience in the course. Korn claims that the radical revision assignment provides an opportunity for writers to gain "thoughtful insights" not only into their own composing processes but also into their "motives and choices" as writers. The letters in my course often illustrate such insights.

For example, one young woman remembers that the radical revision prodded her into experimenting with the structure of her writing.[3] She says,

> When the class was assigned the radical revision, I was pleasantly surprised and relieved to see that there are ways to move away from the five-paragraph essay format. Going from assignment one to assignment two helped me open my eyes to the fact that I was being close-minded and that there are other options for my writing … Changing my essay to a letter of nomination forced me to write to a new audience: to the person who would be choosing whether my nomination deserved the award.

It is hard to say which decision came first: a new purpose, a different audience, or a new genre, but her commentary makes clear that she has become quite aware of how those decisions moved her away from her previous comfort zone of the five-paragraph form.

Another student focuses on how the radical revision assignment affected her belief system about revision

> Before taking this course, I believed that revising a paper meant to fix grammatical and punctuation errors. Now, I agree with the credo statement "I believe revising helps a writer step back, look at the paper from a different perspective and make changes …" For assignment number two, I revised my paper from being a narrative to a letter. The narrative just told the reasons why my teacher had good qualities and had stories to support them, but in the letter I explained why these qualities made my teacher deserving of an award.

This student has not only transformed the genre of her essay, but she has switched her intended audience of readers, and the dissonance of these transformations has produced a change in her conception of the possibilities available in revising.

I also required students to compose a Writer's Memo to accompany each radical revision, a metacommentary on the new draft. These reflective pieces reveal the impact of the radical revision on the students' understanding of the writing process. One student had transformed her personal essay into the first chapter of a hypothetical self-help book. Her memo explains why. "I have a very hard time writing personal things … it is really hard for me to talk about myself in my writing." The self-help book approach resolved her issues by sharing the same information about her influential teacher (she had chosen Buddha) by couching the discussion in terms of how readers might benefit from his teachings instead of revealing her own personal experiences.[4]

Several students chose to transform their personal essay tributes to a favorite teacher into more public pieces of writing, learning along the way how choosing a genre and audience can affect the impact of a draft. As Daniel Collins writes elsewhere in this collection, "the writer is not separate from larger social contexts, and so the writing process does not end until such inquiry is used to in the making of meaning for the writer and for others." One student converted a personal narrative into a newspaper feature story about her teacher and described one of her major changes as reconfiguring her introduction. She chose to incorporate "quotations" from her teacher, primarily remembered as favorite comments the teacher had made, in order to give the new version the sound of a human interest feature story, demonstrating her understanding that readers of newspaper articles have expectations of the genre, expectations that she felt it important to meet.

Harlan's narrative essay became a commencement speech. "By doing this," the memo reveals, "I still shared memories, but directed them in a way that showed everyone how great a teacher she was and how she helped me grow as a student … I selected this approach because I knew she was a great friend to many students in my grade. I felt that this would have been a good tribute to her and a collective farewell." While the genre has changed in this radical revision, it is important to note that the author has also learned that a single piece of writing can have multiple purposes.

In a similar move, Wanda decided to revise her narrative about her favorite instructor into an open letter addressed to younger students at her old high school, the intent of which was to encourage them to take classes with this fine teacher.

> The organization of this paper works better because as a student, I could determine which traits were more important to other students than other traits. Therefore, I could organize the paper from less important traits to most important traits.

> It worked better than in the last paper because my audience was clearer so I could really organize my paper in a way that would be interesting to students.

For Wanda, the radical revision had led to her exploring organizational patterns and considering herself as a member of a specific discourse community: present and former high school students.

For at least two other students, the radical revision increased the complexity of the writing task as they faced decisions about which of their two teacher essays to include in our final course portfolio. Brady decided to transform his film review of a recent movie about a teacher into a report written by the school's principal that collected several first-person eyewitness accounts of a controversial incident documented in the film. He notes "I think that this paper shows the personality of the characters better than the first [paper] ... because it's easier to show personality through what a person says than it is to explain their personality ... I think that the first paper does a better job of showing my analysis of the movie." Brady has made a discovery about the complex relationship of genre, audience, and purpose through his radical revision; the revision has not simplified his writing task, but actually complicated it as he has realized that there are both advantages and disadvantages to his revision decisions.

Natalie also experienced the problematic outcome of radical revision. She began by writing a personal essay about a teacher with whom she had had a complicated relationship. The teacher was a leader in the transcendental meditation (TM) community in the student's hometown, but she was, at the same time, a difficult and challenging person with whom to have a personal relationship. In her radical revision, Natalie chose to rewrite her personal narrative as an imagined obituary for the teacher in the local paper. "I went from writing an essay to writing an obituary, and I went from writing to, well, an audience of whom I wasn't too sure ... but which I think ended up being my fellow classmates, to an audience of two communities [the TM community and her hometown]." She describes how she did "a little research" by reading a number of obituaries, but then she concludes,

> An obituary can be a hard thing to keep interesting! The only thing that I didn't get to express is my negative feelings and criticisms of Kathy, simply because it's not right to be negative in an obituary. That was the only thing that didn't work as well. I almost felt like I wasn't telling the whole story, because I was leaving out that entire side of my opinion of her.

Natalie's reflections make clear that she did not experience revision as how to "correct moments of dissonance" (Welch, 1997, p. 6), but instead ended up facing a difficult choice between two pieces that do different things better (and worse) than one another.

These students' testimonies show how engaging in radical revision required them not only to wrestle with the challenges of reconceiving their previously finished work but also encouraged them to consider how they wanted to define revision and how they chose to learn to deal with its limitations. Nancy DeJoy objects to students' "consuming and applying heuristic processes they had no part in developing" (2004, p. 62), but these students, I want to argue, have indeed developed their own heuristic processes for revision.

BEING CRITICALLY EXPRESSIVIST

The examples I have shared demonstrate that radical revision often encourages students to move away from personal writing into more overtly public writing: newspaper stories, commencement speeches, open letters. In several cases, moves like this led students to engage with the politics of public education and the challenges of writing in a situation where the balance of power resided with the readers. Interestingly, these students had all chosen to write about a memorably bad teacher. Carlee changed her narrative about how a teacher had let her down into a personal letter directly to that teacher. Her Writer's Memo comments on the challenges in this revision: how can she be honest yet still encourage the reader—her former teacher—to read her entire letter? She strikes upon the idea of first praising some of the teacher's methods and then offering advice, showing that she cares about her successors as students in the teacher's class. This approach, she writes in her memo, "gave me the ability to offer suggestions on how she could improve her negative teaching qualities." The radical revision forced her, in other words, to strategize rather than simply venting her feelings, as she had done in the original narrative.

Several other students chose to write formal letters to administrators, voicing their concerns about a teacher's ineffectiveness. One memo explains her thinking:

> Since my new audience would be my teacher's boss I was able to instill a purpose in my writing. Before I felt that my paper lacked a true purpose. I confused many of my ideas into one paper and therefore the paper had no direction. With this paper I was able to give it a purpose, that purpose being to initiate a revision of the way teachers can behave with their students on school trips off of campus. I want my reader to do something about what happened to me on my trip so that no other student can feel this way again.

Once more, however, the task has been more complicated than her first narrative paper was—a story that emphasized her hurt feelings in a somewhat rambling manner. The tone of the new piece is a tricky one lest she alienate her reader and thus undermine her purpose. This student's experience reminds of comments made by Daniel Collins, elsewhere in this collection, who writes, "expressivist writing theory, it seems to me, upholds the idea that to write is to discover oneself amidst an array of others. It honors the importance of the student engaging and making sense out of the world." I see this student explaining how her revision was borne out of an enhanced understanding of her ideas in the context of the larger world that included her anticipated reader, an "other" whom she wished to convince. This "engaging and making sense out of the world" was prompted by the radical revision assignment.

I find Nancy Welch and Nancy DeJoy persuasive when they argue for a more nuanced and problematized conception of revision and of teaching revision. Their theoretical arguments are convincing. Welch urges that "border-talk" between process and post-process pedagogies needs to take place in teaching revision (1997, pp. 163-164). The radical revision assignment, I contend, represents that border talk. Radical revision offers the possibilities of presenting revision in the richer, more complex ways that Welch and DeJoy advocate. In fact, Welch's descriptions of how revision is enacted in her classroom sounds like a description of the radical revision assignment (1997, p. 165).

What I want to argue is that less experienced writers may not yet understand all of the rich possibilities open to them through revision.[5] The "first phase model" of composition instruction, what DeJoy terms "process pedagogy"(2004, p. 4), offers an opportunity to experience revision in writing so that it can be applied in the way that she advocates. DeJoy's empirical data (2004, pp. 34-35) show that the students' placement essays had very little to say about revision, and she later discovers a similar silence when she directly asks her students questions about their revision knowledge (2004, p. 74). DeJoy's notion of "revision" is about a way of thinking—assuming that writers are always "revising the world" by presenting their ideas about the world (in the Burkean sense of joining a conversation and changing it by doing so). To learn to revise texts, however, requires an attention to developing a series of texts, and that is what process pedagogy offers. The radical revision assignment, born out of an expressivist approach to writing instruction, provokes students into discovering that "finished" texts may not be "finished" at all and can be "refinished" into new texts. By being so provoked, students also experience a conception of revision that means more than mere fiddling with commas and word choices, preparing them to continue learning what a rich, complex, and rewarding part of the writing process revision can be.

NOTES

1. It's noteworthy to point out that Welch's book does not cite either of these sources.

2. I chose Bishop's terminology because it seems very direct in telling students what is expected of them: they will produce a second paper that is different while clearly growing out of their first paper. They are not to produce an entirely different text that is only tangentially related to the first—which is not a revision at all—but a recognizable version of the first paper that has been "radically" changed.

3. This student expressed her delight in discovering that the five-paragraph formulaic structure she had learned in high school was not the only effective way to organize a piece of writing. Because she had decided to change her first draft, a traditional five-paragraph theme extolling the virtues of her favorite teacher, into a letter nominating that teacher for an award, she realized that she had to focus on her new readers: the awards committee. That realization freed her to ignore the prescriptive five-paragraph approach, instead concentrating on building a strong and convincing argument for her candidate.

4. Thomas Newkirk notes a potential resemblance between the "traditional, teacher-directed classroom" and pedagogies that rely upon social constructivism and cultural studies (1997, p. 89) and attempts to reclaim personal narrative for the first-year writing classroom, offering an analysis of what expressivism still has to offer in a social-constructionist composition environment. Expressivist classrooms often began with personal narrative, but my initial assignment merely asks the students to write about a memorable teacher. More often than not, this general prompt leads to narrative writing, most likely because it is familiar to the students and because they want to explore a personal relationship, for good or ill, with a specific teacher. I deliberately leave the assignment rather open-ended, however, because I expect the radical revision will lead students to re-examine their initial choices anyway. And it does so—their reexaminations have led students to incorporate self-reflection into personal experience, explore other points of view, modify their purposes, and, as was the case with the self-help book and other examples to follow, even leave personal narrative behind altogether. My examples illustrate a point that Nancy Mack makes elsewhere in this collection when she argues that "writing should open the author to the possibility of agency through the interpretation and representation of memory." In the open-endedness of my original assignment, I would argue that I follow an expressivist pedagogy, and in the required metacognitive reflection that follows, I would argue the assignment presents the students with opportunities to exercise agency by interpreting their own representation of memory.

5. See Lea Povozhaev's "Essai—A Metaphor: Perception of Possibilities and Writing to Show Thinking" in this collection. Povozhaev argues that "the critical, searching spirit of pragmatism encourages trying new things," offering a different path to a similar conclusion reached in this essay.

REFERENCES

Bauerlein, M. (2008, March 14). *Eight reasons why this is the dumbest generation.* Retrieved from Boston.com Web site: http://www.boston.com/lifestyle/gallery/dumbestgeneration/

Bishop, W. (1997). *Elements of alternate style: Essays on writing and revision.* Portsmouth, NH: Heinemann.

Bishop, W. (2002). Steal this assignment: The radical revision. In C. Moore & P. O'Neill (Eds.), *Practice in context* (pp. 205-222). Urbana, IL: NCTE.

Costello, L. A. (2011). The new art of revision: Research papers, blogs, and the first-year writing classroom. *Teaching English in the Two-Year College, 39*(2), 151-167.

DeJoy, N. C. (2004). *Process this: Undergraduate writing in composition studies.* Logan, UT: Utah University Press.

Fulwiler, T. (1993). A lesson in revision. In W. Bishop (Ed.), *The subject is writing: Essays by teaches and students* (pp. 132-149). Portsmouth, NH: Boynton/Cook-Heinemann.

Fulwiler, T. (1992). Provocative revision. *The Writing Center Journal, 12*(2), 190-204.

Fulwiler, T. (1982). Teaching teachers to teach revision. In R. A. Sudol (Ed.), *Revising: New essays for teachers of writing* (pp. 100-108). Urbana, IL: ERIC/NCTE.

Haven, C. (2009). The new literacy: Stanford study finds richness and complexity in students' writing. *Stnanford Report,* 12 October. Retrieved from http://news.stanford.edu/news/2009/october12/lunsford-writing-research-101209.html

Korn, K. H. (1997). Distorting the mirror: Radical revision and writers' shifting perspectives.In W. Bishop (Ed.), *Elements of alternate style: Essays on writing and revision* (pp. 88-95). Portsmouth, NH: Boynton/Cook Publishers-Heinemann.

Korn, K. H. & Bishop, W. (1997). Two instances of the radical revision assignment. In W. Bishop (Ed.), *Elements of alternate style: Essays on writing and revision* (pp. 172-174). Portsmouth, NH: Boynton/Cook Publishers-Heinemann.

Lunsford, A. (n.d.) *Our semi-literate youth? Not so fast.* Retrieved from Stanford University Web site: Retrieved from https://ssw.stanford.edu/sites/default/files/OPED_Our_Semi-Literate_Youth.pdf

Murray, D. M. (1991). *The craft of revision.* Ft. Worth, TX: Holt, Rinehart, and Winston.

Newkirk, T. (1997). *The performance of self in student writing.* Portsmouth, NH: Boynton/Cook Publishers-Heinemann.

Nowacek, R. S. (2011). *Agents of integration: Understanding transfer as a rhetorical act*. Carbondale and Edwardsville, IL: Southern Illinois University Press.

Reither, J. A. (1985). Writing knowing: Toward redefining the writing process. *College English, 47*(6), 620-628.

Sommers, J. (2011). Reflection revisited: The class collage. *Journal of Basic Writing, 30*(1), 99-129.

Sommers, N. (1980). Strategies of student writers and experienced adult writers. *College Composition and Communication, 31*(4), 278-388.

Tobin, L. (1994). Introduction: How the writing process was born—and other conversion narratives. In L. Tobin & T. Newkirk (Eds.), *Taking stock: The writing process movement in the 90s* (pp. 1-14). Portsmouth, NH: Boynton/Cook Publishers-Heinemann.

Welch, N. (1997). *Getting restless: Rethinking revision in writing instruction*. Portsmouth, NH: Boynton/Cook Publishers-Heinemann

Yagelski, R. P. (1994). Who's afraid of subjectivity? The composing process and postmodernism or A student of Donald Murray enters the age of postmodernism. In L. Tobin & T. Newkirk (Eds.), *Taking stock: The writing process movement in the 90s* (pp. 203-217). Portsmouth, NH: Boynton/Cook Publishers-Heinemann.

APPENDIX: RADICAL REVISION ASSIGNMENT SHEET

Assignment #2 (Radical Revision)

What's Expected?

For this assignment, please produce a radical revision of Paper #1. This revision will count as a separate assignment. For example, let's suppose that for paper #1 I've written an essay about my most influential teacher, my high school 11th grade English teacher. I could continue to work on that paper (Assignment #1), telling some new stories about my experiences that show the reader why I hold the opinion that I do. For Assignment #2, however, I might transform that essay into an editorial for the journal that I edit in hopes that it would influence teachers, I might build on it by interviewing some of my old classmates to see what they think about our old teacher, I could limit my topic by focusing entirely on a single interaction I'd had with my teacher as I wrote a major term paper, or I could switch the essay into a third-person description of his teaching prowess. Any one of those four papers would be sufficiently different to count as a radical revision while still being recognizably about the same specific topic, my old English teacher, so I'd now have two different papers on a closely related topic. In your case, you'll have to pick either Asst #1 or Asst #2 for a final grade just before our midterm break.

For suggestions on how to transform your first paper into something sufficiently new to count as Assignment #2, check the Radical Revision Powerpoint. The genre for this paper is up to you: essay, letter, diary, editorial, film critique, etc.

Length requirement: 3 or more pages

Memo #2 (250 words)

1. How is this paper radically revised from your original paper? Why did you select this approach instead of another one? What other radical revisions did you consider?
2. What works better in this paper than in the original paper? What doesn't work as well? Why? What genre is this paper and has that changed from your first paper?
3. What is your purpose in writing this paper? That's another way of asking, "What are your readers supposed to get out of reading your draft?"
4. What questions do you have for me about your draft? (Remember: No yes/no questions …)

CONTRIBUTORS

Jean Bessette is an Assistant Professor at the University of Vermont, where she teaches rhetoric and writing courses that address issues in gender and sexuality, historiography, and multimodality. Her essays have appeared in *Rhetoric Society Quarterly* and *College Composition and Communication*.

Patricia Webb Boyd is an Associate Professor at Arizona State University in Tempe, Arizona. Her work has appeared in *College English* and *Computers and Composition*.

Daniel Collins is an Associate Professor at Manhattan College, where he teaches courses in composition and composition theory. He also directs the Center for Excellence in Learning and Teaching.

Kim M. Davis is an English faculty member at Oakland Community College, where she serves as a coordinator in the school's College Readiness Division. Her work on critical approaches to the teaching of writing includes a contribution to the edited collection *Activism and Rhetoric: Theories and Contexts for Political Engagement* (In S. Kahn & J. Lee (Eds.), 2011, New York: Routledge).

Peter Elbow is Professor of English Emeritus at UMass Amherst. He directed the Writing Program there and earlier at SUNY Stony Brook, and taught at various colleges. He recently published *Vernacular Eloquence: What Speech Can Bring to Writing* (2012, New York: Oxford University Press).

Roseanne Gatto is an Associate Professor with the Institute for Writing Studies at St. John's University. She earned her doctorate in composition and rhetoric at Indiana University of Pennsylvania in 2011. Her research interests include archival research methods and social justice in composition/rhetoric.

Eric Leake is an Assistant Professor of English at Texas State University, where he teaches rhetorical theory and composition pedagogy. His research focuses on empathy and nonrational rhetorics.

Nancy Mack is a Professor of English at Writing at Wright State University, where she teaches undergraduate courses for preservice teachers, as well as graduate courses in composition theory, memoir, and multigenre writing. Her publications include articles in *College English*, *JAC*, *Pedagogy*, *The Writing Instructor*, *Pretext*, *Teaching in the Two Year College*, and *English Journal*. She edited a special issue on Bullying for the *English Journal*.

Contributors

Thomas Newkirk is a Professor of English at the University of New Hampshire, where he teaches writing and directs the New Hampshire Literacy Institutes, a program for teachers now in its 33rd year. He has written on literacy at all levels, most recently, *The Art of Slow Reading* (2012, Portsmouth, NH: Heinemann).

Derek Owens is Vice Provost of Undergraduate Education at St. John's University, where he directs the Institute for Writing Studies. He is author of *Memory's Wake, Composition and Sustainability (Teaching for a Threatened Generation)*, and *Resisting Writings (And the Boundaries of Composition)*.

Anthony Petruzzi received his Ph.D. in Rhetoric and Composition from the University of Connecticut. He was the Director of the Writing Assessment Program at UMASS Boston, where he taught courses in Rhetoric and Composition. A former Fulbright Scholar in Turin Italy, Dr. Petruzzi is the author of several articles in *Hermeneutics, Rhetoric and Composition*, and *Writing Assessment.*

Lea Povozhaev earned her Ph.D. in 2014 from Kent State University. She researches medical rhetoric, and her scholarship appears in *Rhetoric Review*. Her memoir *When Russia Came to Stay* was published in 2012. Currently, her work with narrative weds her passion for writing and healing and its various manifestations in her creative, spiritual, and academic writing.

Tara Roeder is an Associate Professor with the Institute for Writing Studies at St. John's University. She earned her doctorate in English from the CUNY Graduate Center in 2014. Her research focuses on feminist theory and women's memoir; non-oedipal psychoanalytic theory and pedagogy; and queer theory and pedagogy.

Hannah J. Rule is an Assistant Professor of Rhetoric and Composition at University of South Carolina where she teaches courses in first-year writing and writing pedagogy. Her research, which focuses on the sensory and material dimensions of writing and reading processes, has appeared in *Composition Forum* and *Computers and Composition Online*.

Sheri Rysdam is Assistant Professor of Basic Composition at Utah Valley University. In addition to her scholarship on strategies for teacher response to student writing, her publications are on the rhetoric of political economy, issues surrounding contingent faculty, and the impact of social class in the composition classroom.

David Seitz is a Professor of Composition and Rhetoric at Wright State University, where he teaches writing courses, rhetorical theory, composition and literacy studies, and ethnography. He has published *Elements of Literacy* with Julie Lindquist, and *Who Can Afford Critical Consciousness?: Practicing a Pedagogy of*

Humility, in addition to articles in *Pedagogy, College English*, and Comp*osition Studies* and other book chapters.

Jeff Sommers is an Associate Professor of English at West Chester University. He is editor of *Teaching English in the Two-Year College* and 2012 winner of NCTE's Nell Braddock Service Award.

Scott Wagar received his Ph.D. in Composition and Rhetoric from Miami University, where he teaches courses in rhetoric and writing. His research examines composition theory and pedagogy as well as the rhetoric of contemporary spirituality.

Chris Warnick is an Associate Professor at the College of Charleston, where he teaches courses in first-year writing, writing in the disciplines, and literacy studies. His research has appeared in *The Journal of Basic Writing* and *Across the Disciplines*, and he is among the founding editors of the journal *Literacy in Composition Studies*.

Maja Wilson is the author of *Rethinking Rubrics in Writing Assessment* (2006, Portsmouth, NH: Heinemann) which won the 2007 James Britton Award. She has taught high school English, college composition, and literacy methods courses for pre-service and practicing teachers.

www.ingramcontent.com/pod-product-compliance
Lightning Source LLC
Chambersburg PA
CBHW030524230426
43665CB00010B/751